PowerPC™

Microprocessor
Developer's Guide

PUBLISHING

201 West 103rd Street
Indianapolis, Indiana 46290

This book is dedicated to
Leona, Tara, and John.

Trademarks

Overview

Contents

IV Appendixes

Acknowledgments

The authors gratefully acknowledge Greg Galanos, John Golenbieski, Steve Hoxey, Cathy May, Larry Merkel, Ed Silha, and Rick Simpson for help with technical questions. We would also like to thank the IBM and Somerset management team, especially Doug Balser, Chin-Cheng Kau, Joe Fitzgerald, Jan Jannick, Rowland Reed, John Ripley, Susan Tiner, and David Tuttle. Thanks also to Joyce Fitzgerald, George Paap, and Tom Thompson. Finally we would like to thank our families and friends for their support, especially Amy Chu, Tara Ellis, and Leona Slepetis.

About the Authors

John Bunda holds a Ph.D. in Computer Science from the University of Texas at Austin, where he did research in microprocessor and instruction set design, VLSI implementation, and compiler scheduling. Prior to his time at the university, he spent seven years as an assembly language programmer on several mainframe and microprocessor architectures. Dr. Bunda joined the Somerset PowerPC Design Center in 1992 and worked on verification and performance analysis of the PowerPC 601 microprocessor. Currently he is involved in the design of future PowerPC processor implementations.

Terence M. Potter received his bachelor's degree in Electrical Engineering from the University of Texas at Austin in 1991. He was a logic designer on the PowerPC 601 processor, and was responsible for the instruction fetch and dispatch logic, as well as the branch processor. He currently works at the Somerset PowerPC Design Center at Austin, developing future PowerPC microprocessors.

Robert Shadowen received a bachelor's degree in Physics from the University of Texas at Austin in 1990. As part of the design verification team for the PowerPC 601, he developed software tools now used by other PowerPC projects. He is currently working in the design and verification tools group at the Somerset PowerPC Design Center.

What This Book Can and Cannot Tell You

Because PowerPC processors are being used in computers with different system architectures (with some of these running multiple operating systems), the scope of this book is limited to the processors themselves. This book will show you how these processors work, so that you can get the maximum performance out of your PowerPC processor based computer. And even though this book will primarily cover assembly language programming, you will be able to use this knowledge to optimize your programs, even when you are working in a higher-level language, such as C.

The purpose of this book is not to describe interfaces at the system level, nor is it a prescription for how these interfaces should be implemented in hardware or software. Rather, it is intended as a guide (possibly even for the developer of these interfaces or systems) to explain how PowerPC microprocessors work, and to provide enough information so that developers and users of these interfaces can most effectively get these jobs done.

Part 1 of this book is an introduction to the PowerPC architecture. Chapter 1, "PowerPC Concepts," explains what the PowerPC concept is, where it came from, and the ideas behind the PowerPC processor architecture. Chapter 2, "Introduction to the PowerPC Architecture," provides a more detailed view of the architecture, and provides a high-level view of the PowerPC machine environment; the types and number of machine registers, the kinds of instructions available, and the programming constructs the machine was designed to most efficiently support.

Chapters 3, 4, and 5 form Part 2 and give a description of the instruction set. These chapters provide a detailed reference—they are the place to look to find a precise description of the behavior of each PowerPC instruction.

Finally, Part 3 discusses assembly programming on the PowerPC architecture. Chapter 7, "Coding Strategy and Tuning for Performance," covers a series of issues one step removed from the machine architecture. These include the conventions that are adopted to help structure and organize code sequences into subroutines, programs, and libraries (such as call-return linkage conventions, register save and restore requirements, and interface between assembly language and compiler-generated code).

Chapter 7 is more about code strategy than it is about the actual nuts and bolts. It describes in detail how the designers of the PowerPC architecture intended it to be used. This chapter will help you understand the difference between PowerPC code that works, and PowerPC code that works very well. Topics discussed include performance optimization (both general and processor-specific), coding practices to avoid, platform independence, and seamless transition to 64-bit addressing.

The appendixes provide programming examples, as well as a wealth of more detailed information that may not be of general interest, but nonetheless it provides comprehensive reference. Some of the topics covered include operating system memory management and address translation, multiprocessor systems and shared memory, and details of floating point processing.

About the Sample Programs

Because of the range of PowerPC processor-based computer systems, operating systems, and associated development tools, the sample programs are as portable as possible. There are no specific examples of system device programming (such as timer chip programming), as these will vary with your computer system, and your operating system may prevent your accessing them. The examples also avoid heavy use of assembler pseudo-ops (commands to the assembler) as they may vary between specific assemblers. While we discuss calling assembly language routines from C and use of the TOC for XCOFF format object files, this is in the context of AIX, and the specifics may not apply to your operating system.

Conventions Used in This Book

The following typographic conventions are used in this book:

- Code lines, commands, statements, variables, and any text you type or see on the screen appears in a `computer` typeface.
- Placeholders in syntax descriptions appear in an *`italic computer`* typeface. Replace the placeholder with the actual filename, parameter, or whatever element it represents.
- *Italics* highlight technical terms when they first appear in the text and are sometimes used to emphasize important points.

  Pseudocode, a way of explaining in English what a program does, also appears in *italics.*

I

Introduction

This book is a field guide for developers of PowerPC applications and systems software. In researching this book, we found that much of currently available reference information on the PowerPC architecture is written from the processor designer's, rather than the programmer's, point of view. The designer wants to know how each feature works; the programmer wants to know how to use and combine those features most effectively to solve a problem. This is a programmer's book about PowerPC processors.

With modern compilers and ever faster processors, it might seem that assembly language programs would be going the way of relics like punched-paper tape, job control cards, and, well, floppy disks. The advantages of high-level languages—ease of development, maintainability, and portability—are compelling. And, indeed, most software development these days is done in a high-level language.

Nonetheless—it remains that a significant body of the code you execute on your machine (PowerPC or not) each and every time you use it, was coded in assembly language. This includes parts of the operating system, ROM firmware, and run-time library code that is linked into virtually every application program. Why is so much code "still" written in assembler? In some cases, it's because high-level languages don't provide a complete interface to the hardware. They don't provide a direct way to inspect and modify some of the special purpose machine registers, or to execute certain instructions. In these cases, there is no choice but to write some things in assembly language.

Another reason to write assembler is performance. An old hacker's truism states that a "real programmer" can always remove at least one instruction from any program. If this were really the case, all programs could ultimately be reduced to no instructions at all! But seriously, in code that is executed very frequently, removing even that "one instruction" can make a measurable performance difference. If you've ever examined compiler-generated code, even from so-called industrial-strength optimizing compilers, it's not hard to see ways of improving it, even if it is just an instruction or two here or there.

A huge share of the code written in any application is executed so infrequently that an extra instruction here or there won't make much difference, so there's no reason not to use a high-level language. However, there may be some parts of your application that are executed very frequently indeed. If your program isn't fast enough (is it ever?), there may be room to significantly speed it up with some judiciously applied assembly programming muscle.

Even if you are completely satisfied with the performance of your PowerPC application, there are other reasons you might need know about PowerPC assembly language programming. Sometimes, debugging compiled language code requires you to examine the generated assembly output, either to make sure it's correct, or when stepping through it with debugging tools.

This book was written to help make the job of developing software for PowerPC systems easier and more effective. We've gathered a wealth of information from numerous sources to provide you a single reference for the PowerPC architecture, instruction set, and programming conventions used by PowerPC compilers and systems software. We describe the PowerPC architecture and instruction set, and then go on to show you some of the tricks of programming PowerPC machines effectively, what works—and what to avoid—if you want maximum performance from your PowerPC machine.

1

PowerPC Concepts

The History of the PowerPC Microprocessor

In 1992, the PowerPC alliance of IBM, Motorola, and Apple was formed to design and build microprocessors that would meet the needs of all three partners. The instruction set chosen for these processors is a refinement of the set used by IBM's Performance Optimization With Enhanced RISC (POWER) machines. The POWER architecture was introduced in 1989 in IBM's RS/6000 line of workstation computers. The instruction set for this machine has its origins with the 801 minicomputer that was developed at IBM's T.J. Watson Research Lab in the late 1970s.

The evolution of the POWER instruction set to the PowerPC set results in only minor changes to the instruction set and the programmer's view of the machine. Many of the changes affect only system interface instructions that never appear in user programs, but there also were some changes made to user-mode instructions. The most significant change is the addition of instructions to support single-precision (32-bit) floating-point values. Also, some changes were made to allow for upward-compatible extension to 64-bit addresses and data values. The PowerPC 620 is the first available 64-bit PowerPC implementation; it is capable of executing 32-bit PowerPC applications without modification.

While it may seem strange to start with a 32-bit architecture when a 64-bit architecture is seemingly just around the corner, there were important reasons for doing this. First, the PowerPC architecture is close enough to the POWER architecture that existing POWER applications can run unchanged on the 32-bit PowerPC processors. This meant that there was already an existing code base for the new architecture which solves one of the hardest problems associated with introducing a new architecture—nobody buys a system without software, but nobody creates software for a system which no one will buy. Another advantage is that companies which were new to the POWER/PowerPC architectures could start developing software (operating systems, important applications, etc.) before the first PowerPC processors and systems were available by using POWER-based systems. Finally, it is questionable whether the 64-bit operating systems and processors are really just around the corner for all market segments. It will probably be quite some time before 64-bit processors are needed for the consumer desktop and mobile computer markets.

The PowerPC Instruction Set Architecture

An *instruction set architecture* is the set of commands by which the (assembly language) programmer can inspect and alter the state of the machine. The PowerPC microprocessor usually is described as a *Reduced Instruction Set Complexity* (RISC) architecture. Some of the RISC characteristics of the PowerPC microprocessor include a large set of general registers and instructions that perform a single operation rather than a sequence. Instructions that compute (add, shift, and so on), for example, operate only on registers; separate load and store instructions are provided to transfer values between registers and from memory. This approach is different from a CISC architecture, in which a single instruction can perform both a calculation and a load or store.

Understanding the benefits of the RISC approach requires some idea as to how these operations must be implemented in hardware. A simple explanation is that the load from memory usually takes a long time, at least compared to the time it takes to perform the add operation. In the CISC machine, the load operation is started, and the machine must wait for the value to be retrieved from memory before performing the addition. In the RISC machine, the same operation requires two instructions: one for the load, and one for the add. Superficially, this approach seems worse (why use two instructions when one instruction would suffice?). By separating the two operations into two distinct machine instructions, however, the astute programmer (or compiler) is free to move the load instruction earlier in the program, placing other instructions that do not require the memory value between the load and the add instructions. When the value is needed for the computation, it already is available in a register, and the processor does not need to wait idly for the value to be returned from memory.

PowerPC processors go this process one better, in that the processor itself can perform this kind of instruction scheduling on the fly; this is called out-of-order execution, or instruction scheduling. In many cases, the programmer does not need to worry about rearranging the order of instructions, because the processor can look ahead in the instruction stream and do the reordering all by itself. Even so, the hardware can look ahead only so far, and there are limits to the reordering capabilities for each PowerPC implementation. Although PowerPC processors can handle some of the instruction-reordering chores, it still is possible to improve performance by judicious instruction-scheduling and coding practices.

PowerPC Processors

A wide spectrum of PowerPC implementations has been announced or speculated about in the press, from embedded controllers to high-performance server engines. At the time of this writing, four general-purpose PowerPC processor chips are available or officially announced: the PowerPC 601, 603, 604, and 620 processors. IBM and Motorola also are introducing PowerPC processors designed for embedded control applications.

The PowerPC 601 is targeted at the desktop workstation and PC market. The first available PowerPC systems, the IBM RS/6000 Model 250 and Apple's first Power Macintoshes, are based on the 601 processor. The 601 is manufactured by IBM and is marketed by IBM and Motorola. The other three chips in the family are produced by both companies.

The PowerPC 603 processor is a smaller, lower-cost implementation than the 601, designed primarily for use in portable and laptop machines. The 603 features active power management—when execution units are not needed, they are shut down. The 603 also supports software-configurable, low-power, standby modes. The PowerPC 604 is the next-generation, high-performance chip intended for desktop and server applications. The 601, 603, and 604 support 64-bit wide bus data transfers, but are 32-bit PowerPC implementations by virtue of the 32-bit width of their machine registers and memory addresses.

The PowerPC 620 is a high-performance desktop and server engine, and it is the first full 64-bit PowerPC implementation. Registers in the 620 are 64 bits wide, and additional instructions for operating on 64-bit quantities are provided. These extensions are upward-compatible, and the 620 is capable of running all 32-bit PowerPC applications. The principal feature of the 64-bit PowerPC architecture and the 620 is overcoming the 4-gigabyte limit on the effective address space imposed by 32-bit registers. The 64-bit 620 architecture increases the number of addressable memory locations and introduces a new virtual address translation architecture for virtual memory in 64-bit mode. The 620 also supports the 32-bit addressing modes, making it possible to run 32-bit operating systems and applications without modification on a 620 machine.

From the applications programmer's point of view, the various PowerPC processors are virtually indistinguishable. Code sequences of user-mode PowerPC instructions produce identical results on the 601, 603, and 604, and these sequences define the same computation on the 620 (although sequences that exploit the 64-bit wide general-purpose registers (GPRs) in the 620 are not backward-compatible).

Some specific features of the PowerPC 601 also bear mention. In addition to the 32-bit PowerPC instruction set, the 601 provides support for the IBM POWER instructions that were not included in the PowerPC. The intent was to help ease IBM's transition from POWER to PowerPC. These POWER-only instructions are available in all 601-based systems, but it would be prudent to avoid them in code that might need to run on the 603, 604, 620, or future PowerPC processors. In almost all cases, the function provided by a "missing" POWER instruction is available in a more general form in a new PowerPC instruction. The only other difference between the 601 and other PowerPC implementations is in the number of the address translation registers. This difference can be ignored safely everywhere but in the memory-management sections of the operating system.

IBM and Motorola also are introducing PowerPC processors designed for embedded control applications. Most of the material in this book should be germane to programming these devices as well.

PowerPC-Based Systems

The PowerPC architecture is a detailed specification of the machine language. It doesn't specify what happens outside the processor, however, and how a programmer can communicate with other elements of the system. Because PowerPC processors are being used in a wide variety of applications, from automobile engine controllers to video games to personal workstations to high-performance supercomputers, it makes sense to specify the system details separate from the processor architecture.

Even so, it is difficult to develop an interesting application that does not need to interact with devices beyond the processor and memory; video displays, disk drives, keyboards, and other devices occasionally come in handy! The designer of a system must link the external devices to the processor, and the interface to the "outside world" is usually through assignment of special meanings to the reading and writing of specific memory locations and external interrupts. The specifics of such conventions define a system architecture.

The IBM Personal Computer system architecture was defined long ago around the Intel 8088 processor. So that they could run IBM PC software, other PC makers adopted precisely the same system architecture. Despite limitations of the system design, compatibility with the existing software base requires that the conventions defined in the original IBM PC be replicated faithfully in every PC-compatible machine to this day.

Some examples of current PowerPC system architectures include the Apple Power Macintosh, the IBM RS/6000 PowerPC-based workstations, and the Motorola PowerStack machines. These systems are slightly different due to their lineage and to the specific hardware used in these systems. Future portable and multiprocessor systems based on the PowerPC will have their own unique hardware needs.

In modern computer systems, the operating system manages the system devices and provides software interfaces to higher level applications. This approach, however, forces the operating system to have a detailed knowledge of the system architecture of the platform on which it is running, which slows or even prevents porting of operating systems between hardware platforms.

The *PowerPC Reference Platform* (PReP) is a specification for a system architecture that will address these issues by providing a standard layer of abstraction, typically in software, between the operating system and the actual system hardware. This layer not only will allow systems composed of different hardware, but will allow the latest hardware technology to be incorporated into computer systems with little impact on system software. PReP is an open standard being developed and supported by multiple computer manufacturers interested in PowerPC hardware and software development. At the time of this writing, the PReP specification has not been finalized.

PowerPC Operating Systems

Currently, at least six major operating systems are available or under development for PowerPC systems, including Apple Macintosh System 7, IBM AIX, IBM Workplace OS, Taligent, Microsoft Windows NT, and SunSoft Solaris. While all of these operating systems run on at least one other non-PowerPC platform, some of these operating systems currently will run only on a specific PowerPC system, but in the future they may be able to run on any PReP-compliant system. Although this large number of operating systems enables many existing applications to be ported from other hardware platforms, it raises questions when developing new software—for example, for which specific operating system to develop.

In addition, the PowerOpen organization was formed by a set of partners (including IBM, Apple, Bull, Harris, Tadpole Technology, and THOMSON-CSF) interested in developing PowerPC hardware and software. The purpose of the partnership is to develop standards, common interfaces, and the technology necessary to help minimize the cost of developing and distributing PowerPC software. The PowerOpen environment specifies a UNIX type of operating system with the capability to run Macintosh applications, an X Window and Motif-based graphical user interface, and binary compatibility.

2

Introduction to the PowerPC Architecture

In this chapter we will introduce some of the key concepts behind the PowerPC architecture. First we will discuss some more general topics as an introduction to modern computer architecture.

Amdahl's Law

One of the best strategies for increasing performance in modern computer architecture is to optimize the performance of the most common tasks. It is rarely worth investing effort to improve the performance of rare events—a change producing a two-fold increase in performance for a task that accounts for only 2 percent of a program's overall execution time only improves overall performance by 1 percent. Doubling the speed of an event that accounts for 98 percent of the execution time, however, improves overall performance by 96 percent— almost the full factor of two. This effect is known as *Amdahl's Law*, which is one of the foundations of modern computer design. According to Amdahl's Law the general equation for the overall speedup to a system, if a change is made to a single task within the system, is:

$$\text{speedup} = \frac{1}{(1 - \text{Fraction Enhanced}) + \dfrac{\text{Fraction Enhanced}}{\text{Speedup Enhanced}}}$$

Thus for the example above where we increased performance two-fold for the task that accounted for 2 percent of the total execution time of the program, we get

$$\frac{1}{(1 - .02) + \left(\dfrac{.02}{2}\right)} = 1.01$$

For the example above where we increased performance two-fold for the task that accounted for 98 percent of the total execution, we get

$$\frac{1}{(1 - .98) + \left(\dfrac{.98}{2}\right)} = 1.96$$

This law applies equally well to software and hardware, and is why programmers are willing to spend time optimizing loop code and other pieces of code, which accounts for the bulk of a program's execution time.

Much of this book is dedicated to the programmer attempting to optimize critical pieces of code. With modern compiler technology, there is little or no reason to attempt to code entire programs in assembly language. Programmers can write code once and port that code to many different platforms by using a high-level programming language and letting the compiler optimize the bulk of the code. For some programs, a significant performance gain might be available simply by rewriting parts of the code in machine-specific assembly language. This small portion of code would need to be rewritten for different microprocessor targets. By isolating the application of assembly language to small performance-critical sections of code, most of the performance benefits of assembly language coding can be realized without sacrificing general portability.

The Ever Popular RISC Versus CISC Discussion

Different instruction set architectures have different strengths and weaknesses when it comes to the topic of code optimization strategies, particularly in the areas of compiler and hand optimization strategies. One important classification of instruction set architectures is Reduced Instruction Set Complexity (RISC) architectures versus Complex Instruction Set Computer (CISC) architectures. There are many differences between RISC and CISC architectures other than the complexity of the instructions which comprise the architecture. While many of these differences are not exactly part of the definitions of RISC or CISC, they have come to be associated with these two architectural styles (as defining differences).

The first major difference is that RISC architectures are typically load/store architectures, while CISC architectures are not. A load/store instruction set architecture restricts memory access operations to loading and storing values; there are no instructions that perform operations directly on memory locations. A non-load/store architecture not only permits the loading and storing of data, but also combines other data manipulation operations with these memory-access operations in a single machine instruction. The PowerPC architecture is a load/store architecture—data must be loaded from memory into a register before it can be manipulated. Once the data has been manipulated, it must be stored from a register into a memory location.

The Intel X86 and Motorola 68000 instruction sets are not load/store instruction set architectures, because both have instructions that directly manipulate memory. For instance, the X86 instruction set has an add instruction—ADD AX,[BX]—that adds the contents of memory addressed by the value in BX to the contents of the AX register. This instruction would not be appropriate for a load/store architecture because it combines a memory access with an operation on the value in memory.

In order to study the advantages and disadvantages of load/store architectures, one must have an understanding of the system in which the processor is being used. For this discussion, we will assume a typical uniprocessor system (see Figure 2.1).

A modern microcomputer system includes several components. At the core is the microprocessor. The *microprocessor* controls the rest of the system components through the *processor bus*. Almost all general purpose microprocessors in use today are *synchronous processors*—meaning that the flow of data through the processor is controlled by a global clock that divides time into equal-length units called *clock cycles*. Typical microprocessor clock cycles range from about 20 ns to 3 ns. The microprocessor is connected to a processor bus that also is often synchronous. Typical clock cycles for processor buses range from about 40 ns to 10 ns; these frequencies are limited somewhat by the physics associated with long wire runs (from 1 to 5 inches) on Printed Circuit Boards (PCBs). The frequencies at which microprocessors run have been increasing steadily over the past 20 years, while the access times for Dynamic Random-Access Memory (DRAM) used as main memory have been increasing at a much slower rate. The result is that modern microprocessors in microcomputers generally run at a higher frequency than the processor bus and certainly at a much higher frequency than main memory, which generally is made of DRAMs with typical access periods of 60 ns to 80 ns.

FIGURE 2.1.

A typical computer organization.

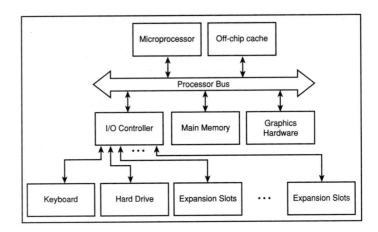

Because of the difference between the access time of on-chip resources such as registers and off-chip resources such as main memory, data within the processor can be manipulated much more quickly than data stored in off-chip resources. This is the reason for the recent trend toward processors which run at higher clock speeds internally than the external interface is running. For instance, the 66MHz Intel 80486DX2 processor has an internal clock rate of 66 MHz, but its external interface runs at 33MHz.

One of the advantages of a load/store architecture is that the long latency memory access can be separated from the short latency data manipulation. This capability enables the compiler or assembly language programmer to schedule short-latency, on-chip, data-manipulation instructions between an access to data contained in an off-chip resource and the use of that data. This capability is known as *code scheduling* and is a very important concept when dealing with RISC/load-store architectures.

The PowerPC Architecture

In this section, we introduce some of the specifics of the PowerPC architecture. This forms the groundwork needed to understand the instruction descriptions in Part II.

Registers

Registers are local memory in the processor where intermediate results are stored. The result of one instruction may be placed in a register, which in turn may be read by another instruction.

There are several different types of registers defined by the PowerPC architecture. They can be classified into four major groups: general-purpose integer registers, floating-point registers, status and control registers, and special-purpose registers (see Table 2.1).

Table 2.1. The basic PowerPC registers set (32-bit architecture).

Name	Size	Number	Description
General-purpose integer registers[a]	32 bits	32	Registers available for integer arithmetic and address calculation.
Floating-point registers	64 bits	32	Registers available for floating-point arithmetic instructions.
Condition register	32 bits	1	Register used to direct branches. It forms the communications path between the data flow and the control flow of a program.
Fixed-point exception register	32 bits	1	This register is used by the integer instructions to store information about exceptional conditions which arise during the execution of instructions.
Floating-point status and control register	32 bits	1	This register is used by the floating-point instructions to store information about exceptional conditions that arise during the execution of instructions. It is used to control the behavior of the floating-point execution unit.

continues

Table 2.1 continued

Name	Size	Number	Description
Link register[a]	32 bits	1	Used for the subroutine linkage address.
Count register[a]	32 bits	1	Used for coding loops with a set number of iterations.
Segment register	32 bits	16	Used for memory management.

[a] In 64-bit implementations these registers are 64 bits wide.

General-purpose registers are used for most operations and are very important to code scheduling. While not a defining characteristic of RISC architectures, the number of general registers is a difference between most current RISC architectures and most current CISC architectures. There are 32 general-purpose integer registers (often referred to simply as GPRs) defined by the PowerPC architecture. In 32-bit implementations, the GPRs are 32 bits wide, while in 64-bit implementations, the GPRs are 64-bits wide. Integer registers are used for integer arithmetic calculations and memory addressing.

There are also 32 floating-point registers each of which can hold a 64-bit IEEE double precision floating-point number or single precision floating-point number (IEEE floating-point numbers will be discussed later in this chapter). Floating-point registers are used for floating-point arithmetic instructions.

The next class of registers are the status and control registers. This includes the condition code register, the fixed-point exception register, and the floating-point status and control register.

There are eight 4-bit condition code register fields within the condition register. These fields behave like a cross between general-purpose and special-purpose registers. The fields are symmetric in most cases, that is, there are instructions that can access any condition register field in place of any other condition register field; however, there are certain non-symmetric cases. Integer arithmetic instructions can be coded to update condition register field zero automatically and floating-point arithmetic instructions can be coded to update condition register field one automatically.

The condition register forms the primary information path between the data flow of a program and the control flow of that program. In other words, if the results of an instruction execution are needed to determine the direction of a branch, then the condition register is used to pass that information from the executing instruction to the dependent branch. This is another important issue relating to code scheduling. The determining event for the branch can be scheduled ahead of the branch so that the branch direction is known as early as possible.

The fixed-point exception register (XER), also refered to as the integer exception register, is used to record exception conditions that arise during the execution of integer instructions. The carry bit is also stored in the XER. The carry bit is set by certain arithmetic operations typically when a result needs an extra bit of precision, for instance, the add carrying instructions will set the carry bit when an addition causes a carry out of the most significant bit. Other instructions read the carry bit as an implicit operand, for instance, the extended add instructions add the carry bit to the other operands.

The floating-point status and control register (FPSCR) is like the XER but for the floating-point unit. It is discussed more thoroughly in Appendix D ("A Detailed Floating-Point Model").

There are several special-purpose registers defined in the PowerPC architecture. Unlike the general-purpose registers, these registers each have a special meaning or purpose. They are generally only accessed by a specialized set of instructions or when certain events occur within the processor. We will leave the discussion of most of these registers until Appendix C ("Operating System Design for PowerPC Processors"), but we will mention two important registers here: the link register and the count register. These registers are associated with the branch instruction portion of the architecture. The primary use of the link register is for subroutine linkage. Branch instructions may be coded to automatically load the subroutine linkage address into the link register. The subroutine linkage address is the return address associated with a subroutine call. The count register is used to control fixed length loop code. If the termination of a loop is determined by the completion of a number of iterations rather than by some condition being met, then the number of iterations can be loaded into the count register. Branch instructions can be coded to automatically decrement the count register and test for the count reaching zero to determine the direction of the branch.

Introduction to Memory

In this section, we give a very brief description of virtual memory on PowerPC processors. This is primarily background information, as the operating system will typically hide memory management from the application programmer. As this section is here for illustrative purposes, only 32-bit memory management is discussed. For a more complete discussion of both 32-bit and 64-bit memory management, see Appendix C ("Operating System Design for PowerPC Processors"). For a really complete discussion of memory management in the PowerPC architecture, we recommend obtaining the PowerPC Architecture Specification (see Appendix G, "Further Reading").

The PowerPC architecture supports *virtual memory*—a method of making a large memory space using a large storage device such as a hard drive for main storage and using the computer's main memory, typically DRAM, as a cache for the main storage (see Figure 2.2). The address used to access virtual memory is called the *virtual address,* and in 32-bit PowerPC processors, the virtual address is 52 bits long. Virtual memory is split into 2^{24} 256-MB segments. Each segment is split into 2^{16} 4-KB pages that can be swapped in and out of memory by the operating system. Finally, a 12-bit offset into the page enables each byte of memory to be addressed.

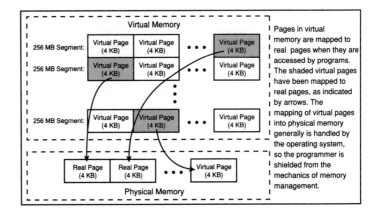

A programmer uses a 32-bit effective address to access memory. The upper order 4 bits access one of 16 segment registers on the processor. Each segment register contains a 24-bit virtual segment ID corresponding to one 256-MB segment. The next 16 bits in the effective address identify the page within the segment that is being accessed. The last 12 bits in the effective address identify the byte within the page being accessed. In order for the processor to access the appropriate page in main memory, it must look in the page table maintained by the operating system. The *page table* maps virtual pages to real pages (physical blocks of 4KB). The processor looks for the virtual segment ID and page from the virtual address in the page table and uses the corresponding real page number as the upper order 20 bits of the physical address. The entire process involves going from a 32-bit effective address to a 52-bit virtual address, and finally to a 32-bit physical address (see Figure 2.3).

FIGURE 2.3.
32-bit address translation.

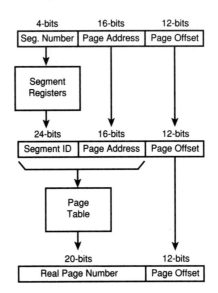

The PowerPC architecture also supports a second way to map virtual memory to physical memory—*block address translation*. Although pages are always 4KB, blocks can range from 128KB to 256MB.

Addressing Modes

Another difference between RISC and CISC architectures is that RISC architectures generally support fewer addressing modes. The X86 architecture includes four major addressing modes: *register addressing, immediate addressing, direct addressing,* and *indirect addressing.* There are three types of indirect addressing: *register indirect addressing, based indirect addressing with displacement,* and *based indirect addressing with index and displacement.* The PowerPC architecture defines instructions that use all but the direct addressing mode and the based indirect addressing with index and displacement, although PowerPC does have based indirect addressing with index. Another difference between PowerPC and X86 or 68000 addressing modes is that load and store instructions are the only instructions that use addressing modes other than register addressing or immediate addressing. With both the 68000 and the X86 architectures, the direct and indirect addressing modes can be used with many of the instructions other than simple data move instructions.

With register addressing mode, the address used identifies some register in the microprocessor (see Table 2.2); for PowerPC architecture, this register can be any of the registers described in Table 2.1, although any given instruction can access only certain registers. The *integer add* instruction, for example, can use only integer general-purpose registers, but the *move from special-purpose register* instruction can use any special-purpose register as a source, and any integer general-purpose register as a target. In the PowerPC architecture, most instructions can use register addressing.

Table 2.2. Examples of register addressing for x86, 68000, and PowerPC architectures.

x86	68000	PowerPC
MOV AX,BX	MOVE D1,D2	or r1,r2,r2
AX ← BX	D2 ← D1	r1 ← r2|r2
ADD AX,BX	ADD D1,D2	add r1,r2,r3
AX ← AX+BX	D2 ← D1+D2	r1 ← r2+r3
SUB AX,BX	SUB D1,D2	subf r2,r2,r3
AX ← AX–BX	D2 ← D2–D1	r2 ← r3–r2

With immediate addressing mode, a constant is used as an operand for the operation (see Table 2.3).

Table 2.3. Examples of immediate addressing for x86, 68000, and PowerPC architectures.

x86	*68000*	*PowerPC*
MOV AX,5	MOVE Q #5, D1	addi r1,r0,5
AX ← 5	D ← 5	r1 ←0+5
MOV CX,0×01234567	MOVE Q D1,#0×01234567	addis r1,r0,0×0123
CX ← 0×01234567	D ← 0×01234567	r1 ← 0+0×01230000
		addi r1,r1,0×4567
		r1 ←
		(r1)+0×00004567
ADD AX,5	ADDI #5,D2	addi r2,r2,5
AX ← (AX)+5	D2 ← (D2)+5	r2 ← (r2)+5
SUB AX,5	SUBI #5,D2	subic r2,r2,5
AX ← AX–5	D2 ← (D2)–5	r2←(r2)–5

Indirect addressing modes use the contents of a register to address memory. Variations on this include using the contents of a register with some constant displacement and using the contents of a register with another register as an index (see Table 2.4).

Table 2.4. Examples of indirect addressing for x86, 68000, and PowerPC architectures.

x86	*68000*	*PowerPC*
MOV AX,[BX]	MOVE (A1) D1	lwzx r1,r0,r2
AX ← [(BX)]	D1 ← [(A1)]	r1 ← [(r2)]
MOV CX,[BX+1]	MOVE (1,A1),D1	lwz r1,
CX ← [(BX)+1]	D1 ← [(A1)+1]	r1 ← [(r2)+1]
ADD AX,[BX+5]	ADD (5,A1),D1	lwz r1,
AX←(AX)+[(BX)+5]	D1←(D1)+[(A1)+5]	r1 ← [(r2)+5]
		add r3,r3,r1
		r3 ← (r3)+(r1)
ADD AX,[BX+S1+4]	ADD (4,A1,A2.32*1),D1	addi r2,r1,4
AX←(AX)+	D1←(D1)+	r2 ← (r1)+4
[(BX)+(S1)+4]	[(A1)+(A2)+4]	lwzx re,r2,r4
		r3 ← [(r2)+(r4)]
		add r5,r5,r3
		r5 ← (r5)+(r3)

Processing Modes (User Versus Supervisor)

The PowerPC architecture supports two processing modes: *user mode* and *supervisor mode*. This architecture enables operating systems to limit the access of machine-critical resources in order to protect the system from wayward user programs. In user mode, certain processor resources cannot be accessed or changed. In addition, memory pages and blocks have two different sets of access permissions: one for user mode and one for supervisor mode. Thus, the operating system can set up memory pages that can be read but not updated by user code, or it even can set up memory pages that cannot be accessed at all by user programs while still maintaining read and/or write permission itself.

Integer Processor Architecture

An *architecture* consists of a framework of instructions and storage elements on which the instructions operate in some consistent manner. This framework is a mathematical model that can be used to solve problems. In order to use this model, you must understand it in addition to understanding the instructions and storage elements that make up the framework. Most of this book is concerned with the framework, but here the underlying mathematical model is introduced, starting with the integer processor architectural model.

Integer Number Representations

The signed integer representation used in the PowerPC architecture is called *two's complement representation*. Using 32 bits, two's complement representation can represent integers between $-2,147,483,648$ and $+2,147,483,647$.

Zero has exactly one representation: 0×00000000. The positive integers are represented by their standard hexadecimal number (1=0×00000001, 12=0×0000000C, and the largest representable positive integer, 2,147,483,647, =0×7FFFFFFF).

The hexadecimal number that is one greater than the largest integer, 0×80000000, represents the largest (magnitude) negative number, $-2,147,483,648$. From the largest negative number through, each time 1 is added, the 1 is added to the number being represented (0×80000001=$-2,147,483,647$, and 0×FFFFFFFF=-1).

In order to negate a two's complement number, the hexadecimal representation is inverted logically and then incremented by 1. So starting with 1, 0×80000001, you invert to get 0×FFFFFFFE, and increment to get 0×FFFFFFFF=-1.

Notice, however, if you start with $-2,147,483,648$=0×80000000, you invert to get 0×7FFFFFFF, and add 1 to get 0×80000000=$-2,147,483,648$. What happened? There is no 32-bit two's complement representation of $+2,147,483,648$; overflow occurred.

Floating-Point Processor Architecture

One of the biggest differences between the PowerPC architecture and Intel's X86 and Motorola's 68000 architectures is in the integrated floating-point unit. Often, scientists and engineers represent numbers in floating-point form; for example:

$1.2375 \times 10^2 \equiv 1.2375e2 \equiv 123.75$

Floating-point numbers contain three parts: a *base*, a *mantissa*, and an *exponent*. In the earlier examples, 1.2345 is the mantissa and 2 is the exponent. The base of the numbers is 10, that is the number raised to the exponent power. In a computer, numbers usually are represented in base 2, and floating-point numbers are not an exception. The mantissa and exponent are represented in base 2 and the base is 2. For example, the following is a floating-point number in base 2:

$1.11101111 \times 2^{110} \equiv 1111011.11 \equiv 111.101111 \times 2^{100} \equiv 123.75.$

Notice that just as binary digits increase by a factor of 2 for each step to the left of the binary point, they also decrease by a factor of 2 for each step to the right of the binary point. Thus, 0.11 in binary is $^1/_2 + ^1/_4 = ^3/_4$. In the preceding example, the same number had two different floating-point representations. Actually, every number has an infinite number of representations. One special representation is when there is a single, non-zero digit to the left of the binary point in the mantissa. Numbers in this form are called *normalized numbers.*

Execution Model

The PowerPC floating-point execution model is based on the IEEE 754-1985 floating-point standard. It supports both single and double precision operations. Single precision floating-point numbers consist of a 24-bit unsigned mantissa, a sign bit, and an 8-bit signed exponent. The leading digit of the mantissa is assumed to be a 1—the number is assumed to be normalized, which enables the 33-bit number to be stored in 32 bits (the leading bit of the mantissa is not stored). Single precision exponents range from –126 to +127. Single precision mantissas can range from 1 to $2^{24}-1$. Finally, the sign bit specifies whether the number is positive or negative.

Double precision floating-point numbers consist of a 53-bit unsigned mantissa, a sign bit, and an 11-bit signed exponent. Again, the numbers are assumed to be normalized, thereby allowing the 53-bit mantissa to be stored in 52 bits, and the entire double precision floating-point number to be stored in 64 bits. Double precision exponents range from –1022 to +1023. Double precision mantissas can range from 1 to $2^{53}-1$. Finally, the sign bit specifies whether the number is positive or negative. With the numbers as defined here, the range of values for single precision floating-point numbers is from $-2^{128}+2^{104}$ to $2^{128}-2^{104}$, or roughly -3.4×10^{38} to 3.4×10^{38}. Double precision numbers can range from $-2^{1024}+2^{972}$ to $2^{1024}-2^{972}$, or roughly -1.8×10^{308} to 1.8×10^{308}.

Notice that with this straightforward encoding, that there is no way to represent the number 0. Because of the implied 1 to the left of the decimal point, the closest number to 0 that can be represented is a fraction of 0 (meaning 1.0000...00) with the minimum exponent. In order to remedy this problem, some special encodings or special numbers have been designated.

Special Numbers

Certain representations have special meanings in the PowerPC architecture. Zero, for example, is represented by a mantissa of 0 with an exponent of e_{min} ((e_{min})=−1032 for double precision, −127 for single precision). The sign bit is ignored for 0 values (+0=−0). Zero really is a special case of a broader set of special numbers called *denormalized numbers*. Denormalized numbers have a 0 to the left of the binary point—they are not normalized and do not have an implicit 1 for the most significant bit of the mantissa. Any number with e_{min} for an exponent value is a denormalized number. Sometimes, support for denormalized numbers is referred to as *gradual underflow*.

Infinity is another special number. For many applications, it is better for a very large number to get clamped at infinity rather than to wrap around to a very small number as integers do—maximum positive integer + 1 = maximum negative integer for signed integer arithmetic, or 0 for unsigned integer arithmetic. Instead, PowerPC floating-point numbers go to infinity. Infinity is represented by fraction of 0 with the maximum exponent value (e_{max})((e_{max})=+1024 for double precision, +128 for single precision). The sign bit differentiates positive and negative infinity.

The final type of special number is called *not a number* (NaN). These numbers are used to represent certain exceptions or the results of invalid operations. These representations come in two forms: *signaling NaNs* and *Quiet NaNs*. Signaling NaNs are represented by a mantissa with the most significant fraction bit set to 1 and an exponent of e_{max}, while quiet NaNs are represented by a mantissa with the most significant fraction bit set to 0 and an exponent of e_{max}. NaNs are discussed in Appendix D, "A Detailed Floating-Point Model."

Rounding

When an operation is performed on floating-point numbers, the result may have greater precision (more digits) than either of the initial operands. For example:

$1.2 \times 10^0 \times 1.2 \times 10^1 = 1.44 \times 10^1$

In this example, each of the operands has a single digit after the decimal place, but the result has two digits after the decimal place. Remember, however, that the floating-point representations in the PowerPC architecture have a fixed number of positions after the binary point. This means that after a calculation is performed, the result is rounded to fit into the mantissa of the appropriate representation.

Four rounding modes are supported by the PowerPC architecture (see Table 2.5). When a number does not fit into the target register, there are two representable numbers that are closest to it. The different rounding modes enable the programmer to specify which of these two numbers is chosen as the final (rounded) result.

Table 2.5. Floating-point rounding modes supported by the PowerPC architecture.

Rounding Mode	*Description*
Round to Nearest	Choose the closest representable value. If the number is exactly between the two closest values, choose the even one.
Round toward zero	Of the two closest representable values, choose the one that is closer to zero.
Round toward positive infinity	Of the two closest representable values, choose the larger one.
Round toward negative infinity	Of the two closest representable values, choose the smaller one.

Registers

The PowerPC architecture defines 32 floating-point registers. Each of these registers can hold one double precision floating-point number or one single precision floating-point number. In addition, there is a 32-bit floating-point status and control register that contains flags which tell the floating-point unit how to perform certain actions (for example, which rounding mode to use) and flags that can tell a programmer about exceptional events (when a divide-by-zero has occurred, for example).

Branch Processor Architecture

The *branch processing* portion, or unit, of the architecture describes a set of registers and instructions that enable the programmer to specify how instructions are fetched from memory. Three of the special-purpose registers described earlier in the chapter are related to the branch processor: the *condition register*, the *link register*, and the *count register*. The condition register is used to direct branch instructions. A branch instruction may test a bit in the condition register to determine whether the target instructions should be fetched, or whether fetching should continue with the instruction immediately following the branch in memory (see Chapter 4, "Branch and Control Flow Functions"). The link register is used for subroutine linkage (see the following section), and the count register is used for several miscellaneous functions.

Subroutine Linkage

The *link register* is used to hold the return address for subroutine calls. A branch instruction that is used to call a subroutine will update the link register with the address of the instruction immediately following the branch in memory. This is the return address for the subroutine. If the subroutine calls another subroutine, then the link register first must be copied into a general integer register and then placed onto the software-maintained link stack—the stack of addresses that corresponds to the function caller stack.

Other Branch Structures

The *count register* is used for other branch structures. The first use is for loop structures. Branches that automatically decrement the count register and branch, based on a comparison of the count register contents to zero, can be used for loop constructs (for...next loops, for example). The count register first is loaded with the iteration variable. The branch instructions then can be coded to perform the loop. The second use for the count register is to supply a target address. This is used for long branches (branching farther in memory than can be coded using other branch instructions, for example), branches to function pointers, and calculated goto-type branches (switch statements in C, for example).

Interrupt Architecture

The PowerPC architecture defines several types of interrupts—each with its own address. The address of an interrupt is the memory location that the program jumps to when the interrupt occurs. The interrupt architecture is described in detail in Appendix C, "Operating System Design for PowerPC Processors." Two interrupts of particular interest to the assembly-language programmer are discussed here: the *system call interrupt* and the *program interrupt*. These are the interrupts a programmer may use to perform some action. When an interrupt occurs, the processor goes into *privileged mode*, which enables code to access certain facilities with restricted access rights and to access data structures in memory that have restricted access rights (see Appendix C). Generally, these are data structures set up by the operating system, which are sensitive in some way (if they are updated inappropriately, for example, the machine may crash). If a programmer wants to access some operating system facility, then he can use a *system call* instruction (see Chapter 4) to cause a system call interrupt. Based on the contents of certain registers, the operating system will perform some service—possibly placing some data in the registers—and then return control back to the program that issued the system call instruction. In essence, the system call instruction is a subroutine call to an operating system subroutine.

The other interrupt of particular interest to the assembly programmer is the *program interrupt*. This interrupt can be caused by a trap instruction (see Chapter 3). Typically, trap instructions check for some error condition and then *trap* (cause a program interrupt) if such an error occurs. From that point, the operating system may try to fix the error or perhaps simply abort the program.

Notation

In the following chapters, the notations shown in Table 2.6 are used. Throughout the book, bits are numbered starting with the most significant bit as 0, and ending with the least significant bit as the operand size minus one. Thus, for a 32-bit number, bit 0 is the most significant bit, and bit 31 is the least significant. This is the convention used for PowerPC bit numbering and may be the reverse of what you are used to seeing for other architectures. In addition, the following symbols are used.

Table 2.6. Notations used in this book.

Notation	Description
(Rx)	Register reference. This means the contents of Rx. Thus, (R2) means the data contained in register R2.
[x]	Memory reference. This means the memory location addressed by the value x.
<-, ←	Assignment statements. The object on the left of the assignment symbol is given the value of the object on the right side of the symbol.
<<	Shift left. A<<B means that A is shifted left by B bits.
>>	Shift right. A>>B means that A is shifted right by B bits.
<	Signed less than. This means less than and uses a signed comparison. Thus, 0×FFFF < 0×0000 (−1 < 0).
u<	Unsigned less than. This means less than and uses an unsigned comparison. Thus, 0×0000 u<0×FFFF (0 u< 65,535).
>	Signed greater than. This means greater than and uses a signed comparison. Thus, 0×0000 > 0×FFFF (0 > −1).
u>	Unsigned greater than. This means greater than and uses an unsigned comparison. Thus, 0×FFFF u> 0×0000 (65,535 u> 0).
==	Equal to. Thus, 0×0000 == 0×0000 (0 == 0).
!=	Not equal to. Thus, 0×0000 != 0×FFFF (0 != −1).
||	Concatenate. Thus, 0×F || 0×D means 0×FD.
&	Boolean AND. 0×F55F & 0×5FAF = 0×550F.
|	Boolean OR. 0×F55F | 0×5FAF = 0×FFFF.
[A]	Boolean NOT. [A] means not A. So [A] | A = 0b1 and [A] & A = 0b0.

Notation	Description
$\oplus$	Boolean XOR. Thus, $\overline{A} \oplus A = 0b1$ and $A \oplus A = 0b0$.
$\equiv$	Boolean equivalence. Thus, $\overline{A} \equiv A = 0b0$ and $A \equiv A = 0b1$.
sign_ext()	Sign extend. sign_ext(0×FF) = 0×FFFF, and sign_ext(0×7F) = 0×007F.
$Rn_{a:b}$	Subfield. Subscripts used in this fashion mean a subfield of the contents of Rn. Thus, $Rn_{0:8}$ means bits 0 through 8 of the register Rn.
^aA	Repeat. This is a repeat symbol. ^aA means to concatenate a copies of A.
+	Addition. 0×0001 + 0×F001 = 0×F002.
−	Subtraction. 0×0444 − 0×0434 = 0×0010.
*, x	Multiplication. 0×0002 * 0×0004 = 0×0008.
%	Modulo. This means modulo or remainder. A%B means the remainder if you divide A by B.
/	Divide. A/B means A divided by B.
?:	Conditional operator. An if...then...else structure. The statement A?B:C takes the value of B if A evaluates to TRUE; otherwise, it takes the value of C.
(Rn)_0	Contents of Rn if n is 1-31, 0 if n is 0.

II

Instruction Descriptions

In this part we describe the PowerPC instruction set and give some programming examples to show how the instructions are used. The PowerPC instruction set can be split into 3 main areas: integer processing instructions, control flow processing instructions, and floating point processing instructions. We will discuss each of these types of instructions below. A fourth area involves processor and system control instructions. These instructions are generally used by an operating system and are not available to user (application) code (see Appendix C, "Operating System Design for PowerPC Processors").

The PowerPC architecture defines extended mnemonics, in addition to the actual hardware-implemented instructions. Extended mnemonics are translated by the assembler into hardware instructions and are only meaningful to the programmer. For instance, the subtract (sub) instruction is an extended mnemonic which is translated into the subtract from (subf) instruction (these instructions are described in more detail below). The subf instruction subtracts the first operand from the second operand. The sub instruction subtracts the second operand from the first operand. When an assembler sees a sub instruction, it simply swaps the first and second operands and changes the sub instruction to a subf instruction. The extended mnemonics can be used to make code easier to read. Extended mnemonics are used throughout this book but are typically noted as extended.

Note that we follow a convention where RT always denotes a target register, while RS, RA, and RB always denote source registers. The processor users' guides and architecture definition use a different (and more complicated) convention for naming the source and destination systems; we chose a simpler scheme that should be more intuitive for programmer's purposes.

3

Integer Instructions

The integer instructions can be split into four subsections: the *arithmetic* instructions, the *logical operation* instructions, the *rotate and shift* instructions, and the *load/store* instructions. All integer instructions operate on data contained in the integer general-purpose registers. In addition, the condition register can be updated by integer instructions, and there is a special register that is used by integer instructions called the *fixed point exception register* or the *XER*.

Arithmetic Instructions

The arithmetic instructions perform the standard integer arithmetic operations—including addition, subtraction, multiplication, and division. The addressing modes supported by these instructions are immediate addressing and register addressing. All these instructions read their sources and store their results into integer general-purpose registers.

For some of these instructions, it is possible to update the condition register with information about the result of the instruction or the XER with information about the execution of the instruction. These registers are known as *implicit targets* because the registers are not explicitly specified in the instruction; instead, a suffix is added to the mnemonic to indicate to the assembler that a slightly different form of the instruction should be used.

To indicate that the condition register should be updated with information about the result, a dot [.] is added to the instruction mnemonic. In this case, the processor updates condition register field zero with a set of flags describing the result. The following four bits of the condition register field are set: bit 0 is set if the result is negative, bit 1 is set if the result is positive, bit 2 is set if the result is zero, thus exactly one of the first three bits is set, and bit 3 is set if this instruction experienced an overflow condition.

To indicate that the XER should be updated with information about the execution of the instruction, an o [o] should be added to the mnemonic. In this case, two bits in the XER may be updated: the overflow bit and the summary overflow bit. The overflow bit is set to 1 if the instruction experienced an overflow condition during execution and to 0 if the instruction completed without overflow. The summary overflow bit is set to 1 if the instruction experienced an overflow condition during execution, and is not changed if it did not experience an overflow condition.

Integer Add Instructions

The PowerPC architecture includes eight integer add instructions. All instructions have two operands and store their primary into general-purpose integer registers. The general form of an add instruction is:

```
add RT, RA, source1
```

The contents of RA are added to source1 and the result is placed into RT. source1 can be the value of an immediate field (immediate addressing mode), the contents of a general-purpose integer register RB (register addressing mode), or implied by the specific instruction used.

Three of the add instructions get source1 from the immediate field. The first two—*add immediate* (addi) and *add immediate shifted* (addis)—can be used together to generate a 32-bit constant in a register. The addi instruction adds RA to the immediate field sign extended to 32 bits, and the addis instruction adds RA to the immediate field shifted left by 16 bits. These two instructions follow the conventions of the load/store address-generation instructions: If RA is registered to 0, then the immediate field is added to 0 rather than to the contents of R0. The next add instruction—*add immediate carrying* with and without condition register record (addic[.])—performs the add of RA and the immediate value sign extended to 32 bits, and places the carry out of the add into the XER register.

Three add instructions use the contents of RB for source1. Each of these three instructions can update the condition register or not, and update the XER with overflow information or not. The basic add instruction (add[o][.]) simply adds the contents of RA to the contents of RB and puts the result in RT. If the carry out of the add is needed, then the *add carrying* instruction should be used (addc[o][.]). The add carrying instruction places the carry out from the addition into the carry bit in the XER. The remaining add instruction, which uses RB, the add extended (adde[o][.]) instruction adds RA and RB to the contents of the carry bit in the XER and places the result into RT.

EXAMPLE 3.1.

Carrying and add extended instructions to perform a 64-bit addition on a 32-bit processor.

Assume that operand A is contained in r1 (high-order 32 bits) and r2 (low-order 32 bits), and that operand B is contained in r3 (high-order 32 bits) and r4 (low-order 32 bits). You want to perform the function A+B, producing a 64-bit result contained in r5 (high-order bits) and r6 (low-order bits).

32-bit machine code:

```
        addc    r6,r2,r4     #  r6<-(r2)+(r4);
                             #  XER_CA<-carry
        adde    r5,r1,r3     #  r5<-(r1)+(r3)+XER_CA;
                             #  XER_CA<-carry
```

The last two add instructions are special cases of the add extended instruction. The first is the *add to minus one extended* instruction (addme[o][.]), which adds RA to –1 and the carry bit in the XER. The second is the *add to zero extended* instruction (addze[o][.]), which adds RA to 0. Table 3.1 lists the add instructions.

Table 3.1. Add instructions.

Instruction	Definition	Format
add immediate	RT <-(RA)_0+sign_ext(SI)	addi RT,RA,SI
add immediate shifted	RT <-(RA)_0+(SI<<16)	addis RT,RA,SI
add immediate carrying	RT <-(RA)+sign_ext(SI) XER_{CA}<-carry_out	addic[.] RT,RA,SI
add	RT <-(RA)+(RB)	add[0][.] RT,RA,RB
add carrying	RT <-(RA)+(RB) XER_{CA}<-carry_out	addc[0][.] RT,RA,RB
add extended	RT <-(RA)+(RB)+XER_{CA} RT,RA,RB XER_{CA}<-carry_out	adde[0][.]
add to minus one extended	RT <-(RA)+XER_{CA}−1 XER_{CA}<-carry_out	addme[0][.] RT,RA
add to zero extended	RT <-(RA)+XER_{CA} XER_{CA}<-carry_out	addze[0][.] RT,RA

Note: If [o] is added, XER_{SO} and XER_{OU} will be set, if [.] is added, CRO will be altered based on the result of the instruction.

Integer Subtract Instructions

The PowerPC architecture includes 12 integer subtract instructions. All instructions have two operands and store their primary into general-purpose integer registers. One of the two operands comes from a general-purpose integer register; the other operand can come from an immediate field, it can come from a general-purpose integer register, or it can be implied by the instruction. The general form of the subtract instructions follows:

```
sub RT, RA, source1
```

RA is subtracted from source1 or source1 is subtracted from RA, depending on the instruction, and the result is placed into RT. source1 is the immediate field for subtract instructions using the immediate addressing mode, a register (RB) for subtract instructions using the register addressing mode, and an implicit value for certain instructions.

There are five immediate mode subtraction instructions. The first two instructions, *subtract immediate* (subi) and *subtract immediate shifted* (subis) are extended mnemonics of the *add immediate* (addi) and *add immediate shifted* (addis) instructions described earlier. The only difference between these instructions and the addi/addis instructions is that RA is added to the 2's complement of the sign extended immediate value (possibly shifted left by 16 bits). The next immediate mode subtract instruction, *subtract immediate carrying* with and without condition register update (subic[.]), is an extended mnemonic of the *add immediate carrying* instruction described earlier. Again, the immediate field is negated (2's complement) and then added to RA. The *subtract from immediate carrying* instruction (subfic) negates RA (2's complement) before performing the addition of RA and the immediate field; thus, RA is subtracted from the immediate field and the result is placed in RT. There also is a single source subtract instruction that negates the source register (neg[o][.]).

Seven subtract instructions use the register addressing mode. The *subtract from* instruction (subf[o][.]) stores RB minus RA into RT. The *subtract from carrying* instruction (subfc[o][.]) subtracts RA from RB and sets the carry bit in the XER as a carry into the subtractor. The result is placed into RT. The *simple subtract* instruction (sub[o][.]) and the *subtract carrying* instruction (subc[o][.]) are extended mnemonics of the subf[o][.] and subfc[o][.] instructions, respectively. Simple subtract and subtract carrying work similarly to subf[o][.] and subfc[o][.], except that RA and RB are reversed so that RT is loaded with RA–RB instead of RB–RA. The last three subtract instructions add carry bit in the XER into the result. *The subtract from extended* instruction (subfe[o][.]) stores RB minus RA with the carry bit in the XER as a borrow from the subtractor (if the carry bit is a 1 then there is no borrow, while if the carry bit is a 0 there is a borrow) into RT. The *subtract from minus one extended* instruction (subfme[o][.]) subtracts RA from –1 with the carry bit in the XER as a borrow from the subtractor. The *subtract from zero extended* instruction (subfze[o][.]) subtracts RA from 0 with the carry bit in the XER as a borrow from the subtractor. Table 3.2 lists the subtract instructions.

Table 3.2. Subtract instructions.

Instruction	Definition	Format
negate	RT <--(RA)	neg[0][.] RT,RA
subtract immediate shifted	RT <-(RA) |0–sign_ext(SI)	subi RT,RA,SI
subtract immediate shifted	RT <-(RA) |0–(SI<<16)	subis RT,RA,SI
subtract immediate carrying	RT <-(RA)–sign_ext(SI) XER_{CA} <-carry_out	subic[.] RT,RA,SI
subtract from immediate carrying	RT <-sign_ext(SI)–(RA) XER_{CA} <-carry_out	subfic RT,RA,SI
subtract	RT <-(RA)–(RB)	sub[0][.] RT,RA,RB
subtract carrying	RT <-(RA)–(RB) XER_{CA} <-carry_out	subc[0][.] RT,RA,RB
subtract from	RT <-(RB)–(RA)	subf[0][.] RT,RA,RB

continues

Table 3.2. continued

Instruction	Definition	Format
subtract from carrying	RT <-(RB)–(RA) XER_{CA} <-carry_out	subfc[0][.] RT,RA, RB
extended subtract from	RT <-(RB)–(RA)–1+ XER_{CA} XER_{CA} <-carry_out	subfe[0][.] RT,RA, RB
extended subtract from minus one	RT <--(RA)+XER_{CA}–2 XER_{CA} <-carry_out	subfme[0][.] RT,RA
extended subtract from zero	RT <--(RA)+XER_{CA}–1 XER_{CA} <-carry_out	subfze[0][.] RT,RA

Note: If [o] is added, XER_{SO} and XER_{OU} will be set, if [.] is added, CRO will be altered based on the result of the instruction.

EXAMPLE 3.2.

Performing 64-bit subtraction on a 32-bit machine using the extended subtraction instruction.

Assume that operand A is contained in r1 (high-order 32 bits) and r2 (low-order 32 bits), and that operand B is contained in r3 (high-order 32 bits) and r4 (low-order 32 bits). You want to perform the function A–B, producing a 64-bit result contained in r5 (high-order bits) and r6 (low-order bits).

32-bit machine code:

```
subfc   r6,r4,r2    # r6<-(r2)-(r4); XER_CA<-carry
subfe   r5,r3,r1    # r5<-(r1)-(r3)+XER_CA;
                    # XER_CA<-carry
```

Integer Multiply Instructions

The PowerPC architecture includes five integer multiply instructions. All these instructions have two operands and store their result primary into a general-purpose integer registers. One of the two operands comes from a general-purpose integer register; the other operand can come from an immediate field (immediate addressing mode), or from a general-purpose integer register (register addressing mode). The general form of the multiply instructions follows:

```
mul RT, RA, source1
```

RA is multiplied by source1, and the result is placed into RT. source1 is the immediate field for multiply instructions using the immediate addressing mode and a register (RB) for multiply instructions using the register addressing mode.

The PowerPC architecture defines multiply instructions to enable a programmer to multiply two integers and get the full range of the results. Note that when two 32-bit numbers are multiplied, the result may require as many as 64 bits to be represented. In order to accommodate this requirement, the multiply instructions are split into two classes: Those that give the upper order bits as the result, and those that give the lower-order bits as the result.

There are three multiply instructions defined for 32-bit implementations of the architecture. The *multiply low immediate* instruction (mulli) multiplies RA by the sign extended immediate field (SI). The low-order half of the 64-bit result is placed into the target register. The *multiply low word* instruction (mullw[o][.]) uses the register addressing mode and multiplies RA by RB, placing the low-order 32 bits of the result into RT. If the mullwo[.] form of the instruction is used, then overflow bit in the XER is set to 1 if the result cannot be represented in 32 bits. The last 32-bit multiply instruction is the *multiply high word* instruction (mulhw[u][.]). This instruction produces the upper-order half of the 64-bit result. RA is multiplied by RB and the upper-order half of the 64-bit result is stored in RT. If the mulhwu[.] form of the instruction is used, then RA and RB are treated as unsigned integers; if the mulhw[.] form of the instruction is used, then RA and RB are treated as signed integers.

EXAMPLE 3.3.

Multiplying two unsigned 64-bit numbers on a 32-bit machine (producing a 128-bit result).

In this example, you multiply two 64-bit numbers. One operand is contained in R1 (high-order 32 bits) and R2 (low-order 32 bits), and the other operand is contained in R3 (high-order 32 bits) and R4 (low-order 32 bits). Multiplying two 64-bit numbers can produce a 128-bit result, which you will place in R5 (high-order 32 bits) through R8 (low-order 32 bits). You will perform the multiplication in the same way that you typically multiply multidigit numbers by hand; remember that multiplying two 32-bit numbers produces a 64-bit result (see Figure 3.1). Table 3.3 lists the 32-bit multiply instructions.

```
mullw    r8,r4,r2      # r8<-((r4) × (r2))32:63
mulhwu   r7,r4,r2      # r7<-((r4) × (r2))0:31
mullw    r10,r4,r1     # r10<-((r4) × (r1))32:63
mulhwu   r6,r4,r1      # r6<-((r4) × (r1))0:31
mullw    r12,r3,r2     # r12<-((r3) × (r2))32:63
mulhwu   r11,r3,r2     # r6<-((r3) × (r2))0:31
mullw    r13,r3,r1     # r13<-((r3) × (r1))32:63
mulhwu   r5,r3,r1      # r6<-((r3) × (r1))0:31
addc     r7,r7,r10     # r7<-(r7)+(r10)
adde     r6,r6,r11     # r6<-(r6)+(r11)+XERCA
addze    r5,r5         # r5<-(r5)+XERCA
addc     r7,r7,r12     # r7<-(r7)+(r12)
                       # i.e. r7<-(r7)+(r10)+(r12)
adde     r6,r6,r13     # r6<-(r6)+(r13)+XERCA
                       # i.e. r6<-(r6)+(r11)+(r13)
addze    r5,r5         # r5<-(r5)+XERCA
```

FIGURE 3.1.

Unsigned multiplication of two 64-bit numbers on a 32-bit machine.

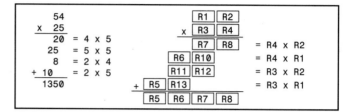

Table 3.3. 32-bit multiply instructions.

Instruction	Definition	Format
multiply low immediate	$RT \leftarrow ((RA)*\text{sign\_ext}(SI))_{32:63}$	mulli RT,RA,SI
multiply low word	$RT \leftarrow ((RA)*(RB))_{32:63}$	mullw[o][.] RT, RA,RB
multiply high word	$RT \leftarrow ((RA)*(RB))_{0:31}$	mullhw[u][.] RT, RA,RB

Note: If [o] is added, XER_{SO} and XER_{OU} will be set, if [.] is added, CR0 will be altered based on the result of the instruction.

Five multiply instructions are defined for 64-bit implementations of the PowerPC architecture. The first three instructions are the instructions that were defined earlier for 32-bit implementations. The *multiply low immediate* instruction (mulli) multiplies RA by the sign extended immediate field (SI) and stores the low-order 64 bits of the 128-bit result in RT. The *multiply low word* instruction (mullw[o][.]) multiplies the low-order 32 bits of RA by the low-order 32 bits of RB and stores the 64-bit result in RT. If the mullwo[.] form of the instruction is used, then the overflow bit in the XER is set to 1 if the result cannot be represented in 32 bits. The *multiply high word* instruction (mulhw[u][.]) multiplies the low-order 32 bits of RA by the low-order 32 bits of RB and stores the high-order 32 bits of the result into the *low-order 32 bits* of RT. The high-order 32-bits of RT are left undefined. If the mulhwu[.] form of the instruction is used, then RA and RB are treated as unsigned; if the mulhw[.] form of the instruction is used, then RA and RB are treated as signed.

The last two multiply instructions are defined only for 64-bit implementations of the architecture. The first instruction, *multiply low doubleword* (mulld[o][.]) is very similar to the mullw[o][.] instruction. The low-order half of the 128-bit product of RA and RB is stored in RT. If the mulldo[.] form of the instruction is used, then the overflow bit in the XER is set to 1 if the product cannot be represented in 64 bits. The *multiply high doubleword* instruction (mulhd[u][.])

is very similar to the mulhw[u][.] defined earlier. The high-order half of the 128-bit product of RA and RB is stored in RT. If the mulhdu[.] form of the instruction is used, then RA and RB are treated as unsigned integers; if the mulhd[.] form of the instruction is used, then RA and RB are treated as signed integers. Table 3.4 lists the 64-bit multiply instructions.

Table 3.4. 64-bit multiply instructions.

Instruction	Definition	Format
multiply low immediate	$RT \leftarrow ((RA) * sign\_ext(SI))_{64:127}$	mulli RT,RA,SI
multiply low word	$RT \leftarrow (RA)_{32:63} * (RB)_{32:63}$ $RT_{0:31} \leftarrow$ undefined	mullw[0][.] RT, RA,RB
multiply high word	$RT_{32:63} \leftarrow ((RA)_{32:63} * (RB)_{32:63})_{0:31}$ $RT_{0:31} \leftarrow$ undefined	mulhw[u][.] RT, RA,RB
multiply low doubleword	$RT \leftarrow ((RA) * (RB))_{64:127}$	mulld[0][.] RT, RA,RB
multiply high doubleword	$RT \leftarrow ((RA) * (RB))_{0:63}$	mulhd[u][.] RT, RA,RB

Note: If [o] is added, XER_{SO} and XER_{OU} will be set, if [.] is added, CRO will be altered based on the result of the instruction.

Integer Divide Instructions

The PowerPC architecture includes two integer divide instructions. Both instructions have two operands and store their primary result into general-purpose integer registers. Both of the operands come from general-purpose integer registers. The general form of the divide instructions follows:

```
div RT, RA, RB
```

RA is divided by RB, and the result is placed into RT. Specifically, RT is set to a value so that the following equation is satisfied:

$$RA = (RT \times RB) + r, \text{ where } -|RA| < r < |RA|.$$

The remainder is not specifically supplied as a result of any of the divide instructions in the PowerPC architecture (see Example 3.4).

EXAMPLE 3.4.

Using the division instructions to calculate a remainder.

The remainder (r) is not supplied as a result of the divide instructions, nor is there any calculate remainder (modulo) instruction. If the remainder is needed, then the sequence of instructions shown to the right can be used.

32-bit machine code:

```
divw    r1,r2,r3    # r1<-(r2) / (r3)
mullw   r4,r1,r3    # r4<-(r1) × (r3)
subf    r1,r4,r3    # r1<-(r2) - (r4)
                    # i.e. r1<-remainder
```

Note: For r2=2^{31}, for r1=−1. Overflow occurs and the remainder isn't correct.

64-bit machine code:

```
divd    r1,r2,r3    # r1<-(r2) / (r3)
mulld   r4,r1,r3    # r4<-(r1) × (r3)
subf    r1,r2,r4    # r1<-(r2) - (r4)
                    # i.e. r1<-remainder
```

Note: For r2=2^{63}, for r1—1. Overflow occurs.

One integer divide instruction is defined for 32-bit implementations of the PowerPC architecture: the *divide word* instruction (divw[u][o][.]). If the divwu[o][.] form of the instruction is used, then RA and RB are treated as unsigned integers; if the divw[o][.] form of the instruction is used, then RA and RB are treated as signed integers. The division is performed as described earlier. Table 3.5 lists the 32-bit divide instructions.

Table 3.5. 32-bit divide instruction.

Instruction	Definition	Format
divide word	RT <- (RA) / (RB)	divw[u][o][.] RT, RA, RB

Note: If [o] is added, XER_{SO} and XER_{OU} will be set, if [.] is added, CRO will be altered based on the result of the instruction.

Two integer divide instructions are defined for 64-bit implementations of the architecture. The first instruction is the divw[u][o][.] instruction from earlier in this chapter. The dividend is formed by sign extending the low-order 32 bits of RA, the divisor is formed by sign extending the low-order bits of RB, and the 32-bit quotient is formed by dividing RA by RB. The quotient then is placed into the low-order 32 bits of RT. The high-order bits of RT are left undefined. If the divwu[o][.] form of the instruction is used, then RA and RB are treated as unsigned integers. If the divw[o][.] form of the instruction is used, then RA and RB are treated as signed integers. The second 64-bit integer divide instruction is the *divide doubleword* instruction (divd[u][o][.]). If the divdu[o][.] form of the instruction is used, then RA and RB are treated as unsigned integers; if the divd[o][.] form of the instruction is used, then RA and RB are treated as signed integers. The division is performed as described earlier. Table 3.6 lists the 64-bit divide instructions.

Table 3.6. 64-bit divide instructions.

Instruction	Definition	Format
divide word	$RT_{32:63} \leftarrow (RA)_{32:63} / (RB)_{32:63}$ $RT_{0:31} \leftarrow$ undefined	divw[u][o][.] RT, RA, RB
divide doubleword	$RT \leftarrow (RA) / (RB)$	divd[u][o][.] RT, RA, RB

Note: If [o] is added, XER_{SO} and XER_{OU} will be set, if [.] is added, CRO will be altered based on the result of the instruction.

Logical Operation Instructions

The logical operations perform Boolean algebraic operations on the integer registers, and some other simple bit-manipulation operations. These instructions will execute on both 32- and 64-bit machines. Some of the logical operation instructions can set condition register field zero with a signed comparison of the result of the operation to 0. These instructions are identified by a dot [.] at the end of the mnemonic. None of the logical instructions updates the overflow bit, summary overflow bit, or carry bit in the XER. The logical operations that require two operands all use one integer register and either another integer register (register addressing mode) or an immediate field in the instruction (immediate addressing mode). The logical operations which only require one operand, get that operand from an integer register.

The immediate addressing mode instructions all have the following basic format:

```
Operation RT, RA, UI
```

Where RT is the target register, RA is the source register, and UI is a 16-bit unsigned immediate value. The immediate value is generally extended to the left with zeros to form an operand of the appropriate width (32 bits on 32-bit implementations, and 64 bits on 64-bit implementations). The logical operation is then performed on RA and the zero-extended immediate operand and the result is placed into RT.

The register addressing mode logical instructions all have the following format:

```
Operation RT, RA, RB
```

Where RT is the target register and is loaded with the result of the operation which is performed on the contents of register RA and the contents of register RB.

The single operand instructions all have the following format:

```
Operation RT, RA
```

RT is the target register, loaded with the results of performing the operation on the contents of register RA. The descriptions below are split up by logical operation.

Boolean Operations

The Boolean operation instructions perform the operations of Boolean algebra in a bitwise manner on the integer registers. This means that, for instance, That bit 0 of the target register is loaded with the result of the Boolean operation performed on bit 0 of the source operands, and bit 1 of the target register is loaded with the results of the Boolean operation performed on bit 1 of the source operands, and so on for each bit of the registers. Note that these operations correspond to C operators like & and | rather than operators like && and ||.

Integer AND Instructions

The integer AND instructions perform a bitwise AND of the two operands. There are two immediate form AND instructions, AND immediate (andi.), and AND immediate shifted (andis.). Both of these instructions use the contents of RA for their first operand. The andi. instruction uses the immediate field left-extended with zeros for the second operand. The andis. instruction uses the immediate field right-extended with 16 zeros. For 32-bit implementations, the 16 zeros concatenated to the 16 bits of the immediate value forms the full 32-bit operand; for 64-bit implementations, the 16 zeros concatenated to the 16-bit immediate field form the low-order 32 bits of the operand; the upper-order 32 bits of the operand are set to zero. Both of these instructions update condition register field zero with a sign compare of the result to zero. These instructions update condition register field 0, and there are no forms of these instructions which do not update condition register field 0.

There are two indexed form AND instructions, AND (and[.]), and AND with complement (andc[.]). These instructions both use the contents of RA and RB as the two operands, however the andc[.] instruction inverts the contents of RB before ANDing it with RA (see Table 3.7).

Integer OR Instructions

The integer OR instructions perform a bitwise OR of the two operands. There are two immediate form OR instructions, OR immediate (ori), and OR immediate shifted (oris). Both of these instructions use the contents of RA for their first operand. The second operand is formed from the immediate field as in the andi. and andis. instructions above.

There are two register addressing mode OR instructions, OR (or[.]), and OR with complement (orc[.]). These instructions both use the contents of RA and RB as the two operands, however the orc[.] instruction inverts the contents of RB before ORing it with RA (see Table 3.7).

Integer XOR Instructions

The integer XOR instructions perform a bitwise XOR of the two operands. There are two immediate form XOR instructions, XOR immediate (xori), and XOR immediate shifted (xoris). Both of these instructions use the contents of RA for their first operand. The second operand is formed from the immediate field as in the andi. and andis. instructions above.

There is one indexed form XOR instructions, XOR (xor[.]). This instruction uses the contents of RA and RB as the two operands (see Table 3.7).

EXAMPLE 3.5.

Swapping the contents of two registers using XOR instructions.

It is possible to swap the contents of two registers using three instructions and no scratch registers. Assume we want to swap the contents of R1 and R2. xor   r1,r1,r2
r1<-(r1)|(r2)

```
xor      r2,r1,r2      # r2<-(r1)¦(r2);
                       # i.e.r2<-original value of R1
xor      r1,r1,r2      # r1<-(r1)¦(r2);
                       # i.e.r1<-original value of R2
```

Integer NAND Instruction

The integer NAND instruction performs a bitwise NAND of the two operands. The only integer NAND instruction is a register addressing mode instruction and uses the contents of RA and RB as the two operands (see Table 3.7).

Integer NOR Instruction

The integer NOR instruction performs a bitwise NOR of the two operands. The only integer NOR instruction is a register addressing form instruction and uses the contents of RA and RB as the two operands (see Table 3.7).

Integer Equivalent (XNOR) Instruction

The integer equivalent instruction performs a bitwise XNOR of the two operands. The only integer equivalent instruction is a register addressing mode instruction and uses the contents of RA and RB as the two operands (see Table 3.7).

Integer NOT Instruction

The integer NOT (not[.]) instruction negates each bit or the operand (RA) and places the result into register RT. This is an extended mnemonic for the nor[.] instruction (see Table 3.7).

Miscellaneous Logical Instructions

These two logical operation instructions are extended mnemonics based on some of the Boolean operation instructions.

Nop Instruction

The no operation (nop) instruction is an extended mnemonic which generates the preferred form of an instruction which does nothing (see Table 3.7).

Integer Register Move Instruction

The integer register move (mr[.]) instruction has one operand which is copied into the target register. This is an extended mnemonic for the or[.] instruction (see Table 3.7).

Integer Sign Extend Instructions

There are two sign extend operations for 32-bit implementations of the PowerPC architecture, and one additional sign extend instruction for 64-bit implementations. The sign extend instructions all have one operand (the contents of RA). The sign extend byte (extsb[.]) instruction uses the most significant bit of the least significant byte of the contents of RA as a sign bit and copies it into all but the least significant byte of RT. The least significant byte of RT is loaded with the least significant byte of RA. Thus the least significant byte of RA is sign extended and placed into RT. The sign extend halfword (extsh[.]) instruction sign extends the least significant halfword of RA and places it into RT (see Table 3.7). The last sign extend instruction is only available on 64-bit implementations. The sign extend word (extsw[.]) instruction places the sign extended least significant word of register RA into RT (see Table 3.8)

Integer Count Leading Zero Instructions

The integer count leading zero instructions place the number of leading zeros in the single operand into the target register. Both 32-bit and 64-bit implementations implement the count leading zeros word (cntlzw[.]) instruction. This instruction counts the number of leading zeros in the least significant word of the contents of register RA. This count is placed into RT (see Table 3.7). The count leading zeros doubleword (cntlzd[.]) instruction is only available on 64-bit implementations and counts the number of leading zeros in the doubleword contained in register RA. Again, the count is placed into register RT (see Table 3.8).

Table 3.7. 32-bit logical operation instructions.

Instruction	Definition	Format
and immediate[a]	RT <- (RA) & ^{16}0 ‖ UI	andi. RT,RA,UI
and immediate shifted[b]	RT <- (RA) &UI ‖ ^{16}0	andis. RT,RA,UI

Instruction	Definition	Format
and[c]	RT <- (RA) & $(\overline{RB})$	and[.] RT,RA,RB
and with complement[c]	RT <- (RA) & $(\overline{RB})$	andc[.] RA,RS,RB
or immediate[a]	RT <- (RA) | $^{16}0$ || UI	ori RT,RA,UI
or immediate shifted[b]	RT <- (RA) | UI || $^{16}0$	oris RT,RA,UI
or[c]	RT <- (RA) | (RB)	or[.] RT,RA,RB
or with complement[c]	RT <- (RA) | $(\overline{RB})$	orc[.] RT,RA,RB
xor immediate[a]	RT <- (RA) $\oplus$ $^{16}0$ || UI	xori RT,RA,UI
xor immediate shifted[b]	RT <- (RA) $\oplus$ UI || $^{16}0$	xoris RT,RA,UI
xor[c]	RT <- (RA) $\oplus$ (RB)	xor[.] RT,RA,RB
nand[c]	RT <- $\overline{(RA) \& (RB)}$	nand[.] RT,RA,RB
nor[c]	RT <- $\overline{(RA) \| (RB)}$	nor[.] RT,RA,RB
equivalent (xnor)[c]	RT <- $\overline{(RA) \oplus (RB)}$	eqv[.] RT,RA,RB
not[c]	RT <- $(\overline{RA})$	not[.] RT, RA nor[.] RT, RA, RA
nop	(nothing)	nop ori r0, r0, 0
move integer register[c]	RT <- (RA)	mr[.] RT,RA or RT,RA,RA
sign extend byte[c]	RT<-$^{24}RA_{24}$||$RA_{24..31}$	sxtsb[.]RT,RA
sign extend halfword[c]	RT<-$^{16}RA_{16}$||$RA_{16..31}$	extsh[.]RT,RA

count leading zeros word[cd]	n=0;
	while (n<32)
	in (RA_n==1) break;
	else n++;
	RT<-n
		cntlzw[.]RT,RA

Note: If [o] is added, XER_{SO} and XER_{OU} will be set, if [.] is added, CRO will be altered based on the result of the instruction.

[a] For 64-bit implementations, the second operand is formed as follows: $^{48}0\_UI$.

[b] For 64-bit implementations, the second operand is formed as follows. $^{37}0\_UI\_{}^{16}0$.

[c] The [.] in the mnemonic indicates that this instruction can be coded with a dot if condition register field 0 should be updated, or without a dot if condition register 0 should not be updated.

[d] Note that for 64-bit implementations the low order word is used , thus n starts at 32 instead of 0, and the while statement should read "while (n<64)."

Table 3.8. 64-bit logical operation instructions.

Instruction	Definition	Format
sign extend byte[a]	$RT \leftarrow {}^{56}RA_{56} \| RA_{56..63}$	extsb[.] RT, RA
sign extend halfword[a]	$RT \leftarrow {}^{48}RA_{48} \| RA_{48..63}$	extsb[.] RT, RA
sign extend word[a]	$RT \leftarrow {}^{32}RA_{32} \| RA_{32..63}$	extsw[.] RT, RA

count leading zeros doubleword	n = 0;
	while (n < 64)
	if (RA_n == 1) break;
	else n++;
	RT <- n
		cntlzd[.] RT, RA

Note: If [o] is added, XER_{SO} and XER_{OU} will be set, if [.] is added, CR0 will be altered based on the result of the instruction.

[a] The [.] in the mnemonic indicates that this instruction can be coded with a dot if condition register field 0 should be updated, or without a dot if condition register 0 should *not* be updated.

Rotate and Shift Instructions

The PowerPC architecture supports several rotate and shift instructions. These instructions use integer registers for their source operands and produce a result that then is stored back into an integer register.

All rotate and shift instructions may update condition register field zero if the record form of the instruction is used (specified with a trailing dot (.) in the mnemonic). In these cases, the condition register field is set with the results of a signed comparison of the result with zero. The overflow bits in the XER are never changed by rotate or shift instructions.

Shift Instructions

Instructions are provided for shifting a register right or left. Some of the shift instructions are defined only for 64-bit PowerPC implementations. These instructions have two operands and one target. The first operand always is contained in a general integer register and is the value to be shifted. The second operand is the shift amount, which comes from a general integer register or from an immediate field in the instruction. There are signed and unsigned shift instructions. With unsigned instructions, the bits that are vacated by shifting left or right are filled with zeros. Signed shift instructions are defined for right shift instructions, and the bits that are vacated by shifting are replaced with copies of the most significant bit of the operand (the sign bit). Thus, with signed shifts, signed numbers keep the same sign. The general form for shift instructions follows:

```
shift[.] RT, RA, RB¦sh
```

Unsigned Shift Instructions

There are eight unsigned shift instructions, four of which are extended mnemonics of rotate instructions (rotate instructions are described later). Four of the unsigned shift instructions operate on words and are defined for all PowerPC implementations; the other four instructions operate on doublewords and are defined only on 64-bit PowerPC implementations.

The *shift left word* (slw[.]) and *shift right word* (srw[.]) instructions shift the contents of a general integer register (RA) by an amount specified in another general integer register (RB). The results are placed in a third integer register (RT). In order to derive the shift amount, the contents of RB are taken modulo 64. If the shift amount is between 32 and 63, then RT is loaded with 0. Zeros are filled into the vacated bits, and bits that are shifted out of the operand are lost. Table 3.9 lists the 32-bit shift instructions. For 64-bit machines bits 0-31 are set to 0. These instructions can be used for shifting data contained in multiple registers (data larger than 32 bits, for example). (See Example 3.6.)

EXAMPLE 3.6.

Using the slw and srw to left-shift data held in multiple registers.

The slw instruction can be used to shift data contained in multiple registers. In this example, you want to shift a 64-bit value contained in register r1 (the leftmost 32-bits) and r2 (the rightmost 32-bits). The result is placed back into these same registers and the shift amount is contained in r3. The shift amount is assumed to be less than 64.

```
    subfic  r4,r3,32      # This is used to
                          # 'right-align' the bits
                          # coming from r2 and going
                          # into r1.

    slw     r1,r1,r3      # Shift r1 to the left by the
                          # shift amount. If the shift
                          # amount is between 32 and 64,
                          # then r1 is zero.

    srw     r5,r2,r4      # get the bits which will
                          # shift out of r2 and into r1.

    or      r1,r1,r6      # combine the bits left in r1
                          # with those coming from r2.

    addi    r4,r3,-32     # If the shift amount was
                          # greater than 32, then you
                          # must put the rightmost bits
                          # of r2 into r1.
```

```
        slw     r5,r2,r4        # This creates the upper order
                                # bits of the result for
                                # shifts of greater than 32.

        or      r1,r1,r5        # Either r1 or r5 is zero, and
                                # the other contains the
                                # leftmost bits of the result.ᵃ

        slw     r2,r2,r3        # Shift R2 to get the
                                # rightmost 32 bits.
```

ᵃ Except when the shift amount is 32, in which case r1=r5=original value of r2.

The *shift left word immediate* (slwi[.]) and *shift right word immediate* (srwi[.]) instructions are extended mnemonics of the *rotate left word immediate then AND with mask* (rlwinm[.]) instruction. The contents of general integer register RA are shifted by the amount specified in the 5-bit immediate field sh. Zeros are filled into the vacated bits, and bits that are shifted out of the operand are lost (see Table 3.9).

The *shift left doubleword* (sld[.]) and *shift right doubleword* (srd[.]) instructions shift the contents of a general integer register (RA) by an amount specified in another general integer register (RB). The results are placed in a third integer register (RT). In order to derive the shift amount, the contents of RB are taken modulo 128. If the shift amount is between 64 and 127, then RT is loaded with 0. Zeros are filled into the vacated bits, and bits that are shifted out of the operand are lost. These instructions are defined only on 64-bit implementations of the PowerPC architecture. Table 3.10 lists the 64-bit shift instructions.

The *shift left doubleword immediate* (sldi[.]) and *shift right doubleword immediate* (srdi[.]) instructions are extended mnemonics of the *rotate left doubleword immediate then clear right* (rldicr[.]) instruction and the *rotate left doubleword immediate then clear left* (rldicl[.]) instruction, respectively. The contents of general integer register RA are shifted by the amount specified in the 6-bit immediate field sh. Zeros are filled into the vacated bits, and bits that are shifted out of the operand are lost. These instructions are defined only on 64-bit implementations of the PowerPC architecture (see Table 3.10).

Signed Shift Instructions

There are four signed shift instructions; all are shift right instructions. The *shift right algebraic word* (sraw[.]) and the *shift right algebraic word immediate* (srawi[.]) instructions are defined for all implementations of the PowerPC architecture. The shift operand (contents of RA) is shifted right by the shift amount. The shift amount is either the contents of the RB modulo 64 (sraw[.] instruction), or the 5-bit immediate field sh (srawi[.] instruction). The vacated bit positions of the shift operand are replaced with the sign bit of that operand. If any bits are shifted out of the shift operand and the shift operand is negative, then the carry bit in the XER is set to 1, otherwise it is set to 0 (see Table 3.9). These instructions can be used to perform fast division by powers of 2 (see Example 3.9).

Table 3.9. 32-bit shift instructions.

Instruction	Definition	Format
shift left word	RT <- (RA) << ((RB)%64)	slw[.] RT, RA, RB
shift right word	RT <- (RA) >> ((RB)%64)	srw[.] RT, RA, RB
shift left word immediate	RT <- (RA) << sh	slwi[.] RT, RA, sh
shift right word immediate	RT <- (RA) >> sh	srwi[.] RT, RA, sh rlwinm[.] RT, RA
shift right algebraic word immediate	RT <- (RA) >> sh[a]	srawi[.] RT, RA, sh
shift right algebraic word	RT <- (RA) >> ((RB)%64)[b]	sraw[.] RT, RA, RB

Note: If [o] is added, XER_{SO} and XER_{OU} will be set, if [.] is added, CR0 will be altered based on the result of the instruction.

[a] XER_{CA} is set if any 1's are shifted out of the operand.

EXAMPLE 3.7.

Using the signed shift instruction to perform division by a power of 2.

(32-bit code shown; 64-bit code would use the sradi instruction in place of srawi.)

The shift right instruction performs a division by 2, and the addze instruction corrects for rounding error on negative numbers. Note that in the –9/2 case, the add of the carry bit is necessary to round toward 0 instead of rounding toward minus infinity. This code matches the normal definition for integer division.

divide 8 by 2 (r2 = 0b001000)

```
srawi    r1,r2,1     # R1<-R2>>1
                     # R1<-0b000100; XER_CA<-0
addze    R1,R1       # R1<-R1+XER_CA
                     # R1<-0b000100 (8/2 = 4)
```

divide 9 by 2 (r2 = 0b001001)

```
srawi    r1,r2,1     # r1<-r2>>1
                     # r1<-0b000100; XER_CA<-0
addze    r1,r1       # r1<-r1+XER_CA
                     # r1<-0b000100 (9/2 = 4)
```

```
divide –8 by 2 (r2 = 0b111000)
srawi    r1,r2,1     # r1<-r2>>1
                     # r1<-0b111100; XER_CA<-0
addze    r1,r1       # r1<-r1+XER_CA
                     # r1<-0b111100 (-8/2 = -4)

divide –9 by 2 (r2 = 0b110111)
srawi    r1,r2,1     # r1<-r2>>1
                     # r1<-0b111011; XER_CA<-1
addze    r1,r1       # r1<-r1+XER_CA
                     # r1<-0b111100 (-9/2 = -4)
```

The *shift right algebraic doubleword* (srad[.]) and the *shift right algebraic doubleword immediate* (sradi[.]) instructions are defined only on 64-bit implementations of the PowerPC architecture. These instructions behave exactly like the 32-bit signed shift instructions described earlier, except that they operate on 64-bit operands and that a shift amount from RB is modulo 128. (see Table 3.10).

Table 3.10. 64-bit shift instructions.

Instruction	*Definition*	*Format*
shift left doubleword	RT <- (RA) << ((RB)%128)	sld[.] RT, RA, RB
shift right doubleword	RT <- (RA) >> ((RB)%128)	srd[.] RT, RA, RB
shift left doubleword immediate	RT <- (RA) << sh	sldi[.] RT, RA, sh rldicr[.] RT, RA, sh, 63–sh
shift right doubleword immediate	RT <- (RA) >> sh	srdi[.] RT, RA, sh rldicl[.] RT, RA, 64–sh, sh
shift right algebraic doubleword immediate	RT <- (RA) >> sh[a]	sradi[.] RT, RA, sh
shift right algebraic doubleword	RT <- (RA) >> ((RB)%128)[a]	srad[.] RT, RA, RB

Note: If [o] is added, XER_{SO} and XER_{OU} will be set, if [.] is added, CRO will be altered based on the result of the instruction.

[a] XER_{CA} is set if any 1's are shifted out of the operand.

Rotate Instructions

The rotate instructions are more elaborate than the shift instructions. All the rotate instructions perform left rotation and include a masking operation. The only special purpose register affected by these instructions is the condition register. The rotate instructions can be used to perform a host of common operations and, as such, there are many extended mnemonics.

The rotate instructions are split into 32-bit and 64-bit rotates. On 64-bit implementations of the PowerPC architecture, the 32-bit rotate instructions behave as if the least significant 32 bits of the operand first are copied into the most significant 32 bits of the operand. This new 64-bit value then is rotated.

Two types of masking are used by these rotate instructions. The first type, *AND with mask*, ANDs the mask with the rotated result. The second type, *mask and insert*, inserts the rotate result into the target register under control of the mask. In this case, if there is a 1 in the corresponding mask bit, then the bit of the rotated result is placed into the result register (at the same bit position); otherwise, the target register bit is left unchanged.

There are three 32-bit rotate instructions and 12 extended mnemonics for these instructions. The form of all the 32-bit rotate instructions follows:

```
rotate RT, RA, sh¦RB, MB, ME
```

The operand to be rotated is contained in RA, and the amount by which to shift left is contained in the immediate field sh or the general integer register RB. A mask is generated with the values contained in the immediate fields MB and ME. MB and ME are 5-bit fields, where MB is the first one bit of the mask and ME is the last one bit of the mask. The bits in the mask between MB and ME (inclusive) are set to 1, while all other bits are set to 0. If MB is greater than ME, then the bits between MB and bit 31 are set to 1 and the bits between bit 0 and ME are set to 1; again, all other bits are set to 0. The 32-bit mask generated by the MB and ME fields then is used to control how the rotated result is placed into the target register RT.

The *rotate left word immediate then AND with mask* (rlwinm[.]) instruction ANDs the rotated result with the generated mask before placing it into RT. There are many uses for this instruction, and several extended mnemonics exist to make coding these uses easier.

The first use is extracting an n-bit field from a 32-bit register and justifying it. The *extract and left justify word immediate* (extlwi[.]) extended mnemonic performs this function with left justification. The form of this mnemonic follows, along with the equivalent rlwinm[.] instruction:

```
extlwi[.] RT,RA,n,b = rlwinm[.] RT,RA,b,0,n-1, (n>0)
```

In this form, RT is the target register, RA is the source register, n is the size in bits of the field to be justified, and b is the starting bit for the field to be justified. The *extract and right justify word immediate* (extrwi[.]) extended mnemonic performs right justification of a bit field.

The next use for the rlwinm instruction is for simple rotate immediate instructions. The *rotate left word immediate* (rotlwi[.]) and *rotate right word immediate* (rotrwi[.]) instructions also are extended mnemonics for the rlwinm instruction.

Next, the rlwinm instruction can be used to clear bits in a register. The *clear left word immediate* (clrlwi[.]) instruction and the *clear right word immediate* (clrrwi[.]) instruction are extended mnemonics that perform this function. The *clear left immediate* instruction is used to copy the source register to the target register and clear (set to 0) the *n* leftmost bits. The *clear right immediate* instruction copies the source register to the target register and clears (sets to 0) the *n* rightmost bits.

The final extended mnemonic of the rlwinm instruction is the *clear left and shift left word immediate* (clrlslwi[.]) instruction, which combines the function of the clear left immediate and the shift left immediate instructions into a single operation:

```
clrlslwi[.] RT,RA,b,n = rlwinm[.] RT,RA,n,b-n,31-n, (n≤b<31)
```

This instruction first sets the leftmost bits up to bit b of RA to 0 and then rotates left by n bits, storing the result in RT.

The *rotate left word then AND with mask* (rlwnm[.]) instruction is very similar to the rlwinm instruction; the only difference is from where the rotate amount comes. In the rlwnm instruction, the rotate amount comes from the 5 least significant bits of the integer general register RB. The only extended mnemonic for the rlwnm instruction is the *rotate left word* (rotlw) instruction, which is a simple left rotate based on the value in RB (the least significant 5 bits or RB modulo 32).

The *rotate left word immediate then mask insert* (rlwimi[.]) instruction again is similar to the rlwinm instruction. The difference here is in how the mask is used. With the rlwimi instruction, the mask is used to control the insertion of the rotate source register into the target register. Wherever there is a 1 bit in the mask, the corresponding bit in the target register is set to the value of the corresponding bit in the rotated source register. Wherever there is a 0 bit in the mask, the corresponding bit in the target is unchanged.

The *insert from left word immediate* (inslwi[.]) instruction and the *insert from right word immediate* (insrwi[.]) instruction are extended mnemonics of the rlwimi[.] instruction. The form of the inslwi instruction follows:

```
inslwi[.] RT,RA,n,b = rlwimi[.] RT,RA,32-b,b,(b+n)-1, (n>0)
```

The *n* leftmost bits of RA are inserted into RT starting at bit b. Thus,

```
inslwi R1,R2,3,5
```

inserts the 3 leftmost bits of R2 into R1, starting at bit 5. Bit 5 of R1 is set to the value of bit 0 of R2, bit 6 of R1 is set the value of bit 1 or R2, and so on. The insrwi instruction has the same form as the inslwi instruction, but the *n* rightmost bits are inserted into the target register starting at bit b (the most significant bit of the rightmost n bits of the source is inserted into bit b of the target register, and so on). Table 3.11 lists the 32-bit rotate instructions.

Table 3.11. 32-bit rotate instructions.

Instruction	Definition	Format
rotate left word immediate then AND with mask	$RT \leftarrow RL_{32}{}^a((RA), sh) \,\&\, MSK_{32}{}^b(mb, me)$	rlwinm[.] RT, RA, sh, mb, me
rotate left word immediate	$RT \leftarrow RL_{32}((RA), n)$	rotlwi[.] RT, RA, n rlwinm[.] RT, RA, n, 0, 31
rotate right word immediate	$RT \leftarrow RL_{32}((RA), 32-n)$	rotrwi[.] RT, RA, n rlwinm[.] RT, RA, 32–n, 0, 31
extract and left justify word immediate	$RT \leftarrow RL_{32}((RA),b) \,\&\, MSK_{32}(0,n-1)$	extlwi[.] RT, RA, n, b rlwinm[.] RT, RA, b, 0, n–1
extract and right justify word immediate	$RT \leftarrow RL_{32}((RA),b+n) \,\&\, MSK_{32}(32-n,31)$	extrwi[.] RT, RA,n,b, rlwinm[.] RT, RA,b+n,32–n, 31
clear left word immediate	$RT \leftarrow (RA) \,\&\, MSK_{32}(n,31)$	clrlwi[.] RT, RA, n rlwinm[.] RT, RA, 0, n, 31
clear right word immediate	$RT \leftarrow (RA) \,\&\, MSK_{32}(0,31-n)$	clrrwi[.] RT, RA, n rlwinm[.] RT, RA, 0, 0, 31–n

continues

Table 3.11. continued

Instruction	Definition	Format
clear left and shift left word immediate	$RT \leftarrow RL_{32}(((RA)\&MSK_{32}(b,31)),n)$	clrlslwi[.] RT,RA,b,n rlwinm[.] RT, RA,n,b−n, 31−n, n<b
rotate left word then AND mask	$RT \leftarrow RL_{32}((RA), (RB)\%32) \& MSK_{32}(mb, me)$	rlwnm[.] RT, with RA, RB, mb, me
rotate left word	$RT \leftarrow RL_{32}((RA), (RB)\%32)$	rotlw[.] RT, RA, RB rlwnm[.] RT, RA, RB, 0, 31
rotate left word immediate then mask insert	$RT \leftarrow INS_{32}{}^{c}(RL_{32}((RA),sh), (RT), mb, me)$	rlwimi[.] RT, RA, sh, mb, me
insert from left word immediate	$RT \leftarrow INS_{32}(RL_{32}((RA), 32-b)(RT), b, b+n-1)$	inslwi[.] RT, RA, n, b rlwimi[.] RT, RA,32−b, b,b+n−1
insert from right word immediate	$RT \leftarrow INS_{32}(RL_{32}((RA), 32-b),(RT), b, b+n-1)$	insrwi[.] RT, RA, n, b rlwimi[.] RT,RA,32−bh −n,b,b+n−1

Note: If [o] is added, XER_{SO} and XER_{OU} will be set, if [.] is added, CRO will be altered based on the result of the instruction.

[a] $RL_{32}(A,B)$ is a function that rotates A to the left by a number of bits as specified B. Thus, $RL_{32}(0\times73333333,2) = 0\times CCCCCCCD$.

[b] $MSK_{32}(A,B)$ is a function that generates a 32-bit binary mask with 1s starting at bit position A and ending at the bit position B. Thus, $MSK_{32}(0,15) = 0\times FFFF0000$, and $MSK_{32}(24,7) = 0\times FF0000FF$.

[c] $INS_{32}(A,B,C,D)$ replaces bits C[nd]D of B with bits C[nd]D of A. Thus, $INS_{32}(0\times CCCCCCCC,0\times FFFFFFFF,4,7) = 0\times FCFFFFFF$.

There also is a set of rotate instructions defined only on 64-bit implementations of the PowerPC architecture. These instructions perform similar functions to the 32-bit rotates described earlier, but there are slight differences in the semantics of the instructions. The primary difference between these instructions and the 32-bit rotate instructions is in how the mask is generated. Instead of generating a mask by specifying the starting and ending bit, the 64-bit rotate instructions can clear some of the leftmost bits of a rotated operand or some of the rightmost bits of the rotated operand. The general form of the 64-bit rotate instructions follows:

```
rotate RT,RA,sh¦RB,mb¦me
```

sh is an immediate rotate amount, while RB%64 is the rotate amount for nonimmediate rotate instructions. The mb field is used for rotate and clear left instructions (the mask has 0s from bit 0 to bit mb, and 1s from bit mb to bit 63), while the me field is used for rotate and clear right instructions (the mask has 1s from bit 0 to bit me, and 0s from bit me to bit 63).

The first two 64-bit rotate instructions, *rotate left doubleword immediate then clear left* (rldicl[.]) and *rotate left doubleword immediate then clear right* (rldicr[.]), can be used together to obtain the 64-bit equivalent of the 32-bit rlwinm[.] instruction (see Example 3.8).

EXAMPLE 3.8.

Using the 64-bit rotates to create the same function as the 32-bit rotate instructions.

To rotate a 32-bit operand (r1) left by 4 bits, and then to clear the upper-order 4 bits and the lower-order 4 bits, use this code:

```
rlwinm  r2,r1,4,4,27
```

To perform this function with 64-bit operands (on a 64-bit implementation), you can use the following code sequence:

```
rldicl  r2,r1,4,4
rldicr  r2,r2,0,59
```

The first instruction performs the rotation by 4 and clears the upper-order 4 bits of the operand, while the second instruction clears the lower-order 4 bits of the operand. Note that the rlwinm instruction is implemented in 64-bit implementations, and as long as the data being operated on is 32-bit data, the rlwinm code shown here would function correctly.

The third 64-bit rotate instruction is the *rotate left doubleword immediate then clear* (rldic[.]) instruction. This instruction clears the leftmost bits as in the rldicl[.] instruction, but it also clears the rightmost bits from bit 63–sh to bit 63. In essence, this instruction behaves similarly to the shift left instructions in that all bits rotated through position 0 to position 63 are cleared (bits that are shifted out of the most significant bit are lost, and 0s are shifted into vacated bit positions).

The *rotate left doubleword then clear left* (rldcl[.]) and the *rotate left doubleword then clear right* (rldcr[.]) instructions are nonimmediate analogs of the rldicl[.] and rldicr[.] instructions.

Finally, the *rotate left doubleword immediate then mask insert* (rldimi[.]) instruction is similar to the rldcr[.] instruction, except that the mask is used to insert the rotated operand into the target register (as in the rlwimi[.] instruction). Table 3.12 lists the 64-bit rotate instructions.

The extended mnemonics of 64-bit rotate instructions are analogous to the 32-bit rotate extended mnemonics. Therefore, they are not described here (they are described in Appendix B, "Detailed Instruction Set Reference"). The equivalent (nonextended) mnemonic is shown below the instruction form in Table 3.13.

Table 3.12. 64-bit rotate instructions.

Instruction	Definition	Format
rotate left double word immediate then	RT <-RL_{64}[a] ((RA),sh)& MSK_{64}[b] (mb,63)	rlldicl[.] RT,RA, sh,mb
rotate left double word immediate then clear right	RT <-RL_{64}((RA),sh)& MSK_{64} (0,me)	rldicr[.] RT,RA,sh, me
rotate left double word immediate then clear	RT <-RL_{64}((RA),sh)& MSK_{64} (mb,63–sh)	rldic[.] RT,RA,sh, mb
rotate left double word then clear left	RT <-RL_{64}((RA),(RB)%64) & MSK_{64} (mb,63)	rldcl[.] RT,RA,RB, mb
rotate left double word then clear right	RT <-RL_{64}((RA),(RB)%64) & MSK_{64} (0,me)	rldcr[.] RT,RA,RB, me
rotate left double word immediate then mask insert	RT <-INS_{64}[c](RL_{64}((RA),sh), (RT),mb,63–sh)	rldimi[.] RT,RA,sh, mb

[a] RL_{64}(A,B) is a function that rotates A to the left by a number of bits as specified B. Thus, RL_{64} (0×73333333 33333333,2) = 0×CCCCCCCC CCCCCCCD.

[b] MSK_{64}(A,B) is a function that generates a 64-bit binary mask with 1s starting at bit position A and ending at the bit position B. Thus, MSK_{64}(0,15) = 0×FFFF0000 00000000, and MSK_{64}(56,7) = 0×FF000000 000000FF.

[c] INS_{64}(A,B,C,D), replaces bit C-D of B with bits C-D of A. Thus INS_{64}(0×CCCCCCCC CCCCCCCC,0×FFFFFFFF FFFFFFFF4,7) = 0×FCFFFFFF FFFFFFFF.

Note: If [o] is added, XER_{SO} and XER_{OU} will be set, if [.] is added, CRO will be altered based on the result of the instruction.

Table 3.13. 64-bit rotate instructions (extended mnemonics).

Instruction	Definition	Format
rotate left doubleword immediate	$RT \leftarrow RL_{64}{}^a((RA), n)$	rotldi[.] RT, RA, n rldicl[.] RT, RA, n, 0
rotate right doubleword immediate	$RT \leftarrow RL_{64}((RA), 64-n)$	rotrdi[.] RT, RA, n rldicl[.] RT, RA, 64– n, 0
extract and left justify doubleword immediate	$RT \leftarrow RL_{64}((RA),b) \&$ $MSK_{64}{}^b(0, n-1)$	extldi[.] RT, RA, n, b rldicr[.] RT, RA, b, n–1
extract and right justify doubleword immediate	$RT \leftarrow RL_{64}((RA),b+n) \&$ $MSK_{64}(64-n, 63)$	extrdi[.] RT, RA, n, b rldicl[.] RT, RA, b+n,64–n
clear left doubleword immediate	$RT \leftarrow (RA) \& MSK_{64}(n,63)$	clrldi[.] RT, RA, n rldicl[.] RT, RA, 0, n
clear right doubleword immediate	$RT \leftarrow (RA) \& MSK_{64}(0,63-n)$	clrrdi[.] RT, RA, n rldicr[.] RT, RA, 0, 63–n
clear left and shift left doubleword immediate	$RT \leftarrow RL_{64}$ $(((RA)\&MSK_{64}(b,63)), n)$	clrlsldi[.] RT, RA, b, n rldic[.] RT, RA, n, b–n, n<b
rotate left doubleword	$RT \leftarrow RL_{64}((RA), (RB)\%64)$	rotld[.] RT, RA, RB

continues

Table 3.13. continued

Instruction	Definition	Format
		rldcl[.] RT, RA, RB, 0
insert from right doubleword immediate	RT <- INS$_{64}$^{c}(RL$_{64}$((RA), 64–b),(RT), b, b+n–1)	insrdi[.] RT, RA, n, b rldimi[.] RT, RA, 64–b–n, b

^{a} RL$_{64}$(A,B) is a function that rotates A to the left by a number of bits as specified B. Thus, RL$_{64}$ (0×733333333 33333333,2) = 0×CCCCCCCC CCCCCCCD.

^{b} MSK$_{64}$(A,B) is a function that generates a 64-bit binary mask with 1s starting at bit position A and ending at the bit position B. Thus, MSK$_{64}$(0,15) = 0×FFFF0000 00000000, and MSK$_{64}$(24,7) = 0×FF000000 000000FF.

^{c} INS$_{64}$(A,B,C,D) replaces bit C[nd]D of B with bits C[nd]D of A. Thus, INS$_{64}$(0×CCCCCCCC CCCCCCCC,0×FFFFFFFF FFFFFFFF,4,7) = 0×FCFFFFFF FFFFFFFF.

Move To/From Special Register Instructions

The only special purpose register described in this section is the *fixed point exception register* (XER). There are two instructions that can be used to move to and from special purpose registers. The *move to special purpose register* (mtspr) instruction is used to copy the contents of an integer register into a special purpose register. The *move from special purpose register* (mfspr) instruction is used to copy the contents of a special purpose register into an integer register. The form of these instructions follows:

```
move RT, SPR
```

The RT field specifies a general integer register that is the source or target of the special purpose register value (depending on whether a move to or move from instruction is being coded). The SPR field specifies one of 34 special registers. Only three of the 34 special registers generally are used by application code; the other registers are used primarily by operating systems (see Appendix C, "Operating System Design for PowerPC Processors"). The three registers that are used by application code are the XER, the link register, and the count register. The link and count registers are described with the branch instructions. The SPR code for the XER register is 1. There also are extended mnemonics for the XER encoding. The *move to XER* (mtxer) and *move from XER* (mfxer) instructions are extended mnemonics used to move values to and from the XER. Table 3.14 lists the move to and from special purpose register instructions.

Table 3.14. Move to and from special purpose register instructions.

Instruction	Definition	Format
move to special purpose register	SPR <- (RT)	mtspr SPR, RT
move from special purpose register	RT <- (SPR)	mfspr RT, SPR
move to fixed point exception register	XER <- (RT)	mtxer RT mtspr 1, RT
move from fixed point exception register	RT <- (XER)	mfxer RT mfspr RT, 1

Load and Store Instructions

Load and store instructions are used to access memory. Because the PowerPC architecture is a load/store architecture, these are the only instructions that can manipulate memory. The PowerPC architecture supports several data types natively. For the integer processor, byte, halfword (16-bit), word (32-bit), and doubleword (64-bit) load and store instructions are provided (for both signed and unsigned data). For the floating-point processor, both IEEE single- and double-precision load and store instructions are provided.

Address Generation

Address generation is performed in the integer processor. The programmer generally sees a flat 32-bit address space (or a 64-bit address space for 64-bit implementations). The operating system manages a 52-bit virtual address space (or an 80-bit virtual address space for 64-bit implementations) so that each program gets its own flat 32-bit address space (called an *effective address space*). Programs therefore cannot interfere with each other and, in general, the programmer can ignore any other application that may be running on the system. For a discussion of virtual memory, see Appendix C. Throughout this section, only references to effective addresses are made, which are what the programmer sees.

An effective address can be calculated in one of two ways. The first method is to add the contents of a general integer register (the base register) to a constant offset (contained in a 16-bit immediate field in the instruction). The second method, *indexed address generation*, is to add the contents of a general integer register (the base register) to the contents of another general integer register (register addressing mode). Most of the load and store instructions give the option of storing the calculated effective address in the base register—this form is called the *update form* of the instruction.

Sometimes it is desirable to use 0 instead of a base register. The architecture supports this by using 0 instead of the contents of register zero if it is specified as the base register.

Endianness

Endianness refers to the way in which bytes are stored in memory. Bytes are stored in two ways.

The first method, *big endian*, stores the most significant byte of a multibyte value in the low address and the least significant byte in the high address. Therefore, if a 4-byte integer is stored at address 0×20000000, then the most significant byte is at 0×20000000 and the least significant byte is at 0×20000003. The 68000 architecture is an example of a big endian architecture.

The second way to store bytes in memory is *little endian*. In this case, the most significant byte of a multibyte value is stored in the high address, while the least significant byte is stored in the low address. Thus, if a 4-byte integer is stored at address 0×20000000, then the most significant byte can be read from address 0×20000003, while the least significant byte can be read from 0×20000000. Intel's x86 architecture is an example of a little endian architecture.

Often, programs are not endian-independent, and this can lead to problems when porting code from one platform to another or when data is generated on one platform and read on another. In general, endian problems arise whenever data is manipulated in multiple sizes (a 32-bit integer which also is manipulated as an 8-bit character or string of 8-bit characters, for example).

Suppose that a program uses the low order 24 bits of a 32-bit integer to store data, and the upper order 8 bits of the integer to store a flag identifying what the data is. The program was written on a little endian machine that supported byte and word (4-byte) loads. In this program, whenever the flag is needed to identify the data, it is loaded by issuing a load to the address of the integer plus 3 (in order to get the high-order byte). Whenever the integer data and flag are wanted, the load address is the address of the integer. When this program is compiled on a big endian machine, the loads that are supposed to load the flag will fail. In the big endian machine, the address of the integer plus 3 will return the least significant byte instead of the most significant byte. In fact, all the byte loads that address a flag in an integer must be changed to the address of the integer in order for the program to work (see Figure 3.2).

FIGURE 3.2.

Little endian versus big endian.

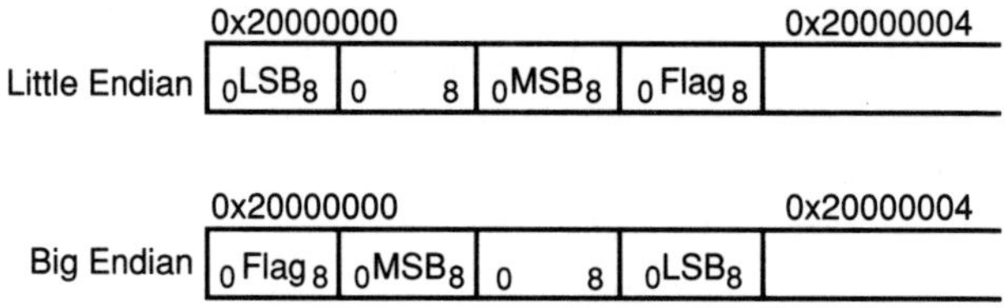

	0x20000000				0x20000004	
Little Endian	$_0LSB_8$	$_0$	8	$_0MSB_8$	$_0Flag_8$	

	0x20000000				0x20000004	
Big Endian	$_0Flag_8$	$_0MSB_8$	$_0$	8	$_0LSB_8$	

The PowerPC architecture uses big endian addressing, but it has support for little endian programs. This support comes in two forms. The first form is the byte reverse load instruction, which reverses the byte order of a word coming into the processor. The second form is a little endian addressing mode, which is described in Appendix E, "Portability Notes."

Integer Load Instructions

Four data sizes are supported for the integer processor. Three are available on any PowerPC implementation: byte (8 bits), halfword (16 bits), and word (32 bits). The last size, doubleword (64 bits), is supported only on 64-bit implementations of the PowerPC architecture. When the data is loaded into a general integer register, it always is right justified (it occupies the least significant bits). These data sizes can be loaded as signed or unsigned values. Signed values are sign extended to the register size (32 bits for 32-bit implementations, 64 bits for 64-bit implementations); unsigned values are zero extended to the register size.

The general form of the integer load instructions follows:

```
load[u][x] RT, RA, D ¦ RB
```

The address is calculated by adding RA to the 16-bit immediate offset D or the 32-bit or 64-bit index contained in register RB. The value at that address is loaded into the integer register RT. If the u form of the instruction is used, the RA is updated with the calculated effective address. If the x form is used, then RB is used to calculate the effective address; otherwise, the immediate offset D is used. Note that the offset form of the instruction generally is written as the following:

```
load[u] RS, D(RA)
```

For all loads except the update forms, if the register 0 is specified for RA, then the value 0 is used instead of the contents of r0. For the load with update instructions, specifying r0 for RA is an invalid form.

There is one byte load instruction: *load byte and zero extend* (lbz[u][x]). It is an unsigned load. The byte at the calculated address is loaded into the least significant byte of the target register and the rest of the register is filled with zeros. In order to get a signed byte, the *extend sign byte* (extsb[.]) must be used following the byte load.

There are two halfword load instructions. The first instruction, *load halfword and zero* (lhz[u][x]), is an unsigned load. The second instruction, *load halfword algebraic* (lha[u][x]), is a signed load. The most significant bit in the halfword is repeated in the upper-order 16 bits of the target register.

There are two word load instructions, but only one is defined for 32-bit implementations. The *load word and zero* instruction (lwz[u][x]) is defined for all implementations of the PowerPC architecture. On 32-bit implementations, the 32-bit word is loaded into the target register (no zero extension is needed because the 32-bit word consumes the entire register). Table 3.15 lists the 32-bit integer load instructions.

Table 3.15. 32-bit integer load instructions.

Instruction	Definition[a]	Format[b]
load byte and zero	RT <- 0^{24} ‖ MEM(sign_ext(D)+(RA) ‖0, 1)	lbz[u] RT, D(RA)
load byte and zero indexed	RT <- 0^{24} ‖ MEM((RB) +(RA)‖0,1)	lbz[u]x RT, RA, RB
load halfword and zero	RT <- 0^{16} ‖ MEM(sign_ext(D)+(RA) ‖0, 2)	lhz[u] RT, D(RA)
load halfword and zero indexed	RT <- 0^{16} ‖ MEM((RB) +(RA)‖0,2)	lhz[u]x RT, RA, RB
load halfword algebraic	RT <- sign_ext(MEM(sign_ext(D)+(RA) ‖0, 2))	lha[u] RT, D(RA)
load halfword algebraic indexed	RT <- sign_ext(MEM((RB)+(RA)‖0, 2))	lha[u]x RT, RA, RB
load word and zero	RT <- MEM(sign_ext(D)+(RA) ‖0, 4))	lwz[u] RT, D(RA)
load word and zero indexed	RT <- MEM((RB)+(RA)?(RA) :0, 4))	lwz[u]x RT, RA, RB

Note: If [o] is added, XER$_{SO}$ and XER$_{OU}$ will be set, if [.] is added, CR0 will be altered based on the result of the instruction.

[a] MEM(A,B) is a function that points to B sequential bytes in memory starting at address A.

[b] [u] in the mnemonic means that the instruction can be coded with the u, meaning update form, or without the u, indicating no update form. In the update form RA is loaded with the effective address of the load. Note that using 0 for RA with the update form of the instruction is invalid and results in an exception.

On 64-bit implementations, the lwz[u][x] instruction loads the 32-bit word into the low-order 32 bits of the target register, and then loads 0s into the upper-order 32 bits of the register. In addition, on 64-bit implementations, there is another load word instruction. The *load word algebraic* (lwa[[u]x]) instruction is defined only for 64-bit implementations of the architecture. The sign bit of the word to be loaded is repeated throughout the upper-order 32 bits of the target register. There is a semantic difference between the offset value for this instruction and the previous ones. The offset is multiplied by 4 (shifted left by 2) before being added to the base register. Note that this only applies to the offset value—not to the index value. Another difference is that although the u and x forms of this instruction are as described earlier, the lwau form does not exist.

The final integer load instruction is the *load doubleword* instruction (ld[u][x]) and is available only on 64-bit implementations of the architecture. This instruction loads the doubleword at the effective address of the load into the target register. There is no sign or zero extension because the doubleword consumes all the bits in the target register. This instruction also multiplies the offset (not index) value by 4 before performing the address calculation. Table 3.16 lists the 64-bit integer load instructions.

Table 3.16. 64-bit integer load instructions.

Instruction	Definition[a]	Format[b]
load word algebraic	RT <- sign_ext (MEM[a](sign_ext(DS||0b00)+ (RA)|0, 4)))	lwa RT, DS(RA)
load word algebraic indexed	RT <- sign_ext (MEM((RB)+(RA)|0, 4)))	lwa[u]x RT, RA, RB
load doubleword and zero	RT <- MEM (sign_ext(DS||0b00)+ (RA)|0, 8))	ldz[u] RT, DS(RA)
load doubleword and zero indexed	RT <- MEM((RB)+(RA) |0, 8))	ldz[u]x RT, RA, RB

Note: If [o] is added, XER_{SO} and XER_{OU} will be set, if [.] is added, CR0 will be altered based on the result of the instruction.

[a] MEM(A,B) is a function that points to B sequential bytes in memory starting at address A.

[b] [u] in the mnemonic means that the instruction can be coded with the u, meaning update form, or without the u, indicating no update form. In the update form RA is loaded with the effective address of the load. Note that using 0 for RA with the update form of the instruction is invalid and results in an exception.

Integer Store Instructions

The same four data sizes that were supported for integer loads are supported for integer stores. There is no distinction, however, between signed and unsigned data. The form of store instructions follows:

```
store[u][x] RS, RA, D ¦ RB
```

The address is calculated by adding RA to the 16-bit immediate offset D or the 32-bit index contained in register RB. The value to be stored is contained in the integer register RS. If the u form of the instruction is used, the RA is updated with the calculated effective address. If the x form is used, then RB is used to calculate the effective address; otherwise, the immediate offset D is used. Note that the offset form of the instruction generally is written as the following:

```
store[u] RS, D(RA)
```

If register zero is specified for RA, except for the store with update instructions, for which setting RA to r0 is an invalid form, then the value 0 is used instead of the contents of RA. There are three integer store instructions specified for 32-bit implementations. The *store byte* instruction (stb[u][x]), the *store halfword* instruction (sth[u][x]), and the *store word* instruction (stw[u][x]) are available on any PowerPC implementation. The store byte instruction stores the least significant byte of RS in the memory location specified by the address calculation. The store halfword instruction stores the least significant halfword contained in RS in the address specified by the effective address calculation (the most significant byte of the halfword is stored at the calculated address, and the least significant byte is stored at the address plus 1). The store word instruction stores the least significant word in register RS starting at the calculated address (the last byte of the word is stored at the address plus 3). Table 3.17 lists the 32-bit integer store instructions.

Table 3.17. 32-bit integer store instructions.

Instruction	*Definition* [a]	*Format* [b]
store byte	$MEM(sign\_ext(D)+(RA)\_0, 1) <- RS_{24:31}$	stb[u] RS, D(RA)
store byte indexed	$MEM((RB)+(RA)\_0,1) <- RS_{24:31}$	stb[u]x RS, RA, RB
store halfword	$MEM(sign\_ext(D)+(RA)\_0, 2) <- RS_{16:31}$	sth[u] RT, D(RA)
store halfword indexed	$MEM((RB)+(RA)\_0,2) <- RS_{16:31}$	sth[u]RT,D (RA)
store word	$MEM(sign\_ext(D)+(RA)\_0, 4)) <- (RS)$	sth[u]x RT, RA, RB
store word indexed	$MEM((RB)+(RA)\_0, 4)) <- (RS)$	stw[u] RT, D(RA)

Note: If [o] is added, XER_{SO} and XER_{OU} will be set, if [.] is added, CRO will be altered based on the result of the instruction.

[a] MEM(A,B) is a function that points to B sequential bytes in memory, starting at address A.

[b] [u] in the mnemonic means that the instruction can be coded with the u, meaning update form, or without the u, indicating no update form. In the update form RA is loaded with the effective address of the load. Note that using 0 for RA with the update form of the instruction is invalid and results in an exception.

There is one more integer store instruction that is available only on 64-bit implementations. The *store doubleword* instruction (std[u][x]) stores the double word contained in register RS starting at the calculated effective address. This instruction multiplies the offset contained in the D field of the instruction by 4 before calculating the effective address (only for non-x forms of the instructions). Table 3.18 lists the 64-bit integer store instructions.

Table 3.18. 64-bit integer store instructions.

Instruction	Definition [a]	Format [b]
store doubleword	MEM[a](sign_ext(DS||0b00)+ (RA)_0,8)) <- (RS)	std[u] RT, DS(RA)
store doubleword indexed	MEM((RB)+(RA)_0, 8)) <- (RS)	std[u]x RT, RA, RB

Note: If [o] is added, XER_{SO} and XER_{OU} will be set, if [.] is added, CR0 will be altered based on the result of the instruction.

[a] MEM(A,B) is a function that points to B sequential bytes in memory, starting at address A.

[b] [u] in the mnemonic means that the instruction can be coded with the u, meaning update form, or without the u, indicating no update form. In the update form RA is loaded with the effective address of the load. Note that using 0 for RA with the update form of the instruction is invalid and results in an exception.

Special Integer Storage Operations

The special integer load/store instructions fall into three categories. The first category is the byte reversal instructions, which give rudimentary support for little endian data. The second category is load and store multiple instructions, which are used primarily for restoring the state of the integer registers from the stack (after a subroutine call). The final category is the move assist instructions, which give basic support for string manipulation.

There are two load byte reversal instructions. The *load halfword byte reverse indexed* (lhbrx) and the *load word byte reverse indexed* (lwbrx) instructions. These instructions are analogous to the lhzx and lwzx instructions, respectively. The difference is that the bytes are loaded in reverse order. In other words, the most significant byte is placed in the least significant byte position in the target register, and the least significant byte is placed in the most significant byte position, which is loaded into the target register (see Figure 3.3).

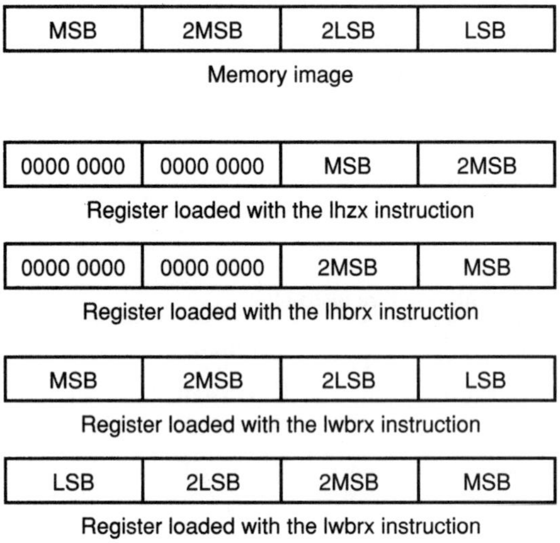

FIGURE 3.3.

Load byte reverse instructions (all instructions address MSB in memory).

MSB	2MSB	2LSB	LSB

Memory image

0000 0000	0000 0000	MSB	2MSB

Register loaded with the lhzx instruction

0000 0000	0000 0000	2MSB	MSB

Register loaded with the lhbrx instruction

MSB	2MSB	2LSB	LSB

Register loaded with the lwbrx instruction

LSB	2LSB	2MSB	MSB

Register loaded with the lwbrx instruction

There are two store byte reversal instructions, which are analogous to the load byte reversal instructions. The *store halfword byte-reverse indexed* instruction (sthbrx) stores the low-order 2 bytes of the source operand (RS) after first reversing the order of the 2 bytes. The *store word byte-reverse indexed* instruction (stwbrx) stores the low-order word of the source operand (RS) after first reversing the order of the 4 bytes.

The load and store multiple instructions can manipulate blocks of memory that span many words. The *load multiple word* instruction (lmw) has the following form:

```
lmw RT, D(RA)
```

The effective address of the load is calculated by adding the contents of RA to the immediate field D. The low-order 32 bits of registers RT–31 are loaded with sequential words in memory, starting at the effective address of the load. The *store multiple word* instruction (stmw) is the dual of the lmw instruction. That is, the low-order 32 bits of registers RS–31 are stored into sequential words in memory, starting at the effective address of the store (RA + D). Table 3.19 lists the 32-bit special integer load/store instructions.

Table 3.19. 32-bit special integer load/store instructions.

Instruction	Definition	Format
load halfword byte reverse indexed	$RT \leftarrow 0^{16}$ || $MEM(1+(RB)+(RA)\|0,1)$ ||$MEM((RB)+(RA)\|0,1)$	lhbrx RT,RA,RB
load word byte reverse indexed	$RT \leftarrow MEM(3+(RB)+(RA)\|0,1)$ || $MEM(2+(RB)+(RA)\|0,1)$ || $MEM(1+(RB)+(RA)\|0,1)$ || $MEM((RB)+(RA)\|0,1)$	lwbrx RT,RA,RB
store halfword byte reverse indexed	$MEM((RB)+(RA)\|0,4) \leftarrow RS_{24:31}\|\|RS_{16:23}\|\|RS_{8:15}\|\|RS_{0:7}$	sthbrx RT,RA,RB
store word byte reverse indexed	$MEM((RB)+(RA)\|0,4) \leftarrow RS_{24:31}\|\|RS_{16:23}\|\|RS_{8:15}\|\|RS_{0:7}$	stwbrx RT,RA,RB
load multiple word[b]	$RT_{0:31}$[c] $: R31_{0:31} \leftarrow MEM(sign\_ext(D)+(RA)\|0, 4*(32-'RT^d))$	lmw RT,D(RA)
store multiple word	$MEM(sign\_ext(D)+(RA)\|0, 4*(32-'RS)) \leftarrow RS_{0:31} : R31_{0:31}$	stmw RT,D(RA)

[a] MEM(A,B) is a function that points to B sequential bytes in memory, starting at address A.

[b] On 64-bit implementations, the load multiple instruction loads only the lower-order 32 bits of each target register (RT). The upper bits are set to zero.

[c] $RT_{0:31}$ refers to the low-order 32 bits of the register on 64-bit implementations or the entire register on 32-bit implementations.

[d] 'RT refers to the register number rather than the contents of that register.

[e] On 64-bit implementations the store multiple instruction stores only the lower-order 32 bits of each store data source register (RS). The upper bits are ignored.

The last four integer load/store instructions are the *move assist* instructions, which manipulate strings of bytes which may be longer than eight bytes (these instructions also may update multiple registers). There are two load string instructions. These instructions are similar to the load multiple word instructions, in that they update multiple registers, but instead of specifying the number of registers to be updated, the number of bytes to be loaded is specified. As many registers as are necessary are loaded (starting at RT, and possibly wrapping around through R0). Again, only the low-order 32 bits of each target register are loaded. The *load string word immediate* instruction (lswi) specifies the number of bytes to load in an immediate field. If 0 bytes is specified, then 32 bytes are loaded. The *load string word indexed* instruction (lswx) specifies the number of bytes to load in bits 25 through 31 of the XER. The *store string word immediate* (stswi) and *store string word indexed* (stswx) instructions are analogous to the lswi and lswx instructions, respectively. Table 3.20 lists the integer move assist instructions.

Table 3.20. Integer move assist instructions.

Instruction	Definition[a][b]	Format

load string word immediate	for (i=0; i< (NB?NB:32); i++)
	 {
	 '$((RT+i/4)\%32)_{((i\%4)*8:(i\%4)*8+7)}$[c] <- 0
	 '$((RT+i/4)\%32)_{((i\%4)*8+32):(((I\%4)*8+7)+32)}$[b]
	 <- MEM[c]$(((RA)?(RA):0)+i, 1)$
	 }
	 '$(RT+NB/4)_{(NB\%4)*8:63}$ <- 0
		lswi RT,RA, NB

load string word indexed	for (i=0; i< $XER_{25:31}$; i++)
	 {
	 '$((RT+i/4)\%32)_{((i\%4)*8:(i\%4)*8+7)}$ <- 0
	 '$((RT+i/4)\%32)_{((i\%4)*8+32):(((I\%4)*8+7)+32)}$
	 <- MEM$((RB)+((RA)?(RA):0)+i, 1)$
	 }
	 '$(RT+NB/4)_{(XER25:31\%4)*8:63}$ <- 0
		lswx RT,RA, RB

store string word immediate	for (i=0; i< (NB?NB:32); i++)
	 {
	 MEM$(((RA)?(RA):0)+i, 1)$ <-
	 '$((RS+i/4)\%32)_{((i\%4)*8+32)}$
		stswi RT,RA, RN

Instruction	Definition[a][b]	Format
	:(((I%4)*8+7)+32) }	

store string word indexed	for (i=0; i< $XER_{25:31}$; i++)
	 {
	 MEM((RB)+((RA)?(RA):0)+i, 1) <-
	 '((RS+i/4)%32)$_{((i\%4)*8+32):}$
	
	 (((I%4)*8+7)+32)
	 }
		stswx RT,RA,
		 RB

[a] MEM(A,B) is a function that points to B sequential bytes in memory, starting as address A.

[b] These instructions only operate on the low order 32 bits of the registers in a 64-bit implementation. The equations are given for a 32-bit implementation with the bit numbers ranging from 0 to 31. For a 64-bit implementation the bit numbers range from 32 to 64 (simply add 32 to the bit numbers given).

[c] RT refers to the register number rather than the contents of that register.

4

Branch and Control Flow Instructions

The *branch and control flow* instructions are used to control the execution of a program. These instructions make things like subroutine calls and for-next loops possible. The PowerPC architecture supports several different branch instructions, all of which direct program execution to one of two possible addresses. The *sequential address* is simply the address of the branch plus 4 (the instruction immediately following the branch in memory). The *target address* is generated by the branch and can be any address in the memory space. If the target address is selected, then the branch is said to be *taken*; if the sequential address is selected, then the branch is said to be *not taken*. Throughout this chapter, references are made to the *program counter*. This is not an architectural register in the PowerPC architecture; instead, it is a convenient way to refer to the address of the instruction being executed. Remember that from the programmer's point of view, the instructions execute one at a time, but in reality the hardware may be executing many instructions at once.

There are four types of branches as classified by how the target address is calculated. The first type, *relative branch*, generates the target address by adding an immediate offset to the current program counter (the address of the branch instruction in memory). The second type, *absolute branch*, generates the address by using an immediate field in the instruction directly. The third type, *branch to link* or *return branch*, uses the contents of the link register as a branch target. The fourth and final type of branch target, *branch to count*, uses the contents of the count register as the target address of the branch. Each of these branches has a purpose, or a set of semantics that programmers should follow. These semantics are described in this chapter.

It also is possible to classify branches based on how the selection between the target and the sequential address is made. The simplest type of branch in this regard is the *unconditional branch*. Unconditional branches always select the target address. The next type of branch, *branch and decrement branches*, subtracts 1 from the value in the count register and then compares the new value of the count register to 0. The address selection is made based on the results of the compare. Finally, any bit in the condition register can be examined and the address selection can be made based on the value of that bit. Note that the condition register and count register tests can be combined into a single test. Also note that unlike many other architectures, it is not possible to base the branch address selection or the target address of the branch directly on an integer register.

Branch Instruction Descriptions

There are four branch instructions, three of which have many forms. There also are many extended mnemonics, which make coding branch instructions much easier. The four instructions are described in detail in this chapter, and Tables 4.2 and 4.4 list the extended mnemonics.

All branch instructions may update the link register with their sequential address. This is coded with an [l] in the instruction mnemonic. The link register is used for subroutine linkage, so when a subroutine is being called, the link register should be updated. The branch to link register instruction then can be used to return from the subroutine (see Example 4.1).

EXAMPLE 4.1.

Using the subroutine linkage convention.

```
START:      bl      SUBROUTINE   # PC<-SUBROUTINE, LK<-(PC)+4
            add     r1,r2,r3     # r1<-(r2)+(r3)

            ....

SUBROUTINE: add     r2,r4,r5     # r2 <- (r4)+(r5)
            bclr                 # PC <- (LK)
```

In this code, the bl instruction is an unconditional subroutine call, which branches to the label SUBROUTINE. The link register is set to the address of the add instruction following the bl instruction. At the end of the subroutine, the bclr instruction is used to return to the add instruction. Note that there generally is more involved with subroutine linkage conventions from a software perspective; this fact is discussed in Chapter 6, "Code Organization and Interfacing."

When coding relative and absolute branches, you typically use a label, rather than an actual address or offset. For instance, in Example 4.1, the first instruction is coded as bl   SUBROU-TINE instead of using some exact offset. The assembler calculates and inserts the exact offset.

The unconditional long branch instruction (b[l][a]) is an unconditional branch with a 24-bit immediate field. The b[l]a form of the instruction uses the immediate field as an absolute address, and the b[l] form of the instruction uses the immediate field as a signed offset from the current program counter. Before being used, the immediate field has two binary zeros appended to the right (the address/offset is multiplied by 4). This gives a word-aligned address, which is required for instructions in the PowerPC architecture.

The branch conditional (bc[l][a]) instruction has many options. The form of the instruction follows:

```
bc BO, BI, BD
```

The BD field is a 16-bit immediate field, and is used as an absolute address (bc[l]a form) or a signed offset from the current program counter (bc[l] form). The BO field is a 5-bit immediate value that describes how the address selection of the branch is performed (see Table 4.1).

Table 4.1. BO field encodings for branch conditional, branch conditional to count, and branch conditional to link instructions.

Encoding[a]	Definition
0b0000yb	Decrement the count register, then branch if the new value in the count register is not 0, and the condition[c] is false.

continues

Table 4.1. continued

Encoding[a]	Definition
0b0001y	Decrement the count register, then branch if the new value in the count register is 0, and the condition is false.
0b0010y	Branch if the condition is false.
0b0100y	Decrement the count register, then branch if the new value in the count register is not 0, and the condition is true.
0b0101y	Decrement the count register, then branch if the new value in the count register is 0, and the condition is true.
0b0110y	Branch if the condition is true.
0b1000y	Decrement the count register, then branch if the new value in the count register is not 0.
0b1001y	Decrement the count register, then branch if the new value in the count register is 0.
0b10100	Branch always.

[a] These are the only valid BO field encodings.

[b] The y-bit is the bit that reverses the default branch prediction.

[c] The condition is determined by the bit in the condition register specified in the BI field. A value of 0 is a false condition, and a value of 1 is a true condition.

Finally, the BI field is a 5-bit immediate field that codes which bit in the condition register should be examined if the condition register actually is examined at all.

The *branch conditional to link register* (bclr[l]) and *branch conditional to count register* (bcctr[l]) instructions are similar to the branch conditional instruction, except that the link register or the count register is used as the target address. The form of these instructions follows:

```
branch BO, BI
```

The BO and BI fields are as defined earlier for the branch conditional instruction, with the exception that the branch and decrement forms are *not valid* with the branch to count register instruction.

At this point, a word about hardware implementation is in order. When a processor is executing an instruction stream, it is common for it to have many instructions executing simultaneously. Often, when a branch instruction is encountered that needs to examine a condition register bit, that condition register bit has not yet been updated by the instruction that sets it. When this occurs, the hardware often tries to predict the direction the branch will take so that it can continue to fetch and execute instructions while waiting for the condition register to be set. If, when the condition register finally is updated, the prediction is determined to be correct, then the processor continues to fetch and execute instructions along the control path it predicted. If, on the other hand, the branch was predicted incorrectly, then the instructions that were being fetched and executed along the predicted control path must be purged (no effects of these instructions are visible to the programmer) and the correct instructions must be fetched and executed. The accuracy of this prediction can have a significant effect on the execution time of a program.

The PowerPC architecture enables the programmer to give hardware a hint about which way it should predict a conditional branch. Normally, branches with negative displacement will be predicted as taken, while those with positive displacement will be predicted as not taken. The least significant bit of the BO field enables the programmer to change this prediction scheme. If this bit is set to 1, then the default prediction is reversed; if the bit is 0, then the prediction is not reversed. Note that hardware is not required to use this prediction scheme, but it is encouraged to use it (all current PowerPC implementations default to this scheme, although some have dynamic prediction schemes as well).

The branch and decrement options (see Table 4.1) are used for coding loops. These options use the count register as the iteration variable and in a single instruction close the loop and decrement that iteration variable (see Table 4.2).

EXAMPLE 4.2.

Using the decrement and branch instruction for coding a for-next style loop.

For this example, assume that the value in the count register is the number of iterations you want to go through the loop and that you always go through at least once. Later, you will see how to put a value in the count register.

```
        addi    r1,r0,0       # R1<-0
LOOP:   addi    r1,r1,1       # increment R1
        bc      16,0,LOOP     # decrement counter and
                              # branch if it isn't 0.
```

When the count reaches 0, then the branch will be not taken, and the value in R1 will be the same as the original value in the count register. Not a very interesting program really.

If you want to add two arrays of integers in memory and store the result back into memory, then you can use a loop similar to the one here. Assume that R1, R2, and R3 contain pointers (starting addresses) to arrays A, B, and C, respectively. You want to add A to B and store the result in C. The size of the arrays minus 1 (they are all the same size, and the size is greater than 1) is contained in the count register.

```
        lwz     r4,o(r1)        # first element of A
        lwz     r5,o(r2)        # first element of B
        add     r6,r4,r5        # r6<-A[0]+B[0]
        stw     r6,o(r3)        # C[0]<-r6
LOOP:   lwzu    r4,4(r1)        # r1 is updated so that
                                # it 'walks' through A
        lwzu    r5,4(r2)
        add     r6,r4,r5
        stwu    r6,4(r3)        # C[i] <- A[i]+B[i]
        bc      16,0,LOOP
```

This code is non-optimized for clarity. Chapter 7, "Performance Tuning and Optimization," discusses ways in which to optimize loops.

There are many extended mnemonics for the three conditional branch instructions, which make coding these branches simpler. Rather than list every one of the extended mnemonics in a single list, this section shows how they are constructed and lists them in Table 4.2.

The first set of extended mnemonics gives a shortcut to coding different BO fields (see Table 4.2). The following shows the form of these instructions:

```
branch BI, target # for absolute branches

branch BI, offset # for relative branches

branch BI # for branches to either the link or count registers
```

Table 4.2. Extended mnemonics for the different BO field encodings.

		Target Address Type		
	(bc)	*(bca)*	*(bclr)*	*(bcctr)*
Branch Semantics (Xª)	*relative*	*absolute*	*to link*	*to count*
branch unconditionally	—	—	blr[l]	nctr[l]
branch if condition true (t)	bt[l]	bt[l]a	btlr[l]	btctr[l]
branch if condition false (f)	bf[l]	bf[l]a	bflr[l]	bfctr[l]
decrement count and branch if count non-zero (dnz)	bdnz[l]	bdnz[l]a	bdnzlr[l]	—

	Target Address Type			
	(bc)	*(bca)*	*(bclr)*	*(bcctr)*
Branch Semantics (X[a])	*relative*	*absolute*	*to link*	*to count*
decrement count and branch if count zero (dz)	bdz[l]	bdz[l]a	bdzlr[l]	—
decrement count and branch if count non-zero and condition true (dnzt)	bdnzt[l]	bdnzt[l]a	bdnztlr[l]	—
decrement count and branch if count non-zero and condition false (dnzf)	bdnzf[l]	bdnzf[l]a	bdnzflr[l]	—
decrement count and branch if count zero and condition true (dzt)	bdzt[l]	bdzt[l]a	bdztlr[l]	—
decrement count and branch if count non-zero and condition false (dzf)	bdzf[l]	bdzf[l]a	bdzflr[l]	—

[a] The building block used to form the mnemonic is shown in parentheses beside the semantic description. The mnemonic for the branch is built out of three components: b[direction mnemonic] [target mnemonic].

The second set of extended mnemonics for the branch instructions has to do with coding the BI field for the branch if condition false and branch if condition true cases. The condition register is conceptually split into eight 4-bit fields. Each of these 4 bits has a meaning related to how it is set by the various instructions. When an integer instruction sets a condition register field (for example, add. automatically updates condition register field zero with a compare of the result to 0), the 4 bits mean *less than, greater than, zero,* and *summary overflow,* respectively. These mnemonics are constructed by concatenating to the branch mnemonic (b) a condition register bit code (see Table 4.3), followed by a target code (see Table 4.4). The form of these instructions follows:

```
b[CR code][target code][l] [CR field],[target]
```

The CR field operand specifies which of the eight condition register fields should be examined, and the target is specified for relative branches (as a signed offset) or absolute branches (as an actual address). If the CR field is left out of the instruction, then condition register field zero is examined.

Table 4.3. Condition register bit codes.

CR Code	Bit	True or False	Meaning
lt	0	true	branch if less than
le	1	false	branch if less than or equal to
eq	2	true	branch if equal to
ge	0	false	branch if greater than or equal to
gt	1	true	branch if greater than
nl	0	false	branch if not less than
ne	2	false	branch if not equal to
ng	1	false	branch if not greater than
so	3	true	branch if summary overflow
ns	3	false	branch if not summary overflow
un	3	true	branch if unordered (see floating point compare instructions)
nu	3	false	branch if not unordered (see floating point compare instructions)

Table 4.4. Extended mnemonics for condition register bit encodings.

	Target address type			
	(bc)	*(bca)*	*(bclr)*	*(bcctr)*
Branch Semantics (X^a)	*relative*	*absolute*	*to link*	*to count*
branch if less than (lt)	blt[l]	blt[l]a	bltlr[l]	bltctr[l]
branch if less than or equal to (le)	ble[l]	ble[l]a	blelr[l]	blectr[l]
branch if equal to (eq)	beq[l]	beq[l]a	beqlr[l]	beqctr[l]
branch if greater than or equal to (ge)	bge[l]	bge[l]a	bgelr[l]	bgectr[l]
branch if greater than (gt)	bgt[l]	bgt[l]a	bgtlr[l]	bgtctr[l]
branch if not less than (nl)	bnl[l]	bnl[l]a	bnllr[l]	bnlctr[l]
branch if not equal to (ne)	bne[l]	bne[l]a	bnelr[l]	bnectr[l]
branch if not greater than (ng)	bng[l]	bng[l]a	bnglr[l]	bngctr[l]

	Target address type			
	(bc)	(bca)	(bclr)	(bcctr)
Branch Semantics (X[a])	relative	absolute	to link	to count
branch if summary overflow (so)	bso[l]	bso[l]a	bsolr[l]	bsoctr[l]
branch if not summary overflow (ns)	bns[l]	bns[l]a	bnslr[l]	bnsctr[l]
branch if unordered (see floating point compare instruction) (un)	bun[l]	bun[l]a	bunlr[l]	bunctr[l]
branch if not unordered (see floating point compare instructions) (nu)	bnu[l]	bnu[l]a	bnulr[l]	bnuctr[l]

[a] The building block that is used to form the mnemonic is shown in parentheses beside the semantic description. The mnemonic for the branch is built out of three components: b[CR code] [target code] [l].

The final extended mnemonic component for the branch instructions gives an easy way to code the prediction bit. If the branch should be predicted as taken, then a plus (+) should be appended to the mnemonic; if the branch should be predicted as not taken, then a minus (-) should be appended to the mnemonic. If the preferred direction is unknown, then neither a plus nor a minus should be appended to the mnemonic. Thus,

```
blt+ CR2, LABEL
```

would be a taken branch if bit 0 of condition register field 2 is a 1. If the branch is predicted, then it will be predicted as taken. The target of the branch is the label LABEL. Assuming that LABEL is five instructions ahead of the branch instruction, it could be coded equivalently as the following:

```
bc 0b01101, 8, 5
```

If LABEL were five instructions behind the branch instruction, then it could be coded as the following:

```
bc 0b01100, 8, -5
```

Note that in the second case, the offset is negative, so it will default to predicted taken. Thus, in the second case, the least significant bit of the BO field is set to 0, meaning use the default prediction.

Compare Instructions, Examples

Now that you have seen how to use the condition register to control the direction of branches, you need to have some way to get data into the condition register. You saw throughout the description of the integer instructions how to set condition register field zero with information about the result of an operation. There are other, more general ways, to set bits in the condition register.

There are a set of eight integer compare instructions that can be used to compare two values and place the results of that compare into any field in the condition register. The form of the compare instructions follows:

```
compare BF,RA,RB¦SI¦UI
```

Where BF is a 3-bit field that identifies one of the eight condition register fields to update. One operand is the contents of general integer register RA. The second operand is one of the contents of RB, the signed immediate field SI, or the unsigned immediate field UI.

The first four compare instructions are available on any PowerPC implementation. The *compare word immediate* instruction (cmpwi) and the *compare word* instruction (cmpw) perform signed compares of the two operands. The cmpwi instruction gets one operand from a general integer register, while the other is the sign extended 16-bit immediate field in the instruction. The cmpw instruction gets both of its operands from general integer registers. These instructions set the following 4 bits of the condition register field selected by BF: bit 0 (LT) is set to 1 if RA < SI¦RB using a signed comparison; bit 1 (GT) is set to 1 if RA>SI¦RB using a signed comparison; bit 2 (EQ) is set to 1 if RA=SI¦RB using a signed comparison; and bit 3 is set to the value of the summary overflow bit in the XER.

The *compare logical word immediate* (cmplwi) and *compare logical word* (cmplw) instructions are similar to the cmpwi and cmpw instructions, except that all comparisons are unsigned, and the immediate field (for cmplwi) is *not* sign extended (see Example 4.3). Table 4.5 lists the 32-bit integer compare instructions.

EXAMPLE 4.3.

Using a compare branch combination.

Compare and branch instructions can be used to direct a program to different pieces of code, depending on the value contained in a general integer register. In Example 3.6, the assumed shift amount was less than 64. But what if you do not know what the shift amount was? In this case, you need to check the shift amount. If it is less than 64, you can take one action, but if it is greater than 64, you can take a different action—an if-then-else construct.

Assume that the data to be shifted is contained in r1 and r2, and the shift amount is contained in r3. Unlike before, however, do not assume anything about the shift amount. For shifts greater than 63, both registers should be set to 0 (all bits are shifted out of the 64-bit number).

```
cmplwi      3,r3,64        # shift amount is unsigned
        blt         3,OLD_CODE    # branch based on cmplwi
        addi        r1,r0,0       # shift >= 64 so r1<-0
        addi        r2,r0,0       # r2<-0
        b           END           # branch to END
OLD_CODE: subfic    r4,r3,32       # shift < 64 use code
        slw         r1,r1,r3      # Example 3.6.
        srw         r5,r2,r4
        or          r1,r1,r5
        addic       r4,r3,-32
        slw         r5,r2,r4
        or          r1,r1,r5
        slw         r2,r2,r3
END:        nop                    # shift is complete.
```

Table 4.5. 32-bit integer compare instructions.

Instruction	Definition	Format
compare word	CR_{BF} <- (RA) < (RB) || (RA) > (RB) || (RA) == (RB) || XER[SO]	cmpw BF, RA, RB
compare word immediate	CR_{BF} <- (RA) < sign_ext(SI)) || (RA) > sign_ext(SI)) || (RA) == sign_ext(SI)) || XER_{SO}	cmpwi BF, RA, SI
compare logical word	CR_{BF} <- (RA) u< (RB) || (RA) u> (RB) || (RA) == (RB) || XER_{SO}	cmplw BF, RA, RB
compare logical word immediate	CR_{BF} <- (RA) u< UI) || (RA) u> UI) || (RA) == UI) || XER_{SO}	cmplwi BF, RA, UI

[a] The relation *u<* is unsigned less than; the relation *u>* is unsigned greater than.

There are four compare instructions, which are available only on 64-bit implementations of the PowerPC architecture. These are analogous to the four word compare instructions, except that they perform their comparison on a doubleword. They are the *compare doubleword* (cmpd), *compare doubleword immediate* (cmpdi), *compare logical doubleword* (cmpld), and *compare logical doubleword immediate* (cmpldi) instructions. Table 4.6 lists the 64-bit integer compare instructions.

Table 4.6. 64-bit integer compare instructions.

Instruction	Definition	Format
compare doubleword	CR_{BF} <- ((RA) < (RB)) ‖ ((RA) > (RB)) ‖ ((RA) == (RB)) ‖ XER_{SO}	cmpd BF, RA, RB
compare doubleword immediate	CR_{BF} <- ((RA) < sign_ext (SI)) ‖((RA) > sign_ext (SI)) ‖ ((RA) == sign_ext (SI)) ‖ XER_{SO}	cmpdi BF, RA, SI
compare logical doubleword RB	CR_{BF} <- ((RA) u< (RB)) ‖ ((RA) u> (RB)) ‖ ((RA) == (RB)) ‖ XER_{SO}a	cmpld BF, RA,
compare logical doubleword immediate	CR_{BF} <- ((RA) u< UI) ‖ ((RA) u> UI) ‖((RA) == UI) ‖ XER_{SO}	cmpldi BF, RA, UI

ª The relation *u<* is unsigned less than; the relation *u>* is unsigned greater than.

Move To/From Special Branch Register Instructions

There are extended mnemonics of the move to and move from special purpose register instructions for the link register and the count register (see "Move To/From Special Register Instructions" in Chapter 3). The *move to link register* (mtlr) and *move from link register* (mflr) instructions are extended mnemonics that are used to move values to and from the link register (LR). The *move to count register* (mtctr) and *move from count register* (mfctr) instructions are extended mnemonics that are used to move values to and from the count register (CTR). See Example 4.4.

EXAMPLE 4.4.

Using a move to count register and branch to count register to build a switch statement.

One of the primary uses of the bcctr instruction is for constructing switch/case statements. In this example, assume that you have the following switch statement:

```
switch (value)
        {
        case 0: SUB_0();
        case 1: SUB_1();
                break;
        case 2: SUB_2();
        case 3: SUB_3();
        default:SUB_ALL();
        }
```

We assume that when we start out, the value in r1 can be anything. With switch statements that have a small number of cases, this may not be the highest performance code, but for large switch statements, it may be quite efficient. We set up a jump table which contains the label corresponding to each of the possible values in the switch variable. At runtime, the appropriate label is loaded from the jump table and put into the count register.

```
# First set up a jump table in memory
                    ZERO,ONE,TWO,THREE,DEFAULT
JMP_TBL:    .long
#Code:
START:      cmpwi    cr2,r1,4
            blt      cr2,SWITCH     # branch if R1 < 4
            addi     r1,r0,4        # R1 <- 4
SWITCH:     lwz      r1,JMP_TBL(r1)# Load the target address
            mtctr    r1             # put target into CTR
            bctr                    # branch to correct case
ZERO:       bl       SUB_0          # case 0:
ONE:        bl       SUB_1          # case 1:
            b        END            # break
TWO:        bl       SUB_2          # case 2:
THREE:      bl       SUB_3          # case 3:
DEFAULT     bl       SUB_ALL        # default:
END:        nop
```

Three move instructions also are used to manipulate the condition register. The *move to condition register field* instruction (mtcrf) moves the contents of a general integer register into the condition register under the control of an 8-bit mask contained in an immediate field. The *move to condition register from XER* instruction (mcrxr) copies the high-order 4 bits of the XER (the summary overflow bit, the overflow bit, the carry bit, and a reserved bit) into a field in the condition register. Finally, the *move from condition register* instruction (mfcr) copies the contents of the condition register into a general integer register. Table 4.7 lists the move to and from branch special purpose register instructions.

Table 4.7. Move to and from branch special purpose register instructions.

Instruction	Definition	Format
move to link register	LR <- (RT)	mtlr RT
		mtspr 8,RT
move from link register	RT <- (LR)	mflr RT
move to count register	CTR <- (RT)	mtctr RT
		mtspr 9,RT
move from count register	RT <- (CTR)	mfctr RT
move to condition register fields	CR <- $((\text{FXM}_0\ \&\ \text{RS}_{00:03})\ \|\ (\overline{\text{FXM}_0}\ \&\ \text{CR}_{00:03}))\ \|$ $((\text{FXM}_1\ \&\ \text{RS}_{04:07})\ \|\ (\overline{\text{FXM}_1}\ \&\ \text{CR}_{04:07}))\ \|$ $((\text{FXM}_2\ \&\ \text{RS}_{08:11})\ \|\ (\overline{\text{FXM}_2}\ \&\ \text{CR}_{08:11}))\ \|$ $((\text{FXM}_3\ \&\ \text{RS}_{12:15})\ \|\ (\overline{\text{FXM}_3}\ \&\ \text{CR}_{12:15}))\ \|$ $((\text{FXM}_4\ \&\ \text{RS}_{16:19})\ \|\ (\overline{\text{FXM}_4}\ \&\ \text{CR}_{16:19}))\ \|$ $((\text{FXM}_5\ \&\ \text{RS}_{20:23})\ \|\ (\overline{\text{FXM}_5}\ \&\ \text{CR}_{20:23}))\ \|$ $((\text{FXM}_6\ \&\ \text{RS}_{24:27})\ \|\ (\overline{\text{FXM}_6}\ \&\ \text{CR}_{24:27}))\ \|$ $((\text{FXM}_7\ \&\ \text{RS}_{28:31})\ \|\ (\overline{\text{FXM}_7}\ \&\ \text{CR}_{28:31}))$	mtcrf FXM,RS
move to condition register from XER	CR_{BF} <- $\text{XER}_{00:03}$	mcrxr BF
move from condition register	RT <- (CR)	mfcr RT

Note that in the move to condition register fields section of the table, for 64-bit implementations $\text{RS}_{32:63}$ are moved into CR. The appropriate bit numbers can be obtained by adding 32 to the numbers given.

CR Logical Instructions

The PowerPC architecture supplies a set of instructions for directly manipulating the condition register bits. These are known as the *condition register* (CR) *logical instructions*; they enable the programmer to perform Boolean operations on bits in the condition register. These instructions are useful for coding multiple condition branches using a single branch. The form of the condition register logical instructions follows:

```
r-logical BT, BA, BB
```

where BT, BA, and BB are 5-bit fields, each specifying a bit of the condition register. The BT bit is loaded with the result of the operation specified by the instruction and performed on the bits specified by the BA and BB fields. There are four extended mnemonics for the condition register logical instructions. These instructions are available on all PowerPC implementations (see Table 4.8).

Table 4.8. Condition register logical instructions.

Instruction	Definition	Format
condition register AND	CR_{BT} <- CR_{BA} & CR_{BB}	crand BT, BA, BB
condition register OR	CR_{BT} <- CR_{BA} | CR_{BB}	cror BT, BA, BB
condition register XOR	CR_{BT} <- $CR_{BA} \oplus CR_{BB}$	crxor BT, BA, BB
condition register NAND	CR_{BT} <- $\overline{CR_{BA} \| CR_{BB}}$	crnand BT, BA, BB
condition register NOR	CR_{BT} <- $\overline{CR_{BA} \& CR_{BB}}$	crnor BT, BA, BB
condition register EQV	CR_{BT} <- $CR_{BA} \equiv CR_{BB}$	creqv BT, BA, BB
condition register AND	CR_{BT} <- CR_{BA} & $\overline{CR_{BB}}$	crandc BT, BA, BB with complement
condition register OR	CR_{BT} <- CR_{BA} | $\overline{CR_{BB}}$	crorc BT, BA, BB with complement
condition register set	CR_{BT} <- 0b1	crset BTcreqv BT, BT, BT
condition register clear	CR_{BT} <- 0b0	crclr BT crxor BT, BT, BT
condition register move	CR_{BT} <- CR_{BA}	crmove BT, BA cror BT,BA, BA
condition register not	CR_{BT} <- $\overline{CR_{BA}}$	crnot BT, BA crnor BT, BA, BA

The *move condition register field* instruction (mcrf) copies the contents of one 4-bit condition register field into another 4-bit condition register field. The form of this instruction follows:

    mcrf BF, BFA

The BF and BFA fields are 3-bits wide, and each field specifies one of the eight 4-bit fields in the condition register. The field specified by BFA is copied into the field specified by BF. Table 4.9 shows the move condition register field instruction.

Table 4.9. Move condition register field instruction.

Instruction	Definition	Format
move condition register field	CR_{BF} <- CR_{BFA}	mcrf BF, BFA

Trap/System Call Instructions

The *trap and system call instructions* enable the programmer to pass control of a program to the operating system. Control may be passed at two points in the system. The system call instruction passes control to the system call interrupt vector; the trap instructions pass control to the system trap handler.

The *system call* instruction (sc) is used to tell the operating system to perform some service. The services available are operating-system dependent. This instruction is similar in function to the INTR instruction in Intel's x86 architecture.

There are four trap instructions. Two of the instructions are available on any PowerPC implementation, and the other two are available only on 64-bit PowerPC implementations. The form of the trap instructions follows:

```
trap TO,RA,SI¦RB
```

The trap instructions perform a function similar to the compare instruction, comparing RA to either SI sign extended to 32 bits (for immediate form trap instructions) or RB (for other trap instructions). The results then are masked by the 5-bit TO field, and action is taken on the masked result. The TO field mask bits have the same meaning on all trap instructions. Table 4.10 lists the trap instruction mask bits for the TO field.

Table 4.10. Trap instruction mask bits (TO field).

Mask Bit	Definition
0	Less than, using signed comparison
1	Greater than, using signed comparison
2	Equal
3	Less than, using unsigned comparison
4	Greater than, using unsigned comparison

If, for any Ob1 in the TO field, the corresponding condition is met, then the trap is taken. If the trap is taken, then control of the program is passed to the system trap handler.

The *trap word* (tw) and *trap word immediate* (twi) instructions are available on any PowerPC implementation and perform the comparison on a 32-bit word (the low-order 32 bits of the registers are used on 64-bit implementations). Table 4.11 lists the 32-bit trap instructions.

Table 4.11. 32-bit trap instructions.

Instruction	Definition	Format

trap word	if ((TO$_0$ & ((RA) < (RB))) |
	 (TO$_1$ & ((RA) > (RB))) |
	 (TO$_2$ & ((RA) == (RB))) |
	 (TO$_3$ & ((RA) <u (RB))) |
	 (TO$_4$ & ((RA) >u (RB))))
	 trap
	 else
	 don't trap
		tw TO, RA, RB

trap word immediate	if ((TO$_0$ & ((RA) < sign_ext(SI))) |
	 (TO$_1$ & ((RA) > sign_ext(SI))) |
	 (TO$_2$ & ((RA) == sign_ext(SI))) |
	 (TO$_3$ & ((RA) <u sign_ext(SI))) |
	 (TO$_4$ & ((RA) >u sign_ext(SI))))
	 trap
	 else
	 don't trap
		twi TO, RA, SI

The *trap doubleword* (td) and *trap doubleword immediate* (tdi) instructions are available only on 64-bit PowerPC implementations and perform their comparison on 64-bit doublewords (the SI field is sign extended to 64 bits for the tdi instruction). Table 4.12 lists the 64-bit trap instructions.

Table 4.12. 64-bit trap instructions.

Instruction	Definition	Format

trap word	if ((TO$_0$ & ((RA) < (RB))) |
	 (TO$_1$ & ((RA) > (RB))) |
	 (TO$_2$ & ((RA) == (RB))) |
	 (TO$_3$ & ((RA) <u (RB))) |
	 (TO$_4$ & ((RA) >u (RB))))
	 trap
	 else
	 don't trap
		td TO, RA, RB

trap word	if ((TO$_0$ & ((RA) < sign_ext(SI))) |	tdi TO, RA, SI

continues

Table 4.12. continued

Instruction	Definition	Format
immediate	$(TO_1$ & $((RA) > sign\_ext(SI)))$ | $(TO_2$ & $((RA) == sign\_ext(SI)))$ | $(TO_3$ & $((RA) <u\ sign\_ext(SI)))$ | $(TO_4$ & $((RA) >u\ sign\_ext(SI))))$ trap else don't trap	

There are several extended mnemonics for the trap instructions. These are similar to the extended mnemonics for the conditional branch instructions. These extended mnemonics are provided for the most commonly used TO field encodings. Table 4.13 lists the TO field encoding for extended mnemonics, and Table 4.14 lists the extended mnemonics for trap instructions.

Table 4.13. TO field encoding for extended mnemonics.

Code	Definition	Decimal TO	<	>	=	<u	>u
lt	less than	16	1	0	0	0	0
le	less than or equal to	20	1	0	1	0	0
eq	equal to	4	0	0	1	0	0
ge	greater than or equal to	12	0	1	1	0	0
gt	greater than	8	0	1	0	0	0
nl	not less than	12	0	1	1	0	0
ne	not equal to	24	1	1	0	0	0
ng	not greater than	20	1	0	1	0	0
llt	logically less than	2	0	0	0	1	0
lle	logically less than or equal to	6	0	0	1	1	0
lge	logically greater than or equal to	5	0	0	1	0	1
lgt	logically greater than	1	0	0	0	0	1
lnl	logically not less than	5	0	0	1	0	1

Code	Definition	Decimal TO	<	>	=	<u	>u
lng	logically not greater than	6	0	0	1	1	0
<none>	unconditional	31	1	1	1	1	1

Table 4.14. Extended mnemonics for trap instructions.

Instruction Semantics	32-Bit Trap Instructions		64-Bit Trap Instructions	
	tw	twi	td	tdi
trap unconditionally	trap	—	—	—
trap if less than	twlt	twlti	tdlt	tdlti
trap if less than or equal to	twle	twlei	tdle	tdlei
trap if equal	tweq	tweqi	tdeq	tdeqi
trap if greater than or equal to	twge	twgei	tdge	tdgei
trap if greater than	twgt	twgti	tdgt	tdgti
trap if not less than	twnl	twnli	tdnl	tdnli
trap if not equal to	twne	twnei	tdne	tdnei
trap if not greater than	twng	twngi	tdng	tdngi
trap if logically less than	twllt	twllti	tdllt	tdllti
trap if logically less than or equal to	twlle	twllei	tdlle	tdllei
trap if logically greater than or equal to	twlge	twlgei	tdlge	tdlgei
trap if logically greater than	twlgt	twlgti	tdlgt	tdlgti
trap if logically not less than	twlnl	twlnli	tdlnl	tdlnli
trap if logically not greater than	twlng	twlngi	tdlng	tdlngi

5

Floating-Point Instructions

The PowerPC architecture includes floating-point instructions and registers that are implemented in the floating-point unit integrated in PowerPC chips. Like the integer instruction set, the floating-point instruction set is a load/store architecture where the only instructions that interface to system memory are load and store instructions, which load data into general floating-point registers and store data from general floating-point registers. There is very little difference in the floating-point architectures of the 32-bit PowerPC architecture and the 64-bit PowerPC architecture. Unless otherwise noted, all instructions are available on all implementations of the PowerPC architecture.

The floating-point unit supports both single and double precision operations, but the floating-point registers support only double precision format. When operations are performed, the inputs are taken as double precision values and an infinitely precise result is formed. This result then is rounded to the target precision (single precision for floating-point single precision operations, and double precision for floating-point double precision operations) under control of the rounding mode (see Chapter 2, "Introduction to PowerPC Architecture").

Floating-Point Load and Store Instructions

There are separate load and store instructions for the floating-point unit. The address for the floating-point load and store instructions, however, is generated in the integer unit just like it was for the integer load instructions. Each of these instructions supports an update mode that is the same as the update mode form of the integer load instructions. All these instructions also support both immediate and indexed addressing modes, just like in the integer load and store instructions.

There are two floating-point load instructions. The *load floating-point single* (lfs[u][x]) instruction loads a 32-bit single precision floating-point number from memory into a general floating-point register. The *load floating-point double* (lfd[u][x]) instruction loads a 64-bit double precision floating-point number from memory into a general floating-point register. When an lfs instruction is used, the data being loaded is extended to a double precision value before it is placed in a register. Single precision positive and negative infinity and Not a Number (NaN) values are translated to double precision infinities and NaNs. Zero is left zero, and normalized numbers are zero extended to the larger mantissa (zeros added to the low-order bit positions). Denormalized numbers are normalized as double precision numbers (see Chapter 2). Table 5.1 lists the floating-point load instructions.

Table 5.1. Floating-point load instructions.

Instruction	Definition	Format
load floating-point single	FRT <- DOUBLE(MEM(sign_ext(D)+(RA)| 0, 4))	lfs[u] FRT, D(RA)

Instruction	Definition	Format
load floating-point single indexed	FRT <- DOUBLE(MEM ((RB)+(RA)|0, 4))	lfs[u]x FRT, RA,RB
load floating-point double	FRT <- MEM(sign_ext(D)+(RA) |0,8)	lfd[u] FRT, D(RA)
load floating-point double indexed	FRT <- MEM((RB)+(RA)|0, 8)	lfd[u]x FRT, RA,RB

a. MEM(A,B) is a function that points to B sequential bytes in memory, starting at address A.

b. The [u] in the mnemonic indicates that the instruction can be coded with the u, meaning update form, or without the u, meaning no update form. In the update form, RA is loaded with the effective address of the load. Note that using 0 for RA with the update form of the instruction is invalid and results in an exception.

There are two floating store instructions. The *store floating-point single* instruction (stfs[u][x]) stores the contents of a general floating-point register as a 32-bit single precision floating-point number into memory. The *store floating-point double* instruction (stfd[u][x]) stores the contents of a general floating-point register as a 64-bit double precision floating-point number into memory. The store floating-point single instruction rounds the double precision value stored in the general floating-point register being stored to a single precision number before storing it. This transformation also may involve taking a double precision normalized number into a single precision denormalized number format. Table 5.2 lists the floating-point store instructions.

Table 5.2. Floating-point store instructions.

Instruction	Definition[a]	Format[b]
store floating-point single	MEM(sign_ext(D)+(RA)?(RA) :0, 4) <- round_single((FRS))	stfs[u] FRS, D(RA)
store floating-point single indexed	MEM((RB)+(RA)?(RA):0, 4) <- round_single((FRS))	stfs[u]x FRS, RA,RB
store floating-point double	MEM(sign_ext(D)+(RA)?(RA) :0, 8) <- (FRS)	stfd[u] FRS, D(RA)
store floating-point double indexed	MEM((RB)+(RA)?(RA):0, 8) <- (FRS)	stfd[u]x FRS, RA,RB

a. MEM(A,B) is a function that points to B sequential bytes in memory, starting at address A.

b. The [u] in the mnemonic indicates that the instruction can be coded with the u, meaning update form, or without the u, meaning no update form. In the update form, RA is loaded with the effective address of the load. Note that using 0 for RA with the update form of the instruction is invalid and results in an exception.

Like many of the integer instructions, many of the floating-point instructions may update the condition register implicitly, in addition to updating the target floating-point register with the result of the operation. Floating-point instructions that update the condition register update field 1 (instead of field 0, which the integer instructions updated). The result of the operation is compared to 0, and the results are stored in the condition register field. The first 4 bits of the FPSCR (FX, FEX, VX, DX) are possibly updated by the instruction and copied into condition register field 1.

In order to have an instruction implicitly update condition register field 1, the instruction mnemonic has a dot [.] appended to it. This form is not available for all floating-point instructions.

Arithmetic Instructions, Examples

The floating-point arithmetic instructions enable the programmer to manipulate floating-point values that have been loaded into the floating-pointt general registers. The arithmetic operations supported include add, subtract, multiply, and divide. The following sections describe a few other arithmetic operations that are supported.

Floating-Point Move Instructions

Four instructions move the contents of one floating-point register into another floating-point register, possibly performing some unary operation as they do so. The general form of these instructions follows:

```
move FRT, FRB
```

These instructions can be coded to update the condition register implicitly, and they can be applied to single or double precision data.

The *floating-point move register* instruction (fmr[.]) simply copies the contents of FRB into FRT. The *floating-point negate* instruction (fneg[.]) copies the additive inverse of the contents of FRB into FRT. Because the mantissa is represented in signed magnitude notation, negation means inverting the sign bit of the mantissa. The *floating-point absolute value* instruction (fabs[.]) stores the absolute value of FRB into FRT. This involves setting the sign bit of the mantissa to 0 as it is stored into FRT. Finally, the *floating-point negative absolute value* instruction (fnabs[.]) finds the absolute value of the contents of FRB, and then negates it before storing it into FRT. Table 5.3 lists the floating-point move instructions.

Table 5.3. Floating-point move instructions.

Instruction	Definition	Format
floating-point register move	FRT <- (FRB)	fmr[.] FRT, FRB
floating-point negate	FRT <- 0 – (FRB)	fneg[.] FRT, FRB

Instruction	Definition	Format
floating-point absolute value	FRT <- |(FRB)|	fabs[.] FRT, FRB
floating-point negative absolute value	FRT <- 0 – |(FRB)|	fnabs[.] FRT, FRB

a. The [.] in the mnemonic indicates that the instruction can be coded with a dot if condition register field 1 should be updated, or without a dot if condition register field 1 should *not* be updated.

Floating-Point Add/Subtract Instructions

There are two floating-point add and two floating-point subtract instructions. The general form of these instructions follows:

```
add FRT, FRA, FRB
```

where the operation specified by the instruction is performed on the contents of floating-point registers FRA and FRB, and the result of the operation is stored into floating-point register FRT. These instructions optionally can update condition register field one, as described earlier.

The *floating-point add single* instruction (fadds[.]) adds two single precision numbers; the *floating-point add double* instruction (fadd[.]) adds two double precision numbers. The main difference between these two instructions is the precision to which the result is rounded. Some implementations may have higher performance with the single precision operation.

The *floating-point subtract single* instruction (fsubs[.]) subtracts two single precision numbers; the *floating-point subtract double* instruction (fsub[.]) subtracts two double precision numbers. The main difference between these two instructions is the precision to which the result is rounded. Table 5.4 lists the floating-point add and subtract instructions.

Table 5.4. Floating-point add and subtract instructions.

Instruction	Definition	Format
floating-point add single precision	FRT <- round_single ((FRA) + (FRB))	fadds[.] FRT,FRA,FRB
floating-point add double precision	FRT <- round_double ((FRA) + (FRB))	fadd[.] FRT, FRA,FRB
floating-point subtract single precision	FRT <- round_single ((FRA) – (FRB))	fsubs[.] FRT,FRA,FRB

continues

Table 5.4. continued

Instruction	Definition	Format
floating-point subtract double precision	FRT <- round_double ((FRA) – (FRB))	fnsub[.] FRT,FRA,FRB

a. round_single(A) is a function which rounds the infinite precision number A to a single precision number (see Appendix D, "A Detailed Floating-point Model").

b. round_double(A) is a function which rounds the infinite precision number A to a double precision number.

c. The [.] in the mnemonic indicates that the instruction can be coded with a dot if condition register field 1 should be updated, or without a dot if condition register field 1 should *not* be updated.

Floating-Point Multiply and Divide Instructions

There are two multiply and two divide instructions, which are analogous to the add and subtract instructions. That is, there is a *floating-point multiply single* (fmuls[.]) and a *floating-point multiply double* (fmul[.]) instruction. The form of the multiply instructions follows:

```
multiply FRT, FRA, FRC
```

These instructions multiply the contents of floating-point registers FRA and FRC, placing the result into FRT. Similarly, there is a *floating point divide single* (fdivs[.]) and a *floating-point divide double* (fdiv[.]) instruction. The form of these instructions follows:

```
divide FRT, FRA, FRB
```

For the divide instructions, the contents of FRA are divided by the contents of FRB, and the result is placed into FRT. Table 5.5 lists the floating-point multiply and divide instructions.

Table 5.5. Floating-point multiply and divide instructions.

Instruction	Definition	Format
floating-point multiply single precision	FRT <- round_single ((FRA) × (FRC))	fmuls[.] FRT, FRA,FRC
floating-point multiply double precision	FRT <- round_double ((FRA) × (FRC))	fmul[.] FRT, FRA,FRC
floating-point divide single precision	FRT <- round_single ((FRA) / (FRB))	fdivs[.] FRT, FRA,FRB
floating-point divide double precision	FRT <- round_double ((FRA) / (FRB))	fdiv[.] FRT, FRB

Instruction	Definition	Format
a. round_single(A) is a function which rounds the infinite precision number A to a single precision number (see Appendix D).		
b. round_double(A) is a function which rounds the infinite precision number A to a double precision number.		
c. The [.] in the mnemonic indicates that the instruction can be coded with a dot if condition register field 1 should be updated, or without a dot if condition register field 1 should *not* be updated.		

Combined Multiply and Add Instructions

The PowerPC architecture supports a set of floating-point instructions that combine multiply and add operations. The general form of these instructions follows:

```
multiply-add FRT, FRA, FRC, FRB
```

The contents of FRA and FRC are multiplied together. The result of the multiplication then is added to the contents of FRB. The result of this whole operation then is placed into FRT.

There are eight multiply-add instructions. The *floating-point multiply add single* (fmadds[.]) and *floating-point multiply add double* (fmadd[.]) instructions perform the exact function described in the preceding example. The *floating-point multiply subtract single* (fmsubs[.]) and *floating-point multiply subtract double* (fmsub[.]) instructions store the result of FRA times FRC minus FRB into FRT. The last four multiply-add instructions are analogous to the first four, except that the final result is negated before being placed into FRT. These instructions are the *floating-point negative multiply add single* (fnmadds[.]), *floating-point negative multiply add double* (fnmadd[.]), *floating-point negative multiply subtract single* (fnmsubs[.]), and *floating-point negative multiply subtract double* (fnmsub[.]) instructions. Table 5.6 lists the floating-point multiply accumulate instructions.

Table 5.6. Floating-point multiply accumulate instructions.

Instruction	Definition	Format
floating-point multiply-add single precision	FRT <- round_single((FRA)×(FRC) + (FRB))	fmadds[.] FRT,FRA,FRB,FRC
floating-point multiply-add double precision	FRT <- round_double((FRA)×(FRC) + (FRB))	fmadd[.] FRT,FRA,FRB,FRC
floating-point multiply-subtract single precision	FRT <- round_single((FRA)×(FRC) – (FRB))	fmsubs[.] FRT,FRA,FRB,FRC

continues

Table 5.6. continued

Instruction	Definition	Format
floating-point multiply-subtract double precision	FRT <- round_double((FRA)×(FRC) – (FRB))	fmsub[.] FRT,FRA,FRB,FRC
floating-point negative multiply-add single precision	FRT <- round_single(0 – ((FRA)×(FRC)+ (FRB)))	fnmadds[.] FRT,FRA,FRB,FRC
floating-point negative multiply-add double precision	FRT <- round_double (0 – ((FRA)×(FRC)+ (FRB)))	fnmadd[.] FRT,FRA,FRB,FRC
floating-point negative multiply-subtract single precision	FRT <- round_single 0 – ((FRA)×(FRC)– FRB)))	fnmsubs[.] FRT,FRA,FRB,FRC
floating-point negative multiply-subtract double precision	FRT <- round_double 0 – ((FRA)×(FRC)– FRB)))	fnmsub[.] FRT,FRA,FRB,FRC

a. round_single(A) is a function which rounds the infinite precision number A to a single precision number (see Appendix D).

b. round_double(A) is a function which rounds the infinite precision number A to a double precision number.

c. The [.] in the mnemonic indicates that the instruction can be coded with a dot if condition register field 1 should be updated, or without a dot if condition register field 1 should *not* be updated.

Floating-Point Compare Instructions, Examples

There are two floating-point compare instructions. These instructions are used to set a condition register field based on a comparison of the contents of two general floating-point registers. The condition register field then can be examined by branch instructions to direct program flow. The form of the floating-point compare instructions follows:

```
compare BF, FRA, FRB
```

The two floating-point compare instructions update the 4-bit condition register field in the same way:

■ Bit 0 is set if (FRA) < (FRB).

■ Bit 1 is set if (FRA) > (FRA).

■ Bit 2 is set if (FRA) = (FRB).

■ Bit 3 is set if (FRA) or (FRB) is not a Number (NaN).

Both floating-point compare instructions also put the results of the comparison into the floating-point condition code bits of the floating-point status and control register. The difference between these two instructions is in how the floating-point status and control register are updated for quiet and signaling NaNs (see Appendix D). The two instructions are the *floating-point compare unordered* (fcmpu) and *floating-point compare ordered* (fcmpo) instructions. Table 5.7 lists the floating-point compare instructions.

Table 5.7. Floating-point compare instructions.

Instruction	Definition	Format
floating-point compare unordered	CR$_{BF}$ <- (FRA)<(FRB) ||(FRA)>(FRB) || (FRA) ==(FRB) ||((FRA) is a NaN or (FRB) is a NaN)	fcmpu BF,FRA,FRB
floating-point compare ordered	CR$_{BF}$ <- (FRA)<(FRB) ||(FRA)>(FRB) || (FRA) ==(FRB) ||((FRA) is a NaN or (FRB) is a NaN)	fcmpo BF,FRA,FRB

Floating-Point Rounding and Conversion Instructions

The PowerPC architecture defines a set of floating-point instructions that can be used to round floating-point numbers and to convert between integer and floating-point formats in the general floating-point registers.

Floating-Point Rounding Instructions

The *floating-point round to single instruction* (frsp[.]) rounds the contents of its one general floating-point register operand (FRB) to single precision, using the rounding mode specified in the floating-point status and control register. If the contents of FRB already are in single precision format, then they are left the same. The result of the rounding is placed into the target register (FRT). This is the only floating-point rounding instruction defined in the PowerPC architecture (see Table 5.8).

Table 5.8. Floating-point rounding instruction.

Instruction	Definition	Format
floating-point round to single	FRT <- round_single ((FRB))	frsp[.] FRT,FRB

a. round_single(A) is a function which rounds the infinite precision number A to a single precision number (see Appendix D).

b. The [.] in the mnemonic indicates that the instruction can be coded with a dot if condition register field 1 should be updated, or without a dot if condition register field 1 should *not* be updated.

Floating-Point Conversion Instructions

The floating-point conversion instructions convert values in the general floating-point registers from integers to floating-point format and from floating-point format to integer format. These instructions are the assembly language equivalent of casting an integer to a floating-point number or vice versa. There are no instructions for moving the contents of a floating-point register into an integer register, so this must be done through memory using loads and stores. The general form of the conversion instructions follows:

```
convert FRT, FRB
```

The contents of FRB are converted and placed into FRT. Any numbers greater than the largest representable integer are set to the maximum representable integer, and any numbers with greater magnitude than the smallest (most negative) representable integer are set to the smallest representable integer.

There are four instructions that convert floating-point numbers to integers. The first two instructions are available on any implementation of the PowerPC architecture. The *floating-point convert to integer word* instruction (fctiw[.]) converts the operand in FRB to a 32-bit integer, using the rounding mode specified in the floating-point status and control register. The *floating-point convert to integer word with round to zero* instruction (fctiwz[.]) converts the operand in FRB to an integer word using round toward zero, regardless of what rounding mode is specified in the floating-point status and control register. Table 5.9 lists the 32-bit floating-point conversion instructions.

Table 5.9. 32-Bit Floating-point conversion instructions.

Instruction	Definition[a]	Format[b]
floating-point convert to integer word	$FRT_{32:63}$ <- convert_to_integer((FRB),32, $FPSCR_{RN}$)$FRT_{0:31}$ <- undefined	fctiw[.] FRT, FRB

Instruction	Definition[a]	Format[b]
floating-point convert to integer word with round to zero	$FRT_{32:63}$ <- convert_to_integer((FRB),32, 0b01) $FRT_{0:31}$ <- undefined	fctiw[.] FRT, FRB

a. convert_to_integer (A,B,C) is a function that converts the floating-point number A into a B-bit integer using rounding specified by C (see Appendix D).

b. The [.] in the mnemonic indicates that the instruction can be coded with a dot if condition register field 1 should be updated, or without a dot if condition register field 1 should *not* be updated.

The second two convert to integer instructions are available only on 64-bit implementations of the PowerPC architecture. The *floating-point convert to integer doubleword* instruction (fctid[.]) converts the operand in FRB to a 64-bit integer using the rounding mode specified in the floating-point status and control register. The *floating-point convert to integer doubleword with round to zero* instruction (fctidz[.]) converts the operand in FRB to an integer doubleword using round toward zero, regardless of what rounding mode is specified in the floating-point status and control register.

There is one instruction that converts from integer to floating-point format; it is available only on 64-bit implementations of the PowerPC architecture. The *floating-point convert from integer doubleword* instruction (fcfid[.]) converts an integer value in floating-point register FRB to a double precision floating-point number. Table 5.10 lists the 64-bit floating-point conversion instructions.

Table 5.10. 64-bit floating-point conversion instructions.

Instruction	Definition	Format
floating-point convert to integer double word	FRT <- convert_to_integer[a]((FRB),64, $FPSCR_{RN}$)	fctid[.] FRT,FRB
floating-point convert to integer doubleword with round to zero	FRT <- convert_to_integer((FRB),64, 0b01)	fctid[.] FRT,FRB
floating-point convert from integer doubleword	FRT <- round_double (convert_from_integer[b] ((FRB), 64)	fcfid[.] FRT,FRB

a. convert_to_integer (A,B,C) is a function that converts the floating-point number A into a B-bit integer using rounding specified by C (see Appendix D).

b. convert_from_integer (A,B) is a function that converts the 64-bit integer in A into a fully precise (64-bit mantissa) floating-point number (see Appendix D).

continues

Table 5.10. continued

Instruction	Definition	Format

c. The [.] in the mnemonic indicates that the instruction can be coded with a dot if condition register field 1 should be updated, or without a dot if condition register field 1 should *not* be updated.

Status and Control Registers, Examples

There are four instructions that can be used to alter fields in the floating-point status and control register (FPSCR). The first two instructions that are used to change the FPSCR are the *move to FPSCR field immediate* (mtfsfi[.]) and the *move to FPSCR fields* (mtfsf[.]) instructions. The mtfsfi[.] instruction copies a 4-bit immediate field into one of eight 4-bit fields in the FPSCR. The form of this instruction follows:

```
mtfsfi[.] BF, U
```

The U field is the 4-bit immediate value, and the BF field specifies which 4-bit field in the FPSCR should be updated. If BF is equal to 0, then the update is handled differently from the other cases. In this case, the floating-point exception summary bit (FX; bit 0) is set to the value of bit 0 of the U field, and the floating-point overflow exception bit (OX; bit 3) is set to the value of bit 3 in the U field. The floating-point enabled exception summary bit (FEX; bit 1) and the floating-point invalid operation exception summary bit (VX; bit 2) are set by the usual rule (see Appendix D), rather than to the values contained in bits 1 and 2 of the U field.

The mtfsf[.] instruction copies the low-order 32 bits from a general floating-point register into the FPSCR under control of an 8-bit mask contained in an immediate field in the instruction. The form of the mtfsf[.] instruction follows:

```
mtfsf[.] FLM, FRB
```

The FLM field is an 8-bit mask that specifies which of the eight 4-bit fields are to be updated from the contents of the source register—FRB. If field 0 is specified (bit 0 of the FLM field is a 1), then field 0 is updated similarly to the mtfsfi[.] instruction. That is, the FX and OX bits are set from the contents of FRB, while the FEX and VX bits are set using the normal rule (see Appendix D).

The second two instructions that are used to set the FPSCR are used to set a single bit to a 1 or a 0. The general form of these instructions follows:

```
set BT
```

The BT field is a 5-bit field that specifies which bit of the FPSCR is to be set, while the value to which it should be set is specified by the instruction. The *reset FPSCR bit* instruction (mtfsb0[.]) is used to set bit BT to 0; the *set FPSCR bit* instruction (mtfsb1[.]) is used to set bit BT of the FPSCR to 1. Neither of these instructions can be used to set or reset the FEX or VX bits (bits 1 and 2) of the FPSCR.

Two instructions enable the programmer to read the FPSCR. The *move from FPSCR* instruction (mffs[.]) copies the contents of the FPSCR into the low-order 32 bits of a floating-point target register. The *move to condition register from FPSCR* instruction (mcrfs) copies a 4-bit field from the FPSCR into one of eight 4-bit fields in the condition register. The form of the mcrfs instruction follows:

```
mcrfs BF, BFA
```

The 3-bit BFA field specifies which field in the FPSCR should be moved, and the 3-bit BF field specifies to which field in the condition register the FPSCR field should be moved. When an exception bit in the FPSCR is copied into the condition register using these instructions, it is set to 0, except for the FEX and VX bits (bits 1 and 2), which are updated in the normal way (see Appendix I). Table 5.11 lists the floating-point status and control register instructions.

Table 5.11. Floating-point status and control register instructions.

Instruction	Definition	Format [a]
move to condition register from FPSCR [b]	$FPSCR_{BF} \leftarrow FPSCR_{BFA}$	mcrfs, BF, BFA
move from FPSCR	$FRT_{32:63} \leftarrow FPSCR$ $FRT_{0:31} \leftarrow$ undefined	mffs[.] FRT
move to FPSCR field immediate	$FPSCR_{BF} \leftarrow U!{=}0?U_{0:3}:U_0$ $\|FEX\|vx\|U_4$	mtfsfi[.]BF, U
move to FPSCR fields	$FPSCR \leftarrow$ $((FLM_0 \& FRB_{32}) \mid (\overline{FLM_0} \& FPSCR_0)) \parallel$ $FEX \parallel VX \parallel$ $((FLM_0 \& FRB_{35}) \mid (\overline{FLM_0} \& FPSCR_3)) \parallel$ $((FLM_1 \& FRB_{36:39}) \mid (\overline{FLM_1} \& FPSCR_{04:07})) \parallel$ $((FLM_2 \& FRB_{40:43}) \mid (\overline{FLM_2} \& FPSCR_{08:11})) \parallel$ $((FLM_3 \& FRB_{44:47}) \mid (\overline{FLM_3} \& FPSCR_{12:15})) \parallel$ $((FLM_4 \& FRB_{48:51}) \mid (\overline{FLM_4} \& FPSCR_{16:19})) \parallel$ $((FLM_5 \& FRB_{52:55}) \mid (\overline{FLM_5} \& FPSCR_{20:23})) \parallel$ $((FLM_6 \& FRB_{56:59}) \mid (\overline{FLM_6} \& FPSCR_{24:27})) \parallel$ $((FLM_7 \& FRB_{60:63}) \mid (\overline{FLM_7} \& FPSCR_{28:31}))$	mtfsf[.] FLM,FRB

continues

Table 5.11. continued

Instruction	Definition	Format[a]
reset FPSCR bit	$FPSCR_{BT} \leftarrow 0b0$	mtfsb0[.] BT
set FPSCR bit	$FPSCR_{BT} \leftarrow 0b1$	mtfsb1[.] BT

a. The [.] in the mnemonic indicates that the instruction can be coded with a dot if condition register field 1 should be updated, or without a dot if condition register field 1 should *not* be updated.

b. Note that $FPSCR_{BFA}$ indicates that the 4-bit field within the FPSCR specified by BFA. Thus for a BFA value of 0, $FPSCR_{BFA} = FPSCR_{0:3} = FPSCR_{FX,FEX,VX,OX}$.

III

Programming in Assembly

6

Code Organization and Interfacing

While an assembly language program has much more freedom to define its own conventions for interfacing between its internal functions, when that code has to interface with other routines certain standard conventions must be followed. This chapter covers the details of those conventions for making function calls, both within your program and to system libraries or compiled code. It also covers object module formats and the impact of dynamic binding on making function calls and writing functions.

Since so many operating systems are being developed for the PowerPC microprocessors, some of this information may not apply to your system. At the time of this writing this information is accurate for all the PowerPC platforms. However, you should consult your system documentation for more details about your specific platform.

Subroutine Linkage Conventions

The current PowerPC development tools follow certain conventions in the programming of the PowerPC processors. These conventions are similar in spirit to the conventions used on the 680x0 based Macintosh or the x86 DOS conventions, but are specific to the PowerPC.

Architecture

These conventions are set by the application binary interface (ABI), not by the PowerPC Architecture. Each operating system may have its own ABI, or may share a common ABI with other operating systems. The ABI illustrated in this chapter is the PowerOpen ABI, which is used by all of the current PowerPC development tools. These conventions are usually known as *subroutine linkage conventions* because they mostly address the programming of function calls.

The basic goal of the linkage conventions is to allow a function to make assumptions about the state of the processor after calling or being called by another function. The other major goal is the fast execution of function calls, achieved mostly by minimizing the amount of interaction with memory during a function call, especially for argument passing.

POWERPC FUNCTION CALLS

The PowerPC architecture has special support for performing function calls and returns. The architecture does not define special function call instructions like other architectures, but instead uses the branch instructions. The *link register* (LR) is used to hold the return address for a function, and the branch-and-link forms of the branch instructions store the return address into the LR. The instructions most commonly used are bl, branch-and-link, to perform the call, and blr, branch-to-link-register, to perform the return.

Register Usage Conventions

The register usage conventions specify which registers are dedicated to certain uses and which registers must have their contents left unchanged by a called function. Those registers whose contents may be changed by a function are known as *volatile registers*, and those whose contents may not be changed are known as *nonvolatile registers*. This doesn't mean a nonvolatile register cannot be changed by a function, but rather that if a function needs to use a nonvolatile register, it must save the contents before the register is modified and restore the original contents before returning to the calling function. That is, it is the called function's responsibility to save and restore nonvolatile register contents, not the calling function's responsibility. This is more efficient because the author of each function knows which registers it needs, and can save and restore only those registers, whereas, if the calling function was responsible, it could be forced to make worst-case assumptions about the behavior of other functions, which would result in unnecessary saving and restoring of registers that are not actually changed by the called function.

GPR Usage Conventions

The register usage conventions for the general purpose registers are shown in Table 6.1. There are two dedicated registers, GPR 1, used as the stack pointer (SP), and GPR 2, used as the TOC pointer (RTOC). For the other volatile GPRs, the table shows a role each register may play during a function call. Notice that since GPRs 0 and 3 – 12 are volatile, if a function can be written to use only these registers in its computations, no registers need to be saved or restored. Also, since GPRs 13 – 31 are nonvolatile, there are essentially 19 words of storage for intermediate values available that can be used when a function needs to call another function, which allows you to save more than just the values in the volatile registers. This will improve the performance of a function that needs to preserve values when making multiple function calls because the nonvolatile register values can be stored to memory once and the registers used freely, instead of storing intermediate values to memory before each function call.

Table 6.1. General-purpose register conventions.

Register	Status	Use
GPR 0	Volatile	In function prologs
GPR 1	Dedicated	Stack pointer (SP)
GPR 2	Dedicated	TOC pointer (RTOC)
GPR 3	Volatile	Argument word 1; Return value word 1
GPR 4	Volatile	Argument word 2; Return value word 2
GPR 5 - GPR 10	Volatile	Argument word 3 - argument word 8

continues

Table 6.1. continued

Register	Status	Use
GPR 11	Volatile	In calls by pointer; Environment pointer in some programming languages (for example, PASCAL)
GPR 12	Volatile	In glink code; In exception handling code in some programming languages
GPR 13 - GPR 31	Nonvolatile	Must be preserved across function calls

When using the nonvolatile GPRs, you should use them starting with GPR 31 and working your way backward, rather than starting with GPR 13. This is historically related to the load-and-store multiple instructions from the POWER architecture, which load or store all registers from a specified register through register 31. In the PowerPC processors, however, the load-and-store multiple instructions can inflict serious performance penalties, so the preferred method of saving and restoring the GPRs is to use a series of load or store word instructions. Allocating nonvolatile GPRs starting with GPR 31 is still useful then, because a single routine performing load or store word instructions can be written with an entry-point at each instruction, corresponding to the lowest numbered nonvolatile GPR used. Using this subroutine can result in smaller code, since potentially large numbers of load-and-store instructions can be omitted from each function call.

FPR Usage Conventions

The usage conventions for the floating-point registers are shown in Table 6.2. There are no floating-point registers with dedicated purposes. Floating-point registers can be used to pass arguments and return values during a function call, much like the GPRs, however, only floating-point values are passed this way. Like the GPRs, the nonvolatile FPRs should be used starting with FPR 31 and working backwards.

Table 6.2. Floating-point register conventions.

Register	Status	Use
FPR 0	Volatile	Scratch
FPR 1	Volatile	FP argument 1; Return FP value 1
FPR 2	Volatile	FP argument 2; Return FP value 2
FPR 3	Volatile	FP argument 3; Return FP value 3
FPR 4	Volatile	FP argument 4; Return FP value 4
FPR 5 - FPR 13	Volatile	FP argument 5 - FP argument 13
FPR 14 - FPR 31	Nonvolatile	Must be preserved across function calls

SPR Usage Conventions

The conventions for using the special purpose registers are shown in Table 6.3. Most of these registers are not explicitly used during a function call and are made volatile because their values are usually not useful for very long. The only nonvolatile values are the condition register fields CR2 - CR4. Since these represent only part of the condition register, to preserve these fields you must save and restore the entire condition register. If you do not use these fields, then you don't need to save and restore the condition register. There are no usage conventions for the SPRs not shown in Table 6.3, as they are usually manipulated only by custom assembly code, typically in the operating system. Compilers will not normally generate any code to manipulate them.

Table 6.3. Special-purpose register conventions.

Register	Status	Use
LR	Volatile	For branching and returning
CTR	Volatile	For branching and loop counts Fixed-point status register Floating-point status register
XER	Volatile	Scratch condition register fields
FPSCR	Volatile	Must be preserved across function calls
CR0, CR1	Volatile	Scratch condition register fields
CR2, CR3, CR4	Nonvolatile	
CR5, CR6, CR7	Volatile	

Stack Usage Conventions

Like the x86 and 680x0 processors, the PowerPC programming model utilizes a stack to store information associated with a function, such as local (automatic) variables, and as a way for functions to transfer data during a function call, such as function arguments. The stack is a last-in first-out (LIFO) data structure, meaning that the last thing you put into a stack is the first thing out. In the context of making function calls, the elements that are being put (or pushed) onto the stack are called *stack frames*, which contain information for the function that is being called. When a function returns, its stack frame is removed (or popped) from the stack, so the currently executing function always has its stack frame at the top of the stack.

As is the convention in most computers, the PowerPC stack grows from higher addresses towards lower addresses. This can be confusing because the end of the stack with the lowest address is actually referred to as the top of the stack. The stack pointer (SP), GPR 1 by convention, always contains the address of the top of the stack, or more precisely, the topmost (lowest addressed) word on the stack. When a stack frame is pushed onto the stack, the SP is decremented by the size of the stack frame, and when a stack frame is popped, the SP is incremented accordingly.

Stack Alignment

The top of the stack is required to be quadword aligned, that is the value in SP must be an multiple of sixteen. Thus each stack frame must be a multiple of sixteen bytes in size. In order to maintain this requirement, each stack frame must include zero to fifteen bytes of alignment padding.

Stack Frame Layout

The structure of a stack frame for a single function is shown in Figure 6.1. The figure shows the various areas of the stack frame, their offsets relative to the SP, the areas that are optional, and the areas that are actually used by the function associated with the stack frame.

FIGURE 6.1.

Layout of a function's stack frame. Grayed areas are not used by this function. Addresses are shown relative to the stack pointer from which they are addressed.

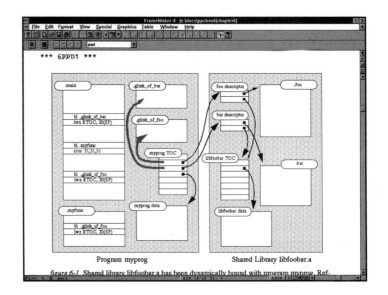

Each area of the stack frame is described in detail below.

Link Area

The link area of the stack frame contains the fields used most often during function calls. The first field contains the address of the top of the caller's stack frame, that is the value in SP when a function is called is stored here before SP is changed. This field is sometimes called the back chain, as it allows you to find each stack frame by tracing the pointers back through the stack. The remainder of the link area is used by any functions called from this function, and so should be considered volatile across these function calls. There are two words reserved for use by the compiler and the binder, and the other three words are used by any called function to store the value of the link register, the condition register, and the RTOC (GPR 2). Note that the current function uses the corresponding fields in its caller's stack frame, though those fields are not shown in the figure. The TOC save area is usually only used when glink (global linkage) helper functions are used to complete a function call.

The link area is required to be in a stack frame and is always exactly 24 bytes long. The link area is addressed in the context of the calling function, that is when SP points to the top of the caller's stack frame, and begins at SP + 0. Functions use the link area of their callers during function entry and exit.

Argument Passing Area

The argument passing area is used by the current function to pass parameters to any functions it may call and to retrieve return values. Space is always allocated for the first eight words of function arguments; however, the current function actually passes these arguments via GPRs 3 through 10. This space is only used by a called function that takes the address of one of its parameters. When a called function wants to do this, it first stores the parameter into the argument passing area of the parent function's stack frame, and then takes the address of that location in the stack. This is more efficient because the author of the called function knows whether it will need to do this, so the store is done only when needed, rather than having the caller always store the first arguments.

Space beyond the first eight words is added into the argument passing area only if the current function will call a function that requires more than eight words of parameters. In that case, the extra parameter data is stored here before calling the function. Notice that this implies that when creating a function's stack frame, you must know the maximum number of arguments required by any function called.

The argument passing area is required and is always at least 32 bytes long. It is addressed in the context of the function associated with the stack frame, that is when SP points to the top of the current function's stack frame (when the caller is storing arguments), or in the context of the calling function, that is when SP points to the top of the stack frame of the function which called the current function (when the called function is retrieving arguments). The argument passing area begins at SP + 24.

Local Stack Area

The local stack area is basically a scratch area for the function associated with the stack frame. The most common use of this area is for storage of local, or automatic, variables.

The local stack area is optional and may be any size. It is usually addressed in the context of the function associated with the stack frame, that is when SP points to the top of the current function's stack frame, and begins at an offset that depends on the size of the argument passing area.

There are zero to fifteen bytes of alignment padding below the local stack area, added to maintain the quadword alignment of SP.

Register Save Areas

The register save areas are used to preserve the initial values of any nonvolatile GPRs and FPRs that are used by the current function. The GPR save area is above the FPR save area, and within each the lowest nonvolatile register used is topmost, and register 31 is bottommost.

The GPR save area is 0 – 76 bytes long and the FPR save area is 0 – 144 bytes long. These areas are usually accessed in the context of the calling function, that is while the SP points to the top of the stack frame of the function which called the current function. The FPR save area begins at SP - 8 * (number of FPRs to save), and the GPR save area begins at SP - 4 * (number of GPRs to save) - 8 * (number of FPRs to save).

Stack Usage: Function Prolog and Epilog

The code that performs the pushing and popping of stack frames during a function call is usually known as the *function prolog* and the *function epilog*. While some parts of the prolog and epilog are optional since some parts of the stack frame are optional, the general steps are well defined. Each function is responsible for constructing and destroying its own stack frame since only the author of a function can know exactly what parts of a stack frame a given function will need, or if it will even need a stack frame at all. So the prolog and epilog code is included in each function, are performed after the actual branch or before the returning branch, and execute in the context of the function's caller, that is the SP should point to the calling function's stack frame. Figure 6.2 shows the stack during the execution of the prolog and epilog. Example 6-1 shows sample code illustrating function prolog and epilog, and stack frame construction and destruction.

Function Prolog

The function prolog code should at the beginning of a function so that it is executed immediately following the branch to the function. At this time the SP will contain the address of the calling function's stack frame. The steps performed by the function prolog are:

- If the function will modify the nonvolatile condition register fields (CR 2- 4), save the CR into the space in the function caller's link area (SP + 4).

- If the function will modify the link register, save the LR into the space in the function caller's link area (SP + 8). This value is normally the return address, the address to branch to when the function is complete.

- If the function will use any nonvolatile FPRs, save them into the function's FPR save area (SP - 8 * number of FPRs).

- If the function will use any nonvolatile GPRs, save them into the function's GPR save area (SP - 4 * number of GPRs - 8 * number of FPRs).

■ After storing nonvolatile registers, the function may load any argument data from the argument passing area into these registers.

Following the function prolog, the function's stack frame is constructed.

FIGURE 6.2.

View of the stack during execution of prolog and epilog code. Grayed areas are not accessed by the prolog or epilog. Some areas shown are optional.

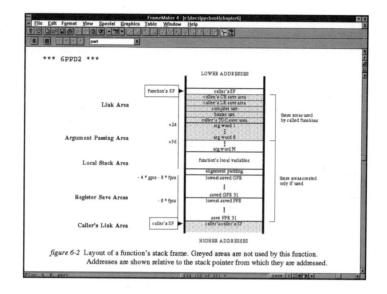

Function Epilog

The function epilog code should located at the end of a function so that it will be executed after the destruction of the current function's stack frame and immediately before the return branch. At this time the SP will contain the address of the calling function's stack frame. The steps performed in the function epilog are:

■ The values of any nonvolatile FPRs that were saved should be restored from the FPR register save area (SP - 8 * number of FPRs).

■ The values of any nonvolatile GPRs that were saved should be restored from the GPR register save area (SP - 4 * number of GPRs - 8 * number of FPRs).

■ If the function will modified the nonvolatile condition register fields (CR 2- 4), restore the CR from the space in the function caller's link area (SP + 4).

■ If the function will modified the link register, restore the LR from the space in the function caller's link area (SP + 8). This value is normally the return address, the address to branch to when the function is complete.

Following the function epilog, the function returns to its caller.

Creating and Destroying the Stack Frame

The actual creation and destruction of the stack frame is simple. All that you need to do is to update the value in the SP to point to the new top of the stack, and in the case of creating a new stack frame you will need to store the back chain (the previous value of SP) in the link area. Some systems may require that the store of the back chain and the update of SP is done atomically (in one instruction), but this requirement is easy to satisfy. The reason for this requirement is that it guarantees that an interrupt cannot occur while the stack is in an invalid state.

The stack frame creation and store of the back chain can be done with the store-word-with-update instruction. This instruction performs the update of SP and the store of the back chain atomically. For stack frames smaller than 32KB the immediate form can be used, and if the stack frame is larger than 32KB the X-form should be used.

The destruction of the stack frame can be done two ways. One way is to subtract the size of the stack frame from SP, and the other way is to load the back chain into SP. The first method is faster, but it may be inconvenient if the size of the stack frame may have changed during execution of the function. The second method is slower, but will always work.

Notice that since the value of SP must be quadword aligned, and that the link area and minimum argument passing areas are required, the minimum stack frame size is 64 bytes: 24 bytes in the link area, 32 bytes in the argument passing area, and 8 bytes of padding.

EXAMPLE 6.1.

Code showing function prolog and epilog, and stack frame construction and destruction.

```
#
# func uses:
#    nonvolatile GPRs N - 31
#    nonvolatile FPRs M - 31
#    any nonvolatile CF fields (CR 2 - 4)
#    the LR
#
# S_SIZE is the total size of func's stack frame #
    .csect  .func[PR]
# function prolog

    mfcr    r0                  # get the CR
    stw     r0,4(SP)            #   and save in caller's link area
    mflr    r0                  # get the return address (in LR)
    stw     r0,8(SP)            #   and save in caller's link area
    stfd    M,-8*(32-M)(SP)     # save FPR M
    stfd    M+1,-8*(31-M)(SP)   # save FPR M+1
#   ...
    stfd    f31,-8(SP)          # save FPR 31
    addi    r12,-8*(32-M)(SP)   # FPR save area
    stw     N,-4*(32-N)(r12)    # save GPR N
    stw     N+1,-4*(31-N)(r12)  # save GPR N+1
```

```
#   ...
    stw     r31,-4(r12)         # save GPR 31
# if S_SIZE is less than 32K
    stwu    SP,-S_SIZE(SP)      # create frame & chain
# if S_SIZE is greater than or equal to 32K
    addis   r12,-S_SIZE & 0xFFFF0000 (r0)          # move -S_SIZE
    ori     r12,-S_SIZE & 0xFFFF (r12)             #   into r12
    stwux   SP,SP,r12           # update SP atomically
#
# function code goes here
#
# if the stack frame size is still S_SIZE

    addi    SP,S_SIZE(SP)       # destroy the stack frame
# if the stack frame may have grown, e.g. with alloca.
    lwz     SP,0(SP)            # load back chain into SP
# function epilog
    lfd     M,-8*(32-M)(SP)     # restore FPR M
    lfd     M+1,-8*(31-M)(SP)   # restore FPR M+1
#   ...
    lfd     f31,-8(SP)          # restore FPR 31
    addi    r12,-8*(32-M)(SP)   # FPR save area
    lwz     N,-4*(32-N)(r12)    # restore GPR N
    lwz     N+1,-4*(31-N)(r12)  # restore GPR N+1
#   ...
    lwz     r31,-4(r12)         # restore GPR 31
    lwz     r0,4(SP)            # get the saved CR value
    mtcr    r0                  #  and restore
    lwz     r0,8(SP)            # get the save return address
    mtlr    r0                  #  and restore to the LR
    blr                         # return
```

Functions Without Stack Frames: Leaf Functions

Leaf functions, that is, functions that do not call any other functions, do not need to create a stack frame at all. The areas in the stack frame of the leaf function's caller allow a leaf function to perform any type of operation any function would, with the exception of making a function call. If a leaf function without a stack frame were to call another function, that function would treat the stack frame of the leaf function's caller as its caller's stack frame, and overwrite any values to leaf function that may have been stored there. A good example is the LR field in the link area. The leaf function stores its return address there, and then calls another function that stores its return address in the same place. When the leaf function attempts to return to its caller, it will instead branch back to the location following the function call it made, creating an infinite loop through the end of the leaf function.

In order to allow a leaf function to save and restore nonvolatile registers, a leaf function may use the register save area above its caller's stack frame. Apple's PowerPC System Software volume of *Inside Macintosh* calls this area the *Red Zone*. The Red Zone is 220 bytes long, since this is the largest possible register save area, and any space not used for preserving registers can be used as a scratch area by the leaf function.

Argument and Return Value Passing on the Stack

The general layout of parameters during parameter passing is as follows:

■ The first argument is the leftmost, and each argument smaller than 32 bits is extended to 32 bits. Structures are passed without changing their internal data layout.

■ Each word of the resulting data is passed through the GPRs and the argument passing area. Note that this includes floating point values. The reason is that C functions may take variable numbers of arguments, and this is necessary for those functions to process their argument list.

■ Any floating-point values are also passed via the FPRs.

From the above rules it becomes clear that C functions can attain maximum benefit from passing arguments in registers by moving all floating-point arguments to the end of their parameter lists.

Return values are passed back in a similar manner, that is, for integer type return values, the value is passed in GPR 3. For floating point return values, the value is returned in both the GPRs and FPRs. An additional special case is when a structure is returned. In this case the calling function places the address of an area in its local variable area in GPR 3. The called function should return the structure by storing the appropriate data into that area. Note that this means that if a function calls another function which returns a structure, it must allocate space in its local variable area for that structure.

Interrupts and the Stack

When an interrupt handler is invoked, it must not destroy the contents of the stack. At entry the handler should assume the following:

■ SP points to the top of the stack, and the top of the stack contains a valid back chain. This should be true because any updates to SP should be atomic.

■ The register save area above the stack should not be touched. This area may be in use either by a function prolog that is saving registers, or by a leaf function.

So, if an interrupt handler needs to use the stack, it should perform a store-with-update, decrementing SP by 224 bytes, creating a valid back chain. And the handler should restore SP before exiting.

Variable Size Stack Frames

Sometimes it is useful to dynamically allocate storage in a function and have that storage automatically deallocated when the function returns. This is done in C with the library function alloca. The way alloca works is that it expands the function's local stack area.

Example 6.2 shows one way to do this on the PowerPC. Notice that GPR 31 is used to save the original value of SP. This is to simplify accessing the caller's argument passing area and the function's data in the original local stack area.

If you implement your own method of expanding the local stack area, you must remember:

■ SP and the back chain value must be updated atomically.

■ Any memory beyond the register save area above SP is volatile because an interrupt could occur and the interrupt handler may use that memory.

EXAMPLE 6.2.

Sample code showing expansion of local stack area.

```
#
# func uses:
# nonvolatile GPRs N - 31
# nonvolatile FPRs M - 31
# any nonvolatile CF fields (CR 2 - 4)
# the LR
#
# IS_SZ is the initial size of func's stack frame
# X_SZ is the size to expand func's local stack area.
#
        .csect   .func[PR]
# function prolog
        mfcr    r0              # get the CR
        stw     r0,4(SP)        #   and save in caller's link area
        mflr    r0              # get the return address (in LR)
        stw     r0,8(SP)        #   and save in caller's link area
        stfd    M,-8*(32-M)(SP)  # save FPR M
        stfd    M+1,-8*(31-M)(SP) # save FPR M-1
#       ...
        stfd    f31,-8(SP)      # save FPR 31
        addi    r12,-8*(32-M)(SP) # FPR save area
        stw     N,-4*(32-N)(r12) # save GPR N
        stw     N+1,-4*(31-N)(r12) # save GPR N+1
#       ...
        stw     r31,-4(r12)     # save GPR 31
# if IS_SZ is less than 32K
        stwu    SP,-IS_SZ(SP)   # create frame & chain
# if IS_SZ is greater than or equal to 32K
        addis   r12,-IS_SZ & 0xFFFF0000 (r0) # move -IS_SZ
        ori     r12,-IS_SZ & 0xFFFF (r12)    #   into r12
        stwux   SP,SP,r12       # update SP atomically
        or      r31,SP,SP       # r31 <- orignal SP
#
# function code
#
# if X_SZ is less than 32K
        lwz     r11,0(SP)       # load back chain
        stwu    r11,-X_SZ(SP)   # update SP atomically
```

```
# if X_SZ is greater than or equal to 32K
        addis   r12,-X_SZ & 0xFFFF0000 (r0) # move -X_SZ
        ori     r12,-X_SZ & 0xFFFF (r12) #   into r12
        lwz     r11,0(SP)       # load back chain
        stwux   r11,SP,r12      # update SP atomically
#
# function code
#

# destroy the stack frame
        lwz     SP,0(SP)        # load back chain into SP
# function epilog
        lfd     M,-8*(32-M)(SP)         # restore FPR M
        lfd     M+1,-8*(31-M)(SP)       # restore FPR M-1
#       ...
        lfd     f31,-8(SP)              # restore FPR 31
        addi    r12,-8*(32-M)(SP)       # FPR save area
        lwz     N,-4*(32-N)(r12)        # restore GPR N
        lwz     N+1,-4*(31-N)(r12)      # restore GPR N+1
#       ...
        lwz     r31,-4(r12)     # restore GPR 31
        lwz     r0,4(SP)        # get the saved CR value
        mtcr    r0              #  and restore
        lwz     r0,8(SP)        # get the save return address
        mtlr    r0              #  and restore to the LR
        blr                     # return
```

Differences for 64-Bit Processors

Operating systems and development tools for the 64-bit PowerPC implementations are currently under development, so it's difficult to be precise about what will happen with the subroutine linkage conventions. However, since the GPRs will be 64-bits wide, the size of the GPR save area will be doubled, and the store-double-word and load-double-word instructions will be used to save and restore the volatile registers.

When to Use the Conventions

The register usage conventions and the subroutine linkage conventions are followed by the current PowerPC compilers, so they should clearly be used when you interface with compiled code. This includes:

■ Compiled code calling your assembly code.

■ Your assembly code calling your compiled code.

■ Your assembly code calling library functions.

Once you are beyond those interfaces, the only other real concern is interrupt handlers and, in the case of a preemptive multitasking operating system, the operating system preempting your program. To avoid problems with these it is best to follow the convention of the SP as GPR 1 and the RTOC as GPR 2, because these registers may be expected to hold those meanings by the interrupting code. In general, though, any interrupting software is expected to be invisible to the currently running software and should restore any machine state that it changes. So you are free to develop whatever standards are convenient for passing parameters amongst your own functions. This is one of the factors that can make well-written assembly code much faster than compiled code.

The PowerPC Object Module Format

The term *object module* refers to a program, or part of a program, which consists of code, data, and control information. Apple's PowerPC System Sooftware volume of *Inside Macintosh* calls PowerPC object modules *fragments*. Object modules are produced by compilers and assemblers. They may contain references to code or data that are not contained within the object module. Multiple object modules are combined together by the linker, or binder, which resolves references between them. The PowerPC development tools and operating systems use a paradigm for object modules that is quite different from the models used for DOS and the 680x0-based Macintosh systems. It is based on the AIX paradigm where one of the major design goals was efficient support for shared libraries. One result is little difference between an executable object module and any other object module because of the capability of load-time binding.

This is necessary for shared libraries because at the time a program loads, any calls to functions in shared libraries must be resolved.

The PowerPC object module format is transparent to most programs written in higher level languages. The compilers will generate the proper code and data automatically. When writing your own assembly language, however, you may have to add this code and data. Most of the time you won't have to.

Non-Shared Object Modules

Most programs are statically bound internally, that is, references to functions and data within the program are resolved at link time. Most programs will only make calls to the operating system's shared libraries, not actually contain shared object modules themselves.

There is no difference in how data is accessed from dynamically or statically bound object modules. However, both when coding functions and when calling them there are slight differences between statically linked and dynamically linked functions. Coding a function or calling a function as if it will be dynamically linked will always work, and this is what compilers usually will do. When a function is coded and called as a dynamically linked function, but the function is actually statically bound, there is very little overhead. Calling a function that is dynamically linked is somewhat more expensive.

Control Sections

A PowerPC object module consists of one or more control sections, known as *csects*. Each csect is a self-contained, relocatable, piece of code or data. The csect is the atomic unit of relocation in an object module, that is csects may be relocated but are never merged or split.

Within an object module the csects are organized into several groups called sections. The text (or code) section contains initialized read-only csects, mostly csects containing executable code, read-only data, and debugger information. The data section contains initialized read-write csects, mostly csects containing the program's static data, the TOC, and any function descriptors. The bss section contains uninitialized read-write data, mostly program data csects.

SECTIONS AND SEGMENTS

The text, data, and bss sections do not correspond directly with segments, as they usually do on the x86 processors in real mode. The PowerPC architecture presents the programmer with a 32-bit or 64-bit flat address space, depending on the processor. This address space is implicitly segmented by using the value of the highest order nibble in the address to select one of the sixteen segment registers. The segment registers contain information for mapping the effective address into a 52-bit or 80-bit virtual address, and for controlling access to that segment, including write permission. The read-only csects of a program, including text csects, will be located in a separate segment than read-write data, but these will just appear to be in two different areas of memory.

When writing assembly language you define the csects that contain your code and data, but you must remember that they may be relocated relative to each other. So you must write your code to be position independent when making references between csects. The main mechanism for doing this is the TOC.

The TOC

The TOC (table of contents) is a special csect that contains the addresses of other csects. There is exactly one TOC for each object module, and when object modules are statically linked their TOCs are merged. When object modules are bound together dynamically they retain separate TOCs. Counter to the name, a module's TOC contains addresses that csects in that module need to use, rather than a list of addresses within the module. Programs use the TOC for two primary purposes, gaining addressability to data and making function calls to dynamically bound functions.

Because csects use the TOC to find the locations of other csects, and the TOC itself is a csect which could be located anywhere, there is a sort of "chicken and egg" problem. So, by convention, GPR 2 (the RTOC) is dedicated to holding the address of the current TOC. All software should maintain this, although code in functions will rarely ever have any need to set the RTOC.

Entries in the TOC consist of a TOC entry name and one or more expressions, usually a csect symbol or a label. If a TOC entry contains only a single expression, it may be combined into other TOC entries with the same name, if the expressions reference the same csect. This combining can potentially change the semantics of your code, for example, causing you to load the wrong address from the TOC, so it is best to choose unique names for all TOC entries.

UNDERSTANDING LABELS

The assembler essentially treats a label as a symbol for a csect symbol plus an offset. A csect symbol represents the 32-bit or 64-bit effective address of that csect, so a label also represents a 32-bit or 64-bit address, and since csect symbols are relocatable, labels are relocatable.

The important exception to this rule is that a label in the TOC csect is always a symbol for that label's offset from the top of the module's TOC. When modules are statically linked their TOCs are merged, and the linker will update the values of any TOC labels.

Also, for relative branch instructions, the assembler will implicitly subtract the address of the branch instruction from the value of the symbol specifying the target address.

Accessing Data Using the TOC

You must use the TOC to find the addresses of any data your code uses from the data and bss sections. Example 6.3 shows a simple example of addressing static data. The address of a counter variable is loaded from the TOC using a TOC label. This example shows why TOC labels are always relative to the top of a module's TOC—because the TOC is accessed using the RTOC as a base register and an immediate offset. If TOC labels represented effective addresses, every TOC access would have an immediate field like "LABEL - TOC[tc0]". The symbol "TOC[tc0]" represents the top of the current module's TOC.

EXAMPLE 6.3.

Function that increments a static counter variable. The TOC is used to find the address of the counter in the data section.

```
        .csect  .incctr[PR]
        .globl  .incctr[PR]
        lwz     r3,Tctr(RTOC)       # get address of counter
                                    # (Tctr is rel to TOC)
        lwz     r4,0(r3)            # load counter value
        addi    r4,r4,1             # increment counter
        stw     r4,0(r3)            # store counter value
        blr                         # return
        .csect  _ctrdata[RW]
```

```
Dctr:   .long    0                       # counter
        .toc                             # TOC csect
Tctr:   .tc      ctrtoc[TC],Dctr         # label Dctr in entry
```

Why can't the label in a data csect, or even a csect symbol, be used directly? The main reason is that there is no way to code a reference like this in the PowerPC architecture. Since all immediate fields on arithmetic and load/store instructions are 16 bits, and a label represents an effective address, the closest you could come to coding this would involve constant expressions for breaking up the label's value into 16-bit pieces, and these type of expressions would require that the expression be preserved and evaluated by linkers and binders whenever relocation occurred.

Example 6.4 illustrates an important way to increase the efficiency of using the TOC. Rather than having TOC entries for every data label, you can load a register with a TOC entry and index from that address. To calculate the immediate fields you can use the difference between a label and the base. This approach is more efficient because only one load of a TOC entry is necessary. The .using pseudo op is used as a convenience. It tells the assembler to implicitly calculate the immediate field based on the value given in the .using statement, and to use the register given in the .using statement as the base register for the instruction. The .using statement does not actually put the value into the register, it tells the assembler to assume that it is there. You must properly load the base register in your code.

EXAMPLE 6.4.

Function that updates a static incrementer and static decrementer.

```
        .csect  .incdec[PR]
        .globl  .incdec[PR]
        lwz     r3,Tdata(RTOC)          # get base addr of data
                                        # (Tdata is rel to TOC)
        .using  _ctrdata[RW],r3         # tell assembler to
                                        # assume r3 <- _ctrdata
        lwz     r4,Dinc # —> (Dinc - _ctrdata[RW])(r3)
        addi    r4,r4,1 # increment counter
        stw     r4,Dinc # store counter value
        lwz     r5,Ddec # —> (Ddec - _ctrdata[RW])(r3)
        addi    r5,r5,-1                 # decrement counter
        stw     r5,Ddec # store counter value
        blr             # return
        .csect  _ctrdata[RW]
Dinc:   .long   0       # incrementer
Ddec:   .long   0x0000FFFF       # decremeter
        .toc                    # TOC csect
Tdata: .tc      dtoc[TC],_ctrdata[RW]            # data section TOC entry
```

FUNCTION ENTRY POINTS

The symbol used to refer to a function is known as the *entry point*. Function entry points may be csect names or labels. If an entry point is a csect name, execution will begin at the first instruction in the csect.

All entry point names must start with a period. Compilers will prefix function names with the period automatically, but the assembler will not. So the C library function printf would be referred to as .printf in assembly code, and an assembly function .myfunc would be called as myfunc from a compiled language.

Statically Bound Functions

Coding and calling statically bound functions on the PowerPC are very similar to performing function calls on the x86 or 680x0 architectures. Basically all that you need to do is to branch-and-link to the function's entry point. If the function is contained in other module, that module must declare the function global with the .globl pseudo op, and in the calling module the entry point must be declared external with the .extern or the .globl pseudo op. Example 6.5 illustrates this for statically bound functions calling between modules.

EXAMPLE 6.5.

Definition and calling of statically bound function .getxer from function .addxer.

```
######## file getxer.s ########
       .csect  .getxer[PR]
       .globl  .getxer[PR]
       mfxer   r3       # r3 <- xer
       br               # return
######## file addxer.s ########
       .extern .getxer
       .csect  .addxer[PR]
       .globl  .addxer[PR]
       mflr    r12      # r12 <- return address
       addc    r3,r3,r4         # add first two arguments
       bl      .getxer # call func to get the xer value
       mtlr    r12      # lr <- return address

       blr              # return
```

Shared Object Modules

Dynamic binding mostly affects the definition and calling of functions. Access to data is still done via the TOC. Defining and calling dynamically bound functions basically involves adding an extra piece of data for each function defined, and an extra instruction at each function call.

Execution of Dynamically Bound Function Calls

When object modules are dynamically bound, they are not merged together as in static linking. One reason for this is that shared libraries could not share a single image of their text section if every image had to be customized. This implies that each object module which is dynamically bound will still have its own TOC, since the object modules are not merged.

Functions in a sharable object are associated with a data structure called the *function descriptor*. Each function in a sharable object module must have a function descriptor. The descriptor contains the address of the function's entry point, and a pointer to the TOC of the module.

Calls to dynamically bound functions are made through glue or glink functions. These functions find the function descriptor for the called function, set the RTOC, and branch to the called function. When the function returns, it does not return to the glink code; instead it returns directly to the original caller. Because the RTOC is set to the TOC of the shared object module when the return branch is taken, the calling function must restore the value of the RTOC.

Figure 6.3 shows program myprog which calls functions from the shared library libfoobar after libfoobar has been loaded and bound with myprog. References to functions in libfoobar have been transformed into references to glink code, which uses the myprog TOC to locate the function descriptors for foo and bar. The function descriptors give the TOC and entry point for the functions. The call to myfunc from main was resolved statically, so it is not made via a glink routine. Note that all references to libfoobar from myprog are located in the TOC, so the code in myprog is correct and complete whether or not libfoobar is loaded.

FIGURE 6.3.

Shared library libfoobar has been dynamically bound with program myprog.

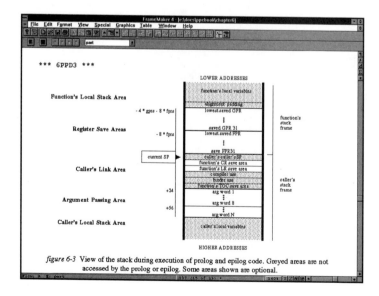

Following the thread of execution of .main's call to .bar:

- .main calls .glink_of_bar.
- .glink_of_bar gets the address of .bar's descriptor from myprog's TOC.
- .glink _of_bar sets the RTOC to point to libfoobar's TOC using .bar's descriptor.
- .glink_of_bar branches to .bar using .bar's descriptor to locate .bar.
- .bar executes
- .bar returns directly to .main
- .main restores the RTOC to point to myprog's TOC.

Example 6.6 shows the code for .glink_of_bar. Notice that the link register is not set in the branch to .bar, as is usually done for a function call. Thus, when .bar performs its return branch, it will return directly to .main.

EXAMPLE 6.6.

Code for .glink_of_bar. TbarFD is a label on the TOC entry containing the address of .bar's function descriptor.

```
.csect  .glink_of_bar[GL]
lwz     r12,TbarFD(RTOC)      # r12 <- bar func desc
stw     RTOC,20(SP)      # store TOC in link area
lwz     r0,0(r12)        # r0 <- .bar
lwz     RTOC,4(r12)      # RTOC <- bar TOC
mtctr   r0               # ctr <- .bar
bctr                     # goto .bar
```

There is one glink routine for each dynamically bound function referenced, per module. This is because the offset into the TOC of .bar's file descriptor is hardcoded into the glink routine by the use of the label TbarFD.

The glink routine destroys the values in GPR 0 and GPR 12. This is fine for functions that are strictly following the register usage conventions, as these registers are volatile and not used to pass function parameters. However, if you write your own dynamically bound assembly language functions with your own calling conventions, you will need to avoid these registers.

A slight variation on the glink routine is shown in Example 6.7. The ptrgl function takes a function pointer in GPR 11 rather than using an entry in the TOC. Recall that function pointers are actually pointers to function descriptors. Note the use of GPR 11 as the environment pointer. The ptrgl code will restore any value saved in the third word of the function descriptor into GPR 11. This allows languages that make use of the environment pointer, such as PASCAL, to set it's value. In languages that do not use the environment pointer, such as C, ptrgl will put garbage into GPR 11, but it is considered a volatile register anyway.

EXAMPLE 6.7.

Code for .ptrgl, glink code for calling via a function pointer.

```
# On entry r11 contains address of func descriptor.
      .csect  .ptrgl[PR]
      lwz     r0,0(r11)        # r0 <- func address
      stw     RTOC,20(SP)      # store TOC in link area
      mtctr   r0               # ctr <- func address
      lwz     RTOC,4(r12)      # RTOC <- func's TOC
      lwz     r11,8(r12)       # r11<- func's ENV
      bctr                     # goto .bar
```

Coding Calls to Dynamically Bindable Functions

Coding calls to dynamically bindable functions is really very easy. The only difference between this and calling any other function is that a special no-op instruction is placed immediately following the branch. The binder will replace this instruction will an instruction which will restore the TOC of the current module if the called function is actually going to be called via glink code. The binder will also replace the target of your calling branch with the location of the glink code if it is needed.

You also do not need to write the glink code or create the function descriptor entry in the TOC. The linker will do both of these for you. Example 6.8 shows a function myfunc which calls a dynamically bindable function foo.

EXAMPLE 6.8.

Function that calls a dynamically bindable function.

```
.extern  .foo
.csect   .myfunc[PR]
mflr     r12              # r12 <- return address
stw      r12,8(SR)        # save in link area
bl       .foo             # call .foo
cror     31,31,31         # no-op
lwz      r12,8(SR)        # r12 <- return address
mtlr     r12              # lr <- r12
blr                       # return
```

Coding Dynamically Bindable Functions

Coding a dynamically bindable function is also very simple. The function itself is coded just like any other function, and the function entry point is exported.

You do need to add the code to generate the function descriptor, and you should export the descriptor's symbol. Example 6.9 shows a dynamically bindable function xor64. Note that the use of .toc is required in the module in order to use the TOC[tc0] symbol.

EXAMPLE 6.9.

Code for a dynamically bindable function.

```
.globl  .xor64[PR].
.globl  xor64[DS]
.csect  .xor64[PR]
xor     r3,r3,r5      # r3 <- r3 xor r5 (high words)
xor     r4,r4,r6      # r4 <- r4 xor r6 (low words)
blr                   # return
.toc                  # .toc csect req'd for TOC[tc0]
.csect  xor64[DS]     # function descriptor
.long   .xor64[PR]    # entry point
.long   TOC[tc0]      # module's TOC
```

Linking For Dynamic Binding

In order for the linker to distinguish between symbols that will be resolved via dynamic binding and those that are actually unresolved, when you link you should use an import list. The import list contains a list of symbols that the linker will assume are present at run time. The import list tells the linker to generate the glink code and to create TOC entries for function descriptors. The import list also tells the linker which object file contains the symbols, so that a list of object files that are required by the program can be generated. This list is used to load all the proper object files when the program is run.

Creating A Shared Object File

You can create an object module that will act like an import list when linked with a program. To do this you use an export list, which is the same as an import list, except that you use it when linking the object files to be dynamically loaded.

Object File Formats

It is the job of the operating system and development tools to read and write object modules to files. So most of the time you will never have to worry about the actual file format used to store an object module.

Historically the PowerPC object modules have been stored in XCOFF (extended common object file format) files. The use of XCOFF files comes from AIX which uses this format exclusively. XCOFF is an extension to the standard UNIX object file format COFF which was formalized in System V, although it was based on the BSD a.out format.

Apple System 7 supports XCOFF files, as well as a newer format PEF (Preferred Executable Format), which is better suited to the Macintosh environment. Although XCOFF files are supported, any programs which depend on UNIX specific shared libraries or system calls will not execute correctly under System 7. Programs written for the Macintosh should use the PEF format.

Macintosh Operating System Considerations

The Macintosh Operating System on PowerPC-based Macintosh computers is designed to be backward compatible with software written for 680x0 based Macintosh computers. In fact many parts of the Macintosh OS are still 680x0 code. The basis for this capability is a 68LC040 emulator and a part of the operating system known as the *Mixed Mode Manager*, which switches between PowerPC (or native) mode and the 68LC040 emulator. For the most part this is transparent, but it does complicate programming in some cases, and because 680x0 code must run unchanged, the burden falls to the PowerPC code.

When performing a cross-mode call, the Mixed Mode Manager needs to know what architecture set the function uses so that it can switch to the correct mode. There are two cases where this problem arises most often: calls to operating system functions, and the passing of function pointers to functions of unknown architecture, especially system functions. Note that there are other scenarios involving cross-mode function calls that may or may not be handled transparently by the Mixed Mode Manager—you should consult *Inside Macintosh* for more details.

Calls to the operating system functions are handling by inserting glue code when the routine is dynamically bound to the calling application. This glue code can perform whatever steps are necessary to switch to the proper mode for the operating system function. For calls from 680x0 code, this is handled by the trap dispatch mechanism in the 68LC040 emulator.

The problem of passing function pointers is handled by using universal procedure pointers in the place of function pointers. A *universal procedure pointer* (UPP) is defined as either a pointer to 680x0 code, or a pointer to a routine descriptor. The routine descriptor is a structure which contains information about the function, including the calling conventions, instruction set architecture, and the actual function pointer (which is really a pointer to a function descriptor, in the case of a PowerPC function). The first element of a routine descriptor is a 680x0 instruction which causes a trap into the Mixed Mode Manager. You should use a UPP rather than a normal function pointer in cases where you are providing a function pointer to be called by external code whose architecture is not certain. In addition, new versions of Macintosh system functions that expect UPPs should be used.

An additional scenario exists which can commonly occur on the Macintosh: When a code resource is invoked, often this is performed by simply branching to the beginning of the resource. To allow the Mixed Mode Manager to intervene, you should place a routine descriptor for your function at the beginning of the resource.

7

Performance Tuning and Optimization

The earlier chapters in this book covered the nuts and bolts of the PowerPC architecture and instruction set. You might be wondering about the story behind some of the features and facilities of the machine, why they were provided, and when you have several options to implement a particular function in your program, which is the best one to choose. This chapter covers some of these issues, and shows you how to best express your program in the language of PowerPC instructions.

Speeding Up an Application Written in a High-Level Language

Most applications are far too large to even talk seriously about wholesale rewriting to address performance problems. In most cases, performance can be improved significantly through relatively simple incremental improvements.

When setting out to improve performance of a program, it is important to follow a strategy. It's all too easy to spend hours of programming effort chasing too little performance gain; performance tuning work expands easily to fill almost any available time. Before starting, it's worth investing some time-setting goals and deciding to what lengths you are willing to go to achieve these goals. Have a plan, set goals, and stay focused.

Using Development Tools

You need a suite of development tools that should include the following:

- *A high-level language compiler.* You will want to do most coding in a high-level language, because it's usually quicker and easier to develop that way.

- *A PowerPC assembler.* You will want an assembler to do machine language coding. Some compilers provide an inlining feature that enables you to code assembly language instructions within a high-level language procedure. This capability can be handy, but it can become awkward for larger coding projects.

- *A debugger.* Unless you write perfect code the first time—every time—you probably will want a debugging tool that enables you to step through assembly code and examine or modify the machine state.

- *A profiler.* This is one of the most important additions to the performance-minded code developer's toolbox. A profiler enables you to instrument an application to discover critical information, such as how often functions and procedures are called and which sections of your code are using the most CPU time.

Ordinarily, most or all of these tools are included with an operating system or as part of a software development system. If you're using AIX for the PowerPC, for example, the IBM XL compilers, an assembler, a linker, a profiler, and several debuggers are available. On the Power Macintosh, Metrowork's CodeWarrior system provides most of this, though it doesn't include an assembler.

Another very important tool is a means of measuring and monitoring actual performance. Depending on your development environment, this might be more of a problem than it first appears. The next section covers some of the problems and pitfalls of performance measurement, and what you can do about them.

DEVELOPING A PERFORMANCE STRATEGY

■ Tools are an important component of any strategy, both for identifying optimization opportunities and pursuing them. If your program is written in a high-level language, use the highest quality, industrial-strength optimizing compiler you can get. Program profiling can be crucial to understanding where your program spends its time (you may be surprised). Profiling is the best way to ensure that you spend your time wisely and get the most performance benefit for your work. Use profiling to identify key routines or places in the code where speedup is most critical.

■ Examine the algorithms used in these critical areas. Make sure that the problem is, in fact, not a programming error or poor algorithm choice. You might be able make a bubble-sort slightly faster with performance tuning, but a switch to a better-behaved algorithm like quicksort is almost always a better tactic. If your program spends a lot of time searching, for example, consider techniques like hashing, balanced trees, or index inversion before recoding.

■ Isolate critical code in a module by itself and try playing with compilation options. Some code responds better to some optimization strategies than others, and most compilers enable you to selectively enable and disable particular optimizations.

■ Sometimes, the program appears to be spending huge chunks of its time in library or system routines. This can be discouraging, because often you cannot exercise any control over these routines. At the same time, library code might be more general in scope than what is called for in your application. You may be able to replace some library or system calls with routines of your own that perform much more efficiently. An example of this appears later in this chapter in the "Putting It All Together" section.

■ When you recode a routine in assembler, make sure that you are building an exact replacement. Also, carefully document your work, being sure to include the code it replaces as the specification.

■ Be very careful not to violate compiler linkage or other conventions of your system. If your code does calls and returns, obey stack- and storage-management rules. Be careful not to clobber nonvolatile registers or memory locations— debugging problems due to wayward stores and registers with mysteriously changing values can be painful, and the problem might not show up immediately. Some debugging tools have additional constraints and methods to enable traceback and stack decoding; be careful to observe these if you want to be able to use your debugger.

■ Be scientific in your approach, and precisely measure performance before and after each step. There usually are enough variables in the mix that an "optimization" actually could make things worse! If this happens, investigate. Monitoring your progress and keeping close track of the benefits of each tactic can go a long way in helping you understand what works and what doesn't. (See the following section, "Measuring Performance.")

■ Test, test, test. Be very careful that your enhancements don't introduce new "features" in your system. If you don't already have one, put together as comprehensive a regression test suite as you can. Select both simple and complicated sample workloads, and be sure to include test cases with unusual edge conditions, such as zero iterations of a loop, or out-of-bounds variable values. Many program bugs begin their lives as performance enhancements; try to avoid this pitfall by making sure that the program behaves the same way with or without your enhancements.

Measuring Performance

In your quest to improve performance, you need a way of checking your progress. There are many ways to measure performance with varying degrees of precision, accuracy, and cost. If you have access to a laboratory reference system with direct instrumentation of the hardware for performance measurement and diagnostics, you are fortunate indeed. This kind of system is truly the hot setup, and can provide invaluable insight into what really is happening inside the box. The bad news is that such systems are terrifically expensive, and few developers can justify the cost. Similar information sometimes can be obtained by using a software timing simulator, which can be less expensive than instrumented hardware, but this still is not necessarily cheap. Also, because software simulation is so much slower than real hardware, the size and scope of the workloads you can measure are limited.

Fortunately, such precision isn't usually necessary, and it's possible to do performance work with tools you probably already have. Your operating system may have facilities for measuring program execution. The UNIX time command, for example, reports the system and user time used during an execution of a program. If an OS measurement tool isn't available, you might be able to build your own using the processor's own time base registers. However, it's not always necessary to resort to complicated hardware or software performance measurement tools. In many cases, you are interested in performance because your application is making you wait, and your wristwatch may provide all the precision you need.

Regardless of the technique you use to measure performance, be careful to control the conditions under which you conduct your experiments. It can be very difficult to get reliable measurements if your machine depends on a network file server or receives a fax in the middle of your timed runs. The best measurements are consistently repeatable timings that don't vary more than a few percent from run to run.

Examining PowerPC Coding Strategy and Instruction Selection

Particular features of any architecture sometimes favor one coding style or approach to a programming problem over another. A list of the available registers and machine instructions doesn't necessarily communicate how the designers intended the machine to be used. Machine language programmers are well aware that different code sequences that compute the same result can yield quite different measured performances. There may be many ways to solve a particular problem, but often one is better than another, and that better way was provided by the machine designers expressly for that purpose. The PowerPC instruction set, for example, provides several types of conditional branch instructions, and several types of load and store addressing. In this chapter, you will learn the rationale for some of these features and how they can be used to extract maximum performance from your PowerPC programs.

In some cases, these features improve performance by reducing the number of instructions required for a computation. Some optimizations, however, improve performance not by reducing the number of instructions *per se*, but by exploiting particular ways in which PowerPC processors are implemented in hardware. All the currently available PowerPC implementations are *pipelined superscalar machines*, meaning that each is capable of working on the execution of several instructions in parallel (see the following sidebar). All implementations can issue and complete at least three instructions per clock cycle. This execution capability is impressive, but limits—of the processor, the system, or your program—can prevent sustaining this peak execution rate for extended periods. Some of these limits are unavoidable; others, however, can be minimized through careful instruction selection, programming style, and code organization.

PIPELINED AND SUPERSCALAR EXECUTION

As in most processors, the instructions of a PowerPC program appear, from the outside, to be executed one after the other, as if one instruction is executed completely before the next is started. In practice, no modern microprocessor actually performs instructions strictly one at a time. Instead, instruction execution is divided into a series of stages, like an assembly line; this process is called *pipelining*. In a pipeline with three stages, for example, the processor can be working on the execution of three instructions, each in a different stage, at the same time. By starting on the second instruction as soon as the first instruction moves out of the first pipeline stage, rather than waiting until the first moves all the way to the end of the pipeline, throughput is increased. If the three-stage pipeline can be kept full, instructions are completed at a rate three times faster than they could be without pipelining. Throughput can be increased even more by adding an additional pipeline alongside the first.

Figure 7.1 shows how pipelining and parallel pipelines can speed up the processing of machine instructions. This example starts with a hypothetical machine that takes three time units to execute an instruction. The leftmost column depicts the flow of instructions through a simple, one-instruction-at-a-time implementation of the architecture. The middle column shows what happens if instruction execution is split into three separate stages, provided that one instruction can be put into the pipeline during each time unit. Notice how it still takes the first instruction three time units (cycles) to complete but, after that, an instruction is completed every cycle.

The rightmost column shows how instructions could flow through an implementation of the same architecture with two execution pipelines in parallel. This type of organization commonly is described as *superscalar*. Feeding these two pipelines requires the machine to issue two instructions per cycle. When this is possible, a pipelined superscalar machine is capable of very high instruction throughput.

FIGURE 7.1.
The advantages of pipelining.

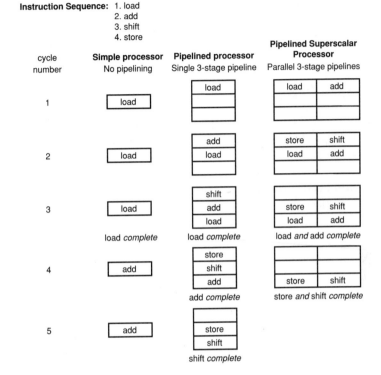

Instruction Sequence: 1. load
2. add
3. shift
4. store

Using Branches and Loops in PowerPC Code

Branch instructions provide the mechanism for altering the simple sequential flow of control in the execution of a program. The PowerPC architecture has several forms of conditional and unconditional branch instructions, and the way the hardware executes the different forms of these instructions has implications for which is best for a given programming situation.

To understand this concept, look at what happens when a branch is encountered. In any pipelined processor, a conditional branch instruction must pass through several stages of the execution pipeline before the hardware can tell which instruction should follow the branch. By that time, some of the instructions at sequential addresses after the branch already may have proceeded through several stages of the execution pipeline. If the branch is *taken* (control is transferred off the sequential path), execution of the partially processed instructions after the branch must be abandoned and cleared out of the pipeline, and the fetch and execution of instructions at the branch target location must be initiated. Thus, the steady flow of instructions through the pipeline is broken. The length of time from the point at which the branch takes effect until the pipeline flow resumes at the target address is called *branch latency*.

Because branches are so frequent, this could create a very serious performance problem. In most programs, 15 percent or more of the instructions can be some form of branch. To avoid the loss of such a large number of processor cycles to branch latency, the PowerPC architecture has several important features to streamline the processing of branch instructions.

Branch Resolution and Prediction

By looking ahead in the instruction stream, it is possible for the processor to identify branch instructions early, and begin processing them several cycles before they would be executed in a strictly sequential fashion. This look-ahead hardware makes it possible to eliminate completely the latency of many branch instructions. This capability depends on being able to correctly determine whether a given branch instruction causes a transfer of control, and it must be possible to make this determination before completely executing all the instructions preceding the branch.

For unconditional branches, this is easy, because control is always transferred. The fetcher can discard safely the sequential path following the branch, and begin prefetching at the branch target as soon as the look-ahead hardware spots the unconditional branch. Things are not so simple for conditional branch instructions, because any instruction preceding the branch could affect whether it is taken. Only after the results of operations the branch depends upon are available can the branch can be treated as unconditional. Until then, the processor can wait for the necessary information or predict which way the branch will go (possibly fixing things up if the guess was wrong).

All current PowerPC implementations prefetch the instruction stream, execute unconditional branches early, and use a prediction mechanism to remove pipeline bubbles after conditional branches. In addition, the PowerPC architecture provides several mechanisms that enable the programmer to help the processor in the branch resolution process and improve program performance.

Using Branch Unit Registers

The PowerPC register set includes a number of special purpose registers designed to hold branch targets, loop counters, and branch conditions. These special registers enable some hardware speedups by simplifying tasks like determining which instructions currently in execution can affect the outcome of a conditional branch. These branch registers were described in Chapter 4; in this chapter, you will learn how to use them most effectively.

Using the Condition Register (CR)

The PowerPC condition register provides a powerful means of controlling conditional branching. It not only allows multiple condition codes, but also logical operations among condition code values. Descriptions of this facility sometimes make it seem more complicated than it really is, so let's get it straight.

The PowerPC condition register (CR) is a single register, 32 bits wide. A conditional branch instruction can be coded to test the binary value of any one of the 32 bits, and branch if it is one or if it is zero. However, the PowerPC comparison instructions treat the condition register as if it were divided into eight four-bit condition codes, or CR fields. A comparison instruction writes all four bits of one of these CR fields. The first three bits indicate less than, equal to, and greater than relations between the values being compared; the fourth bit is overflow.

Don't worry, you don't have to keep CR bit numbers straight—PowerPC assemblers provide extended mnemonics to make CR field selection for comparisons and the bit testing for branch instructions easy and readable. Example 7.1 shows PowerPC instructions to (1) add the values of registers r4 and r5, (2) compare the sum to zero, and (3) branch to label1 if the sum is equal to zero.

EXAMPLE 7.1.

Using the CR for Conditional Branching.

```
add     r3,r4,r5            (1)
        cmpi    cr0,r3,0    (2)
        beq     cr0,label1  (3)
```

It turns out that "comparison with zero" is a frequently needed operation; it also turns out to be fairly easy to implement in hardware. Some PowerPC instructions provide the ability to do a comparison with zero "for free," eliminating the need for an explicit comparison instruction. This capability is called the *record* feature, and is available on many PowerPC integer and floating point instructions. The record feature causes condition field zero (condition field one for floating point operations) to be set with the four-bit condition code generated by comparing the instruction's result to zero. This implicit comparison is specified by apending a dot (.) to the instruction opcode. Example 7.2 shows how the record feature on the PowerPC add instruction can be used to eliminate the comparison instruction from Example 7.1:

EXAMPLE 7.2.

Implicit comparison using the record feature.

```
add     r3,r4,r5
beq     cr0,label1
```

The PowerPC instruction set also provides a set of logical instructions that enables you to combine multiple conditions and use a single branch instruction. The code sequence in Example 7.3 branches to an error handler if the value in register r3 is outside the range {1,2,3,...,25}.

EXAMPLE 7.3.

Operations in condition register values.

```
cmpi    cr0,r3,1     # Less than one
        cmpi    cr1,r3,25   # ..or greater than 25?
        cror    cr2_eq,cr0_lt,cr1_gt
        beq     cr2,out_of_range
```

PROGRAMMING WITH THE CONDITION REGISTER

The record feature on many integer instructions causes cr0 to be updated to reflect an implicit comparison of the result of the instruction with 0, possibly making it unnecessary to code an explicit compare instruction. The record option always is denoted by a dot (.) appended to the opcode mnemonic. For example, in add. versus add, the dotted version specifies record. Most instructions that support the record feature can be specified with or without the dot.

It's not a good idea to specify the record option unless you truly are interested in the result of the comparison. One reason is that an unneeded write of the CR could interfere with branch look-ahead and unnecessarily delay the resolution of a conditional branch. Or, because cr0 is not explicitly mentioned, it's possible for a programmer to overlook the fact that its value is overwritten by the recording instruction. A similar *caveat* applies for cr1, which is written implicitly by floating point records. One way to avoid conflicts with a record is to make a practice of using CR fields other than cr0 or cr1 as the target of explicit comparisons (keeping in mind that CR fields cr2, cr3, and cr4 are nonvolatile and must be preserved across procedure calls).

Although some PowerPC instructions don't have a record option, it is required on both PowerPC and immediate instructions andi. and andis. In many situations, this is handy, or at least does no harm. If you're using the and immediate to extract or clear a contiguous string of bits, you could use one of the variants of the rlwinm instruction (see Chapter 3, "Integer Instructions") to avoid writing the condition register.

Using the Count Register (CTR)

The PowerPC branch unit architecture provides a second conditional branch mechanism via the count register (CTR). The count register was designed specifically to control loop iteration in a way that makes it easy for the branch look-ahead hardware to predict the outcome of a CTR-dependent conditional branch.

Constructing a loop using the CTR can be as easy as moving the loop iteration count from a GPR to the CTR, and closing the loop with a CTR-based branch instruction that is taken whenever the decremented value in the count register is greater than 0. Example 7.4 illustrates a simple loop structure using the count register.

EXAMPLE 7.4.

Loop using the count register.

```
        mtctr    r4           # iteration count to CTR
  loop1:
        <loop body>           # instructions of the loop
        bdnz     loop1        # branch if CTR - 1 > 0
```

This mechanism is less general than branching based on the condition register, but it is sufficient to express many simple loops. Because only conditional branch instructions (and the mtctr instruction) can alter the CTR, in simple loops it is easy for the hardware to determine well in advance of executing the instructions in the loop body whether the loop-closing branch instruction will be taken. Because the CTR always is decremented, some extra care (and instructions) might be needed if the loop iteration count might be 0.

Naturally, it is possible to terminate the loop from within the body with other condition register-based conditional branches. It almost always is a bad idea to modify the CTR within the loop (with a move to CTR instruction), because this interferes with the hardware's capability to resolve the branch in advance, possibly nullifying the performance advantage of using the CTR. The instruction set also enables branches to depend on both the count register and the condition register, making it possible to combine multiple-loop exit conditions in a single branch instruction. However, reading the condition register could delay resolution of the branch compared to a simple count register test.

Some programming situations, such as jump tables, call for computing a branch target address in a general register. The PowerPC instruction set doesn't permit branching directly to an address contained in a general register; the address must first be moved to the count register or link register (with the mtlr or mtctr variants of the mtspr instruction). It's a good practice to reserve the use of the link register (and the bclr instruction) for subroutine linkage (that is, when the branch is a call or return), and the count register (with bcctr) for computed go-to's and jump tables. Not only is it good style, but it can improve performance; the PowerPC 620 processor has a hardware link register that can speed up return from function calls if this convention is followed.

Looking At PowerPC Branch Prediction

Each PowerPC processor implementation has a mechanism for predicting the execution path beyond conditional branch instructions. As long as the predictions prove correct, there can be an uninterrupted flow of instructions through the execution pipeline, and no branch latency performance penalty.

The PowerPC 601 and 603 processors both implement a similar branch-prediction scheme. The mechanism used by both these chips is *static*, because the processor does not "remember" how a particular branch instruction behaved earlier in the execution of the program. The PowerPC 604 and 620 processors both implement dynamic branch prediction, and have on-chip memory dedicated to keeping track of how a particular branch instruction behaved in the past. This information is used by the hardware to predict whether the branch will be taken if it is encountered again during the execution.

Static Prediction in the PowerPC 601 and 603 Processors

The static branch prediction scheme implemented in these PowerPC processors is based on the type of branch instruction and the direction of the branch. When a branch instruction is executed, the processor issues a fetch request for a new block of instructions. If the branch is conditional, and it cannot be immediately determined whether the branch will be taken (because the condition depends on data that is still being computed), the processor guesses which way the branch will go, and begins fetching along that guessed path.

The possibility of an incorrect guess means that the processor must be prepared to abort the execution of any speculatively executed instructions, and resume execution along the correct path. The inability to commit the results of the speculative execution limits the number of instructions that can be executed along the guessed path, and 601 and 603 processors both are limited to execution past a single predicted branch.

The branch-prediction scheme used for unresolved conditional branches by the 601 and 603 processors is simple. If the conditional branch is to the address contained in the link register or count register (a bcctr or bclr instruction that tests a bit in the condition register), the branch is predicted taken. Conditional branches are predicted based on the direction of the branch; the branch is predicted taken if the branch target address is less than the address of the branch instruction, and it is predicted not taken if the branch target address is greater than the branch instruction's address (the hardware simply tests the sign bit of the address offset in the branch instruction). This convention is illustrated in Example 7.5; backward branches are predicted taken, and forward branches are predicted not taken.

EXAMPLE 7.5.

Branch prediction for forward and backward branches (PowerPC 601 and 603).

```
above:
          blt     cr5,below     # predicted not taken
          bgt     cr6,above     # predicted taken
    below:
```

This scheme corresponds to the way branches are most often used. A branch to a negative off-set is commonly the closing instruction of a loop, and therefore usually would be taken. A branch with a positive offset cannot be predicted as accurately, but in many cases these branches are used to exit from loops or to escape to special-case and exception-handling sections of the code, and are less likely to be taken.

These rules are based on broad generalizations, and really just exploit particular coding styles and compiler conventions. It is not difficult to imagine programming situations where these static prediction rules would be incorrect. If you know that the branch is most likely to behave opposite to this prediction convention, it can be reversed by setting the Y bit in the BO field of conditional branch instruction. Rather than worry about whether to set the Y bit, you can indicate explicitly which way the hardware should predict the branch. Appending + to the branch mnemonic tells the hardware to predict the branch taken, and − tells the hardware to predict not taken. The assembler then makes sure that the Y bit is set appropriately, based on the sign of the branch offset. Example 7.6 shows how to force to a forward branch, which is normally predicted not taken, to be predicted taken instead.

EXAMPLE 7.6.

Overriding static branch prediction.

```
        # r3 = min(r3, 100)
        cmpi    cr7,r3,100      #
        bng+    cr7,label1      # predict this branch taken
        li      r3,100          # r3 <= 100
label1:
```

Dynamic Branch Prediction in the PowerPC 604 and 620 Processors

Instead of fixed prediction rules, the PowerPC 604 and 620 processors both have hardware for dynamic branch prediction. The hardware maintains a *branch history table*, indexed by bits of the address of the branch instruction, that tracks how that branch has behaved earlier. When a branch instruction is identified by the look-ahead hardware, the branch history table is consulted. Because most branch instructions will behave in the future much as they have behaved previously, the history table can yield much more accurate predictions than the static rules. This is not to say that the prediction algorithms always are correct. However, unlike static prediction, there's no need to worry about coding the Y bit properly.

Instruction Reordering

One of the guiding principles in the first generation of RISC architectures was to keep the instruction set simple and uniform, permitting the greatest flexibility in reordering instructions to avoid stalls and keep the pipeline flowing smoothly. In the first RISCs, all this reordering was done by instruction-scheduling compilers or assemblers prior to running the program.

The simplicity of RISC instructions also makes it easier to build hardware that does this kind of scheduling dynamically, as the program is executed. One advantage of this approach is that it provides some relief from the necessity of rescheduling code for different implementations of the same architecture that have different optimal scheduling policies. All the current PowerPC implementations provide some capability to execute instructions out of program order. This feature reduces, to some extent, the degree to which the hardware depends on static instruction scheduling to achieve good performance, and makes it possible to write programs that can perform well across a large family of PowerPC implementations.

Therefore, although there are notable differences among PowerPC implementations in their capability to dispatch and reorder instructions, it is not necessary to understand these differences in painstaking detail in order to write PowerPC code that achieves good performance. In fact, excellent performance usually can be achieved by following a few simple rules:

1. Separate compares from dependent branches.

2. Separate uses from loads.

3. Interleave operations of different functional units (integer, branch, load-store, floating point).

The first rule is to help reduce branch misprediction penalty cycles. PowerPC processors look ahead in the instruction stream and predict the outcome of branches to keep the execution pipeline full. This capability is limited, however; even if the direction of a conditional branch is predicted correctly, the hardware can proceed only so far down the predicted path before it has to wait for confirmation of the prediction. If the branch outcome is not predicted correctly, the sooner the processor finds out, the sooner the misprediction recovery process can be started. Therefore, where possible, use a branch that doesn't depend on the CR, but if this is unavoidable, compute the CR value for a branch as early as possible.

The second rule suggests that when you load a value from memory, try not to use that value in an instruction immediately following the load; instead, place the load instruction earlier in the sequence, or in the instruction that uses the loaded value earlier.

Following the third rule helps the dispatcher maximize the number of instructions that can be executed in parallel. PowerPC processors can, to varying degrees, reorder instructions on the fly, but the dispatcher can choose from only a few instructions at any given time. Each PowerPC implementation uses different algorithms and functional unit instruction groupings, so if you are writing code for a specific processor target and want very precise details of the scheduling model, consult the instruction timing section of the User's Guide for that processor.

Programming with PowerPC Memory Instructions

The PowerPC load and store instructions provide a powerful and flexible interface to processor memory. The instructions support several *addressing modes*—the number of ways an address can be formed. Different PowerPC instructions enable an address to be expressed as a constant, the contents of a register, the sum of a register and a constant, or the sum of two registers. Indexed (sum of two register) instructions also can be coded to automatically increment the address index register to the next sequential memory unit.

Instructions are provided to support *access modes* of byte, halfword, word, and doubleword. Several block-mode memory instructions are defined to save or restore multiple general registers and manipulate strings.

PowerPC memory is byte-addressed. Unlike some other RISCs, all the standard PowerPC load and store instructions *require* no alignment of the effective address. However, depending on the processor, there can be a significant performance penalty for an unaligned memory references. Best performance is provided when the alignment of a reference matches its natural mode (doublewords should be aligned on 8-byte boundaries, words on 4-byte boundaries, and halfwords on 2-byte boundaries).

Two principal factors determine the precise performance penalty for an unaligned access. The worst case is when the target data requires two cache accesses in order to complete the reference. Unaligned references that do not span a doubleword boundary are tolerated gracefully by all PowerPC processors, usually requiring one additional cycle compared to an aligned reference. Because misalignment can effectively cut load-store bandwidth in half, however, it is a good idea to align accesses whenever possible.

POWERPC LOAD/STORE MULTIPLE AND STRING INSTRUCTIONS

IBM's POWER architecture has several instructions for loading and storing multiple GPRs at a time. In many cases, these instructions don't execute significantly faster than an equivalent sequence of individual loads and stores, but they do help reduce the size of programs that include a great deal of block memory moves. Most of these instructions were carried forward in the PowerPC architecture, and work fine in the current crop of PowerPC processor chips. Among other things, these instructions enable IBM's exiting base of RS/6000 code to perform well without modification on PowerPC processors.

The PowerPC 601 User's Guide warns that in future PowerPC implementations, these instructions might "have greater latency, and take [a] longer, perhaps much longer, time to execute than the equivalent sequence of individual load or store instructions." The main reason these instructions are being phased out is they don't compatibly extend from 32-bit to 64-bit registers. Also, although PowerPC processors can access memory in big-endian or little-endian mode, the string instructions interrupt to software (as an alignment exception) in little-endian mode.

For now, though, in most cases, the instructions work fine, and you shouldn't necessarily avoid using them if they suit your needs, especially if long code lifetime or 64-bit compatibility is not a pressing concern. Engineering a way to painlessly eliminate these instructions from the code if that becomes desirable is probably a good idea, though.

Putting It All Together

By now, you probably have some ideas about writing good PowerPC code. This section crystallizes some of these ideas in an optimization problem that explores alternative formulations of a simple programming task.

Suppose that while profiling your application, you notice that a huge amount of CPU time is spent in a library routine that copies strings (by the way, be prepared—discovering that some mundane task is chewing up loads of CPU time is not unusual). You discover that the library routine is a bulletproof general-purpose string copy routine that is coded inefficiently with special case checking and other features that your application doesn't need. It's possible that a custom recoding without all the bells and whistles could save a significant amount of CPU time.

The code fragment shown in Example 7.7, bytecopy1, is a naive first cut of a simple assembly language string copy routine. Input to the routine consists of a pointer to the first byte in the source string, a pointer to the first byte of the destination, and the number of bytes to copy.

EXAMPLE 7.7.

A simple byte copy routine.

```
# Simple byte copy routine
        # r3 = pointer to source bytes
        # r4 = pointer to target bytes
        # r5 = nonzero number of bytes
  bytecopy1:
        ldb     r9,0(r3)        # Load from source[r3]
        stb     r9,0(r4)        # Store to target[r4]
        addi    r3,1            # Increment source
        addi    r4,1            # ..and target pointers
        subi    r5,1            # Decrement byte count
        cmpi    cr7,r5,0        # Any more bytes to copy?
        beq+    cr7,bytecopy1   #
        bclr                    # return
```

In this sequence, the first two instructions copy a byte from the source to the target, and the next two instructions increment the addresses to point at the next byte locations. The last three instructions decrement the iteration count, test it for zero, and branch back to the top of the loop.

Using Indexed Load and Store

Three of the seven instructions in the bytecopy1 loop are simply incrementing or decrementing index and counter variables. The PowerPC instruction set has indexed load and store instructions that allow sharing of an index variable, and bytecopy2 shows how using the same index for the load and store instructions enables you to eliminate one of the add immediate instructions. You can eliminate the decrement instruction simply by using the index as the loop control variable, as shown in Example 7.8.

EXAMPLE 7.8.

Using indexed load and store instruction.

```
            # Byte copy using indexed load and store
            # r3 = pointer to source
            # r4 = pointer to target
            # r5 = nonzero number of bytes
bytecopy2:
            li    r13,0           # Starting index2
loop:
            lbzx  r9,r13,r3       # Load next source byte
            cmp   cr7,r13,r5      # Test index
            stbx  r9,r13,r4       # Store target byte
            addi  r13,1           # Increment index
            blt+  cr7,loop        #
            bclr
```

The loop body in Example 7.8 has been reduced from seven to five instructions; however, one cost of this approach is the requirement of an additional register (r13) to hold the index. The compare is scheduled early to avoid delays in resolving the conditional branch; however, to do this, it's necessary to compare the byte count with the index value used in the current, not the next, loop iteration. When reordering instructions in this way, be sure to preserve the meaning of the program. For example, if the compare instruction is placed after, instead of before, the add immediate instruction that increments the index, the branch would need to be coded differently (bng instead of blt) to avoid exiting the loop one iteration too soon.

Using Load and Store with Update

Sometimes it's possible to use an update form of the PowerPC load or store instructions to automatically increment an address. This technique is shown in Example 7.9, which has no explicit increment instructions, but instead uses the update feature to do this automatically. The index register has been eliminated by incrementing the source and target pointers directly. One drawback to this approach is that the addresses must be adjusted to allow for the increment that occurs *before* the very first reference—hence the subtract-immediate instructions above the loop body.

EXAMPLE 7.9.

Using load and store with copy.

```
                # Byte copy using load and store with update
                # r3 = pointer to source
                # r4 = pointer to target
                # r5 = nonzero number of bytes
     bytecopy3:
                subi    r3,1            # Adjust pointers for
                subi    r4,1            # ..update instructions
                add     r8,r5,r3        # Compute end address
     loop:
                lbzu    r9,1(r3)        # Get source[++r3]
                cmpl    cr7,r3,r8       # See if last byte
                stbu    r9,1(r4)        # Store target[++r4]
                blt+    cr7,loop        #
                bclr                    # return
```

To avoid explicit incrementation instructions in the body of the loop, the termination test is based directly on one of the addresses—the add instruction just above the loop label computes the address of the last byte to be copied, which serves as the operand of the compare instruction following the load. You're back to seven total instructions, but three of them are executed only once—the loop body is only four instructions.

Using the Count Register

The count register and the CTR decrement and test capabilities of PowerPC branch instructions can be used to eliminate many explicit compare-and-branch sequences used to control program loops. Using the CTR instead of the CR to control a loop is desirable, because in most cases, the hardware can resolve a CTR-based branch more quickly. Because the number of loop iterations is known, the byte copy loop is an ideal candidate for control with the CTR, as shown in Example 7.10.

EXAMPLE 7.10.

Using the count register.

```
                # Byte copy using the Count Register
                # r3 = pointer to source
                # r4 = pointer to target
                # r5 = nonzero number of bytes
     bytecopy4:
                mtctr   r5              # Initialize Count Register
                subi    r3,1            # Adjust pointers
                subi    r4,1            # ..for update instructions
```

```
loop:
        lbzu    r9,1(r3)    # Get source[++r3]
        stbu    r9,1(r4)    # Store target[++r4]
        bdnz+   loop        # Loop if CTR nonzero
        bclr                # return
```

In some special cases where the memory block size and alignment obey certain rules, it's possible to code a more efficient solution by "unrolling the loop" and reading and writing more than one byte at a time, but bytecopy4 probably is as good as it gets for a small and truly general byte-granular copy routine for PowerPC architecture.

In some programming situations, it is necessary to terminate loops under several different conditions, possibly depending on values computed within the loop body itself. It almost never is desirable to modify the CTR in the body of the loop, because this can defeat the hardware that provides the performance advantage of using CTR-controlled loops in the first place. The CTR still can be used advantageously, however, using CR-based branches for "early exit" conditions. For example, Example 7.11 shows an enhancement of bytecopy4 that takes advantage of the C programming language conventions for strings. In C, a *string* is a sequence of characters terminated by a null (0 byte). The compare and conditional branch instructions inserted in the loop cause exit from the loop if a null byte is reached in the source string before the specified number bytes are copied (thus, the value in register r5 now is used as the maximum number of bytes to copy).

EXAMPLE 7.11.

Early exit from CTR-based loops.

```
            # Copy up to N bytes of a null-terminated string
            # r3 = pointer to source
            # r4 = pointer to target
            # r5 = nonzero byte count limit
bytecopy5a:
            mtctr   r5          # Initialize Count Register
            subi    r3,1        # Adjust pointers
            subi    r4,1        # ..for update instructions
loop:
            lbzu    r9,1(r3)    # Get source[++r3]
            cmpli   cr7,r9,0    # Is it null?
            stbu    r9,1(r4)    # Store target[++r4]
            bne-    cr7,exit    # Exit if null.
            bdnz+   loop        # Loop if not at limit.
exit:
            bclr                # return
```

PowerPC branch instructions can test the CTR, the CR, or both at the same time, and Example 7.12 shows the same loop implemented with a single branch combining tests of both termination conditions!

Incidentally, the name bytecopy was chosen deliberately to avoid confusion with the similar ANSI C library function strncpy. Unlike strncpy, bytecopy will not pad the end of the target string with null bytes, and it doesn't return a result. You could modify bytecopy to mimic this behavior, but that's not the point. There may be situations where zeroing the trailing portion of the target buffer is overhead that you want to eliminate, while retaining the safety and security of a limit that prevents writing past the end of the target buffer.

EXAMPLE 7.12.

CR and CTR testing in a single branch.

```
              # Copy up to N bytes of a null-terminated string
              # Two branches in one!
              # r3 = pointer to source
              # r4 = pointer to target
              # r5 = nonzero byte count limit
bytecopy5b:
              mtctr  r5            # Initialize Count Register
              subi   r3,1          # Adjust pointers
              subi   r4,1          # ..for update instructions
loop:
              lbzu   r9,1(r3)      # Get source[++r3]
              cmpli  cr7,r9,0      # Is it null?
              stbu   r9,1(r4)      # Store target[++r4]
              bdnzf+ 2,loop        # Loop if non-null and
                                   # ..limit not exceeded
              bclr                 # return
```

Dealing with Overflow and Carry

In many high-level languages (C springs to mind), the concepts of overflow and carry don't appear in the language. The tacit assumption is that the programmer is responsible for choosing an integer type that provides enough precision for the computation, and it's up to the user to make sure that the programmer's assumptions aren't violated.

Even though most programming languages and programmers never use the features, almost all microprocessor architectures provide registers and instructions to deal with overflow and carry in fixed-point arithmetic instructions. These features are essential to permit implementation of integer types that are wider than a machine's fixed-point general registers. Techniques for implementing multiple-precision arithmetic on PowerPC processors are described in Appendix A, "Programming Examples." However, the information and capabilities provided also can be useful occasionally in single-precision computing.

In some machines, all integer instructions that could cause overflow set a status register, and the program can check the status if appropriate. Maintaining that status register, however, can restrict the capability of the processor to issue and complete instructions out of order. Because overflow and carry information is used so rarely, most PowerPC fixed-point instructions that can overflow have forms that will set the status register only if the programmer has explicitly requested so.

This results in a potentially confusing array of options on PowerPC integer instructions. For example, when should you use a plain add instruction; and when should you use addo, addc, addco, adde, or addeo? All these instructions add 32-bit integers; the differences among them are the way that carry and overflow conditions are handled—for example, which conditions are recorded in the PowerPC fixed point exception register (XER) or the condition register (CR).

First, if you aren't concerned about overflow or carry situations, just use a simple add. In fact, you should make sure not to use the other forms, because setting overflow bits in the CR or XER could needlessly delay the execution of subsequent dependent instructions.

Variants of the *add carrying* instruction (addc*x*) set the CA bit in the XER. This bit can be carried in to *add extended* instructions (adde*x*) to compute multiple precision results.

The *overflow enable* (OE) forms of these instructions (for example, addo, addco, and addeo) cause the overflow (OV) and summary overflow (SO) bits of the XER to be set if the instruction overflows, which you should use if you want to detect an overflow condition and do something about it later. The SO bit of the XER is *sticky*, meaning that once it is set, it remains set until you explicitly clear it, such as with an mtxer instruction. This instruction enables you to delay checking for an overflow condition until after a lengthy computation sequence; you can sum up a sequence of numbers in a loop, and then check for possible overflow once upon exiting the loop.

Using PowerPC Floating-Point Instructions

One of the biggest advantages of moving to the PowerPC microprocessor from some of the "classic" personal computer microprocessors is a substantial increase in floating point performance. All PowerPC processors provide much higher floating-point processing bandwidth than predecessor architectures.

PowerPC processors support two native floating point modes: 32-bit single precision and 64-bit double precision. Both modes are compatible with the IEEE 754/854 standards for floating-point arithmetic. In most applications, you will want to use double-precision format, which yields the best accuracy.

The performance advantage for single precision is primarily on the 601 and 603 processors, where double-precision multiplies take a cycle longer than single-precision multiplies. The 604 and 620 processors have no execution time penalty for double-precision operations. Actual latency varies by data value, but double-precision division generally takes a little longer on all PowerPC processors. All processors can benefit from the reduced memory space used by single-precision values—see the next section ("Looking At Memory System and Cache Considerations") on memory performance to understand how. If you don't need more than a few significant digits, single-precision values significantly can speed up some applications.

PowerPC processors provide a family of multiply and add instructions for both single and double precision operands. These instructions permit very efficient implementation of some numeric and matrix operations. (See the matrix multiplication example in Appendix A.)

The PowerPC architecture doesn't have instructions for copying values from floating point registers to and from general registers; any communication between the register sets must go through memory. If you convert a floating-point value to an integer, you need to store it in memory and reload it into a GPR to operate on it with integer instructions.

FLOATING POINT AND THE POWER MACINTOSH

If you are porting a floating-point application from a 68K Mac to PowerPC, you can continue to use the SANE (Standard Apple Numeric Environment) library calls, or convert to PowerPC native floating point. "Going native" yields a substantial performance boost, especially because SANE calls are supported in 680x0 emulation. If you were using the SANE 80-bit or 96-bit formats, however, you would sacrifice some precision in switching to the 64-bit native representation. Your development system should provide some tools to ease the conversion. Metroworks CodeWarrior, for example, provides compatible header files and compiler directives to minimize the pain of floating point code conversion.

Looking At Memory System and Cache Considerations

Virtually all modern high-performance microprocessors have on-chip cache memory. On-chip caches help prevent the processor from starving for memory bandwidth, especially in the face of increasing relative latency of off-chip communication and DRAM access times. In most cases, it's not necessary for the programmer to worry or do anything about caches; the beauty of the idea is that caches almost always work well without any intervention or explicit control on the part of application programs. Even so, there are some things you can do to help "optimize" your program's cache performance.

A word of warning, however. Optimizing cache performance can be a very difficult and patience-testing process. First, without hardware instrumentation (or at the very least, simulation tools), it can be very difficult to measure accurately the cache behavior of your program. In many cases, results aren't even reliably reproducible from one execution to another on the same machine, due to context switches and other execution-dependent behavior. Accidents of recompiling, relinking modules in a different order, moving variables in memory, and other seemingly innocent changes sometimes can result in bigger performance swings than your tuning efforts. Moreover, because cache designs and organizations vary so much across the PowerPC processor line (see Table 7.1), it's hard to predict whether a technique that works for 601 chips will yield similar gains on any of the other chips. Having said that, there are some rules of thumb you can follow, and some promising research in cache optimization bears discussion.

Table 7.1. Cache Designs and Organizations in the PowerPC Processor Line.

PowerPC Processor	*Size Instruction/ Data*	*Associativity*	*Replacement Policy*	*Line Size (bytes)*
601	32K Unified	8	LRU	32/64
603	8K/8K	2/2	LRU	32
604	16K/16K	4/4	LRU	32
620	32K/32K	8/8	LRU	64

Even if you aren't conversant with cache-design issues and terminology (see the following sidebar), you still can follow a few simple rules that could improve measurably your program's bottom-line performance.

CACHE BASICS

A *cache* is just a small memory that acts as a buffer between the processor and main memory. On-chip cache access times usually are one or two processor cycles, compared to as many as 20 or 30 for a main memory access. A cache works based on the principle that whenever a program refers to a location in memory, it is likely to refer to it, or to a location very nearby soon thereafter. This phenomenon is called *locality of reference*. On the first reference to a memory location, a block of memory containing the target location is copied from main memory into the cache. Later references to that location, or any others in the containing block, occur directly in the cache, avoiding the wait for main memory. The degree to which a cache is successful in reducing memory latency depends on both the design of the cache and the memory behavior of the target application.

The PowerPC 603, 604, and 620 processors have *split caches*—the processors maintain separate cache memories for instructions and data. The 601 processor has a *unified*, or *mixed* cache, storing instructions and data together in the same cache structure.

Other cache terminology follows:

Cache size. The number of main memory bytes that can be held in the cache at any one time.

Hit or miss. A cache *hit* occurs when the processor finds that a needed memory location already has been copied into the cache, and no transfer from main memory is necessary. A *miss* occurs when the location isn't loaded currently.

Miss penalty. The delay that occurs on a cache miss, usually expressed as the number of processor clock cycles that the processor spends waiting for the data to be loaded from memory.

Cache line. The block of memory in the cache that holds the loaded data. The cache is divided into some number of fixed-size lines.

Cache tag. When a block of memory is loaded into a line of the cache, the tag for that line is set to the main memory address of the loaded block. There is one tag per line, and by looking at the tags, the processor can determine which main memory locations currently are loaded.

Line size. The number of bytes associated with a tag, also usually the number of bytes loaded into the cache on a miss. In a *sectored cache*, the line is subdivided into sectors that may be loaded and cast out independently.

Set-associativity. If any block from main memory can be loaded into any line of the cache, the cache is said to be *fully associative*. To find out whether a memory location is loaded in a fully associative cache, the address must be compared against every tag. Because this normally isn't practical, the number of lines in which a block might reside is limited to some small number. In an eight-way, set-associative cache, a block always will be loaded into one of eight possible cache lines. This method limits the number of tag comparisons the processor must perform to see whether the cache can hold a given address. A one-way set associative cache is said to be *direct-mapped*.

Writeback (or store-in) versus store-through. The way the cache controller deals with updates (store instructions). In a store-through cache, the stored data is posted immediately to main memory when the write occurs. In a writeback or store-in cache, only the image in the cache is updated (the line is marked *dirty*), and posting to main memory is delayed until the line is replaced.

Replacement policy. When a memory block is loaded and all the potential lines that are allowed to hold the block are occupied, the cache controller chooses to replace one of the currently held lines with the new block. Some common replacement policies are *first in-first out* (FIFO), *least recently used* (LRU), and *random*. In a writeback cache, if the line to be replaced is dirty, it must be written back to memory before the new line can be loaded.

L1 cache, L2 cache. In a multilevel memory hierarchy, caches usually are numbered with their distance in levels from the processor. The level of cache closest to the processor is the first-level or L1 cache, and L2 refers to a cache between the first-level cache and main memory. Most processors today have an on-chip L1, and an external L2 cache. Some machines have additional levels of cache (L3, and so on), and recently, processors have been announced with two-level caches on chip.

Working set. Generally, each increase in the size of a cache reduces the number of misses observed during its execution. Beyond a certain point, however, further increases in the size of the cache don't appreciably reduce the number of misses. At this point, the cache is said to have captured the program's *working set.*

Reducing Cache Misses

Cache misses often are classified into three general groups: *compulsory* misses, *capacity* misses, and *conflict* misses. Each of these misses arises due to a different aspect of cache and program behavior. It's possible to formulate strategies for reducing all three types of misses. Which strategy works best depends on the distribution of each type in your program.

Compulsory Misses

The first time any memory block is referenced, the miss is *compulsory*, because the miss would occur regardless of the size or organization of the cache. Compulsory misses are a direct function of the number of memory blocks touched by a program during its execution. Therefore, the only way to reduce compulsory misses is to reduce the total number of touched blocks.

Capacity Misses

When the cache is not large enough to hold all the blocks needed during execution, some blocks are loaded and discarded to make room for other blocks. Reloading such a block is classified as a *capacity miss*. Reducing capacity misses means effectively shortening the span of time during which particular blocks are needed. One way to do this is to partition an application into distinct stages, each of which has a smaller working set. A simple example is to use an algorithm that makes a single pass through a large memory array (in particular, larger than the data cache), rather than an algorithm that makes two or more passes. The first time through, the misses are compulsory; as work progresses through the array, blocks holding portions of the beginning of the array must be discarded to make room for later portions. Returning for the second pass, the beginning of the array must be reloaded, and these are capacity misses.

Conflict Misses

If a cache is fully associative, all misses are compulsory or capacity. If a cache is not fully asso-ciative, it is possible for a block to be discarded to make room for another block that maps to the same set. This is a *conflict miss*. Conflict misses are the trickiest, because you need to pay attention to addresses and layout of program sections. Fortunately, for most applications, any degree of associativity reduces conflict misses to a very small portion of the overall total.

As pointed out earlier, the way to reduce compulsory misses is to reduce the total number of memory blocks that a program touches, which also indirectly reduces capacity misses. One strategy is to try to increase locality—to organize code and data so that instructions or data that are needed frequently are not grouped in blocks with things that rarely are needed. You could generate error and exception-handling code in one area, for example, and the mainline code in another area. This method reduces the likelihood of loading a block containing a se-quence of exception-handling instructions that always are branched around by the mainline.

Reorganizing blocks of code based on execution frequency seems like an ideal job for a tool, and feedback directed program restructuring (FDPR) is available from IBM for the AIX envi-ronment. This tool uses trace profile feedback to reorganize the basic blocks of the executable; experiments show typical speedups of 20 percent.

Even if you don't have access to the tool, you can follow some simple coding practices to try to achieve similar results.

Using Alignment and Cache Block Boundaries

Alignment of branch targets on cache line boundaries can not only help cache performance, but it also can improve instruction parallelism. This is because the PowerPC processor dispatcher depends on being able to fetch several instructions at a time. If the target address of a taken branch is near the end of a cache line, it increases the likelihood that some of the instructions in the block (those above the branch target) are fetched, but then immediately discarded. Then, the fetcher immediately must issue another request for the instructions below the branch tar-get (in the following line). Instructions that might have been issued immediately had they ar-rived with the first fetch are delayed until the second block can be loaded into the instruction dispatch buffer. This situation is especially noticeable in the PowerPC 601 processor, which has a unified cache. Because the instruction fetcher and the load-store unit share the cache port, and the load-store unit always gets priority, a pending load or store instruction could delay the fetch of the next block of instructions for at least one additional cycle. It's a good idea, there-fore, to align frequently executed branch targets on 32-byte boundaries (for 601 processors, which can load up to eight instructions per cycle), 16-byte boundaries (for 604 and 620 pro-cessors, which can load up to four instructions per cycle), or 8-byte boundaries (for 603 pro-cessors, which can load up to two instructions per cycle), *especially* if the target is the top of a loop. If the loop fits in a single cache line, it's a good idea to align the branch target at the top of the loop to a 32- or 64-byte boundary.

For similar reasons, it can be a good idea to align data structures so that they don't span cache-line boundaries. If structures are not accessed sequentially, and the cache is not large enough to hold all the data, it's possible to reduce miss penalty cycles if the structures never span a cache-line boundary. The benefits of this capability, however, must be traded off against the cost of wasted storage if the size of the structure is not a factor or multiple of the line size.

POWERPC CACHE MANAGEMENT INSTRUCTIONS

Because the PowerPC architecture includes a number of instructions for explicit management of instruction and data caches, they bear mention in a discussion of cache performance. The most interesting of these instructions are the *data cache block touch* (dcbt) and *data cache block touch for store* (dcbtst).

The purpose of these instructions is to enable a program to provide "hints" about addresses it is likely to touch in the near future. These instructions essentially are loads without a target—the address request is sent to the cache, but no data is returned. The PowerPC architecture specification gives implementations great freedom in choosing how to carry out these instructions (it even is permitted to do nothing). The idea is to provide a way to explicitly prefetch from main memory into the cache using instructions that don't interrupt and cannot interlock due to a cache miss.

It is possible to improve the performance of some programs using these instructions (hand modification of some of the SPECfp92 programs yielded improvements of up to 15 percent). The payoff is unpredictable for two reasons, however. First, the operations are specified by X-form instructions, meaning that the addressing mode is register + register, rather than register + constant. If the stride or offset to the next cache block is not handy, an additional instruction or register is required to compute the effective address for the touch. Second, the current PowerPC implementations aren't capable of loading the cache block in the background. When a touch instruction misses in the cache (the only interesting case—a touch instruction that hits is redundant), the processor usually cannot proceed much further without having to wait for the touched block to be loaded. If the next instruction is a load, for example, none of the current processors will show noticeable improvement.

IV

Appendixes

A

Programming Examples

Standard Symbol Definitions

The PowerPC assemblers do not natively support symbolic arguments representing registers and registers fields. For example, the assembler expects "7", not "r7", as a GPR argument to an instruction. In order to make source code more readable, it's beneficial to create symbolic constants which can be used as instruction arguments. Example A.1 is the standard set of symbolic constants used for writing the sample programs. This file uses the .set assembler pseudo-op to define the symbolic constants. This file is then included into each assembly language source file. For our examples we use the UNIX m4 macro preprocessor. An implementation of m4 is available from the Free Software Foundation in source code form. An alternative is to change the m4 include command to the C preprocessor's include command. You can then run each source file through the C preprocessor before assembly.

EXAMPLE A.1.

stdhdr.s: Standard symbol definitions for use with the sample programs.

```
#   Example A.1
#
# GPRs
#
    .set    r0,     0
    .set    r1,     1
    .set    r2,     2
    .set    r3,     3
    .set    r4,     4
    .set    r5,     5
    .set    r6,     6
    .set    r7,     7
    .set    r8,     8
    .set    r9,     9
    .set    r10,    10
    .set    r11,    11
    .set    r12,    12
    .set    r13,    13
    .set    r14,    14
    .set    r15,    15
    .set    r16,    16

    .set    r17,    17
    .set    r18,    18
    .set    r19,    19
    .set    r20,    20
    .set    r21,    21
    .set    r22,    22
    .set    r23,    23
    .set    r24,    24
    .set    r25,    25
    .set    r26,    26
    .set    r27,    27
    .set    r28,    28
```

```
        .set    r29,    29
        .set    r30,    30
        .set    r31,    31
        .set    SP,     1
        .set    RTOC,   2
#
# FPRs
#
        .set    f0,     0
        .set    f1,     1
        .set    f2,     2
        .set    f3,     3
        .set    f4,     4
        .set    f5,     5
        .set    f6,     6
        .set    f7,     7
        .set    f8,     8

        .set    f9,     9
        .set    f10,    10
        .set    f11,    11
        .set    f12,    12
        .set    f13,    13
        .set    f14,    14
        .set    f15,    15
        .set    f16,    16
        .set    f17,    17
        .set    f18,    18
        .set    f19,    19
        .set    f20,    20
        .set    f21,    21
        .set    f22,    22
        .set    f23,    23
        .set    f24,    24
        .set    f25,    25
        .set    f26,    26
        .set    f27,    27
        .set    f28,    28
        .set    f29,    29
        .set    f30,    30
        .set    f31,    31
#
# User mode SPRs
#
#    For use in mtspr and mfspr.
#
#    Extended mnemonics cover most of these anyway. #

        .set    mq,     0x000    # 601 only
        .set    xer,    0x001
        .set    lr,     0x008
        .set    ctr,    0x009
        # these are read-only SPRs for user mode
        #  - supervisor mode uses different SPR numbers for mtspr
        .set    rtcu,   0x004    # 601 only
        .set    rtcl,   0x005    # 601 only
        .set    dec,    0x006
```

```
# note that mftb and mftbu cannot be performed with mfspr
#
#  BO bits
#
#  For use in the branch conditional instructions
#
#  Most combinations are already covered by extended mnemonics.
#
    .set    bo_nc,  16    # do not consider cr bit
    .set    bo_c,    0    # consider cr bit
    .set    bo_bt,   8    # branch if cr bit set (condition true)
    .set    bo_bf,   0    # branch if cr bit clear (false)
    .set    bo_ndec,    4               # do not decrement the CTR
    .set    bo_dec, 0     # decrement the CTR
    .set    bo_bz,   2    # branch if dec'd CTR == 0
    .set    bo_nbz,  0    # branch if dec'd CTR != 0
    .set    bo_p,    1    # set prediction bit


#
#  BI bits
#
#  For use in branch conditional instructions.
#
#  Use only for bc forms, and bt, bf extended forms. #
    .set    cr0,     0
    .set    cr0_lt,  0
    .set    cr0_gt,  1
    .set    cr0_eq,  2
    .set    cr0_so,  3
    .set    cr0_un,  3
    .set    cr1,     4
    .set    cr1_lt,  4
    .set    cr1_gt,  5
    .set    cr1_eq,  6
    .set    cr1_so,  7
    .set    cr1_un,  7
    .set    cr2,     8
    .set    cr2_lt,  8
    .set    cr2_gt,  9
    .set    cr2_eq,  10
    .set    cr2_so,  11
    .set    cr2_un,  11
    .set    cr3,     12
    .set    cr3_lt,  12

    .set    cr3_gt,  13
    .set    cr3_eq,  14
    .set    cr3_so,  15
    .set    cr3_un,  15
    .set    cr4,     16
    .set    cr4_lt,  16
    .set    cr4_gt,  17
    .set    cr4_eq,  18
    .set    cr4_so,  19
    .set    cr4_un,  19
    .set    cr5,     20
```

```
        .set    cr5_lt, 20
        .set    cr5_gt, 21
        .set    cr5_eq, 22
        .set    cr5_so, 23
        .set    cr5_un, 23
        .set    cr6,    24
        .set    cr6_lt, 24
        .set    cr6_gt, 25
        .set    cr6_eq, 26
        .set    cr6_so, 27
        .set    cr6_un, 27
        .set    cr7,    28
        .set    cr7_lt, 28
        .set    cr7_gt, 29
        .set    cr7_eq, 30
        .set    cr7_so, 31
        .set    cr7_un, 31

#
#       Use the following with the addition notation,
#       e.g., "cr5+eq".
#
        .set    lt,     0
        .set    gt,     1
        .set    eq,     2
        .set    so,     3
        .set    un,     3
#
#       CR fields
#
#       For use with cmp and mcr instructions.
#
#       Use also for branch conditional extended forms, e.g., "blt".
#
        .set    crf0,   0
        .set    crf1,   1
        .set    crf2,   2
        .set    crf3,   3
        .set    crf4,   4
        .set    crf5,   5
        .set    crf6,   6
        .set    crf7,   7
```

Linking to C

When interfacing with C and using nonvolatile FPRs and GPRs, you can save a substantial amount of code by using the routines in Example A.2. These routines also illustrate how to use a label as an entry point by prefixing the label with a period. The technique of jumping into a table-like series of instructions is often useful in assembly language programming when you may want to perform some action using a register or set of registers that is not known until runtime.

EXAMPLE A.2.

svNrst.m4: Code for saving and restoring GPRs and FPRs.

```
#     Example A.2
include('stdhdr.s')
##########################################################################
#
#     This module contains routines for saving and restoring volatile
#     registers.  They are useful for function prologs and epilogs.
#
#     The save and restore GPR routines expect r12 to contain the
#     address of the start of the FPR save area.  If there is no
#     FPR save area, then this will just be the top of the stack.
#
        .csect save_registers[PR]
#
# sv_gprNN:     stw     rNN,-4*(32-NN)(r12)     # save gpr NN
#
.sv_gpr13:     stw     r13,-4*(32-13)(r12)     # save gpr 13
.sv_gpr14:     stw     r14,-4*(32-14)(r12)     # save gpr 14
.sv_gpr15:     stw     r15,-4*(32-15)(r12)     # save gpr 15
.sv_gpr16:     stw     r16,-4*(32-16)(r12)     # save gpr 16
.sv_gpr17:     stw     r17,-4*(32-17)(r12)     # save gpr 17
.sv_gpr18:     stw     r18,-4*(32-18)(r12)     # save gpr 18
.sv_gpr19:     stw     r19,-4*(32-19)(r12)     # save gpr 19
.sv_gpr20:     stw     r20,-4*(32-20)(r12)     # save gpr 20
.sv_gpr21:     stw     r21,-4*(32-21)(r12)     # save gpr 21
.sv_gpr22:     stw     r22,-4*(32-22)(r12)     # save gpr 22
.sv_gpr23:     stw     r23,-4*(32-23)(r12)     # save gpr 23
.sv_gpr24:     stw     r24,-4*(32-24)(r12)     # save gpr 24
.sv_gpr25:     stw     r25,-4*(32-25)(r12)     # save gpr 25
.sv_gpr26:     stw     r26,-4*(32-26)(r12)     # save gpr 26
.sv_gpr27:     stw     r27,-4*(32-27)(r12)     # save gpr 27
.sv_gpr28:     stw     r28,-4*(32-28)(r12)     # save gpr 28
.sv_gpr29:     stw     r29,-4*(32-29)(r12)     # save gpr 29
.sv_gpr30:     stw     r30,-4*(32-30)(r12)     # save gpr 30
.sv_gpr31:     stw     r31,-4*(32-31)(r12)     # save gpr 31
    blr        # return
#
# sv_fprNN:     stfd    fNN,-8*(32-NN)(r1)      # save fpr NN
#
.sv_fpr14:     stfd    f14,-8*(32-14)(r1)      # save fpr 14
.sv_fpr15:     stfd    f15,-8*(32-15)(r1)      # save fpr 15
.sv_fpr16:     stfd    f16,-8*(32-16)(r1)      # save fpr 16
.sv_fpr17:     stfd    f17,-8*(32-17)(r1)      # save fpr 17
.sv_fpr18:     stfd    f18,-8*(32-18)(r1)      # save fpr 18
.sv_fpr19:     stfd    f19,-8*(32-19)(r1)      # save fpr 19
.sv_fpr20:     stfd    f20,-8*(32-20)(r1)      # save fpr 20
.sv_fpr21:     stfd    f21,-8*(32-21)(r1)      # save fpr 21
.sv_fpr22:     stfd    f22,-8*(32-22)(r1)      # save fpr 22
.sv_fpr23:     stfd    f23,-8*(32-23)(r1)      # save fpr 23
.sv_fpr24:     stfd    f24,-8*(32-24)(r1)      # save fpr 24
.sv_fpr25:     stfd    f25,-8*(32-25)(r1)      # save fpr 25
.sv_fpr26:     stfd    f26,-8*(32-26)(r1)      # save fpr 26
.sv_fpr27:     stfd    f27,-8*(32-27)(r1)      # save fpr 27
```

```
.sv_fpr28:    stfd    f28,-8*(32-28)(r1)    # save fpr 28
.sv_fpr29:    stfd    f29,-8*(32-29)(r1)    # save fpr 29
.sv_fpr30:    stfd    f30,-8*(32-30)(r1)    # save fpr 30
.sv_fpr31:    stfd    f31,-8*(32-31)(r1)    # save fpr 31
    blr           # return
#
# rst_gprNN:    lwz     rNN,-4*(32-NN)(r12)    # restore gpr NN
#
.rst_gpr13:    lwz     r13,-4*(32-13)(r12)    # restore gpr 13
.rst_gpr14:    lwz     r14,-4*(32-14)(r12)    # restore gpr 14
.rst_gpr15:    lwz     r15,-4*(32-15)(r12)    # restore gpr 15
.rst_gpr16:    lwz     r16,-4*(32-16)(r12)    # restore gpr 16
.rst_gpr17:    lwz     r17,-4*(32-17)(r12)    # restore gpr 17
.rst_gpr18:    lwz     r18,-4*(32-18)(r12)    # restore gpr 18
.rst_gpr19:    lwz     r19,-4*(32-19)(r12)    # restore gpr 19
.rst_gpr20:    lwz     r20,-4*(32-20)(r12)    # restore gpr 20
.rst_gpr21:    lwz     r21,-4*(32-21)(r12)    # restore gpr 21
.rst_gpr22:    lwz     r22,-4*(32-22)(r12)    # restore gpr 22
.rst_gpr23:    lwz     r23,-4*(32-23)(r12)    # restore gpr 23
.rst_gpr24:    lwz     r24,-4*(32-24)(r12)    # restore gpr 24
.rst_gpr25:    lwz     r25,-4*(32-25)(r12)    # restore gpr 25
.rst_gpr26:    lwz     r26,-4*(32-26)(r12)    # restore gpr 26
.rst_gpr27:    lwz     r27,-4*(32-27)(r12)    # restore gpr 27
.rst_gpr28:    lwz     r28,-4*(32-28)(r12)    # restore gpr 28
.rst_gpr29:    lwz     r29,-4*(32-29)(r12)    # restore gpr 29
.rst_gpr30:    lwz     r30,-4*(32-30)(r12)    # restore gpr 30
.rst_gpr31:    lwz     r31,-4*(32-31)(r12)    # restore gpr 31
    blr           # return
#
# rst_fprNN:    lfd     fNN,-8*(32-NN)(r1)    # restore fpr NN
#
.rst_fpr14:    lfd     f14,-8*(32-14)(r1)    # restore fpr 14
.rst_fpr15:    lfd     f15,-8*(32-15)(r1)    # restore fpr 15
.rst_fpr16:    lfd     f16,-8*(32-16)(r1)    # restore fpr 16
.rst_fpr17:    lfd     f17,-8*(32-17)(r1)    # restore fpr 17
.rst_fpr18:    lfd     f18,-8*(32-18)(r1)    # restore fpr 18
.rst_fpr19:    lfd     f19,-8*(32-19)(r1)    # restore fpr 19
.rst_fpr20:    lfd     f20,-8*(32-20)(r1)    # restore fpr 20
.rst_fpr21:    lfd     f21,-8*(32-21)(r1)    # restore fpr 21
.rst_fpr22:    lfd     f22,-8*(32-22)(r1)    # restore fpr 22
.rst_fpr23:    lfd     f23,-8*(32-23)(r1)    # restore fpr 23
.rst_fpr24:    lfd     f24,-8*(32-24)(r1)    # restore fpr 24
.rst_fpr25:    lfd     f25,-8*(32-25)(r1)    # restore fpr 25
.rst_fpr26:    lfd     f26,-8*(32-26)(r1)    # restore fpr 26
.rst_fpr27:    lfd     f27,-8*(32-27)(r1)    # restore fpr 27
.rst_fpr28:    lfd     f28,-8*(32-28)(r1)    # restore fpr 28
.rst_fpr29:    lfd     f29,-8*(32-29)(r1)    # restore fpr 29
.rst_fpr30:    lfd     f30,-8*(32-30)(r1)    # restore fpr 30
.rst_fpr31:    lfd     f31,-8*(32-31)(r1)    # restore fpr 31
    blr           # return
    .globl    .sv_gpr13
    .globl    .sv_gpr14
    .globl    .sv_gpr15
    .globl    .sv_gpr16
    .globl    .sv_gpr17
    .globl    .sv_gpr18
```

```
.globl    .sv_gpr19
.globl    .sv_gpr20
.globl    .sv_gpr21
.globl    .sv_gpr22
.globl    .sv_gpr23
.globl    .sv_gpr24
.globl    .sv_gpr25
.globl    .sv_gpr26
.globl    .sv_gpr27
.globl    .sv_gpr28
.globl    .sv_gpr29
.globl    .sv_gpr30
.globl    .sv_gpr31
.globl    .sv_fpr14
.globl    .sv_fpr15
.globl    .sv_fpr16
.globl    .sv_fpr17
.globl    .sv_fpr18
.globl    .sv_fpr19
.globl    .sv_fpr20
.globl    .sv_fpr21
.globl    .sv_fpr22
.globl    .sv_fpr23
.globl    .sv_fpr24
.globl    .sv_fpr25
.globl    .sv_fpr26
.globl    .sv_fpr27
.globl    .sv_fpr28
.globl    .sv_fpr29
.globl    .sv_fpr30
.globl    .sv_fpr31
.globl    .rst_gpr13
.globl    .rst_gpr14
.globl    .rst_gpr15
.globl    .rst_gpr16
.globl    .rst_gpr17
.globl    .rst_gpr18
.globl    .rst_gpr19
.globl    .rst_gpr20
.globl    .rst_gpr21
.globl    .rst_gpr22
.globl    .rst_gpr23
.globl    .rst_gpr24
.globl    .rst_gpr25
.globl    .rst_gpr26
.globl    .rst_gpr27
.globl    .rst_gpr28
.globl    .rst_gpr29
.globl    .rst_gpr30
.globl    .rst_gpr31
.globl    .rst_fpr14
.globl    .rst_fpr15
.globl    .rst_fpr16
.globl    .rst_fpr17
.globl    .rst_fpr18
.globl    .rst_fpr19
```

```
.globl    .rst_fpr20
.globl    .rst_fpr21
.globl    .rst_fpr22
.globl    .rst_fpr23
.globl    .rst_fpr24
.globl    .rst_fpr25
.globl    .rst_fpr26
.globl    .rst_fpr27
.globl    .rst_fpr28
.globl    .rst_fpr29
.globl  .rst_fpr30
.globl  .rst_fpr31
```

The function framework shown in Example A.3 can be used as a model for functions that are called from a compiled language. The full prolog, full epilog, and the function descriptor are shown. As discussed in Chapter 6, some of the steps shown are optional.

EXAMPLE A.3.

framewrk.m4: Basic framework for a function showing prolog and epilog, and the function descriptor.

```
#     Example A.3
###########################################################################
#
#     Framework for function func().
#
#     func uses:
#         nonvolatile GPRs N - 31
#         nonvolatile FPRs M - 31
#         any nonvolatile CF fields (CR 2 - 4)
#         the LR
#
#     S_SIZE is the total size of func's stack frame
#
          .csect    .func[PR]
          .globl    .func[PR]
# full function prolog
          mfcr    r0                        # get the CR
          stw     r0,4(SP)                  #   and save in caller's link area

    mflr    r0    # get the return address (in LR)
    stw   r0,8(SP)   #   and save in caller's link area
    bl    .sv_fprM   # save FPRs
    addi    r12,SP,-8^(32-M)   # calculate beginning of FPR save area
    bl    .sv_gprN   # save GPRs
# if S_SIZE is less than 32K
    stwu    SP,-S_SIZE(SP)    # create the stack frame & chain
# if S_SIZE is greater than or equal to 32K
    addis    r12,-S_SIZE & 0xFFFF0000 (r0)   # move -S_SIZE
    ori    r12,-S_SIZE & 0xFFFF (r12)    #   into r12
    stwux    SP,SP,r12                # update SP atomically
```

```
####
#### function code goes here
####
# if the stack frame size is still S_SIZE, and S_SIZE < 32K
    addi    SP,S_SIZE(SP)    # destory the stack frame
# if the stack frame may have grown, e.g. with alloca, or S_SIZE >= 32K
    lwz     SP,0(SP)         # load back chain into SP
# full function epilog

    bl      .rst_fprM    # restore FPRs
    addi    r12,SP,-8*(32-M)    # calculate beginning of FPR save area
    bl      .rst_gprN    # restore GPRs
    lwz     r0,4(SP)     # get the saved CR value
    mtcr    r0    # and restore
    lwz     r0,8(SP)     # get the save return address
    mtlr    r0    # and restore to the LR
    blr          # return
# function descriptor
    .toc          # TOC csect required for use of TOC[tc0]
    .csect  func[DS]
    .globl  func[DS]
    .long   .func[PR]
    .long   TOC[t0]
```

Program Timing

One key aspect of tuning for performance is being able to measure the performance of code. Example A.4 shows aixtimer.h, a C header file which defines macros for timing. The timer facilities are POSIX specific, so this code should be portable to most operating systems with little modification. One important point to note is that in a multitasking operating system there is a difference between real (or wall clock) time and the time spent running any one program, since the operating system can switch between several processes. This timer shows the wall clock time, the system time, time spent running operating system code on behalf of the program, and user time, the time spent actually running the program's code. User time will also include time spent running library code. One problem with this type of timer is that it is often not very accurate due to the overhead of maintaining times for all running programs. On AIX 3.2, this timer has a resolution of ten milliseconds, so in order to get accurate results, functions must have their run times extended either by increasing the amount of data processed, or by repeatedly invoking the function. Example A.5 shows a C program which uses the macros from aixtimer.h to time mxmul on an extended data set. The source code for mxmul is shown in Example A.15.

Note that on the Macintosh you should be able to get higher resolution times by simply using the move-from-time-base instructions (move-from-real-time-clock for the 601), since the Macintosh Operating System does not perform preemptive multitasking.

EXAMPLE A.4.

aixtimer.h: C header file for timing called assembly functions.

```
/*  Example A.4  */
#include <stdio.h>
#ifndef _POSIX_SOURCE
#define _POSIX_SOURCE
#endif
#include <sys/times.h>
#define    START_TIMER    StartClk = times(&StartTMS);
#define    STOP_TIMER     StopClk = times(&StopTMS);
#define    PRINT_TIME     printTime();
static struct tms      StartTMS, StopTMS;
static clock_t         StartClk, StopClk;
static void printTime()
{
    clock_t    s, u;
s = StopTMS.tms_stime - StartTMS.tms_stime;

    u = StopTMS.tms_utime - StartTMS.tms_utime;
printf("Time:  wall = %.2f, sys = %.2f, user = %.2f (proc = %.2f)\n", (StopClk
- StartClk) / 100.0, s/100.0, u/100.0, (u + s)/100.0);
}
```

EXAMPLE A.5.

try_mxmul.c: C program that uses aixtimer.h to time assembly language function mxmul.

```
/*  Example A.5  */
#include <stdio.h>
#include <malloc.h>
#include "aixtimer.h"
extern void mxmul(int h, int n, int w, float A[][], float B[][], float
R[][]);
/*
        R = A * B
        A is n x h
        B is w x n
        R is w x h
*/
#define        HEIGHT           128
#define        SIZE             256
#define        WIDTH            512

main()
{
    float      A[HEIGHT][SIZE];
    float      B[SIZE][WIDTH];
    float      R[HEIGHT][WIDTH];
    int        i, j, k;
```

```
    for (i=0; i<SIZE; ++i)
    {
        for (j=0; j<HEIGHT; ++j)
A[j][i] = (float) (i + j + 1);
        for (j=0; j<WIDTH; ++j)
B[i][j] = (float) (i + j + 1);
    }
    START_TIMER;
mxmul(HEIGHT, SIZE, WIDTH, A, B, R);
    STOP_TIMER;
    for (i=0; i<4; ++i)
    {
        for (j=0; j<4; ++j)
printf("%.2f ", R[i][j]);
        putc('\n', stdout);
    }
    PRINT_TIME;
}
```

Runtime Environment

Often times it is important to know something about the mode the processor is running in, and the main problem is that user mode programs often cannot access the status registers which hold this information. Two modes of interest to user programs are little versus big endian and 32- versus 64-bit mode. While the operating system may provide an API for discovering this information, Example A.6 and Example A.7 illustrate methods of detecting these modes for user mode programs. Example A.6 shows detecting 32- or 64-bit mode by taking advantage of the fact that 0x00000000FFFFFFFF is positive in 64-bit mode and negative in 32-bit mode. The detection of the endian mode shown in Example A.7 relies on the endian mode-specific behavior of the load and store instructions.

64- or 32-Bit Mode

EXAMPLE A.6.

is64mode.m4: Function for checking whether the processor is in 32- or 64-bit mode.

```
#     Example A.6
include('stdhdr.s')
#################################################################
#
#     is64mode
#
#     Returns non-zero if processor is in 64 bit mode.
#
```

```
#     int is64mode();
#
        .csect    .is64mode[PR]
        .globl    .is64mode[PR]
        li    r3,-1    # r3 <- 0xFFFFFFFF_FFFFFFFF or 0xFFFFFFFF
        rlwinm. r3,r3,0,0,31    # r3 <- 0x00000000_FFFFFFFF or 0xFFFFFFFF
        bgt    done    # if r3 considered positive, must be 64 bit mode
        li    r3,0    # else 32 bit mode

done:    blr        # return
*** end example ***
Endian mode
*** begin example ***
Example A.7. isLEmode.m4: Function for checking whether the processor is in
little endian mode.
#     Example A.7
include('stdhdr.s')
####################################################################
#
#    isLEmode
#
#    Returns non-zero if processor is in little endian mode.
#
#    int isLEmode();
#
        .csect    .isLEmode[PR]
        .globl    .isLEmode[PR]
        lwz    r4,T.data(RTOC) # get the data address
        lbz    r3,0(r4)    # load byte at address
                # r3 <- 0 in big endian mode
        # r3 <- 1 in little endian mode blr        # return
        .align    3    # guarantee doubleword alignment
        .csect    _isLEmode[RW]
        .long    0x00000000
        .long    0x00000001
        .toc
T.data:    .tc    _isLEmode[TC],_isLEmode[RW]
```

64-Bit Integer Math on 32-Bit Machines

These functions illustrate 64-bit unsigned arithmetic for 32-bit machines. By far the most complex operation is division, since it doesn't easily break down into some combination of several 32-bit divides. Therefore, a shift-add method is used. Note the use of the condition register logical instructions to check for special cases near the top of Example A.11. When evaluating complex logical statements, you can either use the condition register logical instructions or construct a series of branch conditionals. Which method is better varies from situation to situation.

Notice that since a structure is returned by these functions, the caller implicitly passes the address for the return value as the first argument.

Also, note in the shift routines in Example A.12 that no branches or comparisons are used due to the support for 64-bit shifts on 32-bit processors.

Addition and Subtraction

EXAMPLE A.8.

add64.m4: Function that performs 64-bit integer addition.

```
#     Example A.8
include('stdhdr.s')
############################################################################
#
#     add64
#
#     Performs addition of 64 bit numbers.
#
#     struct unsigned64
#     {
#       unsigned    hi;
#       unsigned    lo;
#     }
#
#     unsigned64 add64(unsigned64 *a, unsigned64 *b)
#
#     Expects
#
#         r3     pointer to struct unsigned64 result
#         r4     pointer to struct unsigned64 a
#         r5     pointer to struct unsigned64 b
#
#     Uses
#
#         r3     pointer to result
#         r4     pointer to a
#         r5     pointer to b
#         r6     high order word of a (a.hi), high word of sum
#         r7     low order word of a (a.lo), low word of sum
#         r8     high order word of b (b.hi)
#         r9     low order word of b (b.lo)
#
#     Returns
#
#         r3     high order word of sum (result.hi)
#         r6     high order word of sum (result.hi)
#         r7     low order word of sum (result.lo)
#
            .globl    .add64[PR]
            .csect    .add64[PR]
            lwz     r7,4(r4)      # r7 <- a.lo
            lwz     r9,4(r5)      # r9 <- b.lo
            lwz     r6,0(r4)      # r6 <- a.hi
            addc    r7,r7,r9      # r7 <- sum lo, set CA
            lwz     r8,0(r5)      # r8 <- b.hi
```

```
        stw    r7,4(r3)    # result.lo <- r7
        adde   r6,r6,r8    # r6 <- sum hi w/ CA
        stw    r6,0(r3)    # result.hi <- r6
        blr                # return
```

EXAMPLE A.9.

sub64.m4: Function that performs 64-bit integer subtraction.

```
#    Example A.9
include('stdhdr.s')
##################################################################### #
#    sub64
#
#    Performs subtraction of 64 bit numbers.
#
#    struct unsigned64
#    {
#      unsigned    hi;
#      unsigned    lo;
#    }
#
#    unsigned64 sub64(unsigned64 *a, unsigned64 *b)
#
#  Expects
#
#    r3    pointer to struct unsigned64 result
#    r4    pointer to struct unsigned64 a
#    r5    pointer to struct unsigned64 b
#
#  Uses
#
#    r3    pointer to result
#    r4    pointer to a
#    r5    pointer to b
#    r6    high order word of a (a.hi), high word of difference
#    r7    low order word of a (a.lo), low word of difference
#    r8    high order word of b (b.hi)
#    r9    low order word of b (b.lo)
#
#  Returns
#
#    r3    high order word of difference (result.hi)
#    r6    high order word of difference (result.hi)
#    r7    low order word of difference (result.lo)
#
      .globl   .sub64[PR]
      .csect   .sub64[PR]
      lwz    r7,4(r4)    # r7 <- a.lo
      lwz    r9,4(r5)    # r9 <- b.lo
      lwz    r6,0(r4)    # r6 <- a.hi
      subfc  r7,r9,r7    # r7 <- difference.lo, set CA
      lwz    r8,0(r5)    # r8 <- b.hi
```

```
        stw     r7,4(r3)    # result.lo <- r7
        subfe   r6,r8,r6    # r6 <- difference.hi w/ CA
        stw     r6,0(r3)    # result.hi <- r6
        blr         # return
```

Multiplication

EXAMPLE A.10.

mull64.m4: Returns low-order 64 bits of the product of two 64-bit numbers.

```
#     Example A.10
include('stdhdr.s')
#####################################################################
#
#     mull64
#
#     Performs the low-order multiplication of 64 bit numbers.
#
#     struct unsigned64
#     {
#       unsigned    hi;
#       unsigned    lo;
#     }
#
#     unsigned64 mull64(unsigned64 *a, unsigned64 *b)
#

    .globl    .mull64[PR]
    .csect    .mull64[PR]
    lwz     r7,4(r4)    # r7 <- a.lo
    lwz     r9,4(r5)    # r9 <- b.lo
    lwz     r8,0(r5)    # r8 <- b.hi
    mulhwu  r10,r7,r9   # r10 <- high word (a.lo * b.lo)
    lwz     r6,0(r4)    # r6 <- a.hi
    mullw   r11,r7,r8   # r11 <- low word (a.lo * b.hi)
    mullw   r12,r6,r9   # r12 <- low word (a.hi * b.lo)
    mullw   r7,r7,r9    # r7 <- low word (a.lo * b.lo)
    add     r6,r11,r12  # add low words from cross term
    add     r6,r6,r10   #     plus high word from low term
    stw     r6,0(r3)    # result.hi <- r6
    stw     r7,4(r3)    # result.lo <- r7
    blr         # return
```

Division

div64.m4: Performs 64-bit division using shift-add algorithm.

```
#  Example A.11
include('stdhdr.s')
############################################################################ #
#  div64
#
#     Performs division of 64 bit operands on a 32 bit machine.
#
#     struct unsigned64
#     {
#       unsigned    hi;
#       unsigned    lo;
#     }
#
#     unsigned64 div64(unsigned64 *rmndr,unsigned64 *dvdnd,unsigned64 *dvsr);
#
#     Input:
#     r3 = pointer to struct unsigned64 quotient
#     r4 = pointer to struct unsigned64 remainder
#     r5 = pointer to struct unsigned64 dividend
#     r6 = pointer to struct unsigned64 divisor
#
#     Output:
#     r3 = quotient.hi
#     r4 = quotient.lo
#     r5 = remainder.hi
#     r6 = remainder.lo
#
          .globl    .div64[PR]
          .csect    .div64[PR]
          stw    r3,8(SP)     # store quotient pointer in link area
          lwz    r3,0(r5)     # r3 <- dividend.hi
          stw    r4,12(SP)    # store remainder pointer in link area
          lwz    r4,4(r5)     # r4 <- dividend.lo
          cmpi    crf5,0,r3,0    # crf5 <- dividend.hi == 0 ??
          lwz    r5,0(r6)     # r5 <- divisor.hi
          cmpi    crf6,0,r4,0    # crf6 <- dividend.lo == 0 ??
          lwz    r6,4(r6)     # r6 <- divisor.lo
          cmpi    crf7,0,r5,0    # crf7 <- divisor.hi == 0 ??
          cmpi    crf1,0,r6,0    # crf1 <- divisor.lo == 0 ??
          crand    cr5_gt,cr1_eq,cr7_eq    # cr5_gt <- (r.lo==0) & (r.hi==0)
          crand    cr5_lt,cr5_eq,cr7_eq    # cr5_lt <- (d.hi==0) & (r.hi==0)
          bt    cr5_gt,divByZero    # handle divide by zero
          bt    cr5_lt,div32    # both divisor and dividend are 32 bit
          cmpl    crf5,0,r3,r5    # crf5 <- cmp dividend.hi, divisor.hi
          cmpl    crf6,0,r4,r6    # crf6 <- cmp dividend.lo, divisor.lo
          blt    crf5,divTooSmall    # handle case: dividend < divisor
          crand    cr0_eq,cr5_eq,cr6_lt    # cr0_eq <- (d.hi==r.hi) &
              ➥(d.lo<r.lo)
          bt    cr0_eq,divTooSmall    # handle dividend < divisor
```

```
        beq    crf7,divSmall    # goto divSmall if divisor.hi == 0
                                 # else continue to divLarge
#######################################################################
#
#     divLarge
#
#     Performs division when dividend and divisor are 64 bit numbers.
#
#     Input:
#     r3 = dividend.hi
#     r4 = dividend.lo
#     r5 = divisor.hi
#     r6 = divisor.lo
#
#     Uses:
#     r4     quotient.lo
#     r5     shift.hi
#     r6     shift.lo
#     r7     -divisor.hi
#     r8     -divisor.lo
#     r9     diff.hi
#     r10    diff.lo
#     r11    dividend.lo
#     r12    scratch
#
#     Output:
#     r3 = quotient.hi
#     r4 = quotient.lo
#     r5 = remainder.hi
#     r6 = remainder.lo
#
#     Notes:
#
#     assumes divisor.hi != 0
#
divLarge:
        nor    r7,r5,r5     # calc ~divisor.hi
        subfic r8,r6,0      # calc -divisor.lo, set CA
        addze  r7,r7        # ~divisor.hi += CA
        or     r6,r3,r3     # shift.lo <- dividend.hi (divisor.hi>0)
        or     r11,r4,r4    # r11 = dividend.lo
        # try to shift ahead, skipping initial uneccessary shifting loops
        cntlz  r12,r5       # find order of divisor.hi
        subfic r3,r12,32    # calc shift = 32 - order
        srw    r5,r6,r12    # shift.hi <- shift ahead of shift.lo
        slw    r6,r6,r3     # shift ahead shift.lo
        srw    r4,r11,r12   # get shifted part of dividend.lo
        or     r6,r6,r4     # add to shift.lo
        slw    r11,r11,r3   # shift ahead dividend.lo
        addi   r12,r12,1    # setup for looping
        mtctr  r12          #
        xor    r3,r3,r3     # clear quotient.hi
        xor    r4,r4,r4     # clear quotient.lo
        b   ldiff    # skip first round of shifts
        .align  6    # align loop to 64-byte boundary
```

```
lshift:
    rlwinm  r5,r5,1,0,30     # shift.hi <<= 1
    rlwimi  r5,r6,1,31,31     # shift.hi[31] = shift.lo[0]
    rlwinm  r6,r6,1,0,30     # shift.lo <<= 1
rlwimi  r6,r11,1,31,31 # shift.lo[31] = dividend.lo[0] rlwinm  r11,r11,1,0,30
➡# dividend.lo <<= 1
    rlwinm  r4,r4,1,0,30     # quotient.lo <<= 1
ldiff:
    addc    r10,r6,r8    # diff.lo = shift.lo-divisor.lo, set CA
    adde.   r9,r5,r7     # diff.hi = shift.hi - divisor.hi + CA
    blt     lloop    # loop if diff < 0
    or      r6,r10,r10    # shift.lo = diff.lo
    or      r5,r9,r9    # shift.hi = diff.hi
    ori     r4,r4,1    # set bit in quotient
lloop:
    bdnz    lshift

        b           divDone           # goto exit code
########################################################################### #
#    divSmall
#
#    Performs division when dividend is 64 bit and divisor is 32 bit.
#
#    Input:
#    r3 = dividend.hi
#    r4 = dividend.lo
#    r5 = divisor.hi
#    r6 = divisor.lo
#
#    Uses:
#    r3    quotient.hi
#    r4    quotient.lo
#    r5    shift.hi
#    r6    shift.lo
#    r7    -divisor.lo
#    r8    diff.lo
#    r9
#    r10   dividend.hi
#    r11   dividend.lo
#    r12   scratch
#
#    Output:
#    r3 = quotient.hi
#    r4 = quotient.lo
#    r5 = remainder.hi
#    r6 = remainder.lo
#
#   Notes:
#
#   assumes divisor.hi == 0
#
divSmall:
    or      r7,r6,r6    # r7 = divisor.lo
    or      r10,r3,r3    # r10 = dividend.hi
    or      r11,r4,r4    # r11 = dividend.lo
    xor     r5,r5,r5    # clear shift.hi
    xor     r6,r6,r6    # clear shift.lo
```

```
        # try to shift ahead, skipping initial uneccessary shifting loops
        cntlz    r12,r7    # find order of divisor.lo
        subfic   r3,r12,32    # calc shift = 32 - order
        srw      r6,r10,r12    # shift.lo <- shift ahead of dividend.hi
        slw      r10,r10,r3    # shift ahead dividend.hi
        srw      r4,r11,r12    # get shifted part of dividend.lo
        or       r10,r10,r4    # add to dividend.hi
        slw      r11,r11,r3    # shift ahead dividend.lo
        addi     r12,r12,33    # setup for looping
        mtctr    r12    #
        xor      r3,r3,r3    # clear quotient.hi
        xor      r4,r4,r4    # clear quotient.lo
        b        sdiff    # skip first round of shifting


        .align  6    # align loop to 64-byte boundary
sshift:
        rlwinm   r6,r6,1,0,30    # shift.lo <<= 1
rlwimi   r6,r10,1,31,31 # shift.lo[31] = dividend.hi[0] rlwinm   r10,r10,1,0,30
➡# dividend.hi <<= 1
rlwimi   r10,r11,1,31,31 # dividend.hi[31] = dividend.lo[0] rlwinm
➡r11,r11,1,0,30 # dividend.lo <<= 1
        rlwinm   r3,r3,1,0,30    # quotient.hi <<= 1
        rlwimi   r3,r4,1,31,31    # quotient.hi[31] = quotient.lo[0]
        rlwinm   r4,r4,1,0,30    # quotient.lo <<= 1
sdiff:
        subf.    r8,r7,r6    # diff.lo = shift.lo - divisor.lo
        blt      sloop    # loop if diff < 0
        or       r6,r8,r8    # shift.lo = diff.lo
        ori      r4,r4,1    # set bit in quotient
sloop:
        bdnz     sshift
        b        divDone    # goto exit code
######################################################################## #
#    div32
#
#    Performs division when both dividend and divisor are 32 bit numbers.
#
#    Input:
#    r3 = dividend.hi
#    r4 = dividend.lo
#    r5 = divisor.hi
#    r6 = divisor.lo
#
#    Uses:
#    r3    quotient.hi
#    r4    quotient.lo
#    r5 = remainder.hi
#    r6 = remainder.lo
#    r7    product of quotient.lo and divisor.lo
#
#    Output:
#    r3 = quotient.hi (always zero)
#    r4 = quotient.lo
#    r5 = remainder.hi (always zero)
#    r6 = remainder.lo
#
```

```
div32:
        divwu    r3,r4,r6     # r3 <- quotient
        mullw    r7,r6,r3     # r7 <- r6 * int(r4 / r6)
        subf     r6,r7,r4     # r6 <- remainder.lo
        mr    r4,r3    # r4 <- quotient.lo
        li    r3,0    # r3 <- quotient.hi (0)
        li    r5,0    # r5 <- remainder.hi (0)
        b     divDone    # goto exit code
####################################################################### #
#    divByZero
#
#    Handles attempted division by zero.
#
#    Input:
#    r3 = dividend.hi
#    r4 = dividend.lo
#    r5 = divisor.hi
#    r6 = divisor.lo
#
#    Output:
#    r3 = quotient.hi (always -1)
#    r4 = quotient.lo (always -1)
#    r5 = remainder.hi (always -1)
#    r6 = remainder.lo (always -1)
#
divByZero:
        addi     r3,r0,-1    # r3 <- -1
        addi     r4,r0,-1    # r4 <- -1
        addi     r5,r0,-1    # r5 <- -1
        addi     r6,r0,-1    # r6 <- -1
        b     divDone    # goto exit code
####################################################################### #
#    divTooSmall
#
#    Handles division when the divisor is greater than the dividend.
#
#    Input:
#    r3 = dividend.hi
#    r4 = dividend.lo
#    r5 = divisor.hi
#    r6 = divisor.lo
#
#    Output:
#    r3 = quotient.hi (always zero)
#    r4 = quotient.lo (always zero)
#    r5 = remainder.hi (always dividend.hi)
#    r6 = remainder.lo (always dividend.lo)
#
divTooSmall:
        mr    r5,r3    # remainder.hi <- dividend.hi
        mr    r6,r4    # remainder.lo <- dividend.lo
        li    r3,0    # quotient.hi <- 0
        li    r4,0    # quotient.lo <- 0
        b     divDone    # goto exit code
####################################################################### #
#    divDone
#
```

```
#       Returns from div64.
#
#       Input:
#       r3 = quotient.hi
#       r4 = quotient.lo
#       r5 = remainder.hi
#       r6 = remainder.lo
#
#       8(SP)     pointer to struct unsigned64 quotient
#       12(SP)    pointer to struct unsigned64 remainder
#
#       Returns:
#       r3 = quotient.hi (C return value)
#       r4 = quotient.lo
#       r5 = remainder.hi
#       r6 = remainder.lo
#
divDone:
        lwz     r7,8(SP)        # r7 <- &Q
        lwz     r8,12(SP)       # r8 <- &R
        stw     r3,0(r7)        # Q.hi <- quotient.hi
        stw     r4,4(r7)        # Q.lo <- quotient.lo
        stw     r5,0(r8)        # R.hi <- remainder.hi
        stw     r6,4(r8)        # R.lo <- remainder.lo
        blr             # return
```

Shifts

EXAMPLE A.12.

shift64.m4: Performs shifts on 64-bit numbers.

```
#       Example A.12
include('stdhdr.s')
######################################################################## #
#       shr64
#
#       Performs right shifts on 64 bit numbers.
#
#       unsigned64 shr64(unsigned64 *val, unsigned n)
#
        .globl    .shr64[PR]
        .csect    .shr64[PR]
        lwz     r11,4(r4)       # r11 <- a.lo
        subfic  r6,r5,32        # r6 <- 32 - n
        lwz     r10,0(r4)       # r10 <- a.hi
        addi    r7,r5,-32       # r7 <- n - 32
        srw     r11,r11,r5      # result.lo <- val.lo >> n
        slw     r8,r10,r6       # tmp1 <- val.hi << (32 - n)
        srw     r9,r10,r7       # tmp2 <- val.hi >> (n - 32)
        srw     r10,r10,r5      # result.hi <- val.hi >> n
```

```
        or     r11,r11,r8   # result.lo |= tmp1
        or     r11,r11,r9   # result.lo |= tmp2
        stw    r10,0(r3)    # result.hi <- r10
        stw    r11,4(r3)    # result.lo <- r11
        mr     r3,r10    # r3 <- result.hi
        blr          # return
################################################################### #
#    sh164
#
#    Performs left shifts on 64 bit numbers.
#
#    unsigned64 sh164(unsigned64 *val, unsigned n)
#

        .globl   .sh164[PR]
        .csect   .sh164[PR]
        lwz    r10,0(r4)    # r10 = a.hi
        subfic r6,r5,32     # r6 = 32 - n
        lwz    r11,4(r4)    # r11 = a.lo
        addi   r7,r5,-32    # r7 = n - 32
        slw    r10,r10,r5   # result.hi = val.hi << n
        srw    r8,r11,r6    # tmp1 = val.lo >> (32 - n)
        slw    r9,r11,r7    # tmp2 = val.lo << (n - 32)
        slw    r11,r11,r5   # result.lo = val.lo << n
        or     r10,r10,r8   # result.hi |= tmp1
        or     r10,r10,r9   # result.hi |= tmp2
        stw    r10,0(r3)    # result.hi = r10
        stw    r11,4(r3)    # result.lo = r11
        blr          # return
```

String Operations

Example A.13 shows the code for a simple string hash. The hash function simply XORs each character into an unsigned word, looping through the word byte-by-byte.

The code for a Boyer-Moore type string search is shown in Example A.14. Notice that this example contains subfunctions, unlike most of the examples, and that the interfaces to these functions are tailored to the exact needs of their caller (and would not be callable from a compiled language as they do not follow the subroutine calling conventions). This is one of the ways in which well-written assembly language code can outperform compiled languages—the programmer can use exact knowledge of the algorithm and the machine state to make the function calls as efficient as possible.

String Hash

EXAMPLE A.13.

strhash.m4: Performs simple xor hash of a string.

```
#     Example A.13
include('stdhdr.s')
############################################################################ #
#     strhash
#
#     Performs simple xor hash for null terminated data.
#
#     Callable from C as:
#
#         unsigned strhash(char *str);
#
#     Expects
#
#         r3      string pointer
#
#     Uses
#
#         r3      string pointer
#         r4      hash key
#         r5      string character
#         r6      shift counter
#         crf0
#
#     Returns
#
#         r3      hash value
#
        .csect    .strhash[PR]
        .globl    .strhash[PR]

    lbz     r5,0(r3)    # get first character
    xor     r4,r4,r4    # r4 <- 0 (initial hash value)
    xor     r6,r6,r6    # r6 <- 0 (initial shift count)
loop:
    cmpi    crf0,0,r5,0    # crf0 <- is character NULL ??
    rlwnm    r5,r5,r6,0,31    # shift character left
    xor     r4,r4,r5    # xor into hash value
    lbzu    r5,1(r3)    # load next byte
    addi    r6,r6,8     # next character shift count
    bne     loop    # loop if character was not NULL
    mr      r3,r4    # return hash value
    blr        # return
```

Boyer-Moore String Search

EXAMPLE A.14.

strsrch.m4: Peforms a Boyer-Moore style string search.

```
#  Example A.14
include('stdhdr.s')
define('SSIZE','(56 + 12)')
define('CBSIZE',16)


##################################################################### #
#    strsrch
#
#    Performs Boyer-Moore style string search.
#
#    char *strsrch(char *key, char *buff, int bufflen);
#
#    If key is NULL, the previous key will be reused to search buff, and
#    in this case the storage containing the key string should not be
#    altered between calls.
#
#    Expects
#
#        r3    address of string to search for (target)
#        r4    address of string to search (source)
#        r5    length of source string
#
#    Uses
#
#        r0    scratch
#        r3    address of target string
#        r4    pointer into source string
#        r5    pointer past end of source string
#        r6    length of target string
#        r7    scratch ptr
#        r8    scratch ptr
#        r9
#        r10   work space for target string
#        r11   work space for search string
#        r12   address of skip table
#

#  Returns
#    r3    address of first match
#
    .csect    .strsrch[PR]
    .globl    .strsrch[PR]
    mflr   r0     # r0 <- return address
    stw    r0,8(SP)    # save in link area
    stwu   SP,-(SSIZE)(SP) # create stack frame and back chain
    lwz    r12,T.data(RTOC)   # r12 <- address of skip table
    .using _strsrch[RW],r12    # use r12 as implicit base
             #  for data csect access
    cmpi   cr0,0,r3,0   # is target pointer NULL?
```

```
        bz    ss_ldptr   # if so, use saved target info
                  # else
        bl    rsttbl    # clear skip table
        bl    bldtbl    # build skip table
        stw   r3,_tgtptr   # save target pointer
        stw   r6,_tgtlen   # save target length
        b   ss_srch   # start searching
ss_ldptr:
        lwz   r3,_tgtptr   # reload saved target pointer
        lwz   r6,_tgtlen   # reload saved target length
ss_srch:
        add   r5,r5,r4   # calculate address past end of source
        xor   r11,r11,r11   # set last character compared to NULL
        add   r4,r6,r4   # set initial source pointer

ss_loop:
        cmp   cr0,0,r4,r5   # is source pointer past end of string??
        bgt   ss_fail    # if so, goto failure exit
        bl    strrncmp   # do string compare
        beq   ss_cmp   # if found, goto ss_cmp
        lbzx   r0,r11,r12   # get skip table value for character
        subf   r0,r0,r6   # calculate skip ahead in source
        add   r7,r8,r0   # calculate skip ahead target address
        cmp   cr0,0,r7,r4   # compare skip and next addresses
        ble   ss_nxt   # if next >= skip, goto ss_nxt
        mr   r4,r7   # use skip address
ss_nxt:
        addi   r4,r4,1   # use next address
        b   ss_loop   # loop
ss_fail:
        xor   r3,r3,r3   # not found, return NULL
        b   ss_done
ss_cmp:
        mr   r3,r8   # return pointer to matched string
ss_done:
        addi   SP,SP,SSIZE   # destroy stack frame
        lwz   r0,8(SP)   # get the return address
        mtlr   r0   # LR <- return address
        blr          # return
######################################################################## #
#  strrncmp - string reverse n-byte compare (right to left)

#
#    Expects
#
#        r3    starting address of target string (leftmost byte)
#        r4    address past end of source string (past rightmost byte)
#        r6    length to compare
#
#    Uses
#
#        r7    pointer into target string
#        r8    pointer into source string
#        r10   data from target string
#        r11   data from source string
#        ctr
#        cr0
```

```
#
#     Returns
#
#         r8      address of last character compared in source string
#         r11     last character compared in source string
#         cr0     result of last character compare
#
#     Notes
#
#     Uses load byte instructions rather than using load word with
#     loop unrolling in order to avoid alignment problems.  Detecting
#     and handling all the alignment cases will give significant overhead
#     with few payoffs because many times the miscompare will happen
#     within the first few bytes.
#
strrncmp:
        mtctr   r6

        add     r7,r6,r3
        mr      r8,r4
sc_loop:
        lbzu    r10,-1(r7)    # get character from target string
        lbzu    r11,-1(r8)    # get character from source string
        cmp     cr0,0,r10,r11    # compare characters
        bdnzt   eq,sc_loop    # exit if not equal or compared n bytes
        blr           # return
######################################################################### #
#     bldtbl
#
#     Builds the skip table for the target string
#
#     Expects
#         r3      address of target string
#         r12     address of skip table
#
#     Uses
#         r6      length of target string
#         r7      current character of target string
#         r10     current word buffer for target string
#         cr0
#
#     Returns
#         r6      length of target string
#
#     Notes
#

#     Due to instruction ordering, the length in r6 is always
#     incremented before testing for the terminating NULL.  Thus
#     the length is decremented before returning.  Also note that
#     the count is stored before the test for the NULL, so the
#     value in the table for a character is its offset plus one.
#
bldtbl:
        xor     r6,r6,r6    # r6 <- 0
bt_loop:
        lwzx    r10,r3,r6    # load next 4 chars of target
```

```
rlwinm. r7,r10,8,24,31  # r0 <- first char, set cr0 addi    r6,r6,1    #
➥increment the length
        stbx    r6,r7,r12   # store count into skip table
        bz    bt_done   # done if it's NULL
rlwinm. r7,r10,16,24,31 # r0 <- second char, set cr0 addi    r6,r6,1    #
➥increment the length
        stbx    r6,r7,r12   # store count into skip table
        bz    bt_done   # done if it's NULL
rlwinm. r7,r10,24,24,31 # r0 <- third char, set cr0 addi    r6,r6,1    #
➥increment the length
        stbx    r6,r7,r12   # store count into skip table
        bz    bt_done   # done if it's NULL
        andi.   r7,r10,0xFF   # r0 <- fourth char, set cr0
        addi    r6,r6,1   # increment the length
        stbx    r6,r7,r12   # store count into skip table
        bz    bt_done   # done if it's NULL

        b    bt_loop        # loop until we find NULL
bt_done:
        addi    r6,r6,-1        # decrement the length
        blr                    # return
#################################################################### #
#     rsttbl
#
#     Resets the skip table to contain all zeroes.
#
#     Expects
#       r12    table address
#
#     Uses
#       r0        scratch
#       ctr    loop count
#
#     Notes
#
#       Uses the data cache block zero (dcbz) instruction for performance.
#
rsttbl:
        li    r0,256/CBSIZE   # calc number of loops
        mtctr    r0    #   and place in CTR
        mr    r0,r12   # save table address
rt_loop:
        dcbz    0,r12    # clear cache block to zeroes
        addi    r12,r12,CBSIZE    # calc next block
        bdnz    rt_loop   # and loop until table reset

    mr    r12,r0   # restore table addr to r12
    blr        # return
#
#   Data segment and TOC
#
    .csect  _strsrch[RW]
    .space  256   # skip table
_tgtptr:
    .long    0    # pointer to last target string
```

```
_tgtlen:
      .long    0     # length of last target string
      .toc
T.data:   .tc    _strsrch[TC], _strsrch[RW]
```

Matrix Multiplication

Example A.15 shows the code for a matrix multiply function. The matrices consist of single-precision floating-point numbers and may be any size.

EXAMPLE A.15.

mxmul.m4: Performs matrix multiplication of two single-precision matrices.

```
#   Example A.15
include('stdhdr.s')
########################################################################
#
#     mxmul
#
#     Performs matrix multiplication.
#
#     Input
#         r3    h
#         r4    n
#         r5    w (stride for b)
#         r6    address of A (n x h)
#         r7    address of B (w x n)
#         r8    address of R (w x h)
#     Uses
#         r0    scratch
#         r3    h
#         r4    n
#         r5    size of row of B in bytes (w * 4) [Brow]
#         r6    size of row of A in bytes (n * 4) [Arow]
#         r7    ptr before start of B (&B - w * 4) [Btop]
#         r8
#         r9    ptr into A [Aptr]
#         r10   ptr into B [Bptr]
#         r11   ptr into R [Rptr]
#         r12   ptr to last element of R [Rend]
#         r13   ptr to last element of B [Bend]
#         r14   ptr to top of next column in B [Bnxt]
#         r15
#
#         f1    fp accumulator
#         f2    A term 1
#         f3    B term 1
#         f4    A term 2
#         f5    B term 2
```

```
#    f6    A term 3
#    f7    B term 3
#
    .csect   .mxmul[PR]
    .globl   .mxmul[PR]
    rlwimi  r5,r5,2,0,31    # r5 <- Brow
    addi    r9,r6,-4     # r9 <- Atop (&A - 4)
    rlwimi  r6,r4,2,0,31    # r6 <- Arow
    addi    r11,r8,-4    # r11 <- Rtop
    mullw   r0,r3,r5     # r0 <- size of R (h * w * 4)
    add     r12,r8,r0    # r12 <- Rend + 4 (past end)
    addi    r12,r12,-4   # r12 <- Rend
    mullw   r0,r4,r5     # r0 <- size of B (n * w * 4)
    add     r13,r7,r0    # r13 <- Bend + 4 (past end)
    addi    r13,r13,-4   # r13 <- Bend
    subf    r7,r5,r7     # r7 <- Btop (&B - Brow)
    or      r10,r7,r7    # r10 <- Btop
next:
    addi    r14,r10,4    # Bnxt <- Bptr + 4
    fsub    f1,f1,f1     # clear f1
    mtctr   r4      # ctr <- number of terms to mult-add
loop:
    lfsu    f2,4(r9)     # f2 <- A term, Aptr <- addr
    lfsux   f3,r10,r5    # f3 <- B term, Bptr <- addr
    fmadds  f1,f2,f3,f1    # f1 <- f1 + (A term * B term)
    bdnz    loop
    stfsu   f1,4(r11)    # store result term into R
    cmp   cr0,1,r12,r11   # is Rptr == Rend ??
    bz    done    #   - if so, we're done,
          #     else...
    cmp   cr0,1,r13,r10   # is Bptr == Bend ??
    bz    resetB   #   - if so, reset Bptr to Btop,
          #     else...
    or    r10,r14,r14    # Bptr <- Bnxt
    subf    r9,r6,r9    # reset Aptr (Aptr -= Arow)
    b    next    # do next term
resetB:
    or    r10,r7,r7    # Bptr <- Btop
    b    next    # do next term
done:
    blr       # return
```

B

Detailed Instruction Set Reference

In this section, we give detailed descriptions of each instruction in the PowerPC instruction set. The notation used throughout this chapter is consistent with the rest of the book. (See Table B.1.)

Table B.1. Notations used in this book.

Notation	Description
(RT)	Register reference. This means the contents of RT. Thus, (R2) means the data contained in register R2.
[x]	Memory reference. This means the memory location addressed by the value x.
<-, [la]	Assignment statements. The object on the left of the assignment symbol is given the value of the object on the right side of the symbol.
<<	Shift left. A<<B means that A is shifted left by B bits.
>>	Shift right. A>>B means that A is shifted right by B bits.
<	Signed less than. This means less than and uses a signed comparison. Thus, 0×FFFF < 0×0000 (−1 < 0).
u<	Unsigned less than. This means less than and uses an unsigned comparison. Thus, 0×0000 u<0×FFFF (0 u< 65,535).
>	Signed greater than. This means greater than and uses a signed comparison. Thus, 0×0000 > 0×FFFF (0 > −1).
u>	Unsigned greater than. This means greater than and uses an unsigned comparison. Thus, 0×FFFF u> 0×0000 (65,535 u> 0).
==	Equal to. Thus, 0×0000 == 0×0000 (0 == 0).
!=	Not equal to. Thus, 0×0000 != 0×FFFF (0 != −1).
||	Concatenate. Thus, 0×F || 0×D means 0×FD.
&	Boolean AND. 0×F55F & 0×5FAF = 0×550F.
|	Boolean OR. 0×F55F | 0×5FAF = 0×FFFF.
$\overline{A}$	Boolean NOT. $\overline{A}$ means not A. So $\overline{A}$ | = 0b1 and $\overline{A}$ & A = 0b0.
$\overline{C}$	Boolean XOR. Thus, $\overline{A} \oplus A$ = 0b1 and A $\oplus$ A = 0b0.
$\overline{E}$	Boolean equivalence. Thus, $\overline{A} \equiv A$ = 0b0 and A $\equiv$ A = 0b1.
sign_ext()	Sign extend. sign_ext(0×FF) = 0×FFFF, and sign_ext(0×7F) = 0×007F.
$Rn_{a:b}$	Subfield. Subscripts used in this fashion mean a subfield of the contents of Rn. Thus, $Rn_{0:8}$ means bits 0 through 8 of the register Rn.
aA	Repeat. This is a repeat symbol. aA means to concatenate a copies of A.
+	Addition. 0×0001 + 0×F001 = 0×F002.
−	Subtraction. 0×0444 − 0×0434 = 0×0010.

Notation	Description
*, x	Multiplication. 0×0002 * 0×0004 = 0×0008.
%	Modulo. This means modulo or remainder. A%B means the remainder if you divide A by B.
÷	Divide. A/B means A divided by B.
?:	Conditional operator. An if then else structure. The statement A?B:C takes the value of B if A evaluates to true; otherwise, it takes the value of C.

Throughout this reference, we use bit values associated with the 32-bit PowerPC architecture except for those instructions that are only available on 64-bit implementations. When no bit numbering is given, either a note is made for 64-bit implementations showing the appropriate bit numbering, or the 64-bit operation only operates on the low-order 32-bits (bits 32-63) of the operands. In the latter case, the bit numbering for 64-bit implementations can be obtained by adding 32 to each bit number.

Fields which are reserved are marked with a forward slash (/). These fields should always be set to 0.

add[o][.]
integer add instruction

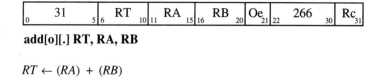

| 0 | 31 | 5 | 6 | RT | 10 | 11 | RA | 15 | 16 | RB | 20 | 21 | Oe | 22 | 266 | 30 | Rc | 31 |

add[o][.] RT, RA, RB

$RT \leftarrow (RA) + (RB)$

The add instruction stores the sum of RA and RB into RT.

If the addo[.] form of the instruction is used, then the overflow and summary overflow bits of the XER are set if overflow occurs. The overflow bit is cleared if overflow does not occur.

If the add[o]. form of the instruction is used, then CR0 is updated.

addc[o][.]
integer add carrying instruction

| 0 | 31 | 5 | 6 | RT | 10 | 11 | RA | 15 | 16 | RB | 20 | 21 | Oe | 22 | 10 | 30 | Rc | 31 |

addc[o][.] RT, RA, RB

$RT \leftarrow (RA) + (RB)$

The addc instruction stores the sum of RA and RB into RT. The XERCA bit is set to the carry-out of the addition.

If the addco[.] form of the instruction is used, then the overflow and summary overflow bits of the XER are set if overflow occurs. The overflow bit of the XER is cleared if overflow does not occur.

If the addc[o]. form of the instruction is used, then CR0 is updated.

adde[o][.]
integer add extended

0	31	5	6	RT	10	11	RA	15	16	RB	20	21	Oe	22	138	30	Rc	31

adde[o][.] RT, RA, RB

$$RT \leftarrow (RA) + (RB) + XER_{CA}$$

The add extended instruction performs an add with the carry bit in the XER as an implicit operand. Thus RT is loaded with the sum of RA, RB and the carry bit in the XER. The XERCA bit is set by the carry out of this addition.

If the addeo[.] form of the instruction is used, then the overflow and summary overflow bits of the XER are set if overflow occurs. The overflow bit of the XER is cleared if overflow does not occur.

If the adde[o]. form of the instruction is used, then CR0 is updated.

addi
integer add immediate

0	14	5	6	RT	10	11	RA	15	16	si	31

addi[.] RT, RA, si

$$RT \leftarrow (RA) + \left({}^{16}si_{16} \parallel si_{16.\,31} \right)$$

The add immediate instructions perform an add of RA to the sign extended 16-bit immediate field, placing the result into RT.

If the addi form of the instruction is used with RA = 0, then 0 is used instead of the contents of RA. Thus regardless of the contents of r0, addi r1, r0, 4 would load the constant 4 into r1 (see the li instruction).

addic[.]
integer add immediate carrying

6	Rc	RT	RA	si
0 4	5 6	10 11	15 16	31

addic[.] RT, TA, si

$$RT \leftarrow (RA) + \left({}^{16}si_{16} \parallel si_{16, 31} \right)$$

The add immediate instructions perform an add of RA to the sign extended 16-bit immediate field, placing the result into RT. The XERCA bit is updated with the carry out of the addition.

If the addic. form of the instruction is used, then CR0 is updated.

addis
integer add immediate shifted

15	RT	RA	si
0 5 6	10 11	15 16	31

addis RT, RA, si

$$RT \leftarrow (RA) + \left(si \parallel {}^{16}0 \right)$$

The add immediate shifted instruction performs an addition of RA to the immediate field left shifted by 16 bit (that is the immediate field with 16 zeros concatenated to the right), placing the result into RT.

If the addis instruction is used with RA = 0, then 0 is used instead of the contents of RA. Thus regardless of the contents of RA, addis r1, r0, 4 would load the constant 4∥160 = 262,144 into r1 (see the lis instruction).

addme[o][.]
integer add extended to minus one

31	RT	RA	/	Oe	234	Rc
0 5 6	10 11	15 16	20	21 22	30	31

addme[o][.] RT, RA

$$RT \leftarrow (RA) + XER_{CA} - 1$$

The add extended to minus one instruction performs an add with the carry bit in the XER as an implicit operand. Thus RT is loaded with the sum of RA , -1 and XERCA. The XERCA bit is set by the carry out of this addition.

If the addmeo[.] form of the instruction is used, then the overflow and summary overflow bits of the XER are set if overflow occurs, The overflow bit of the XER is cleared if overflow does not occur.

If the addme[o]. form of the instruction is used, then CR0 is updated.

addze[o][.]
integer add extended to zero

| 0 | 31 | 5 6 | RT | 10 11 | RA | 15 16 | / | 20 | Oe 21 22 | 202 | 30 | Rc 31 |

addze[o][.] RT, RA, RB

$RT \leftarrow (RA) + XER_{CA}$

The add extended to zero instruction performs an add with the carry bit in the XER as an implicit operand. Thus RT is loaded with the sum of RA and XERCA. The XERCA bit is set by the carry out of this addition.

If the addzeo[.] form of the instruction is used, then the overflow and summary overflow bits of the XER are set if overflow occurs. The overflow bit of the XER is cleared if overflow does not occur.

If the addze[o]. form of the instruction is used, then CR0 is updated.

and[.]
logical AND

| 0 | 31 | 5 6 | RA | 10 11 | RT | 15 16 | RB | 20 21 | 28 | 30 | Rc 31 |

and[.] RT, RA, RB

$RT \leftarrow (RA) \wedge (RB)$

The and[.] instruction performs a logical AND of register RA with register RB. The result of this is then stored into register RT.

If the Rc bit is set (and.), then CR0 is updated.

andc[.]
logical AND with compliment

| 0 | 31 | 5 6 | RA | 10 11 | RT | 15 16 | RB | 20 21 | 60 | 30 | Rc 31 |

andc[.] RT, RA, RB

$RT \leftarrow (RA) \wedge (\overline{RB})$

The andc[.] instruction performs a logical AND of register RA with the logical negation of register RB. The result of this is then stored into register RT.

If the Rc bit is set (andc.), then CR0 is updated.

andi.
logical AND immediate

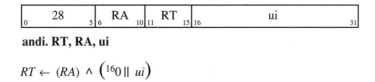

andi. RT, RA, ui

$$RT \leftarrow (RA) \wedge \left(^{16}0 \parallel ui\right)$$

The andi. instruction performs a logical AND of the low-order 16 bits of the contents of register RA with the immediate field ui; the high-order 16 bits of RA are unchanged. The result of this is then stored into register RT.

For this instruction, CR0 is always updated.

andis.
logical AND shifted immediate

andis. RT, RA, ui

$$RT \leftarrow (RA) \wedge \left(ui \parallel {}^{16}0\right)$$

The andis. instruction performs a logical AND register RA with the immediate field ui. The result of this is then stored into register RT.

For this instruction, CR0 is always updated.

b[l]
unconditional branch

18		Li		AA	LK
0	5 6		29	30	31

b[l][a] target_addr

$$\textbf{b[l]a: } PC \leftarrow \left(^{6}Li_{6} \parallel Li_{6,\,29} \parallel {}^{2}0\right)$$

$$\textbf{b[l]: } PC \leftarrow PC + \left(^{6}Li_{6} \parallel Li_{6,\,29} \parallel {}^{2}0\right)$$

b[l]a: b[l]: The unconditional branch instruction transfers control to the instruction at the target address (target_addr). Note that target_addr must be divisible by four (that is quad-word aligned).

The absolute unconditional branch (b[l]a) instructions uses the sign extended immediate field of the instruction (Li) with two binary zeros appended to it as the target address.

The relative unconditional branch (b[l]) instruction current value of the program counter (PC) added to the sign extended immediate field of the instruction (Li) with two binary zeros appended to it as the target address.

If the bl[a] form of the instruction is used, then the link register is loaded with the old value of the PC added to 4 (that is the address of the branch, plus four).

bc[l][a]
conditional branch

16	BO	BI	BD	AA	LK
0 5	6 10	11 15	16 29	30	31

bc[l][a] BO, BI, target_addr

bc[l]a: $PC \leftarrow \left({}^{16}BD_{16} \parallel BD_{16, 29} \parallel {}^{2}0\right)$ **iff condition**

bc[l]: $PC \leftarrow PC + \left({}^{16}BD_{16} \parallel BD_{16, 29} \parallel {}^{2}0\right)$ **iff condition**

bc[l]a: bc[l]: The conditional branch instruction may transfer control to the instruction at the target address (target_addr). Note that target_addr must be divisible by four (that is quad-word aligned). Control is transfered only if some condition is met. The BO field defines the condition which must be met (see Table B.2). There are many extended mnemonics associated with this instruction which are used to specify the BO and BI fields implicitly (see Tables B.3 and B.4).

The absolute conditional branch (bc[l]a) instruction uses the sign extended immediate field of the instruction (BD) with two binary zeros appended to it as the target address.

The relative conditional branch (bc[l]) instruction uses the current value of the program counter (PC) added to the sign extended immediate field of the instruction (BD) with two binary zeros appended to it as the target address.

If the bcl[a] form of the instruction is used, then the link register is loaded with the old value of the PC added to 4 (that is the address of the branch, plus four).

Table B.2. BO field encodings for branch conditional, branch conditional to count, and branch conditional to link instructions.

encoding[a]	definition
0b0000y[b]	Decrement the count register; then branch if the new value in the count register is not 0, and the condition[c] is false.

encoding[a]	definition
0b0001y	Decrement the count register; then branch if the new value in the count register is 0, and the condition is false.
0b0010y	Branch if the condition is false.
0b0100y	Decrement the count register; then branch if the new value in the count register is not 0, and the condition is true.
0b0101y	Decrement the count register; then branch if the new value in the count register is 0, and the condition is true.
0b0110y	Branch if the condition is true.
0b1000y	Decrement the count register, then branch if the new value in the count register is not 0.
0b1001y	Decrement the count register, then branch if the new value in the count register is 0.
0b10100	Branch always.

a. These are the only valid BO field encodings.

b. The y-bit is the bit which reverses the default branch prediction.

c. The condition is determined by the bit in the condition register specified in the BI field. A value of 0 is a false condition while a value of one is a true condition.

Table B.3. Extended mnemonics for the different BO field encodings.

Branch Semantics (X^a)	(bc) relative	Target address type (bca) absolute	(bclr) to link	(bcctr) to count
branch unconditionally	—	—	blr[l]a	bctr[l]
branch if condition true (t)	bt[l]	bt[l]a	btlr[l]	btctr[l]
branch if condition false (f)	bf[l]	bf[l]a	bflr[l]	bfctr[l]
decrement count and branch if count non-zero (dnz)	bdnz[l]	bdnz[l]a	bdnzlr[l]	—
decrement count and branch if count zero (dz)	bdz[l]	bdz[l]a	bdzlr[l]	—

continues

Table B.3. continued

Branch Semantics (X[a])	(bc) relative	(bca) absolute	(bclr) to link	(bcctr) to count
		Target address type		
decrement count and branch if count non-zero and condition true (dnzt)	bdnzt[l]	bdnzt[l]a	bdnztlr[l]	—
decrement count and branch if count non-zero and condition false (dznf)	bdnzf[l]	bdnzf[l]a	bdnzflr[l]	—
decrement count and branch if count zero and condition true (dzt)	bdzt[l]	bdzt[l]a	bdztlr[l]	—
decrement count and branch if count non-zero and condition false (dzf)	bdzf[l]	bdzf[l]a	bdzflr[l]	—

a.   The building block which is used to form the mnemonic is shown in parentheses beside the semantic description. The mnemonic for the branch is built out of three components: b[CR code][target code][1] or b[CR code][1][target code].

Table B.4. Extended mnemonics for condition register bit encodings.

Branch Semantics (X[a])	(bc) relative	(bca) absolute	(bclr) to link	(bcctr) to count
		Target address type		
branch if less than (lt)	blt[l]	nlt[l]a	bltlr[l]	bltctr[l]
branch if less than or equal to (le)	ble[l]	ble[l]a	blelr[l]	blectr[l]
branch if greater than or equal to (ge)	bge[l]	bge[l]a	bgelr[l]	bgectr[l]
branch if greater than (gt)	bgt[l]	bgt[l]a	bgtlr[l]	bgctr[l]
branch if not less than (nl)	bnl[l]	bnl[l]a	bnllr[l]	bnlctr[l]

Branch Semantics (X^a)	(bc) relative	(bca) absolute	(bclr) to link	(bcctr) to count
		Target address type		
branch if not equal to (ne)	bne[l]	bne[l]a	bnelr[l]	bnectr[l]
branch if not greater than (ng)	bng[l]	bng[l]a	bnglr[l]	bngctr[l]
branch if summary overflow (so)	bso[l]	bso[l]a	bsolr[l]	bsoctr[l]
branch if not summary overflow (ns)	bns[l]	bns[l]a	bnslr[l]	bnsctr[l]
branch if unordered (see floating-point compare instructions below) (un)	bun[l]	bun[l]a	bunlr[l]	bunctr[l]
branch if not unordered (see floating-point compare instructions below) (nu)	bnu[l]	bnu[l]a	bnulr[l]	bnuctr[l]

a. The building block which is used to form the mnemonic is shown in parentheses beside the semantic description. The mnemonic for the branch is built out of three components: b[CR code][target code] [l].

bcctr[l]
conditional branch to count register

19	BO	BI	/	528	LK
0 5	6 10	11 15	16 20	21 30	31

bcctr[l] BO, BI

bcctr[l]: $PC \leftarrow CTR_{0,29} \parallel {}^2 0$ **iff condition**

The conditional branch to count register instruction may transfer control to the instruction at the address contained in the count register. Control is transfered only if some condition is met. The BO field defines the condition which must be met (see Table B.2). There are many extended mnemonics associated with this instruction which are used to specify the BO and BI fields implicitly (see Tables B.3 and B.4). Note that settings of the BO field which correspond to type branches are not valid with this instruction (see Tables B.2 and B.3).

If the bcctrl form of the instruction is used, then the link register is loaded with the old value of the PC added to 4 (that is the address of the branch, plus four).

bclr[l]
conditional branch to link register

19		BO		BI		/		16		LK
0	5	6	10 11		15 16		20 21		30	31

bclr[l] BO, BI

bclr[l]: $PC \leftarrow LR_{0, 29} \parallel {}^{2}0$ **iff condition**

The conditional branch to link register instruction may transfer control to the instruction at the address contained in the link register. Control is transfered only if some condition is met. The BO field defines the condition which must be met (see Table B.2). There are many extended mnemonics associated with this instruction which are used to specify the BO and BI fields implicitly (see Tables B.3 and B.4).

If the bclrl form of the instruction is used, then the link register is loaded with the old value of the PC added to 4 (that is the address of the branch, plus four).

clrldi[.]
clear left doubleword immediate

30		RA		RT		0		n		0	0	Rc
0	5	6	10 11		15 16		20 21		26 27	29	30	31

clrldi[.] RT, RA, n (n<64)

$$RT \leftarrow {}^{n}0 \parallel RA_{n, 63}$$

The clrldi[.] instruction clears the n leftmost bits of RA and places the result in RT. This is an extended mnemonic for the rotate left doubleword immediate and clear left (rldicl[.]) instruction:

rldicl[.] RT, RA, 0, n

If the record bit is set (clrldi.), then CR0 is updated.

This instruction is only defined for 64-bit implementations.

clrlsldi[.]
clear left and shift left doubleword immediate

0	30	5	6	RA	10	11	RT	15	16	$n_{1:5}$	20	21	b-n	26	27	2	29	n_0	30	Rc	31

clrlsldi[.] RT, RA, b, n (*n   b* < 64)

$$RT \leftarrow {}^{b-n}0 \parallel RA_{b,\,63} \parallel {}^{n}0$$

The clrlsldi[.] instruction clears the b leftmost bits of RA, then left shifts that by n bits and places the result in RT. This is an extended mnemonic for the rotate left doubleword immediate and clear (rldic[.]) instruction:

rldic[.] RT, RA, n, b-n

If the record bit is set (clrlsldi.), then CR0 is updated.

This instruction is only defined for 64-bit implementations.

clrlslwi[.]
clear left and shift left word immediate

0	21	5	6	RA	10	11	RT	15	16	n	20	21	b-n	25	26	31-n	30	Rc	31

clrlslwi[.] RT, RA, b, n ($n \le b$ < 32)

$$RT \leftarrow {}^{b-n}0 \parallel RA_{b,\,31} \parallel {}^{n}0$$

The clrlslwi[.] instruction clears the b leftmost bits of RA, then left shifts that by n bits and places the result in RT. This is an extended mnemonic for the rotate left word immediate then AND with mask (rlwinm[.]) instruction:

rlwinm[.] RT, RA, n, b-n, 31-n

If the record bit is set (clrlslwi.), then CR0 is updated.

clrlwi[.]
clear left word immediate

0	21	5	6	RA	10	11	RT	15	16	0	20	21	n	26	27	31	30	Rc	31

clrlwi[.] RT, RA, b, n (n<32)

$$RT \leftarrow {}^{n}0 \parallel R_{n,\,31}$$

The clrlwi[.] instruction clears the n leftmost bits of RA and places the result in RT. This is an extended mnemonic for the rotate left word immediate then AND with mask (rlwinm[.]) instruction:

rlwinm[.] RT, RA, 0, n, 31

If the record bit is set (clrlwi.), then CR0 is updated.

clrrdi[.]
clear right doubleword immediate

30		RA		RT		0		63-n		1	0	Rc
0	5 6	10	11	15	16	20	21	26	27	29	29	31

clrldi[.] RT, RA, n (n<64)

$$RT \leftarrow RA_{0,\,63\text{-}n} \,\|\, {}^{n}0$$

The clrrdi[.] instruction clears the n rightmost bits of RA and places the result in RT. This is an extended mnemonic for the rotate left doubleword immediate and clear right (rldicr[.]) instruction:

rldicr[.] RT, RA, 0, 63-n

If the record bit is set (clrrdi.), then CR0 is updated.

This instruction is only defined for 64-bit implementations.

clrrwi[.]
clear right word immediate

21		RA		RT		0		0		31-n	Rc
0	5 6	10	11	15	16	20	21	26	27	30	31

clrrwi[.] RT, RA, n (n<32)

$$RT \leftarrow R_{0,\,31\text{-}n} \,\|\, {}^{n}0$$

The clrrwi[.] instruction clears the n rightmost bits of RA and places the result in RT. This is an extended mnemonic for the rotate left word immediate then AND with mask (rlwinm[.]) instruction:

rlwinm[.] RT, RA, 0, 0, 31-n

If the record bit is set (clrrwi.), then CR0 is updated.

cmp
integer compare

31		BF	/	L	RA		RB		0		/
0	5 6	8	9	10 11	15	16	20	21	30	31

cmp BF, L, RA, RB

$$CR_{BF} \leftarrow (RA) < (RB) \,\|\, (RA) > (RB) \,\|\, (RA) \equiv (RB) \,\|\, XER_{SO}$$

The cmp instruction performs a signed word or signed doubleword comparison of the contents of RA and RB. A word compare is done if the L-bit is a 0, while a doubleword compare is performed if the L-bit is a 1. The doubleword compare form is only defined for 64-bit implementations.

cmpd
compare doubleword

31		BF	/	1	RA	RB	0	/
0	5 6	8	9	10 11	15 16	20 21	30	31

cmpd BF, RA, RB

$$CR_{BF} \leftarrow (RA) < (RB) \parallel (RA) > (RB) \parallel (RA) \equiv (RB) \parallel XER_{SO}$$

The cmpd instruction performs a signed doubleword compare of the contents of RA and RB. This is an extended mnemonic for the compare (cmp) instruction:

cmp BF, 1, RA, RB

It is only defined for 64-bit implementations.

cmpdi
compare doubleword immediate

11		BF	/	1	RA	si
0	5 6	8	9	10 11	15 16	31

cmpdi BF, RA, si

$$CR_{BF} \leftarrow (RA) < si \parallel (RA) > si \parallel (RA) \equiv si \parallel XER_{SO}$$

The cmpdi instruction performs a signed doubleword compare of the contents of RA to the sign extended value si. This is an extended mnemonic for the compare immediate (cmpi) instruction:

cmpi bf, 1, RA, si

It is only defined for 64-bit implementations.

cmpld
compare logical (unsigned) doubleword

31		BF	/	1	RA	RB	32	/
0	5 6	8	9	10 11	15 16	20 21	30	31

cmpld BF, RA, RB

$$CR_{BF} \leftarrow (RA) < (RB) \parallel (RA) > (RB) \parallel (RA) \equiv (RB) \parallel XER_{SO}$$

The cmpld instruction performs an unsigned doubleword compare of the contents of RA and RB. This is an extended mnemonic for the compare logical (cmpl) instruction:

cmpl bf, 1, RA, RB

It is only defined for 64-bit implementations.

cmpldi
compare logical (unsigned) doubleword immediate

10	BF	/	1	RA	ui
0 5	6 8	9	10 11	15 16	31

cmpldi BF, RA, ui

$$CR_{BF} \leftarrow (RA) < ui \, \| \, (RA) > ui \, \| \, (RA) \equiv ui \, \| \, XER_{SO}$$

The cmpldi instruction performs an unsigned doubleword compare of the contents of RA to the value ui. This is an extended mnemonic for the compare logical immediate (cmpli) instruction:

cmpli bf, 1, RA, ui

It is only defined for 64-bit implementations.

cmpi
integer compare immediate

11	BF	/	L	RA	si
0 5	6 8	9	10 11	15 16	31

cmpi BF, L, Ry

$$CR_{Bf} \leftarrow (RA) < si \, \| \, (RA) > si \, \| \, (RA) \equiv si \, \| \, XER_{SO}$$

The compare immediate (cmpi) instruction performs a signed word or signed doubleword comparison of the contents of RA to the sign extended value si. A word compare is done if the L-bit is a 0, while a doubleword compare is performed if the L-bit is a 1. The doubleword compare form is only defined for 64-bit implementations.

cmpl
compare logical (unsigned)

31	BF	/	L	RA	RB	32	31
0 5	6 8	9	10 11	15 16	20 21	30	10

cmpl BF, L, RA, RB

$$CR_{BF} \leftarrow (RA) < (RB) \, \| \, (RA) > (RB) \, \| \, (RA) \equiv (RB) \, \| \, XER_{SO}$$

The compare logical (cmpl) instruction performs an unsigned word or unsigned doubleword comparison of the contents of RA and RB. A word compare is done if the L-bit is a 0, while a doubleword compare is performed if the L-bit is a 1. The doubleword compare form is only defined for 64-bit implementations.

cmpli
compare logical (unsigned) immediate

10	BF	/	L	R_y	ui
0 5	6 8	9	10 11	15	16 31

cmpli bf, L, Ry,ui

$$CRBF \leftarrow (RA) < ui \parallel (RA) > ui \parallel (RA) \equiv ui \parallel XER_{SO}$$

The compare immediate (cmpli) instruction performs an unsigned word or unsigned doubleword comparison of the contents of RA to the value ui. A word compare is done if the L-bit is a 0, while a doubleword compare is performed if the L-bit is a 1. The doubleword compare form is only defined for 64-bit implementations.

cmpw
compare word

31	BF	/	0	RA	RB	0	/
0 5	6 8	9	10 11	15 16	20 21	30	31

cmpw BF, RA, RB

$$CR_{BF} \leftarrow (RA) < (RB) \parallel (RA) > (RB) \parallel (RA) \equiv (RB) \parallel XER_{SO}$$

The cmpw instruction performs a signed word compare of the contents of RA and RB. This is an extended mnemonic for the compare (cmp) instruction:

cmp BF, 0, RA, RB

cmpwi
compare word immediate

11	BF 0	/	RA	si
0 5	6 8	9	10 11 15 16	31

cmpwi BF, RA, si

$$CR_{BF} \leftarrow (RA) < si \parallel (RA) > si \parallel (RA) \equiv si \parallel XER_{SO}$$

The cmpwi instruction performs an signed word compare of the contents of RA to the sign extended value si. This is an extended mnemonic for the compare immediate (cmpi) instruction:

cmpi bf, 0, RA, si

cmplw
compare logical (unsigned) word

31		Bf	/	0	RA	RB	32	/
0	5 6	8	9	10 11	15 16	20 21	30	31

cmplw BF, RA, RB

$$CR_{BF} \leftarrow (RA) < (RB) \parallel (RA) > (RA) \parallel (RB) \equiv (RB) \parallel XER_{SO}$$

The cmplw instruction performs an unsigned word compare of the contents of RA and RB. This is an extended mnemonic for the compare logical (cmpl) instruction:

cmpl bf, 0, RA, RB

cmplwi
compare logical (unsigned) word immediate

10		BF	/	0	RA	ui	
0	5 6	8	9	10 11	15 16		31

cmplwi BF, Ry, si, ui

$$CR_{BF} \leftarrow (RA) < ui \parallel (RA) > ui \parallel (RA) \equiv ui \parallel XER_{SO}$$

The cmplwi instruction performs an unsigned word compare of the contents of RA to the value ui. This is an extended mnemonic for the compare logical immediate (cmpli) instruction:

cmpli BF, 0, RA, ui

cntlzd[.]
count leading zeros doubleword

31		RA	RT	/	58	Rc
0	5 6	10 11	15 16	20 21	30	31

cntlzd[.] RT, RA

The cntlzd[.] instruction counts the number of leading zeros in RA and places the count into RT. The count ranges from 0 to 64 inclusive. This instruction is defined only on 64-bit implementations.

If the record bit is set (cntlzd.) then CR0 is updated.

cntlzw[.]
count leading zeros word

0	31	5	6	RA	10	11	RT	15	16	/	20	21	26	30	Rc	31

cntlzw[.] RT, RA

The cntlzw[.] instruction counts the number of leading zeros in RA and places the count into RT. The count ranges from 0 to 32, inclusive. This instruction is defined on both 32-bit and 64-bit implementations.

If the record bit is set (cntlzw.) then CR0 is updated.

crand
condition register AND

0	19	5	6	BT	10	11	BA	15	16	BB	20	21	257	30	/	31

crand BT, BA, BB

$$CR_{BT} \leftarrow CR_{BA} \wedge CR_{BB}$$

The crand instruction performs a logical AND of CR bit BA (CRBA) and CR bit BB (CRBB) and places the result into CR bit BT (CRBT).

crandc
condition register AND with compliment

0	19	5	6	BT	10	11	BA	15	16	BB	20	21	129	30	/	31

crandc BT, BA, BB

$$CR_{BT} \leftarrow CR_{BA} \wedge \overline{CR_{BB}}$$

The crandc instruction performs a logical AND of condition register bit BA (CRBA) and the logical negation of condition register bit BB (CRBB) and places the result into condition register bit BT (CRBT).

crclr
condition register clear

0	19	5	6	BT	10	11	BT	15	16	BT	20	21	193	30	/	31

crclr BT

$$CR_{BT} \leftarrow 0$$

The crclr instruction clears condition register bit BT (CRBT). This is an extended mnemonic for the condition register XOR (crxor) instruction:

crxor BT, BT, BT

creqv
condition register equivalent (XNOR)

19	BT	BA	BB	289	/
0	5 6	10 11	15 16	20 21	30 31

creqv BT, BA, BB

$$CR_{BT} \leftarrow CR_{BA} \equiv CR_{BB}$$

The creqv instruction performs a logical equivalence (XNOR) of condition register bit BA (CRBA) and condition register bit BB (CRBB) and places the result into condition register bit BT (CRBT).

crmove
condition register move

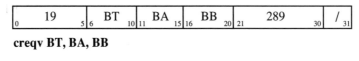

19	BT	BA	BA	449	/
0	5 6	10 11	15 16	20 21	30 31

crmove BT, BA

$$CR_{BT} \leftarrow CR_{BA}$$

The crmove instruction copies condition register bit BA (CRBA) into condition register bit BT (CRBT). This is an extended mnemonic for the condition register OR (cror) instruction:

cror BT, BA, BA

crnand
condition register NAND

19	BT	BA	BB	225	/
0	5 6	10 11	15 16	20 21	30 31

crnand BT, BA, BB

$$CR_{BT} \leftarrow \overline{CR_{BA} \wedge CR_{BB}}$$

The crnand instruction performs a logical NAND of condition register bit BA (CRBA) and condition register bit BB (CRBB) and places the result into condition register bit BT (CRBT).

crnor
condition register NOR

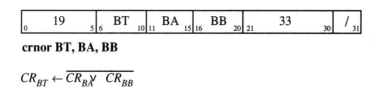

crnor BT, BA, BB

$$CR_{BT} \leftarrow \overline{CR_{BA} \lor CR_{BB}}$$

The crnor instruction performs a logical NOR of condition register bit BA (CRBA) and condition register bit BB (CRBB) and places the result into condition register bit BT (CRBT).

crnot
condition register not

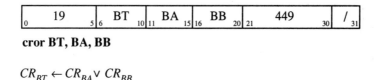

crnot BT, BA

$$CR_{BT} \leftarrow \overline{CR_{BA}}$$

The crnot instruction performs a logical negation of condition register bit BA (CRBA) and places the result into condition register bit BT (CRBT). This is an extended mnemonic for the condition register NOR (crnor) instruction:

crnor BT, BA, BA

cror
condition register OR

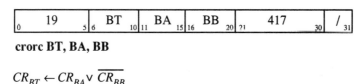

cror BT, BA, BB

$$CR_{BT} \leftarrow CR_{BA} \lor CR_{BB}$$

The cror instruction performs a logical OR of condition register bit BA (CRBA) and condition register bit BB (CRBB) and places the result into condition register bit BT (CRBT).

crorc
condition register OR with compliment

19	BT	BA	BB	417	/
0	5 6	10 11	15 16	20 21	30	31

crorc BT, BA, BB

$$CR_{BT} \leftarrow CR_{BA} \lor \overline{CR_{BB}}$$

The crorc instruction performs a logical OR of condition register bit BA (CRBA) and the logical negation of condition register bit BB (CRBB) and places the result into condition register bit BT (CRBT).

crset
condition register set

19		BT		BT		BT		289		/	
0	5 6		10 11		15 16		20 21		30		31

crset BT

$$CR_{BT} \leftarrow 1$$

The crset instruction sets condition register bit BT (CRBT) to one. This is an extended mnemonic for the condition register equvalence (creqv) instruction:

creqv BT, BT, BT

crxor
condition register XOR

19		BT		BA		BB		193		/	
0	5 6		10 11		15 16		20 21		30		31

crxor BT, BA, BB

$$CR_{BT} \leftarrow CR_{BA} \oplus CR_{BB}$$

The crxor instruction performs a logical XOR of condition register bit BA (CRBA) and condition register bit BB (CRBB) and places the result into condition register bit BT (CRBT).

dcbf
data cache block flush

31		/		RA		RB		86		/	
0	5 6		10 11		15 16		20 21		30		31

dcbf RA, RB

The dcbf instruction flushes a cache block into memory. If RA is 0 (r0), then the contents of RB are used as the effective address, otherwise, the sum of the contents of RA and the contents of RB is used as the effective address. The cache block addressed by this effective address is flushed from the data cache.

The exact action taken depends on whether memory coherence is enforced for that address (see Virtual Memory), and on the state of that address in the cache.

1. Coherence required

   unmodified block: Invalidate all copies of the block in the data caches of all processors.

   modified block: Store the block back to main memory (from whichever caches have the modified data) then invalidate all copies of the block in the data caches of all processors.

   absent block: If the block is absent from the cache, then store back any modified copies of the block in other caches (if there are any), and then invalidate all copies of the block in the data caches of all processors.

2. Coherence not required

   unmodified block: Invalidate all copies of the block in the data caches of this processor.

   modified block: Store the block back to main memory (from whichever caches in this processor have the modified data) then invalidate all copies of the block in the data caches of this processor.

   absent block: Do nothing.

dcbi
data cache block invalidate

| 0 | 31 | 5 6 | /// | 10 11 | RA | 15 16 | RB | 20 21 | 470 | 30 | / | 31 |

dcbi RA, RB

The dcbi instruction invalidates a cache block. If RA is 0 (r0), then the contents of RB are used as the effective address, otherwise, the sum of the contents of RA and the contents of RB is used as the effective address. The cache block addressed by this effective address is invalidated from the data cache.

The exact action taken depends on whether memory coherence is enforced for that address (see Virtual Memory), and on the state of that address in the cache.

1. Coherence required

   unmodified block: Invalidate all copies of the block in the data caches of all processors.

   modified block: invalidate all copies of the block in the data caches of all processors (this discards the modified data).

   absent block: If the block is absent from the cache, then invalidate all copies of the block in the data caches of all processors (possibly discarding modified data).

2. Coherence not required

   unmodified block: Invalidate all copies of the block in the data caches of this processor.

modified block: Invalidate all copies of the block in the data caches of this processor (discard the modified contents).

absent block: Do nothing.

This instruction is privileged (see Appendix C).

dcbst
data cache block store

31		/		RA		RB		54		/	
0	5	6	10	11	15	16	20	21	30	31	

dcbst RA, RB

The dcbst instruction stores a cache block into memory. If RA is 0 (r0), then the contents of RB are used as the effective address, otherwise, the sum of the contents of RA and the contents of RB is used as the effective address. The data cache block addressed by this effective address is stored into main memory.

The exact action taken depends on whether memory coherence is enforced for that address (see Virtual Memory), and on the state of that address in the cache.

1. Coherence required

   unmodified block: If any other processor has a modified copy of the cache block, then store it back to memory.

   modified block: Store the block back to main memory. If any other processor has a modified copy of the cache block, then store it back to memory.

   absent block: If the block is absent from the cache, then store back any modified copies of the block in other caches (if there are any).

2. Coherence not required

   unmodified block: Do nothing.

   modified block: Store the block back to main memory.

   absent block: Do nothing.

dcbt
data cache block touch

31		/		RA		RB		278		/	
0	5	6	10	11	15	16	20	21	30	31	

dcbt RA, RB

The dcbt instruction is a hint to the processor that an access to the address of this instruction will occur in the near future. If RA is 0 (r0), then the contents of RB are used as the effective address, otherwise, the sum of the contents of RA and the contents of RB is used as the effective address.

This instruction can be used to reduce the cache miss penalty on predictable accesses in a program (typically, a processor will treat this instruction as a byte load without a register target).

dcbtst
data cache block touch for store

31	/	RA	RB	246	/
0 5	6 10	11 15	16 20	21 30	31

dcbtst RA, RB

The dcbtst instruction is a hint to the processor that a store access to the address of this instruction will occur in the near future. If RA is 0 (r0), then the contents of RB are used as the effective address, otherwise, the sum of the contents of RA and the contents of RB is used as the effective address.

This instruction can be used to reduce the cache miss penalty on predictable store accesses in a program (typically, a processor will treat this instruction as a byte load without a register target but will initiate a read-with-intent-to-modify operation).

dcbz
data cache block zero

31	/	RA	RB	1014	/
0 5	6 10	11 15	16 20	21 30	31

dcbz RA, RB

The dcbz instruction sets a cache block to 0. If RA is 0 (r0), then the contents of RB are used as the effective address, otherwise, the sum of the contents of RA and the contents of RB is used as the effective address. The data cache block addressed by this instruction is set to 0.

If the block to be zeroed is not in the cache, but is caching allowed, then it is established in the cache (in a modified state) without fetching from main memory. if theaddress of the instruction is cache inhibited or write-through required, then either all bytes corresponding to that cache block are set to 0 in main memory, or the system alignment interrupt handler is initiated. Note that this instruction discards modified data in this cache (or any other processor's cache, if coherent).

divd[o][.]
integer divide doubleword

31	RT	RA	RB	Oe	489	Rc
0 5	6 10	11 15	16 20	21 22	30	31

divd[o][.] RT, RA, RB

$RT \leftarrow (RA) \div (RB)$

The divd[o][.] instruction divides RA by RB and stores the result into RT. Both the operands and the quotient are signed doubleword integers. Division by 0 (contents of RB are 0) or division of the maximum negative integer by -1 leaves RT undefined.

If the divdo[.] form of the instruction is used, then the overflow and summary overflow bits of the XER are set if overflow occurs. Division by 0 or division of the maximum negative integer by -1 sets the overflow bit.

If the divd[o]. form of the instruction is used, then CR0 is updated. Division by 0 (contents of RB are 0) leaves the LT, GT, and EQ, fields of CR0 undefined if this form is used or division of the maximum negative integer by -1.

This instruction is only available on 64-bit implementations.

divdu[o][.]
unsigned integer divide doubleword

31	RT	RA	RB	Oe	457	Rc
0 5	6 10	11 15	16 20	21 22	30	31

divdu[o][.] RT, RA, RB

$RT \leftarrow (RA) \div (RB)$

The divdu[o][.] instruction divides RA by RB and stores the result into RT. Both the operands and the quotient are unsigned doubleword integers. Division by 0 (contents of RB are 0) leaves RT undefined.

If the divduo[.] form of the instruction is used, then the overflow and summary overflow bits of the XER are set if overflow occurs. Division by 0 sets the overflow bit.

If the divdu[o]. form of the instruction is used, then CR0 is updated. Division by 0 (contents of RB are 0) leaves the LT, GT, and EQ, fields of CR0 undefined if this form is used.

This instruction is only available on 64-bit implementations.

divw[o][.]
integer divide word

31		RT		RA		RB		Oe	491		Rc
0	5 6		10 11		15 16		20	21 22		30	31

divw[o][.] RT, RA, RB

$RT \leftarrow (RA) \div (RB)$

The divw[o][.] instruction divides RA by RB and stores the result into RT. Both the operands and the quotient are signed word integers. Division by 0 (contents of RB are 0) or division of the maximum negative integer by -1 leaves RT undefined.

If the divwo[.] form of the instruction is used, then the overflow and summary overflow bits of the XER are set if overflow occurs. Division by 0 or division of the maximum negative integer by -1 sets the overflow bit.

If the divw[o]. form of the instruction is used, then CR0 is updated. Division by 0 (contents of RB are 0) leaves the LT, GT, and EQ, fields of CR0 undefined if this form is used, or division of the maximum negative integer by -1.

divwu[o][.]
unsigned integer divide word

31		RT		RA		RB		Oe	459		Rc
0	5 6		10 11		15 16		20	21 22		30	31

divwu[o][.] RT, RA, RB

$RT \leftarrow (RA) \div (RB)$

The divwu[o][.] instruction divides RA by RB and stores the result into RT. Both the operands and the quotient are unsigned word integers. Division by 0 (contents of RB are 0) leaves RT undefined.

If the divwuo[.] form of the instruction is used, then the overflow and summary overflow bits of the XER are set if overflow occurs. Division by 0 sets the overflow bit.

If the divwu[o]. form of the instruction is used, then CR0 is updated. Division by 0 (contents of RB are 0) leaves the LT, GT, and EQ, fields of CR0 undefined if this form is used.

eciwx
external control word in

31		RT		RA		RB		Oe	310		/
0	5 6		10 11		15 16		20	21 22		30	31

eciwx RT, RA, RB

The eciwx instruction translates the effective address then sends a load word request for this address to the device specified by the RID field in the external access register (EAR) (see

Appendix C). If RA is 0 (r0), then the contents of RB are used as the effective address, otherwise, the sum of the contents of RA and the contents of RB is used as the effective address.

This instruction is used to send a real address to a device that does not support translation. A status word is received from the device and placed into RT. The cache is always bypassed by this instruction.

ecowx
external control word out

31	RT	RA	RB	438	/
0 5	6 10	11 15	16 20	21 30	31

ecowx RT, RA, RB

The ecowx instruction translates the effective address then sends a store word request for this address to the device specified by the RID field in the external access register (EAR) (see Appendix C). If RA is 0 (r0), then the contents of RB are used as the effective address; otherwise, the sum of the contents of RA and the contents of RB is used as the effective address.

This instruction is used to send a real address along with a control word (the contents of register RT) to a device (which does not suport translation). The cache is always bypassed by this instruction.

eieio
enforce in-order execution of I/O

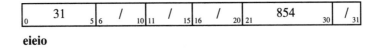

31	/	/	/	854	/
0 5	6 10	11 15	16 20	21 30	31

eieio

The eieio instruction forms a fence between certain storage operations. Operations that occur before the eieio instruction are completed with respect to main storage before operations within the same group that follow the eieio are initiated. Operations are split into two groups and ordering only occurs within each group.

The first group includes loads and stores to storage that are both cache inhibited and guarded, and stores to storage that are write-through required (see Virtual Memory in Appendix C).

The second group includes stores to storage that are not cache inhibited, not write-through required, and memory coherent.

No ordering is forced between accesses from different groups. For stronger ordering, see the sync instruction.

eqv[.]
logical equivalent (XNOR)

31		RA		RT		RB		284		Rc
0	5	6	10	11	15	16	20	21	30	31

eqv[.] RA, RT, RB

$RT \leftarrow (RA) \oplus (RB)$

The eqv[.] instruction performs a bitwise logical equivalence between the contents of RA and the contents of RB, placing the result into RT.

If the record bit is set (eqv.), then CR0 is updated.

extldi[.]
extract and left justify doubleword immediate

30		RA		RT		b		n-1		2	b	Rc
0	5	6	10	11	15	16	20	21	26	27 29	30	31

extldi RT, RA, n, b (n>0)

$RT \leftarrow (RA)_{b, b+n-1} \,\|\, {}^{64-n}0$

The extldi[.] instruction extracts n bits from RA starting at bit position b, left justifies them, and places the result into RT (remaining bits in RT are cleared).

If the Rc bit is set (extldi.), then CR0 is updated.

This is an extended mnemonic for the rotate left doubleword immediate then clear right (rldicr[.]) instruction:

rldicr[.] RT, RA, b, n-1

This instruction is defined only for 64-bit implementations.

extlwi[.]
extract and left justify word immediate

21		RA		RT		b		0		n-1	Rc
0	5	6	10	11	15	16	20	21	25	26 30	31

extlwi[.] RT, RA, n, b (n>0)

$RT \leftarrow (RA)_{b, b+n-1} \,\|\, {}^{32-n}0$

The extlwi[.] instruction extracts n bits from RA starting at bit position b, left justifies them, and places the result into RT (remaining bits in RT are cleared).

If the Rc bit is set (extlwi.), then CR0 is updated.

This is an extended mnemonic for the rotate left word immediate then AND with mask (rlwinm[.]) instruction:

rlwinm[.] RT, RA, b, 0, n-1

extrdi[.]
extract and right justify doubleword immediate

| 0 | 30 | 5 | 6 | RA | 10 | 11 | RT | 15 | 16 | $(b+n)_{1:4}$ | 20 | 21 | 64-n | 26 | 27 | 0 | 29 | $(b+n)_0$ | 30 | Rc | 31 |

extrdi[.] RT, RA, n, b (n>0)

$$RT \leftarrow {}^{64-n}0 \,\|\, (RA)_{b,\, b+n-1}$$

The extrdi[.] instruction extracts n bits from RA starting at bit position b, right justifies them, and places the result into RT (remaining bits in RT are cleared).

If the Rc bit is set (extrdi.) then CR0 is updated.

This is an extended mnemonic for the rotate left doubleword immediate then clear right (rldicl[.]) instruction:

rldicl[.] RT, RA, b+n, 64-n

This instruction is defined only for 64-bit implementations.

extrwi[.]
extract and right justify word immediate

| 0 | 21 | 5 | 6 | RA | 10 | 11 | RT | 15 | 16 | b | 20 | 21 | 0 | 25 | 26 | n-1 | 30 | Rc | 31 |

extrwi[.] RT, RA, n, b (n>0)

$$RT \leftarrow {}^{32-n}0 \,\|\, (RA)_{b,\, b+n-1}$$

The extrwi[.] instruction extracts n bits from RA starting at bit position b, left justifies them, and places the result into RT (remaining bits in RT are cleared).

If the Rc bit is set (extrwi.) then CR0 is updated.

This is an extended mnemonic for the rotate left word immediate then AND with mask (rlwinm[.]) instruction:

rlwinm[.] RT, RA, b+n, 32-n, 31

extsb[.]
sign-extend byte

31	RA	RT	/	954	Rc
0	5 6	10 11	15 16	20 21	30 31

extsb[.] RT, RA

$$RT \leftarrow\ ^{24}(RA)_{24} \parallel (RA)_{24, 31}$$

The extsb[.] instruction sign extends the least significant byte of RA then stores the result into RT.

If the Rc bit is set (extsb.), then CR0 is updated. Note that on 64-bit implementations, RT<-^{56}(RA)$_{56}$__(RA)$_{56:63}$.

extsh[.]
sign-extend half-word

31	RA	RT	/	922	Rc
0	5 6	10 11	15 16	20 21	30 31

extsh[.] RT, RA

$$RT \leftarrow\ ^{16}(RA)_{16} \parallel (RA)_{16, 31}$$

The extsh[.] instruction sign extends the least significant half-word of RA then stores the result into RT.

If the Rc bit is set (extsh.), then CR0 is updated. Note that on 64-bit implementations, RT<-^{48}(RA)$_{48}$(RA)$_{48:63}$.

extsw[.]
sign-extend word

31	RA	RT	/	986	Rc
0	5 6	10 11	15 16	20 21	30 31

extsw[.] RT, RA

$$RT \leftarrow\ ^{32}(RA)_{32} \parallel (RA)_{32, 63}$$

The extsw[.] instruction sign extends the least significant word of RA then stores the result into RT.

If the Rc bit is set (extsw.), then CR0 is updated.

This instruction is defined only on 64-bit implementations.

fabs[.]
floating-point absolute value

0	63	5 6	FRT	10 11	/	15 16	FRA	20 21	264	30	Rc	31

fabs[.] FRT, FRA

$$FRT \leftarrow \left| (FRA) \right|$$

The fabs[.] instruction calulates the absolute value of the contents of floating-point register FRA and stores this into floating-point register FRT.

If the Rc bit is set (fabs.), then CR1 is updated.

fadd[.]
floating-point add double precision

0	63	5 6	FRT	10 11	FRA	15 16	FRB	20 21	/	25 26	21	30	Rc	31

fadd[.] FRT, FRA, FRB

$$FRT \leftarrow (FRA) + (FRB)$$

The fadd[.] instruction performs a double precision add of the contents of floating-point registers FRA and FRB, and stores this into floating-point register FRT.

If the Rc bit is set (fadd.), then CR1 is updated.

The following FPSCR fields may be updated by this instruction (see Appendix D):

FPRF, FR, FI, FX, OX, UX, XX, VXSNAN, and VXISI

fadds[.]
floating-point add single precision

0	59	5 6	FRT	10 11	FRA	15 16	FRB	20 21	/	25 26	21	30	Rc	31

fadds[.] FRT, FRA, FRB

$$FRT \leftarrow (FRA) + (FRB)$$

The fadds[.] instruction performs a double precision add of the contents of floating-point registers FRA and FRB, rounds this to single precision, and then stores it into floating-point register FRT.

If the Rc bit is set (fadds.), then CR1 is updated.

The following FPSCR fields may be updated by this instruction (see Appendix D):

FPRF, FR, FI, FX, OX, UX, XX, VXSNAN, and VXISI

fcfid[.]
convert integer doubleword to floating-point

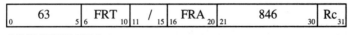

fcfid[.] FRT, FRA

The fcfid[.] instruction converts the contents of floating-point register FRA from a doubleword integer into a double precision floating-point value and stores this into floating-point register FRT.

If the Rc bit is set (fcfid.), then CR1 is updated.

The following FPSCR fields may be updated by this instruction (see Appendix D):

FPRF, FR, FI, FX, and XX

This instruction is available only on 64-bit implementations.

fcmpo
floating-point compare ordered

fcmpo bf, FRA, FRB

$$CR_{bf} \leftarrow (FRA) < (FRB) \;||\; (FRA) > (FRB) \;||\; (FRA) \equiv (FRB) \;||\; \text{unordered}$$

The fcmpo instruction compares the contents of floating-point registers FRA and FRB and stores the result into condition register field bf (CRbf). Unordered (bit three of the CR field) is set if either of the operands is not a number (NaN).

The following FPSCR fields may be updated by this instruction (see Appendix D):

FPCC, FX, VXSNAN, and VXVC

fcmpu
floating-point compare unordered

fcmpu bf, FRA, FRB

$$CR_{bf} \leftarrow (FRA) < (FRB) \;||\; (FRA) > (FRB) \;||\; (FRA) \equiv (FRB) \;||\; \text{unordered}$$

The fcmpu instruction compares the contents of floating-point registers FRA and FRB and stores the result into condition register field bf (CRbf). Unordered (bit three of the CR field) is set if either of the operands is not a number (NaN).

The following FPSCR fields may be updated by this instruction (see Appendix D):

FPCC, FX, and VXSNAN

fctid[.]
convert floating-point to integer doubleword

0 63 5	6 FRT 10	11 / 15	16 FRA 20	21 814 30	Rc 31

fctid[.] FRT, FRA

The fctid[.] instruction converts the contents of floating-point register FRA from a double precision floating-point number into a signed doubleword integer value and stores this into floating-point register FRT.

If the Rc bit is set (fctid.) then CR1 is updated.

The following FPSCR fields may be updated by this instruction (see Appendix D):

FPRF (undefined), FR, FI, FX, XX, VXSNAN, and VXCVI

This instruction is available only on 64-bit implementations.

fctidz[.]
convert floating-point to integer doubleword with round toward zero

0 63 5	6 FRT 10	11 / 15	16 FRA 20	21 815 30	Rc 31

fctidz[.] FRT, FRA

The fctidz[.] instruction converts the contents of floating-point register FRA from a double precision floating-point number into a signed doubleword integer value and stores this into floating-point register FRT. The rounding mode used in this instruction is round toward zero, regardless of the setting in the FPSCR (see Appendix D).

If the Rc bit is set (fctidz.) then CR1 is updated.

The following FPSCR fields may be updated by this instruction (see Appendix D):

FPRF (undefined), FR, FI, FX, XX, VXSNAN, and VXCVI

This instruction is available only on 64-bit implementations.

fctiw[.]
convert floating-point to integer word

63	FRT	/	FRA	14	Rc
0 5	6 10	11 15	16 20	21 30	31

fctiw[.] FRT, FRA

The fctiw[.] instruction converts the contents of floating-point register FRA from a double precision floating-point number into a signed word integer value and stores this into the low-order 32 bits of floating-point register FRT.

If the Rc bit is set (fctiw.) then CR1 is updated.

The following FPSCR fields may be updated by this instruction (see Appendix D):

FPRF (undefined), FR, FI, FX, XX, VXSNAN, and VXCVI

fctiwz[.]
convert floating-point to integer word with round toward zero

63	FRT	/	FRA	15	Rc
0 5	6 10	11 15	16 20	21 30	31

fctiwz[.] FRT, FRA

The fctiwz[.] instruction converts the contents of floating-point register FRA from a double precision floating-point number into a signed word integer value and stores this into the low-order 32 bits of floating-point register FRT. The rounding mode used in this instruction is round toward 0, regardless of the setting in the FPSCR (see Appendix D).

If the Rc bit is set (fctiwz.) then CR1 is updated.

The following FPSCR fields may be updated by this instruction (see Appendix D):

FPRF (undefined), FR, FI, FX, XX, VXSNAN, and VXCVI

fdiv[.]
floating-point divide double precision

63	FRT	FRA	FRB	/	18	Rc
0 5	6 10	11 15	16 20	21 25	26 30	31

fdiv[.] FRT, FRA, FRB

$FRT \leftarrow (FRA) \div (FRB)$

The fdiv[.] instruction performs a double precision divide of the contents of floating-point registers FRA and FRB (FRA divided by FRB), and stores this into floating-point register FRT.

If the Rc bit is set (fdiv.) then CR1 is updated.

The following FPSCR fields may be updated by this instruction (see Appendix D):

FPRF, FR, FI, FX, OX, UX, ZX, XX, VXSNAN, VXIDI, and VXZDZ

fdivs[.]
floating-point divide single precision

59		FRT	FRA	FRB	/	18	Rc
0	5 6	10 11	15 16	20 21	25 26	30	31

fdivs[.] FRT, FRA, FRB

$$FRT \leftarrow (FRA) \div (FRB)$$

The fdivs[.] instruction performs a double precision divide of the contents of floating-point registers FRA and FRB (FRA divided by FRB), rounds this to single precision, and stores the result into floating-point register FRT.

If the Rc bit is set (fdivs.) then CR1 is updated.

The following FPSCR fields may be updated by this instruction (see Appendix D):

FPRF, FR, FI, FX, OX, UX, ZX, XX, VXSNAN, VXIDI, and VXZDZ

fmadd[.]
floating-point multiply accumulate double precision

63		FRT	FRA	FRB	FRC	29	Rc
0	5 6	10 11	15 16	20 21	25 26	30	31

fmadd[.] FRT, FRA, FRB, FRB

$$FRT \leftarrow ((FRA) \times (FRC)) + (FRB)$$

The fmadd[.] instruction performs a double precision multiply of the contents of floating-point registers FRA and FRC, adds to this the contents of floating-point register FRB, and stores this into floating-point register FRT. The intermediate result of FRA times FRC is not rounded before the addition (see Appendix D).

If the Rc bit is set (fmadd.) then CR1 is updated.

The following FPSCR fields may be updated by this instruction (see Appendix D):

FPRF, FR, FI, FX, OX, UX, XX, VXSNAN, VXISI, and VXIMZ

fmadds[.]
floating-point multiply accumulate single precision

| 0 | 59 | 5 | 6 | FRT | 10 | 11 | FRA | 15 | 16 | FRB | 20 | 21 | FRC | 25 | 26 | 29 | 30 | Rc | 31 |

fmadds[.] FRT, FRA, FRB, FRB

$FRT \leftarrow ((FRA) \times (FRC)) + (FRB)$

The fmadds[.] instruction performs a double precision multiply of the contents of floating-point registers FRA and FRC, and adds this to the contents of floating-point register FRB. This result is rounded to single precision and then stored into floating-point register FRT. The intermediate result of FRA times FRC is not rounded before the addition (see Appendix D).

If the Rc bit is set (fmadds.) then CR1 is updated.

The following FPSCR fields may be updated by this instruction (see Appendix D):

FPRF, FR, FI, FX, OX, UX, XX, VXSNAN, VXISI, and VXIMZ

fmr[.]
floating-point move register

| 0 | 63 | 5 | 6 | FRT | 10 | 11 | / | 15 | 16 | FRA | 20 | 21 | 72 | 30 | Rc | 31 |

fmr[.] FRT, FRA

$FRT \leftarrow (FRA)$

The fmr[.] instruction moves the contents of floating-point register FRA into floating-point register FRT.

If the Rc bit is set (fmr.), then CR1 is updated.

fmsub[.]
floating-point multiply subtract double precision

| 0 | 63 | 5 | 6 | FRT | 10 | 11 | FRA | 15 | 16 | FRB | 20 | 21 | FRC | 25 | 26 | 28 | 30 | Rc | 31 |

fmsub[.] FRT, FRA, FRC, FRB

$FRT \leftarrow ((FRA) \times (FRC)) - (FRB)$

The fmsub[.] instruction performs a double precision multiply of the contents of floating-point registers FRA and FRC, subtracts from this the contents of floating-point register FRB, and stores this into floating-point register FRT. The intermediate result of FRA times FRC is not rounded before the addition (see Appendix D).

If the Rc bit is set (fmsub.), then CR1 is updated.

The following FPSCR fields may be updated by this instruction (see Appendix D):

FPRF, FR, FI, FX, OX, UX, XX, VXSNAN, VXISI, and VXIMZ

fmsubs[.]
floating-point multiply subtract single precision

0	63	5 6	FRT	10 11	FRA	15 16	FRB	20 21	FRC	25 26	28	30	Rc	31

fmsubs[.] FRT, FRA, FRC, FRB

$$FRT \leftarrow ((FRA) \times (FRC)) - (FRB)$$

The fmsubs[.] instruction performs a double precision multiply of the contents of floating-point registers FRA and FRC, subtracts from this the contents of floating-point register FRB. This result is then rounded to single precision and then stored into floating-point register FRT. The intermediate result of FRA times FRC is not rounded before the addition (see Appendix D).

If the Rc bit is set (fmsubs.), then CR1 is updated.

The following FPSCR fields may be updated by this instruction (see Appendix D):

FPRF, FR, FI, FX, OX, UX, XX, VXSNAN, VXISI, and VXIMZ

fmul[.]

0	63	5 6	FRT	10 11	FRA	15 16	/	20 21	FRC	25 26	25	30	Rc	31

fmul[.] FRT, FRA, FRC

$$FRT \leftarrow (FRA) \times (FRC)$$

floating-point multiply double precision

The fmul[.] instruction performs a double precision multiply of the contents of floating-point registers FRA and FRC, then stores this into floating-point register FRT.

If the Rc bit is set (fmul.), then CR1 is updated.

The following FPSCR fields may be updated by this instruction (see Appendix D):

FPRF, FR, FI, FX, OX, UX, XX, VXSNAN, and VXIMZ

fmuls[.]
floating-point multiply single precision

0	59	5 6	FRT	10 11	FRA	15 16	/	20 21	FRC	25 26	25	30	Rc	31

fmuls[.] FRT, FRA, FRC

$$FRT \leftarrow (FRA) \times (FRC)$$

The fmuls[.] instruction performs a double precision multiply of the contents of floating-point registers FRA and FRC. This result is then rounded to single precision and then stored into floating-point register FRT.

If the Rc bit is set (fmuls.), then CR1 is updated.

The following FPSCR fields may be updated by this instruction (see Appendix D):

FPRF, FR, FI, FX, OX, UX, XX, VXSNAN, and VXIMZ

fnabs[.]
floating-point negative absolute value

63	FRT	/	FRA	136	Rc
0 5	6 10	11 15	16 20	21 30	31

fnabs[.] FRT, FRA

$$FRT \leftarrow |(FRA)|$$

The fnabs[.] instruction calulates the absolute value of the contents of floating-point register FRA, negates it, then stores it into floating-point register FRT.

If the Rc bit is set (fnabs.), then CR1 is updated.

fneg[.]
floating-point negate

63	FRT	/	FRA	40	Rc
0 5	6 10	11 15	16 20	21 30	31

fneg FRT, FRA

$$FRT \leftarrow (FRA)$$

The fneg[.] instruction negates the contents of floating-point register FRA and stores this into floating-point register FRT.

If the Rc bit is set (fneg.), then CR1 is updated.

fnmadd[.]
floating-point negate multiply accumulate double precision

63	FRT	FRA	FRB	FRC	31	Rc
0 5	6 10	11 15	16 20	21 25	26 30	31

fnmadd[.] FRT, FRA, FRC, FRB

$$FRT \leftarrow -(((FRA) \times (FRC)) + (FRB))$$

The fnmadd[.] instruction performs a double precision multiply of the contents of floating-point registers FRA and FRC, adds to this the contents of floating-point register FRB, negates this result, then stores it into floating-point register FRT. The intermediate result of FRA times FRC is not rounded before the addition (see Appendix D).

If the Rc bit is set (fnmadd.), then CR_1 is updated.

The following FPSCR fields may be updated by this instruction (see Appendix D):

FPRF, FR, FI, FX, OX, UX, XX, VXSNAN, VXISI, and VXIMZ

fnmadds[.]
floating-point negate multiply accumulate single precision

0	59	5	6	FRT	10	11	FRA	15	16	FRB	20	21	FRC	25	26	31	30	Rc	31

fnmadd[.] FRT, FRA, FRC, FRB

$$FRT \leftarrow -(((FRA) \times (FRC)) + (FRB))$$

The fnmadds[.] instruction performs a double precision multiply of the contents of floating-point registers FRA and FRC, and adds this to the contents of floating-point register FRB. This result is then negated, rounded to single precision, and then stored into floating-point register FRT. The intermediate result of FRA times FRC is not rounded before the addition (see Appendix D).

If the Rc bit is set (fnmadds.), then CR_1 is updated.

The following FPSCR fields may be updated by this instruction (see Appendix D):

FPRF, FR, FI, FX, OX, UX, XX, VXSNAN, VXISI, and VXIMZ

fnmsub[.]
floating-point negate multiply subtract double precision

0	63	5	6	FRT	10	11	FRA	15	16	FRB	20	21	FRC	25	26	30	30	Rc	31

fnmadd[.] FRT, FRA, FRC, FRB

$$FRT \leftarrow -((FRA) \times (FRC)) + (FRB))$$

The fnmsub[.] instruction performs a double precision multiply of the contents of floating-point registers FRA and FRB, subtracts this from the contents of floating-point register FRB, negates the result, then stores it into floating-point register FRT. The intermediate result of FRA times FRB is not rounded before the subtraction(see Appendix D).

If the Rc bit is set (fnmsub.) then CR1 is updated.

The following FPSCR fields may be updated by this instruction (see Appendix D):

FPRF, FR, FI, FX, OX, UX, XX, VXSNAN, VXISI, and VXIMZ

fnmsubs[.]
floating-point negate multiply subtract single precision

59	FRT	FRA	FRB	FRC	30	Rc
0 5	6 10	11 15	16 20	21 25	26 30	31

fnmsubs[.] FRT, FRA, FRC, FRB

$$FT \leftarrow -((FRA) \times (FRC)) + (FRB))$$

The fnmsubs[.] instruction performs a double precision multiply of the contents of floating-point registers FRA and FRC, and subtracts this from the contents of floating-point register FRB. This result is then negated, rounded to single precision, and then stored into floating-point register FRT. The intermediate result of FRA times FRC is not rounded before the subtraction (see Appendix D).

If the Rc bit is set (fnmsubs.), then CR_1 is updated.

The following FPSCR fields may be updated by this instruction (see Appendix D):

FPRF, FR, FI, FX, OX, UX, XX, VXSNAN, VXISI, and VXIMZ

fres[.]
floating-point reciprocal estimate single precision

59	FRT	/	FRA	/	24	Rc
0 5	6 10	11 15	16 20	21 25	26 30	31

fres[.] FRT, FRA

$$FRT \leftarrow \frac{1}{(FRA)}$$

The fres[.] instruction estimates the reciprocal of the contents of floating-point register FRA. This result is then rounded to single precision and stored into floating-point register FRT. The accuracy of the estimate is as follows:

$$\left| \frac{\text{estimate} - \frac{1}{(FRA)}}{\frac{1}{(FRA)}} \right| \leq \frac{1}{256}$$

If the Rc bit is set (fres.), then CR1 is updated.

The following FPSCR fields may be updated by this instruction (see Appendix D):

FPRF, FR (undefined), FI (undefined), FX, OX, UX, ZX, and VXSNAN.

This instruction is optional and may not be implemented in every processor. Check the Users' Manual of the implementation you are using.

frsp[.]
floating-point round to single precision

63	FRT	/	FRA	12	Rc
0 5	6 10	11 15	16 20	21 30	31

frsp[.] FRT, FRA

The frsp[.] instruction converts the contents of floating-point register FRA from a double precision floating-point number into a single precision floating-point value and stores this into floating-point register FRT.

If the Rc bit is set (frsp.), then CR1 is updated.

The following FPSCR fields may be updated by this instruction (see Appendix D):

FPRF, FR, FI, FX, OX, UX, XX, and VXSNAN

frsqrte[.]
floating-point estimate reciprocal square root double precision

63	FRT	/	FRA	/	26	Rc
0 5	6 10	11 15	16 20	21 25	26 30	31

frsqrte[.] FRT, FRA

$$FRT \leftarrow \frac{1}{\sqrt{(FRA)}}$$

The fsqrte[.] instruction estimates the reciprocal of the square root of the contents of floating-point register FRA. This result is then stored into floating-point register FRT. The accuracy of the estimate is as follows:

$$\left| \frac{\text{estimate} - \frac{1}{\sqrt{(FRA)}}}{\frac{1}{\sqrt{(FRA)}}} \right| \leq \frac{1}{32}$$

If the Rc bit is set (fsqrte.) then CR1 is updated.

The following FPSCR fields may be updated by this instruction (see Appendix D):

FPRF, FR (undefined), FI (undefined), FX, ZX, VXSNAN, and VXSQRT.

This instruction is optional and may not be implemented in every processor. Check the Users' Manual of the implementation you are using.

fsel[.]
floating-point select

0	63	5	6	FRT	10	11	FRA	15	16	FRB	20	21	FRC	25	26	30	30	Rc	31

fsel[.] FRT, FRA, FRB, FRB

$$FRT \leftarrow ((FRA) \geq 0) ? (FRB) : (FRC)$$

The fsel[.] instruction moves the contents of FRB into FRT if the contents of FRA are greater than or equal to zero; otherwise, it moves the contents of FRC into FRT.

If the Rc bit is set (fsel.), then CR1 is updated.

This instruction is optional and may not be implemented in every processor. Check the Users' Manual of the implementation you are using.

fsqrt[.]
floating-point square root double precision

0	63	5	6	FRT	10	11	/	15	16	FRA	20	21	/	25	26	22	30	Rc	31

frsqrt[.] FRT, FRA

$$FRT \leftarrow \sqrt{(FRA_y)}$$

The fsqrt[.] instruction calculates the square root of the contents of floating-point register FRA and stores the result into floating-point register FRT.

If the Rc bit is set (fsqrt.), then CR1 is updated.

The following FPSCR fields may be updated by this instruction (see Appendix D):

FPRF, FR, FI, FX, XX, VXSNAN, and VXSQRT.

This instruction is optional and may not be implemented in every processor. Check the Users' Manual of the implementation you are using.

fsqrts[.]
floating-point square root single precision

59		FRT		/		FRA		/		22		Rc	
0	5	6	10	11	15	16	20	21	25	26	30	31	

frsqrts[.] FRT, FRA

$$FRT \leftarrow \sqrt{(FRA)}$$

The fsqrts[.] instruction calculates the square root of the contents of floating-point register FRA. This result is then rounded to single precision and stored into floating-point register FRT.

If the Rc bit is set (fsqrts.), then CR1 is updated.

The following FPSCR fields may be updated by this instruction (see Appendix D):

FPRF, FR, FI, FX, XX, VXSNAN, and VXSQRT.

This instruction is optional and may not be implemented in every processor. Check the Users' Manual of the implementation you are using.

fsub[.]
floating-point subtract double precision

63		FRT		FRA		FRB		/		20		Rc	
0	5	6	10	11	15	16	20	21	25	26	30	31	

fsub[.] FRT, FRA, FRB

$$FRT \leftarrow (FRA) - (FRB)$$

The fsub[.] instruction performs a double precision subtraction of the contents of floating-point register FRB from the contents of floating-point register FRA, and stores the result into floating-point register FRT.

If the Rc bit is set (fsub.), then CR1 is updated.

The following FPSCR fields may be updated by this instruction (see Appendix D):

FPRF, FR, FI, FX, OX, UX, XX, VXSNAN, and VXISI

fsubs[.]
floating-point subtract single precision

59		FRT		FRA		FRB		/		20		Rc	
0	5	6	10	11	15	16	20	21	25	26	30	31	

fsubs[.] FRT, FRA, FRB

$$FRT \leftarrow (FRA) - (FRB)$$

The fsubs[.] instruction performs a double precision subtraction of the contents of floating-point register FRB from the contents of floating-point register FRA. This result is then rounded to single precision and stored into floating-point register FRT.

If the Rc bit is set (fsubs.) then CR1 is updated.

The following FPSCR fields may be updated by this instruction (see Appendix D):

FPRF, FR, FI, FX, OX, UX, XX, VXSNAN, and VXISI

icbi
instruction cache block invalidate

31	/	RA	RB	982	/
0 5	6 10	11 15	16 20	21 30	31

icbi RA, RB

The icbi instruction invalidates a cache block. If RA is 0 (r0), then the contents of RB are used as the effective address; otherwise, the sum of the contents of RA and RB is used as the effective address. The cache block addressed by this effective address is invalidated from the instruction cache.

The exact action taken depends on whether memory coherence is enforced for that address (see Virtual Memory), and on the state of that address in the cache.

1. Coherence required

   unmodified block: Invalidate all copies of the block in the instruction caches of all processors.

   absent block: If the block is absent from the cache, then invalidate all copies of the block in the instruction caches of all other processors.

2. Coherence not required

   unmodified block: Invalidate all copies of the block in the instruction caches of this processor.

   absent block: Do nothing.

inslwi[.]
insert from left word immediate

20	RA	RT	32-b	b	b+n-1	Rc
0 5	6 10	11 15	16 20	21 25	26 30	31

inslwi RT, RA, n, b (n>0; (b+n)<32)

$$RT \leftarrow (RT)_{0, b-1} \parallel (RA)_{0, n-1} \parallel (RT)_{(b+n-1), 31}$$

The inslwi[.] instruction extracts n bits from RA starting at bit position 0, and inserts them into RT starting at bit position b (remaining bits in RT are unchanged).

If the Rc bit is set (inslwi.) then CR0 is updated.

This is an extended mnemonic for the rotate left word immediate with mask insert (rlwimi[.]) instruction:

rlwimi[.] RT, RA, 32-b, b, b+n-1

insrdi[.]
insert from right doubleword immediate

0	30	5	6	RA	10	11	RT	15	16	(64-b-n)$_{1:5}$	20	21	b	26	27	3	29	(64-b-n)$_0$	30	Rc	31

insrdi RT, RA, n, b (n>0)

$$RT \leftarrow (RT)_{0,\,b-1} \;\|\; (RA)_{64-n,\,63} \;\|\; (RT)_{(b+n-1),\,63}$$

The insrdi[.] instruction extracts the n rightmost bits from RA and inserts them into RT starting at bit b (remaining bits in RT are unchanged).

If the Rc bit is set (insrdi.), then CR0 is updated.

This is an extended mnemonic for the rotate left doubleword immediate then mask insert (rldimi[.]) instruction:

rldimi[.] RT, RA, 64-b-n, b

This instruction is defined only for 64-bit implementations.

insrwi[.]
insert from right word immediate

0	20	5	6	RA	10	11	RT	15	16	32-b	20	21	b	25	26	b+n-1	30	Rc	31

insrwi RT, RA, n, b (n>0; (b+n)<32)

$$RT \leftarrow (RT)_{0,\,b-1} \;\|\; (RA)_{32-n,31} \;\|\; (RT)_{(b+n-1),\,31}$$

The insrwi[.] instruction extracts the n rightmost bits from RA, and inserts them into RT starting at bit position b (remaining bits in RT are unchanged).

If the Rc bit is set (insrwi.), then CR0 is updated.

This is an extended mnemonic for the rotate left word immediate with mask insert (rlwimi[.]) instruction:

rlwimi[.] RT, RA, 32-b-n, b, b+n-1

isync
instruction synchronize

isync

The isync instruction waits for all previous instructions to complete and then discards all prefetched instructions. This is a context syncronizing instruction (see Appendix C).

la
load address

0	14	5 6	RT	10 11	RA	15 16	D	31

la RT, D(RA)

$$RT \leftarrow (RA) + \left({}^{16}D_{16} \parallel D_{16, 31} \right)$$

The la instruction performs an add of RA to the sign extended 16-bit immediate field, placing the result into RT.

If the la instruction is used with RA = 0, then 0 is used instead of the contents of RA. Thus regardless of the contents of r0, addi RT, RA, D, la r1,4(r0) would load the constant 4 into r1.

lbz
load byte and zero-extend immediate

0	34	5 6	RT	10 11	RA	15 16	D	31

lbz RT, D(RA)

$$RT \leftarrow {}^{24}0 \parallel \left(MEM \left[\left((RA) + \left({}^{16}D_{16} \parallel D_{16, 31} \right) \right), 1 \right] \right)$$

The lbz instruction loads the byte contained at the effective address of the instruction into the low-order byte of RT. The effective address of the instruction is found by adding the contents of RA to the sign extended 16-bit immediate field, unless RA is 0 (r0), in which case the effective address is the sign extended immediate field. The remaining bytes in RT are set to 0.

lbzu
load byte and zero-extend immediate with update

35	RT	RA	D
0 5	6 10	11 15	16 31

lbzu RT, D(RA)

$$RT \leftarrow {}^{24}0 \;\|\; \left(\text{MEM}\,[(\,(RA) + ({}^{16}D_{16} \;\|\; D_{16,31})),\, 1]\right)$$

$$RA \leftarrow (RA) + \left({}^{16}D_{16} \;\|\; D_{16,31}\right)$$

The lbzu instruction loads the byte contained at the effective address of the instruction into the low-order byte of RT. The effective address of the instruction is found by adding the contents of RA to the sign extended 16-bit immediate field. The remaining bytes in RT are set to 0. RA=RT or RA=0 is invalid for this instruction.

In addition, the effective address of the instruction is loaded into RA.

lbzux
load byte and zero-extend with update

31	RT	RA	RB	119	/
0 5	6 10	11 15	11 15	16 30	31

lbzux RT, RA, RB

$$RT \leftarrow {}^{24}0 \;\|\; (\text{MEM}\,[\,(\,(RA) + (RB)\,),\, 1\,])$$

$$RA \leftarrow (RA) + (RB)$$

The lbzux instruction loads the byte contained at the effective address of the instruction into the low-order byte of RT. The effective address of the instruction is found by adding the contents of RA to the contents of RB, unless RA is 0 (r0), in which case the effective address is RB. The remaining bytes in RT are set to 0. RA=RT or RA=0 is invalid for this instruction.

In addition, the effective address of the instruction is loaded into RA.

lbzx
load byte and zero-extend

31	RT	RA	RB	87	/
0 5	6 10	11 15	11 15	16 30	31

lbzx RT, RA, RB

$$RT \leftarrow {}^{24}0 \;\|\; (\text{MEM}\,[\,(\,(RA) + (RB)\,),\, 1\,])$$

The lbzx instruction loads the byte contained at the effective address of the instruction into the low-order byte of RT. The effective address of the instruction is found by adding the contents of RA to the contents of RB, unless RA is 0 (r0), in which case the effective address is RB. The remaining bytes in RT are set to 0.

ld
load doubleword immediate

34	RT	RA	DS	0
0 5	6 10	11 15	16 29	30 31

ld RT, DS(RA)

$$RT \leftarrow \left(\text{MEM} \left[\left((RA) + \left(^{48}DS_{16} \parallel DS_{16,29} \parallel {}^{2}0 \right) \right), 8 \right] \right)$$

The ld instruction loads the doubleword contained at the effective address of the instruction into RT. The effective address of the instruction is found by adding the contents of RA to the sign extended 14-bit immediate field with two binary zeros concatenated to the right, unless RA is 0 (r0), in which case the effective address is just the sign extended immediate field with two binary zeros concatenated to the right.

This instruction is available only on 64-bit implementations.

ldarx
load doubleword and reserve

31	RT	RA	RB	84	/
0 5	6 10	11 15	11 15	16 30	31

ldarx RT, RA, RB

$$RT \leftarrow (\text{MEM} \left[((RA) + (RB)), 8 \right])$$

The ldarx instruction loads the doubleword contained at the effective address of the instruction into RT. The effective address of the instruction is found by adding the contents of RA to the contents of RB, unless RA is 0 (r0), in which case the effective address is RB. The effective address must be a multiple of 8 (doubleword aligned).

In addition, a reservation is created in this processor for use by the store doubleword conditional (stdcx.) instruction. An address calculated from the effective address of this instruction is associated with the reservation (see Appendix C). This instruction is available only on 64-bit implementations.

ldu
load doubleword immediate with update

58	RT	RA	DS	1
0 5	6 10	11 15	16 29	30 31

ldu RT, DS(RA)

$$RT \leftarrow \left(\text{MEM} \left[\left((RA) + \left({}^{48}DS_{16} \parallel DS_{16,\,29} \parallel {}^{2}0 \right) \right), 8 \right] \right)$$

$$RT \leftarrow (RA) + \left({}^{48}DS_{16} \parallel DS_{16,\,29} \parallel {}^{2}0 \right)$$

The ldu instruction loads the doubleword contained at the effective address of the instruction into RT. The effective address of the instruction is found by adding the contents of RA to the sign extended 14-bit immediate field with two binary zeros concatenated to the right. RA=RT or RA=0 is invalid for this instruction.

In addition, the effective address of the instruction is loaded into RA.

This instruction is available only on 64-bit implementations.

ldux
load doubleword with update

31	RT	RA	RB	53	/
0 5	6 10	11 15	11 15	16 30	31

ldux RT, RA, RB

$$RT \leftarrow (\text{MEM} [((RA) + (RB)), 8])$$

$$RA \leftarrow (RA) + (RB)$$

The ldux instruction loads the doubleword contained at the effective address of the instruction into RT. The effective address of the instruction is found by adding the contents of RA to the contents of RB. RA=RT or RA=0 is invalid for this instruction.

In addition, the effective address of the instruction is loaded into RA.

This instruction is available only on 64-bit implementations.

ldx
load doubleword

31		RT		RA		RB		21		/
0	5 6		10 11		15 11		15 16		30	31

ldx RT, RA, RB

$$RT \leftarrow (MEM[((RA) + (RB)), 8])$$

The ldx instruction loads the doubleword contained at the effective address of the instruction into RT. The effective address of the instruction is found by adding the contents of RA to the contents of RB, unless RA is 0 (r0), in which case the effective address is just the contents of RB.

This instruction is available only on 64-bit implementations.

lfd
load double precision floating-point immediate

50		FRT		RA		D	
0	5 6		10 11		15 16		31

lfd FRT, D(RA)

$$FRT \leftarrow \left(MEM\left[\left((RA) + \left(^{16}D_{16} \parallel D_{16,31}\right)\right), 8\right]\right)$$

The lfd instruction loads the doubleword contained at the effective address of the instruction into floating-point register FRT. The effective address of the instruction is found by adding the contents of RA to the sign extended 16-bit immediate field, unless RA is 0 (r0), in which case the effective address is just the sign extended immediate field.

lfdu
load double precision floating-point immediate with update

51		FRT		RA		D	
0	5 6		10 11		15 16		31

lfdu FRT, D(RA)

$$FRT \leftarrow \left(MEM\left[\left((RA) + \left(^{16}D_{16} \parallel D_{16,31}\right)\right), 8\right]\right)$$

$$RA \leftarrow (RA) + \left(^{16}D_{16} \parallel D_{16,31}\right)$$

The lfdu instruction loads the doubleword contained at the effective address of the instruction into floating-point register FRT. The effective address of the instruction is found by adding the contents of RA to the sign extended 16-bit immediate field. If RA=0 the instruction form is invalid.

In addition, The effective address is loaded into register RA.

lfdux
load double precision floating-point with update

31	FRT	RA	RB	631	/
0 5	6 10	11 15	16 20	21 30	31

ldux RT, RA, RB

$$FRT \leftarrow (MEM [((RA) + (RB)), 8])$$

$$RA \leftarrow (RA) + (RB)$$

The lfdux instruction loads the doubleword contained at the effective address of the instruction into floating-point register FRT. The effective address of the instruction is found by adding the contents of RA to the contents of RB. If RA=0 the instruction form is invalid.

In addition, the effective address is loaded into register RA.

lfdx
load double precision floating-point

31	FRT	RA	RB	599	/
0 5	6 10	11 15	16 20	21 30	31

lfdx RT, RA, RB

$$FRT \leftarrow (MEM [((RA) + (RB)), 8])$$

The lfdx instruction loads the doubleword contained at the effective address of the instruction into floating-point register FRT. The effective address of the instruction is found by adding the contents of RA to the contents of RB, unless RA is 0 (r0), in which case the effective address is just the contents of RB.

lfs
load single precision floating-point immediate

48	FRT	RA	D
0 5	6 10	11 15	16 31

lfs FRT, DS(RA)

$$FRT \leftarrow \left(MEM [((RA) + \left(^{16}D_{16} \parallel DS_{16, 31}\right)), 4]\right)$$

The lfs instruction loads the word contained at the effective address of the instruction into floating-point register FRT. The effective address of the instruction is found by adding the contents of RA to the sign extended 16-bit immediate field, unless RA is 0 (r0), in which case the effective address is just the sign extended immediate field. The word is treated as a single precision floating-point number and extended to double precision before being loaded into FRT.

lfsu
load single precision floating-point immediate with update

49	FRT	RA	D
0 5	6 10	11 15	16 31

lfsu FRT, D(RA)

$$FRT \leftarrow \left(\text{MEM}\left[\left((RA) + \left(^{16}D_{16} \parallel D_{16,31}\right)\right), 4\right]\right)$$

$$FRT \leftarrow (RA) + \left(^{16}D_{16} \parallel DS_{16,31}\right)$$

The lfsu instruction loads the word contained at the effective address of the instruction into floating-point register FRT. The effective address of the instruction is found by adding the contents of RA to the sign extended 16-bit immediate field. The word is treated as a single precision floating-point number and extended to double precision before being loaded into FRT. If RA=0 the instruction form is invalid.

In addition, the effective address is loaded into register RA.

lfsux
load single precision floating-point with update

31	FRT	RA	RB	567	/
0 5	6 10	11 15	16 20	21 30	31

lfsux RT, RA, RB

$$FRT \leftarrow (\text{MEM}\,[\,(\,(RA) + (RB)\,), 4\,])$$

$$RA \leftarrow (RA) + (RB)$$

The lfsux instruction loads the word contained at the effective address of the instruction into floating-point register FRT. The effective address of the instruction is found by adding the contents of RA to the contents of RB. The word is treated as a single precision floating-point number and extended to double precision before being loaded into FRT. If RA=0 the instruction form is invalid.

In addition, the effective address is loaded into register RA.

lfsx
load single precision floating-point

31	FRT	RA	RB	535	/
0 5	6 10	11 15	16 20	21 30	31

lfsx RT, RA, RB

$$FRT \leftarrow (\text{MEM}\,[\,(\,(RA) + (RB)\,), 4\,])$$

The lfsx instruction loads the word contained at the effective address of the instruction into floating-point register FRT. The effective address of the instruction is found by adding the contents of RA to the contents of RB, unless RA is 0 (r0), in which case the effective address is just the contents of RB. The word is treated as a single precision floating-point number and extended to double precision before being loaded into FRT.

lha
load halfword algebraic immediate

42	RT	RA	D
0 5	6 10	11 15	16 31

lha RT, D(RA)

$$RT \leftarrow {}^{16}(MEM[((RA)+({}^{16}D_{16} \parallel D_{16,31})), 2])_0 \parallel (MEM[((RA)+({}^{16}D_{16} \parallel D_{16,31})), 2])$$

The lha instruction loads the half-word contained at the effective address of the instruction into the low-order 2 bytes of RT. This halfword is sign-extended into the upper-order 2 bytes of RT. The effective address of the instruction is found by adding the contents of RA to the sign extended 16-bit immediate field, unless RA is 0 (r0), in which case the effective address is the sign extended immediate field.

lhau
load halfword algebraic immediate with update

43	RT	RA	D
0 5	6 10	11 15	16 31

lhau RT, D(RA)

$$RT \leftarrow {}^{16}(MEM[((RA)+({}^{16}D_{16} \parallel D_{16,31})), 2])_0 \parallel (MEM[((RA)+({}^{16}D_{16} \parallel D_{16,31})), 2])$$

$$RA \leftarrow (RA) + ({}^{16}D_{16} \parallel D_{16,31})$$

The lhau instruction loads the half-word contained at the effective address of the instruction into the low-order 2 bytes of RT. This halfword is sign-extended into the upper-order 2 bytes of RT. The effective address of the instruction is found by adding the contents of RA to the sign extended 16-bit immediate field. If RA=0 or RA=RT the instruction form is invalid.

In addition, the effective address is loaded into register RA.

lhaux
load halfword algebraic with update

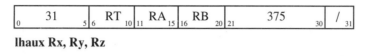

lhaux Rx, Ry, Rz

$$RT \leftarrow {}^{16}(MEM[((\widetilde{RA}) + (RB)), 2])_0 \parallel (MEM[((RA) + (RB)), 2])$$

$$RA \leftarrow (RA) + (RB)$$

The lhaux instruction loads the half-word contained at the effective address of the instruction into the low-order 2 bytes of RT. This halfword is sign-extended into the upper-order 2 bytes of RT. The effective address of the instruction is found by adding the contents of RA to the contents of RB. If RA=0 or RA=RT the instruction form is invalid.

In addition, the effective address is loaded into register RA.

lhax
load halfword algebraic

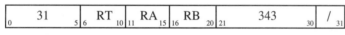

lhax RT, RA, RB

$$RT \leftarrow {}^{16}(MEM[((RA) + (RB)), 2])_0 \parallel (MEM[((RA) + (RB)), 2])$$

The lhax instruction loads the half-word contained at the effective address of the instruction into the low-order 2 bytes of RT. This halfword is sign-extended into the upper-order 2 bytes of RT. The effective address of the instruction is found by adding the contents of RA to the contents of RB, unless RA is 0 (r0), in which case the effective address is just the contents of RB.

lhbrx
load halfword and reverse bytes

0	31	5	6	RT	10	11	RA	15	11	RB	15	16	790	30	/	31

lhbrx RT, RA, RB

$$RT \leftarrow {}^{16}0 \parallel (MEM[((RA) + (RB) + 1), 1]) \parallel (MEM[((RA) + (RB)), 1])$$

The lhbrx instruction loads the half-word contained at the effective address of the instruction into the low-order 2 bytes of RT. The effective address of the instruction is found by adding the contents of RA to the contents of RB, unless RA is 0 (r0), in which case the effective address is RB. The remaining bytes in RT are set to 0. The two bytes of the loaded halfword are reversed (swapped) before being placed into RT.

lhz
load half-word and zero-extend immediate

40		RT		RA		D	
0	5 6	10	11	15	16		31

lhz RT, D(RA)

$$RT \leftarrow {}^{16}0 \parallel \left(\text{MEM} \left[\left((RA) + \left({}^{16}D_{16} \parallel D_{16,31} \right) \right), 2 \right] \right)$$

The lhz instruction loads the half-word contained at the effective address of the instruction into the low-order 2 bytes of RT. The effective address of the instruction is found by adding the contents of RA to the sign extended 16-bit immediate field, unless RA is 0 (r0), in which case the effective address is the sign extended immediate field. The remaining bytes in RT are set to 0.

lhzu
load half-word and zero-extend immediate with update

41		RT		RA		D	
0	5 6	10	11	15	16		31

lhzu RT, D(RA)

$$RT \leftarrow {}^{16}0 \parallel \left(\text{MEM} \left[\left((RA) + \left({}^{16}D_{16} \parallel D_{16,31} \right) \right), 2 \right] \right)$$

$$RA \leftarrow (RA) + \left({}^{16}D_{16} \parallel D_{16,31} \right)$$

The lhzu instruction loads the half-word contained at the effective address of the instruction into the low-order 2 bytes of RT. The effective address of the instruction is found by adding the contents of RA to the sign extended 16-bit immediate field. If RA=0 or RA=RT the instruction form is invalid. The remaining bytes in RT are set to 0.

In addition, the effective address of the instruction is loaded into RA.

lhzux
load half-word and zero-extend with update

31		RT		RA		RB		311		/	
0	5 6	10	11	15	11	15	16		30		31

lhzux RT, RA, RB

$$RT \leftarrow {}^{16}0 \parallel \left(\text{MEM} \left[\left((RA) + (RB) \right), 2 \right] \right)$$

$$RA \leftarrow (RA) + (RB)$$

The lhzux instruction loads the half-word contained at the effective address of the instruction into the low-order 2 bytes of RT. The effective address of the instruction is found by adding the contents of RA to the contents of RB. If RA=0 or RA=RT the instruction form is invalid. The remaining bytes in RT are set to 0.

In addition, the effective address of the instruction is loaded into RA.

lhzx
load half-word and zero-extend

31	RT	RA	RB	279	/
0 5	6 10	11 15	11 15	16 30	31

lhzx RT, RA, RB

$$RT \leftarrow {}^{16}0 \parallel (\text{MEM} [((RA) + (RB)), 2])$$

The lhzx instruction loads the half-word contained at the effective address of the instruction into the low-order 2 bytes of RT. The effective address of the instruction is found by adding the contents of RA to the contents of RB, unless RA is 0 (r0), in which case the effective address is RB. The remaining bytes in RT are set to 0.

li
load immediate

14	RT	0	D
0 5	6 10	11 15	16 31

li RT, D

$$RT \leftarrow \left({}^{16}D_{16} \parallel D_{16, 31} \right)$$

li RT, D

The li instruction loads the sign extended 16-bit immediate field into RT. This is an extended mnemonic for the add immediate (addi) instruction:

addi RT, r0, D

lis
load immediate shifted

15	RT	0	D
0 5	6 10	11 15	16 31

lis RT, D

$$RT \leftarrow \left(D_{16, 31} \parallel {}^{16}0 \right)$$

The lis instruction loads the 16-bit immediate field into the upper-order bits of RT, zeroing the low-order bits of RT. This is an extended mnemonic for the add immediate shifted (addis) instruction:

addis RT, r0, D

lmw
integer load multiple word

0	46	5 6	RT	10 11	RA	15 16	D	31

lmw RT, D(RA)

$$RT,R_{31} \leftarrow \left(\text{MEM} \left[\left((RA) + \left(^{16}D_{16} \parallel D_{16,31} \right) \right), (4 \times (32{-}RT)) \right] \right)$$

Registers RT through R_{31} are loaded with consecutive words read from memory starting at the effective address of the instruction. The effective address of the instruction is found by adding the contents of RA to the sign extended 16-bit immediate field, unless RA is 0 (r0), in which case the effective address is the sign extended immediate field. RA must be less than RB; the form is invalid if RA is in the range of registers to be loaded. The effective address must be a multiple of 4 (word aligned).

On 64-bit implementations, only the low-order 32 bits of each register are loaded; the high-order 32 bits are set to 0.

lswi
load string word immediate

0	31	5 6	RT	10 11	RA	15 16	n	20 21	597	30	/	31

lswi RT, RA, n
N6= (N=0)? 32in

$$RT, R_{\left(x + \frac{n}{4} \right)} \leftarrow (\text{MEM} \left[(RA), n \right])$$

Starting with RT, registers are loaded (only the low-order 4 bytes of 64-bit registers) with n consecutive bytes read from memory starting at the effective address of the instruction. The effective address of the instruction is the contents of RA, unless RA is 0 (r0), in which case the effective address is 0. The instruction is invalid if RA is in the range of registers to be loaded. If n=0 32 bytes are loaded. High-order 4 bytes of 64-bit registers are zeroed. Unfilled low-order bytes of last register are set to 0.

lswx
load string word indexed

| 0 | 31 | 5\|6 | RT | 10\|11 | RA | 15\|16 | RB | 20\|21 | 533 | 30\| | / | 31 |

lswx RT, RA, RB

$$RT, R_{\left(x + \frac{XER_{25,31}}{4}\right)} \leftarrow (\text{MEM}\ [\ (RA) + (RB)),\ XER_{25,31}\ ])$$

Starting with RT, registers are loaded (only the low-order 4 bytes of 64-bit registers) with consecutive bytes read from memory starting at the effective address of the instruction. The number of bytes to be loaded is stored in XER25:31. The effective address of the instruction is the contents of RA, unless RA is 0 (r0), in which case the effective address is 0. The instruction is invalid if RA is in the range of registers to be loaded. Unfilled low-order bytes of the last register are set to 0.

lwa
load word algebraic immediate

| 0 | 58 | 5\|6 | RT | 10\|11 | RA | 15\|16 | DS | 29\|30 | 2 | 31 |

lwa RT, D(RA)

$$RT \leftarrow {}^{32}(\text{MEM}[((RA)+({}^{16}DS_{16}\ \|\ DS_{16,29}\ \|{}^20),\ 4])_0\ \|\ (\text{MEM}[((RA)+({}^{16}DS_{16}\ \|\ DS_{16,29}\ \|{}^20),\ 4])$$

The lwa instruction loads the word contained at the effective address of the instruction into the low-order 4 bytes of RT. This word is sign-extended into the upper-order 4 bytes of RT. The effective address of the instruction is found by adding the contents of RA to the sign extended 14 bit immediate field, concatenated on the right with two binary zeros, unless RA is 0 (r0), in which case the effective address is the sign extended immediate field, concatenated on the right with two binary zeros.

This instruction is defined only for 64-bit implementations.

lwarx
load word and reserve

| 0 | 31 | 5\|6 | RT | 10\|11 | RA | 15\|11 | RB | 15\|16 | 20 | 30\| | / | 31 |

lwarx RT, RA, RB

$$RT \leftarrow (\text{MEM}\ [\ (\ (RA) + (RB)\ ),\ 4])$$

The lwarx instruction loads the word contained at the effective address of the instruction into RT. The effective address of the instruction is found by adding the contents of RA to the contents of RB, unless RA is 0 (r0), in which case the effective address is RB. The remaining bytes in RT are set to 0. The effective address must be a multiple of 4 (word aligned).

In addition, a reservation is created in this processor for use by the store word conditional (stwcx.) instruction. An address calculated from the effective address of this instruction is associated with the reservation (see Appendix C).

lwaux
load word algebraic with update

lwaux RT, RA, RB

$$RT \leftarrow {}^{32}(MEM[((RA) + (RB) + 4])_0 \parallel (MEM[((RA) + (RB) + 4])$$

$$RA \leftarrow (RA) + (RB)$$

The lwaux instruction loads the word contained at the effective address of the instruction into the low-order 4 bytes of RT. This word is sign-extended into the upper-order 4 bytes of RT. The effective address of the instruction is found by adding the contents of RA to the contents of RB. If Ra=0 or RA=RT the instruction form is invalid.

In addition, the effective address is loaded into register RA.

This instruction is defined only for 64-bit implementations.

lwax
load word algebraic

	31		RT		RA		RB		341		/
0		5 6		10 11		15 16		20 21		30	31

lwax RT, RA, RB

$$RT \leftarrow {}^{32}(MEM[((RA) + (RB)), 4])_0 \parallel (MEM[((RA) + (RB)), 4])$$

The lwax instruction loads the word contained at the effective address of the instruction into the low-order 4 bytes of RT. This word is sign-extended into the upper-order 4 bytes of RT. The effective address of the instruction is found by adding the contents of RA to the contents of RB, unless RA is 0 (r0), in which case the effective address is just the contents of RB.

This instruction is defined only for 64-bit implementations.

lwbrx
load word and reverse bytes (indexed addressing form)

31		RT		RA		RB		534		/
0	5 6		10 11		15 16		20 21		30	31

lwbrx RT, RA, RB

$$RT \leftarrow (\text{MEM}[((RA) + (RB)) + 3), 1]) \, \| \, (\text{MEM}[((RA) + (RB)) + 2), 1]) \, \|$$
$$(\text{MEM}[((RA) + (RB)) + 1), 1]) \, \| \, (\text{MEM}[((RA) + (RB)), 1])$$

The lwbrx instruction loads the word contained at the effective address of the instruction into RT. The effective address of the instruction is found by adding the contents of RA to the contents of RB, unless RA is 0 (r0), in which case the effective address is RB. The remaining bytes in RT are set to 0. The order of the four bytes of the loaded word are reversed before being placed into RT.

lwz
load word and zero-extend immediate

32		RT		RA		D	
0	5 6		10 11		15 16		31

lwz RT, D(RA)

$$RT \leftarrow \left(\text{MEM} \left[\left((RA) + \left({}^{16}D_{16} \, \| \, D_{16, 31} \right) \right), 4 \right] \right)$$

The lwz instruction loads the word contained at the effective address of the instruction into RT. The effective address of the instruction is found by adding the contents of RA to the sign extended 16-bit immediate field, unless RA is 0 (r0), in which case the effective address is the sign extended immediate field.

lwzu
load word and zero-extend immediate with update

33		RT		RA		D	
0	5 6		10 11		15 16		31

lwzu RT, D(RA)

$$RT \leftarrow \left(\text{MEM} \left[\left((RA) + \left({}^{16}D_{16} \, \| \, D_{16, 31} \right) \right), 4 \right] \right)$$

$$RA \leftarrow (RA) + \left({}^{16}D_{16} \, \| \, D_{16, 31} \right)$$

The lwzu instruction loads the word contained at the effective address of the instruction into RT. The effective address of the instruction is found by adding the contents of RA to the sign extended 16-bit immediate field, unless RA is 0 (r0), in which case the effective address is the sign extended immediate field. If Ra=0 or RA=RT the instruction form is invalid.

In addition, the effective address of the instruction is loaded into RA.

lwzux
load word and zero-extend with update

31		RT		RA		RB		55		/	
0	5	6	10	11	15	11	15	16	30		31

lwzux RT, RA, RB

$$RT \leftarrow (MEM [((RA) + (RB)), 4])$$

$$RA \leftarrow (RA) + (RB)$$

The lwzux instruction loads the word contained at the effective address of the instruction into RT. The effective address of the instruction is found by adding the contents of RA to the contents of RB, unless RA is 0 (r0), in which case the effective address is RB. The remaining bytes in RT are set to 0. If Ra=0 or RA=RT the instruction form is invalid.

In addition, the effective address of the instruction is loaded into RA.

lwzx
load word and zero-extend

31		RT		RA		RB		23		/	
0	5	6	10	11	15	11	15	16	30		31

lwzx RT, RA, RB

$$RT \leftarrow (MEM [((RA) + (RB), 4])$$

The lwzx instruction loads the word contained at the effective address of the instruction into RT. The effective address of the instruction is found by adding the contents of RA to the contents of RB, unless RA is 0 (r0), in which case the effective address is RB. The remaining bytes in RT are set to 0.

mcrf
move condition register field

19		BF		/		BFA		/		/		0		/	
0	5	6	8	9	10	11	13	14	15	16	20	21	30		31

mcrf BF, BFA

$$CR_{BF} \leftarrow (CR_{BFA})$$

The mcrf instruction copies condition register field BA (CRBA) into condition register field BF (CR$_{BF}$).

mcrfs
move FPSCR to condition register

0	63	5	6	BT	8	9	/	10	11	BA	13	14	/	15	16	/	20	21	64	30	/	31

mcrfs BT, BA

$$CR_{BT} \leftarrow (FPSCR_{BA})$$

The mcrfs instruction copies FPSCR field by $(FPSCR_{BA})$ into condition register field BT (CR_{BT}).

The following FPSCR fields may be updated by this instruction (see Appendix D):

FX, OX, UX, ZX, XX, VXSNAN, VXISI, VXIDI, VXZDZ, VXIMZ, VXVC, VXSOFT, VXSQRT, and VXCVI.

mcrxr
move XER to condition register

0	31	5	6	BF	8	9	/	10	11	/	15	16	/	20	21	512	30	/	31

mcrxr BF

$$CR_{BF} \leftarrow XER_{0:\,3}$$
$$XER_{0:3} \leftarrow OBOOOO$$

The mcrxr instruction copies XER bits 0–3 into condition register field BF (CR_{BF}). In addition, XER bits 0–3 are set to 0.

mfcr
move from condition register

0	31	5	6	RT	10	11	/	15	16	/	20	21	19	30	/	31

mfcr RT

$$RT \leftarrow (CR)$$

The mfcr instruction copies the contents of the condition register into the register RT.

mfctr
move from count register (CTR)

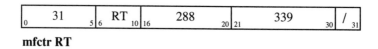

mfctr RT

$$RT \leftarrow (CTR)$$

The mfctr instruction copies the contents of the count register into the register RT. This is an extended mnemonic of the move from SPR (mfspr) instruction:

mfspr RT, 9

mffs[.]
move from FPSCR

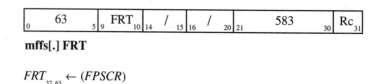

mffs[.] FRT

$$FRT_{32, 63} \leftarrow (FPSCR)$$

The mffs[.] instruction copies the contents of the FPSCR into the low-order 32 bits of floating-point register FRT.

If the Rc bit is set (mffs.), then CR_1 is updated.

mflr
move from link register (LR)

| 0 | 31 | 5 | 6 | RT | 10 | 16 | 256 | 20 | 21 | 339 | 30 | / | 31 |

mflr RT

$$RT \leftarrow (LR)$$

The mflr instruction copies the contents of the link register into the register RT. This is an extended mnemonic of the move from SPR (mfspr) instruction:

mfspr RT, 8

mfmsr
move from machine state register

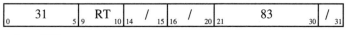

mfmsr RT

$RT \leftarrow (MSR)$

The mfmsr instruction copies the contents of the MSR into register RT.

This instruction is privileged (see Appendix C).

mfspr
move from special purpose register

mfspr RT

$RT \leftarrow (SPR)$

The mfspr instruction copies the contents of the special purpose register identified by the SPR field into the register RT (see Table B.5). Note that the decimal values used in the instruction mnemonic do not correspond exactly to the SPR field values. This is because the SPR field is split with the upper-order 5 bits to the right of the lower-order five bits.

Table B.5. SPR encodings.

Special Purpose Register	Encoding Decimal	SPR field	Privileged	Read/ Write
Integer Exception Register (XER)	1	0x020	no	R/W
Link Register (LR)	8	0x100	no	R/W
Count Register (CTR)	9	0x120	no	R/W
Data Storage Interrupt Status Register (DSISR)	18	0x240	yes	R/W
Data Address Register (DAR)	19	0x260	yes	R/W
Decrementor (DEC)	22	0x2C0	yes	R/W
Storage Descriptor Register 1 (SDR1)	25	0x320	yes	R/W
Machine Status Save/Restore Register 0 (SRR0)	26	0x340	yes	R/W

continues

Table B.5. continued

Special Purpose Register	Decimal	Encoding SPR field	Privileged	Read/ Write
Machine Status Save/Restore Register 1 (SRR1)	27	0x360	yes	R/W
Software Use SPR 0 (SPRG0)	272	0x208	yes	R/W
Software Use SPR 1 (SPRG1)	273	0x228	yes	R/W
Software Use SPR 2 (SPRG2)	274	0x248	yes	R/W
Software Use SPR 3 (SPRG3)	275	0x268	yes	R/W
Address Space Register (ASR)[1]	280	0x308	yes	R/W
External Access Register (EAR)	282	0x348	yes	R/W
Time Base Lower (TBL)	284	0x388	yes	W
Time Base Upper (TBU)	285	0x3A8	yes	W
Processor Version Register (PVR)	287	0x3E8	yes	R
Instruction Block Address Translation Upper Register 0 (IBAT0U)	528	0x210	yes	R/W
Instruction Block Address Translation Lower Register 0 (IBAT0L)	529	0x230	yes	R/W
Instruction Block Address Translation Upper Register 1 (IBAT1U)	530	0x250	yes	R/W
Instruction Block Address Translation Lower Register 1 (IBAT1L)	531	0x270	yes	R/W
Instruction Block Address Translation Upper Register 2 (IBAT2U)	532	0x290	yes	R/W
Instruction Block Address Translation Lower Register 2 (IBAT2L)	533	0x2B0	yes	R/W
Instruction Block Address Translation Upper Register 3 (IBAT3U)	534	0x2D0	yes	R/W

Special Purpose Register	Encoding				Read/ Write
		Decimal	SPR field	Privileged	
Instruction Block Address Translation Lower Register 3 (IBAT3L)		535	0x2F0	yes	R/W
Data Block Address Translation Upper Register 0 (DBAT0U)		536	0x310	yes	R/W
Data Block Address Translation Lower Register 0 (DBAT0L)		537	0x330	yes	R/W
Data Block Address Translation Upper Register 1 (DBAT1U)		538	0x350	yes	R/W
Data Block Address Translation Lower Register 1 (DBAT1L)		539	0x370	yes	R/W
Data Block Address Translation Upper Register 2 (DBAT2U)		540	0x390	yes	R/W
Data Block Address Translation Lower Register 2 (DBAT2L)		541	0x3B0	yes	R/W
Data Block Address Translation Upper Register 3 (DBAT3U)		542	0x3D0	yes	R/W
Data Block Address Translation Lower Register 3 (DBAT3L)		543	0x3F0	yes	R/W
Data Address Breakpoint Register (DABR)	1013	0x2BF	yes	R/W	

[1] 64-bit implementations only.

mfsr
move from segment register

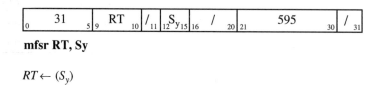

mfsr RT, Sy

$RT \leftarrow (S_y)$

The mfsr instruction copies the contents of segment register Sy into register RT.

This instruction is privileged (see Appendix C). This instruction is defined only for 32-bit implementations.

mfsrin
move from segment register indirect

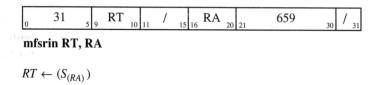

mfsrin RT, RA

$RT \leftarrow (S_{(RA)})$

The mfsrin instruction copies the contents of the segment register pointed to by the high-order 4 bits of register RA into register RT.

This instruction is privileged (see Appendix C). This instruction is defined only for 32-bit implementations.

mftb
move from time base register

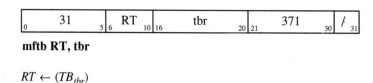

mftb RT, tbr

$RT \leftarrow (TB_{tbr})$

The mftb instruction copies the contents of the either the time base or time base upper register into the register RT (see Table B.6). Notice that the decimal encoding used in the mnemonic is different from the encoding used in the tbr field; the 5-bit halves of the tbr field are reversed.

Table B.6. TBR encodings for mftb instruction.

| | Encoding | | |
Time Base Regsiter	Decimal	TBR field	Privileged
Time Base (TB)	268	0x188	no
Time Base Upper (TBU)	269	0x1A8	no

mftb
move from time base register

31	RT	392	371	/
0 5	6 10	16 20	21 30	31

mftb RT

$RT \leftarrow (TB)$

The mftb instruction copies the contents of the time base (TB) register into the register RT. On 64-bit implementations, this instruction loads the entire 64-bit time base register into RT, while on 32-bit implementations only the low-order 32-bits of the time base register are loaded into RT. This is an extended mnemonic of the move from time base (mftb) instruction (the difference being the number of operands):

mftb RT, 268

mftbu
move from time base register upper

31	RT	424	371	/
0 5	6 10	16 20	21 30	31

mftbu RT

$RT \leftarrow (TBU)$

The mftbu instruction copies the contents of the time base upper (TBU) register into the register RT. On 64-bit implementations, this instruction loads the upper-order 32-bits of the time base register into the low-order 32-bits of register RT. This is an extended mnemonic of the move from time base (mftb) instruction:

mftb RT, 269

mfxer
move from integer exception register (XER)

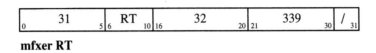

mfxer RT

$RT \leftarrow (XER)$

The mfxer instruction copies the contents of the fixed point exception register into the register RT. This is an extended mnemonic of the move from SPR (mfspr) instruction:

mfspr RT, 1

mr[.]
move register

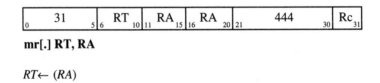

mr[.] RT, RA

$RT \leftarrow (RA)$

mr[.] RT, RA

The mr[.] instruction copies the contents of register RA into register RT. This is an extended mnemonic for the logical OR (or[.])instruction:

or[.] RT, RA, RA

If the Rc bit is set (mr.), then CR0 is updated.

mtcr
move to condition register

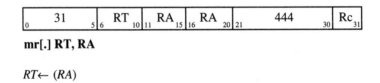

mtcr RA

$CR \leftarrow (RA)$

The mtcr instruction copies the contents of register RA into the condition register. This is an extended mnemonic for the move to condition register fields (mtcrf) instruction:

mtcrf 0xFF, RA

mtcrf
move to condition register fields

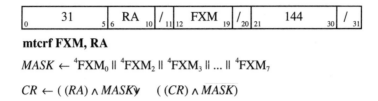

mtcrf FXM, RA

$$MASK \leftarrow {}^4FXM_0 \parallel {}^4FXM_2 \parallel {}^4FXM_3 \parallel ... \parallel {}^4FXM_7$$

$$CR \leftarrow ((RA) \wedge MASK) \parallel ((CR) \wedge \overline{MASK})$$

mtcrf FXM, RA

The mtcrf instruction copies the contents of register RA into the condition register under the control of the immediate field FXM. If there is a one in a bit position in the FXM field, then the corresponding field in the condition register is updated from RA. Otherwise, the field is left unchanged.

mtctr
move to count register (CTR)

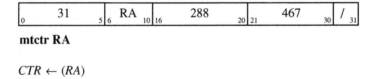

mtctr RA

$$CTR \leftarrow (RA)$$

The mtctr instruction copies the contents of register RA into the count register. This is an extended mnemonic of the move to SPR (mtspr) instruction:

mtspr RA, 9

mtfsb0[.]
move to FPSCR bit 0 (reset FPSCR bit)

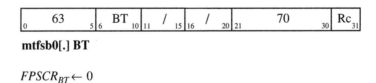

mtfsb0[.] BT

$$FPSCR_{BT} \leftarrow 0$$

The mtfsb0[.] instruction sets FPSCR bit BT (FPSCRBT) to 0.

If the Rc bit is set (mtfsb0.), then CR1 is updated. Note that bits 1 and 2 (FEX and VX) cannot be explicitly reset.

mtfsb1[.]
move to FPSCR bit 1 (set FPSCR bit)

| 0 | 63 | 5 | 6 | BT | 10 | 11 | / | 15 | 16 | / | 20 | 21 | 38 | 30 | Rc | 31 |

mtfsb1[.] BT

$FPSCR_{BT} \leftarrow 1$

The mtfsb1[.] instruction sets FPSCR bit BT (FPSCRBT) to one.

If the Rc bit is set (mtfsb1.), then CR1 is updated. Note that bits 1 and 2 (FEX and VX) cannot be explicitly reset.

mtfsf[.]
move to FPSCR fields

| 0 | 63 | 5 | / | 6 | 7 | FLM | 14 | / | 15 | 16 | FRA | 20 | 21 | 711 | 30 | Rc | 31 |

mtfsf[.] FLM, FRA

$MASK \leftarrow (\, ^4FLM_0 \, \| \, ^4FLM_1 \, \| \, ^4FLM_2 \, \| \, ... \, \| \, ^4FLM_7)$

$FPSCR \leftarrow (\, (FRA) \wedge MASK) \vee (\, (FPSCR) \wedge \overline{MASK})$

The mtfsf[.] instruction copies the contents of floating-point register FRA into the FPSCR under control of the 8-bit immediate field FLM. If there is a one bit in FLM, then the corresponding 4-bit field of the FPSCR is updated from the contents of FRA.

If the Rc bit is set (mtfsb1.), then CR1 is updated. Note that if field 0 is specified, bits 1 and 2 retain their meaning on new bit values (summary of exceptions), rather than being assigned directly from FRA.

mtfsfi[.]
move to FPSCR field immediate

| 0 | 63 | 5 | 6 | BF | 8 | 9 | / | 10 | 11 | / | 15 | 16 | U | 19 | / | 20 | 21 | 134 | 30 | Rc | 31 |

mtfsfi[.] BF, U

$FPSCR_{BF} \leftarrow U$

The mtfsfi[.] instruction sets FPSCR field BF (FPSCR_BF) to the value in the immediate field U.

If the Rc bit is set (mtfsfi.), then CR1 is updated. Note that if BT=0, bits 1 and 2 retain their meaning on the new bit values, rather than being set from U.

mtlr
move to link register (LR)

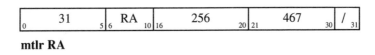

mtlr RA

LR ← (RA)

The mtlr instruction copies the contents of register RA into the link register. This is an extended mnemonic of the move to SPR (mtspr) instruction:

mtspr RA, 8

mtmsr
move to machine state register

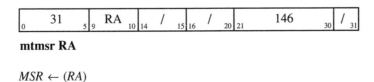

mtmsr RA

MSR ← (RA)

The mtmsr instruction copies the contents of register RA into the MSR.

This instruction is privileged (see Appendix C).

mtspr
move to special purpose register

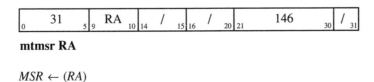

mtspr RA

SPR$_{spr}$ ← (RA)

The mtspr instruction copies the contents of register RA into the special purpose register specified by the SPR field (see Table B.5).

mtsr
move to segment register

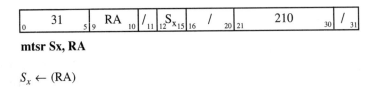

mtsr Sx, RA

$S_x \leftarrow (RA)$

The mtsr instruction copies the contents of register RA into segment register S_x.

This instruction is privileged (see Appendix C). This instruction is defined only for 32-bit implementations.

mtsrin
move to segment register indirect

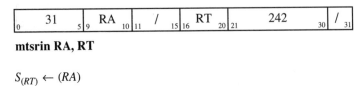

mtsrin RA, RT

$S_{(RT)} \leftarrow (RA)$

The mtsrin instruction copies the contents of register RA into the segment register pointed to by the high-order 4 bits of register RT.

This instruction is privileged (see Appendix C). This instruction is defined only for 32-bit implementations.

mtxer
move to integer exception register (XER)

0	31	5	6	RA	10	16	32	20	21	467	30	/	31

mtxer RA

$XER \leftarrow (RA)$

The mtxer instruction copies the contents of register RA into the fixed point exception register. This is an extended mnemonic of the move to SPR (mtspr) instruction:

mtspr RA, 1

mulhd[.]
multiply integer doubleword, return high doubleword

31		RT		RA		RB		/		73		Rc	
0	5	6	10	11	15	16	20	21	22		30		31

mulhd[.] RT, RA, RB

$$RT \leftarrow ((RA) \times (RB))_{0, 63}$$

The mulhd[.] instruction stores the upper-order 64 bits of the product of the contents of RA and the contents of RB into RT. The contents of RA, RB, and the result are signed doubleword integers.

If the mulhd. form of the instruction is used, then CR0 is updated.

This instruction is defined only for 64-bit implementations.

mulhdu[.]
multiply integer doubleword unsigned, return high doubleword

31		RT		RA		RB		/		9		Rc	
0	5	6	10	11	15	16	20	21	22		30		31

mulhdu[.] RT, RA, RB

$$RT \leftarrow ((RA) \times (RB))_{0, 63}$$

The mulhdu[.] instruction stores the upper-order 64 bits of the product of the contents of RA and the contents of RB into RT. The contents of RA, RB, and the result are unsigned doubleword integers.

If the mulhdu. form of the instruction is used, then CR0 is updated.

This instruction is defined only for 64-bit implementations.

mulhw[.]
multiply integer word, return high word

31		RT		RA		RB		/		75		Rc	
0	5	6	10	11	15	16	20	21	22		30		31

mulhw[.] RT, RA, RB

$$RT \leftarrow ((RA) \times (RB))_{0, 31}$$

The mulhw[.] instruction stores the upper-order 32 bits of the product of the contents of RA and the contents of RB into RT. The contents of RA, RB, and the result are signed word integers.

If the mulhw. form of the instruction is used, then CR0 is updated. Note that if Rc=1 and in 64-bit mode, $CR_{0:2}$ are undefined.

mulhwu[.]
multiply integer word unsigned , return high word

| 0 | 31 | 5 | 6 | RT | 10 | 11 | RA | 15 | 16 | RB | 20 | / | 21 | 22 | 11 | 30 | Rc | 31 |

mulhwu[.] RT, RA, RB

$RT \leftarrow ((RA) \times (RB))_{0,\,31}$

The mulhwu[.] instruction stores the upper-order 32 bits of the product of the contents of RA and the contents of RB into RT. The contents of RA, RB, and their result are unsigned word integers.

If the mulhw. form of the instruction is used, then CR0 is updated.

mulld[o][.]
multiply integer doubleword, return low doubleword

| 0 | 31 | 5 | 6 | RT | 10 | 11 | RA | 15 | 16 | RB | 20 | Oe | 21 | 22 | 233 | 30 | Rc | 31 |

mulld[o][.] RT, RA, RB

$RT \leftarrow ((RA) \times (RB))_{64,\,127}$

The mulld[o][.] instruction stores the lower-order 64 bits of the product of the contents of RA and the contents of RB into RT. The contents of RA, RB, and their result are double-word integers.

If the mulldo[.] form of the instruction is used, then the overflow and summary overflow bits of the XER are set if overflow occurs.

If the mulld[o]. form of the instruction is used, then CR0 is updated.

This instruction is defined only for 64-bit implementations.

mulli
multiply integer immediate, return low word

| 0 | 7 | 5 | 6 | RT | 10 | 11 | RA | 15 | 16 | si | 31 |

mulli RT, RA, si

$RT \leftarrow \left((RA) \times \left({}^{16}si_{16} \parallel si_{16,\,31} \right) \right)_{32,\,63}$

The mulli instruction stores the lower-order 32 bits of the product of the contents of RA and the sign extended immediate value into RT. On 32-bit implementations, the contents of RA and the result are signed word integers. On 64-bit implementations, the contents of RA and the result are signed doubleword integers.

mullw[o][.]
multiply integer word, return low word

31		RT		RA		RB		Oe		235		Rc
0	5 6	10	11	15	16	20	21	22		30	31

mullw[o][.] RT, RA, RB

$$RT \leftarrow ((RA) \times (RB))_{32, 63}$$

The mullw[o][.] instruction stores the lower-order 32 bits of the product of the contents of RA and the contents of RB into RT. The contents of both RA and RB, and the result are word integers.

If the mullwo[.] form of the instruction is used, then the overflow and summary overflow bits of the XER are set if overflow occurs.

If the mullw[o]. form of the instruction is used, then CR0 is updated.

nand[.]
logical NAND

31		RA		RT		RB		476		Rc
0	5 6	10	11	15	16	20	21		30	31

nand[.] RT, RA, RB

$$RT \leftarrow \overline{(RA) \wedge (RB)}$$

The nand[.] instruction performs a logical NAND of the contents of register RA with the contents of register RB. The result of this is then stored into register RT.

If the Rc bit is set (nand.), then CR0 is updated.

neg[o][.]
integer negate

31		RT		RA		/		Oe		104		Rc
0	5 6	10	11	15	16	20	21	22		30	31

neg[o][.] RT, RA

$$RT \leftarrow -(RA)$$

The neg[o][.] instruction stores the arithmetic negation of the contents of RA into RT.

If the nego[.] form of the instruction is used, then the overflow and summary overflow bits of the XER are set if overflow occurs.

If the neg[o]. form of the instruction is used, then CR0 is updated.

nop
no operation

24	0	0	0
0 5	6 10	11 15	16 30

nop

[nothing]

The nop instruction does nothing. This is an extended mnemonic for the logical OR (or[.]) instruction:

or 0, 0, 0

nor[.]
logical NOR

The nor[.] instruction performs a logical NOR of the contents of register RA with the con-

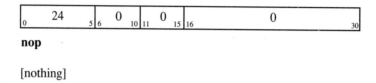

nor[.] RT, RA, RB

$RT \leftarrow \overline{(RA) \vee (RB)}$

tents of register RB. The result of this is then stored into register RT.

If the Rc bit is set (nor.), then CR0 is updated.

not[.]
logical NOT

31	RA	RT	RA	124	Rc
0 5	6 10	11 15	16 20	21 30	31

not[.] RT, RA

$RT \leftarrow \overline{(RA)}$

The not[.] instruction performs a logical negation of the contents of register RA. The result of this is then stored into register RT. This is an extended mnemonic for the logical NOR (nor[.]) instruction:

nor[.] RT, RA, RA

If the Rc bit is set (nor.), then CR0 is updated.

or[.]
logical OR

31	RA	RT	RB	444	Rc
0 5	6 10	11 15	16 20	21 30	31

or[.] RT, RA, RB

$$RT \leftarrow (RA) \vee (RB)$$

The or[.] instruction performs a logical OR of the contents of register RA with the contents of register RB. The result of this is then stored into register RT.

If the Rc bit is set (or.), then CR0 is updated.

orc[.]
logical OR with compliment

31	RA	RT	RB	412	Rc
0 5	6 10	11 15	16 20	21 30	31

orc[.] RT, RA, RB

$$RT \leftarrow (RA) \vee (\overline{RB})$$

The orc[.] instruction performs a logical OR of the contents of register RA with the logical negation of the contents of register RB. The result of this is then stored into register RT.

If the Rc bit is set (orc.), then CR0 is updated.

ori
logical OR immediate

24	RA	RT	ui
0 5	6 10	11 15	16 31

ori RT, RA, ui

$$RT \leftarrow (RA) \vee \left({}^{16}0 \parallel ui \right)$$

The ori instruction performs a logical OR of the low-order 16 bits of the contents of register RA with the immediate field ui; the high-order 16 bits of RA are unchanged. The result of this is then stored into register RT.

oris
logical OR shifted immediate

25		RA		RT		ui	
0	5 6		10 11		15 16		31

oris RT, RA, ui

$$RT \leftarrow (RA)\text{v} \left(ui \, \| \, {}^{16}0 \right)$$

The oris instruction performs a logical OR register RA with the immediate field ui. The result of this is then stored into register RT.

rfi
return from interrupt

19		/		/		/		50		/	
0	5 6		10 11		15 16		20 21		30		31

rfi

This instruction is used to return control to a user application from an interrupt handler. The MSR is updated from SRR1, and control is passed to the instruction at the address contained in SRR0 (see Appendix C).

This instruction is privileged and context synchronizing.

rldcl[.]
rotate left doubleword, then clear left

30		RA		RT		RB		mb		8		Rc
0	5 6		10 11		15 16		20 21		26 27		30	31

rldcl[.] RT, RA, RB, MB

$$MB = mb_{26} \, \| \, mb_{21:25}$$

$$RT \leftarrow \text{ROT} \left((RA), (RB) \right) \wedge \text{MASK} \left((mb_{26} \, \| \, mb_{21,25}), 63 \right)$$

The rldcl[.] instruction rotates the contents of register RA left by the number of bits specified in the low-order 6 bits of register RB, then performs a logical AND of this with a mask consisting of MB zeros followed by 64-MB ones. This result is then stored into RT.

If the Rc bit is set (rldcl.), then CR0 is updated.

This instruction is defined only for 64-bit implementations.

rldcr[.]
rotate left doubleword then clear right

0	30	5	6	RA	10	11	RT	15	16	RB	20	21	me	26	27	9	29	Rc	31

rldcr[.] RT, RA, RB, ME

$ME = me_{26} \parallel me_{21:26}$

$RT \leftarrow \text{ROT} ((RA), (RB)) \wedge \text{MASK} (0, (me_{26} \parallel me_{21, 25}))$

The rldcr[.] instruction rotates the contents of register RA left by the number of bits specified in the low-order 6 bits of register RB, then performs a logical AND of this with a mask consisting of ME+1 ones followed by 63-ME zeros. This result is then stored into RT.

If the Rc bit is set (rldicr.), then CR0 is updated.

This instruction is defined only for 64-bit implementations.

rldic[.]
rotate left doubleword then clear

0	30	5	6	RA	10	11	RT	15	16	$sh_{1:5}$	20	21	mb	26	27	2	29	sh_0	30	Rc	31

rldic[.] RT, RA, sh, MB

$MB = mb_{26} \parallel mb_{21:25}$

$R_x \leftarrow \text{ROT} ((R_y), sh) \wedge \text{MASK} ((mb_{26} \parallel mb_{21, 25}), (63 - sh))$

The rldic[.] instruction rotates the contents of register RA left by sh bits then performs a logical AND of this with a 64-bit mask consisting of ones starting at bit MB and continuing (possibly wrapping) until bit 64-sh. This result is then stored into RT.

If the Rc bit is set (rldic.) then CR0 is updated.

This instruction is defined only for 64-bit implementations.

rldicl[.]
rotate left doubleword immediate then clear left

0	30	5	6	RA	10	11	RT	15	16	$sh_{1:5}$	20	21	mb	26	27	0	29	sh_0	30	Rc	31

rldicl[.] Rx, Ry, sh, MB

$MB = mb_{26} \parallel mb_{21:25}$

$RT \leftarrow \text{ROT} ((RA), sh) \wedge \text{MASK} ((mb_{26} \parallel mb_{21, 25}), 63)$

The rldicl[.] instruction rotates the contents of register RA left by sh bits then performs a logical AND of this with a mask consisting of MB zeros followed by 64-MB ones. This result is then stored into RT.

If the Rc bit is set (rldicl.), then CR0 is updated.

This instruction is defined only for 64-bit implementations.

rldicr[.]
rotate left doubleword immediate then clear right

30	RA	RT	$sh_{1:5}$	me	1	sh_0	Rc
0 5	6 10	11 15	16 20	21 26	27 29	30	31

rldicr[.] RT, RA, sh, ME

$ME = me_{26} \parallel me_{21:25}$

$RT \leftarrow \text{ROT} ((RA), sh) \wedge \text{MASK} (0, (me_{26} \parallel me_{21,25}))$

The rldicr[.] instruction rotates the contents of register RA left by sh bits, then performs a logical AND of this with a mask consisting of ME+1 ones followed by 63-ME zeros. This result is then stored into RT.

If the Rc bit is set (rldicr.), then CR0 is updated.

This instruction is defined only for 64-bit implementations.

rldimi[.]
rotate left doubleword immediate then insert mask

30	RA	RT	$sh_{1:5}$	mb	3	sh_0	Rc
0 5	6 10	11 15	16 20	21 26	27 29	30	31

rldimi[.] RT, RA, sh, MB

$MB = mb_{26} \parallel mb_{21:25}$

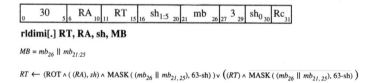

$RT \leftarrow (\text{ROT} \wedge ((RA), sh) \wedge \text{MASK} ((mb_{26} \parallel mb_{21,25}), 63\text{-}sh)) \vee ((RT) \wedge \text{MASK} ((\overline{mb_{26} \parallel mb_{21,25}}), 63\text{-}sh))$

The rldimi[.] instruction rotates the contents of register RA left by sh bits, then inserts this into register RT under control of a 64-bit mask consisting of ones starting at bit MB and continuing (possibly wrapping) until bit 63-sh. Wherever there is a one in the mask, the bit is taken from the rotated register RA, and wherever there is a 0, the bit is taken from the contents of RT. The result is stored into RT.

If the Rc bit is set (rldimi.) then CR0 is updated.

This instruction is defined only for 64-bit implementations.

rlwimi[.]
rotate left word immediate then insert mask

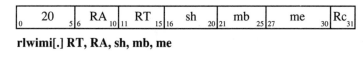

rlwimi[.] RT, RA, sh, mb, me

$RT \leftarrow (\text{ROT}(\,(RA),\,sh) \wedge \text{MASK}\,(mb, me)\,), \vee \,((RT) \wedge \overline{\text{MASK}\,(mb, me)}\,)$

The rlwimi[.] instruction rotates the contents of register RA left by sh bits, then inserts this into register RT under control of a 64-bit mask consisting of ones starting at bit MB and continuing (possibly wrapping) until bit 63-sh. Wherever there is a one in the mask, the bit is taken from the rotated register RA, and wherever there is a 0, the bit is taken from the contents of RT. The result is stored into RT.

If the Rc bit is set (rlwimi.), then CR0 is updated.

rlwinm[.]
rotate left word immediate then AND with mask

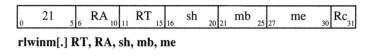

rlwinm[.] RT, RA, sh, mb, me

$RT \leftarrow (\text{ROT}(\,(RA),\,sh) \wedge \text{MASK}\,(mb, me)\,)$

The rlwinm[.] instruction rotates the contents of register RA left by sh bits then performs a logical bitwise AND of this with a 64-bit mask consisting of ones starting at bit MB and continuing (possibly wrapping) until bit 63-sh. The result is stored into RT.

If the Rc bit is set (rlwinm.), then CR0 is updated.

rlwnm[.]
rotate left word then AND with mask

| 0 | 23 | 5\|6 | RA | 10\|11 | RT | 15\|16 | RB | 20\|21 | mb | 25\|27 | me | 30 | Rc | 31 |

rlwnm[.] RT, RA, RB, mb, me

$RT \leftarrow (\text{ROT}(\,(RA),\,(RB)\,) \wedge \text{MASK}\,(mb, me)\,)$

The rlwnm[.] instruction rotates the contents of register RA left by the amount specified in the low-order 5 bits of the contents of RB, then performs a logical bitwise AND of this with a 64-bit mask consisting of ones starting at bit MB and continuing (possibly wrapping) until bit 63-sh. The result is stored into RT.

If the Rc bit is set (rlwnm.), then CR0 is updated.

rotld[.]
rotate left doubleword

0	30	5	6	RA	10	11	RT	15	16	RB	20	21	0	26	27	8	30	Rc	31

rldcl[.] RT, RA, RB

$RT \leftarrow ROT((RA), (RB))$

The rotld[.] instruction rotates the contents of register RA left by the number of bits specified in the low-order six bits of register RB, then stores this result into RT. This is an extended mnemonic for the rotate left doubleword and clear left (rldcl[.]) instruction:

rldcl[.] RT, RA, RB, 0

If the Rc bit is set (rldcl.), then CR0 is updated.

This instruction is defined only for 64-bit implementations.

rotldi[.]
rotate left doubleword immediate

0	30	5	6	R_y	10	11	R_x	15	16	$n_{1:5}$	20	21	0	26	27	0	29	n_0	30	Rc	31

rotldi[.] RT, RA, n

$RT \leftarrow ROT((RA), n)$

The rotldi[.] instruction rotates the contents of register RA left by n bits, then stores this result into RT. This is an extended mnemonic for the rotate left doubleword and clear left (rldcl[.]) instruction:

rldicl[.] RT, RA, n, 0

If the Rc bit is set (rotldi.) then CR0 is updated.

This instruction is defined only for 64-bit implementations.

rotlw[.]
rotate left word

0	23	5	6	RA	10	11	RT	15	16	RB	20	21	0	25	27	31	30	Rc	31

rotlw[.] RT, RA, RB

$RT \leftarrow ROT((RA), (RB))$

The rotlw[.] instruction rotates the contents of register RA left by the amount specified in the low-order 5 bits of the contents of RB, then stores this result into RT. This is an extended mnemonic for the rotate left word then AND with mask (rlwnm[.]) instruction:

rlwnm[.] RT, RA, RB, 0, 31

If the Rc bit is set (rlwnm.), then CR0 is updated.

rotlwi[.]
rotate left word immediate

0	21	5	6	RA	10	11	RT	15	16	n	20	21	0	25	27	31	30	Rc	31

rotlwi[.] RT, RA, n

$RT \leftarrow ROT\ (\ (RA),\ n)$

The rotlwi[.] instruction rotates the contents of register RA left by n bits then store this result into RT. This is an extended mnemonic for the rotate left word immediate then AND with mask (rlwinm[.]) instruction:

rlwinm[.] RT, RA, n, 0, 31

If the Rc bit is set (rotlwi.), then CR0 is updated.

rotrdi[.]
rotate right doubleword immediate

0	30	5	6	RA	10	11	RT	15	16	$(64-n)_{1:5}$	20	21	0	26	27	0	29	$(64-n)_0$	30	Rc	31

rotrdi[.] RT, RA, n

$RT \leftarrow ROT\ (\ (RA),\ n)$

The rotrdi[.] instruction rotates the contents of register RA right by n bits, then stores this result into RT. This is an extended mnemonic for the rotate left doubleword and clear left (rldicl[.]) instruction:

rldicl[.] RT, RA, 64-n, 0

If the Rc bit is set (rotrdi.) then CR0 is updated.

This instruction is defined only for 64-bit implementations.

rotrwi[.]
rotate right word immediate

rotrwi[.] RT, RA, n

$$RT \leftarrow ROT\,(\,(RA),\ (32{-}n)\,)$$

The rotrwi[.] instruction rotates the contents of register RA right by n bits, then stores this result into RT. This is an extended mnemonic for the rotate left word immediate then AND with mask (rlwinm[.]) instruction:

rlwinm[.] RT, RA, 32-n, 0, 31

If the Rc bit is set (rotrwi.) then CR0 is updated.

sc
system call

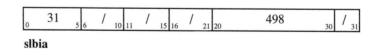

sc

The sc instruction is used to call the system to perform a service. When this instruction is executed, the system call interrupt handler is initiated. The contents of registers after this instruction (when control has been passed back to the program) depends on the register conventions of the system call interface.

slbia
SLB invalidate all

0	31	5	6	/	10	11	/	15	16	/	21	20	498	30	/	31

slbia

The slbia instruction invalidates all SLB entries in the processor (see Appendix C).

This instruction is privileged.

This instruction is available only on 64-bit implementations.

This instruction is optional. Check the Users' Guide for the implementation you are interested in.

slbie
SLB invalidate entry

31		/		/	RA		434		/
0	5	6	10	11	15	16	21	20		30	31

slbie RA

The slbie instruction invalidates an SLB entry (see Appendix C). The effective address of the instruction is the contents of RA, and if there is an SLB entry associated with that address in the processor, then that entry is invalidated.

This instruction is privileged.

This instruction is available only on 64-bit implementations.

This instruction is optional. Check the Users' Guide for the implementation you are interested in.

sld[.]
shift left doubleword

31		RA		RT		RB		27		Rc
0	5	6	10	11	15	16	20	21		30	31

sld[.] RT, RA, RB

$$RT \leftarrow (RA) \ll (RB)_{57, 63}$$

The sld[.] instruction shifts the contents of register RA left by the amount specified in the low-order 7 bits of the contents of RB. This result is stored in RT. Bits shifted out of bit 0 are lost, and zeros are supplied into vacated bit positions.

If the Rc bit is set (sld.), then CR0 is updated.

This instruction is available only on 64-bit implementations.

sldi[.]
shift left doubleword immediate

30		RA		RT		$n_{1:5}$		63-n		1		n_0	Rc
0	5	6	10	11	15	16	20	21		26	27		29	30	31

sldi[.] RT, RA, n (n < 64)

$$RT \leftarrow (RA) \ll n$$

The sldi[.] instruction shifts the contents of register RA left by n bits. This result is stored in RT. Bits shifted out of bit 0 are lost, and zeros are supplied into vacated bit positions. This is an extended mnemonic for the rotate left doubleword immediate then clear right (rldicr[.]) instruction:

rldicr[.] RT, RA, n, 63-n

If the Rc bit is set (sldi.), then CR0 is updated.

This instruction is available only on 64-bit implementations.

slw[.]
shift left word

| 0 | 31 | 5 6 | RA | 10 11 | RT | 15 16 | RB | 20 21 | 24 | 30 | Rc | 31 |

slw[.] RT, RA, RB

$RT \leftarrow (RA) \ll (RB)_{26, 31}$

The slw[.] instruction shifts the contents of register RA left by the amount specified in the low-order 6 bits of the contents of RB. This result is stored in RT. Bits shifted out of bit 0 are lost, and zeros are supplied into vacated bit positions.

If the Rc bit is set (slw.), then CR0 is updated.

slwi[.]
shift left word immediate

| 0 | 21 | 5 6 | RA | 10 11 | RT | 15 16 | n | 20 21 | 0 | 25 26 | 31-n | 30 | Rc | 31 |

slwi[.] RT, RA, n (n < 32)

$RT \leftarrow (RA) \ll n$

The slwi[.] instruction shifts the contents of register RA left by n bits. This result is stored in RT. Bits shifted out of bit 0 are lost, and zeros are supplied into vacated bit positions. This is an extended mnemonic for the rotate left word immediate then AND with mask (rlwinm[.]) instruction:

rlwinm[.] RT, RA, n, 0, 31-n

If the Rc bit is set (slwi.), then CR0 is updated.

srad[.]
shift right algebraic doubleword

| 0 | 31 | 5 6 | RA | 10 11 | RT | 15 16 | RB | 20 21 | 794 | 30 | Rc | 31 |

srad[.] RT, RA, RB

$RT \leftarrow (RA) \gg (RB)_{57, 63}$

The srad[.] instruction shifts the contents of register RA right by the amount specified in the low-order 7 bits of the contents of RB. This result is stored in RT. If any one bits are shifted out of bit position 63 and RA is negative, then the XERCA bit is set. The sign bit of RA (bit 0) is supplied into vacated bit positions.

If the Rc bit is set (srad.), then CR0 is updated.

This instruction is available only on 64-bit implementations.

sradi[.]
shift right algebraic doubleword immediate

| 0 | 31 | 5 6 | RA | 10 11 | RT | 15 16 | $n_{1:5}$ | 20 21 | 413 | 30 | n_0 31 | Rc 31 |

sradi[.] RT, RA, n

$RT \leftarrow (RT) \gg n$

The sradi[.] instruction shifts the contents of register RA right by n bits. This result is stored in RT. If any one bits are shifted out of bit position 63 and RA is negative, then the XERCA bit is set. The sign bit of RA (bit 0) is supplied into vacated bit positions.

If the Rc bit is set (sradi.) then CR0 is updated.

This instruction is available only on 64-bit implementations.

sraw[.]
shift right algebraic word

| 0 | 31 | 5 6 | RA | 10 11 | RT | 15 16 | RB | 20 21 | 792 | 30 | Rc | 31 |

sraw[.] RT, RA, RB

$RT \leftarrow (RA) \gg (RB)_{26, 31}$

The sraw[.] instruction shifts the contents of register RA right by the amount specified in the low-order 6 bits of the contents of RB. This result is stored in RT. If any one bits are shifted out of bit position 31 and RA is negative, then the XERCA bit is set to one. Copies of the sign bit of RA (RA bit 0) are supplied into vacated bit positions.

If the Rc bit is set (sraw.) then CR0 is updated.

srawi[.]
shift right algebraic word immediate

31	RA	RT	n	824	Rc
0 5	6 10	11 15	16 20	21 30	31

srawi[.] RT, RA, n

$$RT \leftarrow (RA) \gg n$$

The srawi[.] instruction shifts the contents of register RA right by n bits. This result is stored in RT. If any one bits are shifted out of bit position 31 and RA is negative, then the XERCA bit is set to one. Copies of the sign bit of RA (RA bit 0) are supplied into vacated bit positions.

If the Rc bit is set (sraw.), then CR0 is updated.

srd[.]
shift right doubleword

31	RA	RT	RB	539	Rc
0 5	6 10	11 15	16 20	21 30	31

srd[.] RT, RA, RB

$$RT \leftarrow (RA) \gg (RB)_{57, 63}$$

The srd[.] instruction shifts the contents of register RA right by the amount specified in the low-order 7 bits of the contents of RB. This result is stored in RT. Bits shifted out of bit position 63 are lost, and zeros are supplied into vacated bit positions.

If the Rc bit is set (srd.), then CR0 is updated.

This instruction is available only on 64-bit implementations.

srdi[.]
shift right doubleword immediate

30	RA	RT	$(64-n)_{1:5}$	n	0	$(64-n)_0$	Rc
0 5	6 10	11 15	16 20	21 26	27 29	30	31

srdi[.] RT, RA, n

$$RT \leftarrow (RA) \gg n$$

The srdi[.] instruction shifts the contents of register RA right by n bits. This result is stored in RT. Bits shifted out of bit position 63 are lost, and zeros are supplied into vacated bit positions. This is an extended mnemonic for the rotate left doubleword immediate then clear left (rldicl[.]) instruction:

rldicl[.] RT, RA, 64-n, n

If the Rc bit is set (srdi.), then CR0 is updated.

This instruction is available only on 64-bit implementations.

srw[.]
shift right word

31	RA	RT	RB	536	Rc
0 5	6 10	11 15	16 20	21 30	31

srw[.] RT, RA, RB

$$RT \leftarrow (RA) \gg (RB)_{26, 31}$$

The srw[.] instruction shifts the contents of register RA right by the amount specified in the low-order 6 bits of the contents of RB. This result is stored in RT. Bits that are shifted out of bit position 31 are lost, and zeros are supplied into vacated bit positions.

If the Rc bit is set (srw.), then CR0 is updated.

srwi[.]
shift right word immediate

21	RA	RT	32-n	n	31	Rc
0 5	6 10	11 15	16 20	21 25	26 30	31

srwi[.] RT, RA, n

$$RT \leftarrow (RA) \gg n$$

The srwi[.] instruction shifts the contents of register RA right by n bits. This result is stored in RT. Bits shifted out of bit position 31 are lost, and zeros are supplied into vacated bit positions. This is an extended mnemonic for the rotate left word immediate then AND with mask (rlwinm[.]) instruction:

rlwinm[.] RT, RA, 32-n, n, 31

If the Rc bit is set (srwi.), then CR0 is updated.

stb
store byte immediate

38	RS	RA	D
0 5	6 10	11 15	16 31

stb RS, D(RA)

$$\text{MEM} \left[\left((RA) + \left(^{16}D_{16} \parallel D_{16,31} \right) \right), 1 \right] \leftarrow (RS)_{24,31}$$

The stb instruction stores the least significant byte contained in RS at the effective address of the instruction. The effective address of the instruction is found by adding the contents of RA to the sign extended 16-bit immediate field, unless RA is 0 (r0), in which case the effective address is the sign extended immediate field.

stbu
store byte immediate with update

39	RS	RA	D
0 5	6 10	11 15	16 31

stbu RS, D(RA)

$$\text{MEM} \left[\left((RA) + \left(^{16}D_{16} \parallel D_{16,31} \right) \right), 1 \right] \leftarrow (RS)_{24,31}$$

$$RA \leftarrow (RA) + \left(^{16}D_{16} \parallel D_{16,31} \right)$$

The stbu instruction stores the least significant byte contained in RS at the effective address of the instruction. The effective address of the instruction is found by adding the contents of RA to the sign extended 16-bit immediate field. If RA=0 the instruction form is invalid.

In addition, the effective address of the instruction is loaded into RA.

stbux
store byte with update

31	RS	RA	RB	247	/
0 5	6 10	11 15	11 15	16 30	31

stbux RS, RA, RB

$$\text{MEM} \left[\left((RA) + (RB) \right), 1 \right] \leftarrow (RS)_{24,31}$$

$$RA \leftarrow (RA) + (RB)$$

The stbux instruction stores the least significant byte contained in RS at the effective address of the instruction. The effective address of the instruction is found by adding the contents of RA to the contents of RB. If RA=0 the instruction form is invalid.

In addition, the effective address of the instruction is loaded into RA.

stBT
store byte

31		RS		RA		RB		215		/	
0	5	6	10	11	15	11	15	16	30		31

stbx RS, RA, RB

$$\text{MEM} [((RA) + (RB)), 1] \leftarrow (RS)_{24, 31}$$

The stBT instruction stores the least significant byte contained RS at the effective address of the instruction. The effective address of the instruction is found by adding the contents of RA to the contents of RB, unless RA is 0 (r0), in which case the effective address is RB.

std
store doubleword immediate

62		RS		RA		DS		0	
0	5	6	10	11	15	16	29	30	31

std RS, DS(RA)

$$\text{MEM} [((RA) + (^{48}DS_{16} \| DS_{16, 29} \| {}^2 0)), 8] \leftarrow (RS)$$

The std instruction stores the doubleword contained in register RS at the effective address of the instruction. The effective address of the instruction is found by adding the contents of RA to the sign extended 14-bit immediate field with two binary zeros concatenated to the right, unless RA is 0 (r0), in which case the effective address is just the sign extended immediate field with two binary zeros concatenated to the right.

This instruction is available only on 64-bit implementations.

stdcx.
conditional store doubleword

31		RS		RA		RB		214		1	
0	5	6	10	11	15	11	15	16	30		31

stdcx. RS, RA, RB

$$\text{MEM} [((RA) + (RB)), 8] \leftarrow (RS)$$

The stdcx. instruction stores the doubleword contained in register RS at the effective address of the instruction if and only if a reservation exists in the processor, and the address of the reservation corresponds to the address of this instruction. The effective address of the instruction is found by adding the contents of RA to the contents of RB, unless RA is 0 (r0), in which case the effective address is just the contents of RB. If the store is successful (that is the correct reservation exists), and $CR_{0:1}$ is set to 0, then the reservation is cleared, and the EQ bit of CR0 is set to 1. If the store is unsuccessful, the the EQ bit of CR0 is set to 0 and $CR_{0:1}$ is set to 0. The effective address of this instruction must be a multiple of 8 (doubleword aligned).

If the reservation exists, but the address of the reservation does not correspond to the address of the instruction, it is undefined whether (RS) is stored into the doubleword in storage addressed by EA.

This instruction is defined only for 64-bit implementations.

stdu
store doubleword immediate with update

62	RS	RA	DS	1
0 5	6 10	11 15	16 29	30 31

stdu RS, DS(RA)

$$\text{MEM} [((RA) + (^{48}DS_{16} \| DS_{16, 29} \| {}^2 0)), 8] \leftarrow (RS)$$

$$RA \leftarrow (RA) + (^{48}DS_{16} \| DS_{16, 29} \| {}^2 0)$$

The stdu instruction stores the doubleword contained in register RS at the effective address of the instruction. The effective address of the instruction is found by adding the contents of RA to the sign extended 14-bit immediate field with two binary zeros concatenated to the right.

In addition, the effective address of the instruction is loaded into RA.

If RA=0 the instruction form is invalid.

This instruction is available only on 64-bit implementations.

stdux
store doubleword with update

31	RS	RA	RB	181	/
0 5	6 10	11 15	11 15	16 30	31

stdux RS, RA, RB

$$\text{MEM} [((RA) + (RB)), 8] \leftarrow (RS)$$

$$RA \leftarrow (RA) + (RB)$$

The stdux instruction stores the doubleword contained in register RS at the effective address of the instruction. The effective address of the instruction is found by adding the contents of RA to the contents of RB, unless RA is 0 (r0), in which case the effective address is just the contents of RB. If RA=0 the instruction form is invalid.

In addition, the effective address of the instruction is loaded into RA.

This instruction is available only on 64-bit implementations.

stdx
store doubleword

31	RS	RA	RB	149	/
0 5	6 10	11 15	11 15	16 30	31

stdx RS, RA, RB

MEM [((RA) + (RB)), 8] ← (RS)

The stdx instruction stores the doubleword contained in register RS at the effective address of the instruction. The effective address of the instruction is found by adding the contents of RA to the contents of RB, unless RA is 0 (r0), in which case the effective address is just the contents of RB.

This instruction is available only on 64-bit implementations.

stfd
store double precision floating-point immediate

54	FRS	RA	D
0 5	6 10	11 15	16 31

stfd FRS, D(RA)

$$\text{MEM} \left[\left((RA) + \left({}^{16}D_{16} \parallel D_{16.31} \right) \right), 8 \right] \leftarrow (FRS)$$

The stfd instruction stores the double precision floating-point value contained in floating-point register FRS at the effective address of the instruction. The effective address of the instruction is found by adding the contents of RA to the sign extended 16-bit immediate field, unless RA is 0 (r0), in which case the effective address is just the sign extended immediate field.

stfdu
store double precision floating-point immediate with update

| 0 | 55 | 5 | 6 | FRS | 10 | 11 | RA | 15 | 16 | D | 31 |

stfdu FRS, D(RA)

$$MEM\left[\left((RA) + \left(^{16}D_{16} \parallel D_{16, 31}\right)\right), 8\right] \leftarrow (FRS)$$

$$RA \leftarrow (RA) + \left(^{16}D_{16} \parallel D_{16, 31}\right)$$

The stfdu instruction stores the double precision floating-point value contained in floating-point register FRS at the effective address of the instruction. The effective address of the instruction is found by adding the contents of RA to the sign extended 16-bit immediate field. If RA=0 the instruction form is invalid.

In addition, the effective address is loaded into register RA.

stfdux
store double precision floating-point with update

| 0 | 31 | 5 | 6 | FRS | 10 | 11 | RA | 15 | 16 | RB | 20 | 21 | 759 | 30 | / | 31 |

stfdux FRS, RA, RB

$$MEM\left[\left((RA) + (RB)\right), 8\right] \leftarrow (FRS)$$

$$RA \leftarrow (RA) + (RB)$$

The stfdux instruction stores the double precision floating-point value contained in floating-point register FRS at the effective address of the instruction. The effective address of the instruction is found by adding the contents of RA to the contents of RB. If RA=0 the instruction form is invalid.

In addition, the effective address is loaded into register RA.

stfdx
store double precision floating-point

| 0 | 31 | 5 | 6 | FRS | 10 | 11 | RA | 15 | 16 | RB | 20 | 21 | 727 | 30 | / | 31 |

stfdx FRS, RA, RB

$$MEM\left[\left((RA) + (RB)\right), 8\right] \leftarrow (FRS)$$

The stfdx instruction stores the double precision floating-point value contained in floating-point register FRS at the effective address of the instruction. The effective address of the instruction is found by adding the contents of RA to the contents of RB, unless RA is 0 (r0), in which case the effective address is just the contents of RB.

stfiwx
store floating-point as integer word

31		FRS		RA		RB		983		/
0	5 6	10	11	15 16		20 21			30	31

stfiwx FRS, RA, RB

$$\text{MEM} [((RA) + (RB)), 4] \leftarrow (FRS_{32:63})$$

The stfiwx instruction stores the low-order 32 bits of the contents of floating-point register FRT at the effective address of the instruction without any conversion. The effective address of the instruction is found by adding the contents of RA to the contents of RB, unless RA is 0 (r0), in which case the effective address is just the contents of RB. This instruction is optional.

stfs
store single precision floating-point immediate

52		FRS		RA		D	
0	5 6	10	11	15 16			31

stfs FRS, D(RA)

$$\text{MEM} [\left((RA) + \left(^{16}D_{16} \parallel D_{16, 31}\right)\right), 4] \leftarrow \text{Convert\_to\_Single} ((FRS))$$

The stfs instruction converts the contents of floating-point register FRS to single precision and then stores this single precision floating-point value at the effective address of the instruction. The effective address of the instruction is found by adding the contents of RA to the sign extended 16-bit immediate field, unless RA is 0 (r0), in which case the effective address is just the sign extended immediate field.

stfsu
store single precision floating-point immediate with update

53		FRS		RA		D	
0	5 6	10	11	15 16			31

stfsu FRS, D(RA)

$$\text{MEM} [\left((RA) + \left(^{16}D_{16} \parallel D_{16, 31}\right)\right), 4] \leftarrow \text{Convert\_to\_Single} ((FRS))$$

$$RA \leftarrow (RA) + \left(^{16}D_{16} \parallel D_{16, 31}\right)$$

stfsu FRT, D(RA)

The stfsu instruction converts the contents of floating-point register FRS to single precision and then stores this single precision floating-point value at the effective address of the instruction. The effective address of the instruction is found by adding the contents of RA to the sign extended 16-bit immediate field. If RA=0 then the instruction form is invalid.

In addition, the effective address is loaded into register RA.

stfsux
store single precision floating-point with update

31	FRS	RA	RB	695	/
0 5	6 10	11 15	16 20	21 30	31

stfsux FRS, RA, RB

MEM [((RA) + (RB)), 4] ← Convert_to_Single ((FRS))

RA ← (RA) + (RB)

The stfsux instruction converts the contents of floating-point register FRS to single precision and then stores this single precision floating-point value at the effective address of the instruction. The effective address of the instruction is found by adding the contents of RA to the contents of RB. If RA=0 then the instruction form is invalid.

In addition, the effective address is loaded into register RA.

stfsx
store single precision floating-point

31	FRS	RA	RB	663	/
0 5	6 10	11 15	16 20	21 30	31

stfsx FRS, Ry, Rz

MEM [((RA) + (RB)), 4] ← Convert_to_Single ((FRS))

The stfsx instruction converts the contents of floating-point register FRS to single precision and then stores this single precision floating-point value at the effective address of the instruction. The effective address of the instruction is found by adding the contents of RA to the contents of RB, unless RA is 0 (r0), in which case the effective address is just the contents of RB.

sth
store integer halfword

44	RS	RA	D
0 5 6	10 11	15 16	31

sth RS, D(RA)

$$\text{MEM} \left[\left((RA) + \left({}^{16}D_{16} \parallel D_{16, 31} \right) \right), 2 \right] \leftarrow (RS)_{16, 31}$$

The sth instruction stores the least-significant halfword contained in RS at the effective address of the instruction. The effective address of the instruction is found by adding the contents of RA to the sign extended 16-bit immediate field, unless RA is 0 (r0), in which case the effective address is the sign extended immediate field.

sthbrx
store integer halfword with bytes reversed

31	RS	RA	RB	918	/
0 5 6	10 11	15 11	15 16	30	31

sthbrx RS, RA, RB

$$\text{MEM} \left[\left((RA) + (RB) \right), 2 \right] \leftarrow \left((RS)_{24, 31} \parallel (RS)_{16, 23} \right)$$

The sthbrx instruction stores the least-significant halfword contained in RS at the effective address of the instruction. The two bytes in the halfword are swapped before being stored. The effective address of the instruction is found by adding the contents of RA to the contents of RB, unless RA is 0 (r0), in which case the effective address is RB.

sthu
store halfword immediate with update

45	RS	RA	D
0 5 6	10 11	15 16	31

sthu RS, D(RA)

$$\text{MEM} \left[\left((RA) + \left({}^{16}D_{16} \parallel D_{16, 31} \right) \right), 2 \right] \leftarrow (RS)_{16, 31}$$

$$RA \leftarrow (RA) + \left({}^{16}D_{16} \parallel D_{16, 31} \right)$$

The sthu instruction stores the least-significant halfword contained in RS at the effective address of the instruction. The effective address of the instruction is found by adding the contents of RA to the sign extended 16-bit immediate field. If RA=0 then the instruction form is invalid.

In addition, the effective address of the instruction is loaded into RA.

sthux
store halfword with update

0 31 5	6 RS 10	11 RA 15	11 RB 15	16 439 30	/ 31

sthux RS, RA, RB

MEM [((RA) + (RB)), 2] ← (RS)$_{16, 31}$

RA ← (RA) + (RB)

The sthux instruction stores the least-significant halfword contained RS at the effective address of the instruction. The effective address of the instruction is found by adding the contents of RA to the contents of RB. If RA=0 then the instruction form is invalid.

In addition, the effective address of the instruction is loaded into RA.

sthx
store halfword

0 31 5	6 RS 10	11 RA 15	11 RB 15	16 407 30	/ 31

sthx RS, RA, RB

MEM [((RA) + (RB)), 2] ← (RS)$_{16, 31}$

The sthx instruction stores the least-significant halfword contained in RS at the effective address of the instruction. The effective address of the instruction is found by adding the contents of RA to the contents of RB, unless RA is 0 (r0), in which case the effective address is RB.

stmw
store multiple integer word

0 47 5	6 RS 10	11 RA 15	16 D 31

stmw RS, D(RA)

MEM [((RA) + ($^{16}D_{16} \parallel D_{16, 31}$)), (4 × 32–RT))] ← (RS), (R_{31})

The contents of registers RS through R_{31} are stored to consecutive words in memory starting at the effective address of the instruction. The effective address of the instruction is found by adding the contents of RA to the sign extended 16-bit immediate field, unless RA is 0 (r0), in which case the effective address is the sign extended immediate field. The effective address must be a multiple of 4 (word aligned).

On 64-bit implementations, only the low-order 32 bits of each register are stored.

stswi
store string immediate

31	RS	RA	n	725	/
0 5	6 10	11 15	16 20	21 30	31

stswi RS, RA, n

$$MEM\,[\,(RA),\ n]\leftarrow(RS),\left(R_{\left(x\,+\frac{n}{4}\right)}\right)$$

Starting with RS, registers are stored (only the low-order 4 bytes of 64-bit registers) to n consecutive bytes in memory starting at the effective address of the instruction. The effective address of the instruction is the contents of RA, unless RA is 0 (r0), in which case the effective address is 0. Data is taken from as many consecutive registers as necessary to fill the number of bytes being stored to (r0 follows R_{31}).

stswx
store string

31	R_x	R_y	R_z	661	/
0 5	6 10	11 15	16 20	21 30	31

stswx Rx, Ry, Rz

(Ry) + (Rz)

$$MEM\,[\,(R_y),\ XER_{25,\,31}]\leftarrow(R_x),\left(R_{\left(x\,+\,\frac{XER_{25,\,31}}{4}\right)}\right)$$

Starting with RS, registers are stored (only the low-order 4 bytes of 64-bit registers) to a number consecutive bytes in memory starting at the effective address of the instruction. The number of bytes is specified in bits 25 through 31 of the XER. The effective address of the instruction is the contents of RA and the contents of RB, unless RA is 0 (r0), in which case the effective address is the contents of RB. Data is taken from as many consecutive registers as necessary to fill the number of bytes being stored to (r0 follows R_{31}).

stw
store integer word

36	RS	RA	D
0 5	6 10	11 15	16 31

stw RS, D(RA)

$$MEM\,[\,\left(\,(RA)+\left({}^{16}D_{16}\,\|\,D_{16,\,31}\right)\right),4\,]\leftarrow(RS)$$

The stw instruction stores the word contained RS at the effective address of the instruction. The effective address of the instruction is found by adding the contents of RA to the sign extended 16-bit immediate field, unless RA is 0 (r0), in which case the effective address is the sign extended immediate field.

stwbrx
store integer word with bytes reversed

31	RS	RA	RB	662	/
0 5	6 10	11 15	11 15	16 30	31

stwbrx RS, RA, RB

$$\text{MEM} \left[((RA) + (RB), 4 \right] \leftarrow ((RS)_{24, 31} \,\|\, (RS)_{16, 23} \,\|\, (RS)_{8, 15} \,\|\, (RS)_{0, 7})$$

The stwbrx instruction stores the word contained RS at the effective address of the instruction. The order of the four bytes in the word is reversed before the word is stored. The effective address of the instruction is found by adding the contents of RA to the contents of RB, unless RA is 0 (r0), in which case the effective address is RB.

stwu
store word immediate with update

37	RS	RA	D
0 5	6 10	11 15	16 31

stwu RS, D(RA)

$$\text{MEM} \left[\left((RA) + \left({}^{16}D_{16} \,\|\, D_{16, 31} \right) \right), 4 \right] \leftarrow (RS)$$

$$RA \leftarrow (RA) + \left({}^{16}D_{16} \,\|\, D_{16, 31} \right)$$

The stwu instruction stores the word contained in RS at the effective address of the instruction. The effective address of the instruction is found by adding the contents of RA to the sign extended 16-bit immediate field. If RA=0 then the instruction form is invalid.

In addition, the effective address of the instruction is loaded into RA.

stwux
store word with update

31	RS	RA	RB	183	/
0 5	6 10	11 15	11 15	16 30	31

stwux RS, RA, RB

$$\text{MEM} \left[((RA) + (RB)), 4 \right] \leftarrow (RS)$$

$$RA \leftarrow (RA) + (RB)$$

The stwux instruction stores the word contained in RS at the effective address of the instruction. The effective address of the instruction is found by adding the contents of RA to the contents of RS. If RA=0 then the instruction form is invalid.

In addition, the effective address of the instruction is loaded into RA.

stwx
store word

31	RS	RA	RB	151	/
0 5	6 10	11 15	11 15	16 30	31

stwx RS, RA, RB

MEM [((RA) + (RB)), 4] ← (RS)

The stwx instruction stores the word contained in RS at the effective address of the instruction. The effective address of the instruction is found by adding the contents of RA to the contents of RB, unless RA is 0 (r0), in which case the effective address is RB.

stwcx.
conditional store word

31	RS	RA	RB	150	1
0 5	6 10	11 15	11 15	16 30	31

stwcx RS, RA, RB

MEM [((RA) + (RB)), 4] ← (RS)

The stwcx. instruction stores the word contained in register RT at the effective address of the instruction if and only if a reservation exists in the processor, and the address of the reservation corresponds to the address of this instruction. The effective address of the instruction is found by adding the contents of RA to the contents of RB, unless RA is 0 (r0), in which case the effective address is just the contents of RB. If the store is successful (that is the correct reservation exists), then the reservation is cleared, and the EQ bit of CR0 is set to 1. If the store is unsuccessful, the the EQ bit of CR0 is set to 0. The effective address of this instruction must be a multiple of 4 (word aligned).

sub[o][.]
subtract

0	31	5	6	RT	10	11	RB	15	16	RA	20	Oe	31	22	40	30	Rc	31

sub[o][.] RT, RA, RB

$RT \leftarrow (RA) - (RB)$

The sub[o][.] instruction subtracts the contents of RB from the contents of RA and places the result in RT. This is an extended mnemonic for the subtract from (subf[o][.]) instruction:

subf[o][.] RT, RB, RA

If the subo[.] form of the instruction is used, then the overflow and summary overflow bits of the XER are set if overflow occurs.

If the sub[o]. form of the instruction is used, then CR0 is updated.

subc[o][.]
subtract carrying

0	31	5	6	RT	10	11	RB	15	16	RA	20	Oe	21	22	8	30	Rc	31

subc[o][.] RT, RA, RB

$RT \leftarrow (RA) - (RB)$

The subc[o][.] instruction subtracts the contents of RB from the contents of RA and places the result in RT. This instruction sets the XERCA bit. This is an extended mnemonic for the subtract from (subfc[o][.]) instruction:

subfc[o][.] RT, RB, RA

If the subco[.] form of the instruction is used, then the overflow and summary overflow bits of the XER are set if overflow occurs.

If the subc[o]. form of the instruction is used, then CR0 is updated.

subf[o][.]
integer subtract from

0	31	5	6	RT	10	11	RA	15	16	RB	20	Oe	31	22	40	30	Rc	31

subf[o][.] RT, RA, RB

$RT \leftarrow (RB) - (RA)$

The subf[o][.] instruction subtracts the contents of RA from the contents of RB and places the result in RT.

If the subfo[.] form of the instruction is used, then the overflow and summary overflow bits of the XER are set if overflow occurs.

If the subf[o]. form of the instruction is used, then CR0 is updated.

subfc[o][.]
integer subtract from carrying

0	31	5	6	RT	10	11	RA	15	16	RB	20	Oe	21	22	8	30	Rc	31

subfc[o][.] RT, RA, RB

$$RT \leftarrow (RB) - (RA)$$

The subfc[o][.] instruction subtracts the contents of RA from the contents of RB and places the result in RT. This instruction sets the XERCA bit.

If the subfco[.] form of the instruction is used, then the overflow and summary overflow bits of the XER are set if overflow occurs.

If the subfc[o]. form of the instruction is used, then CR0 is updated.

subfe[o][.]
integer sutract from extended

0	31	5	6	RT	10	11	RA	15	16	RB	20	Oe	21	22	136	30	Rc	31

subfe[o][.] RT, RA, RB

$$RT \leftarrow (RB) + \overline{(RA)} + XER_{CA}$$

The subfe[o][.] instruction subtracts the contents of RA from the contents of RB and uses the carry bit from the XER (XER$_{CA}$) as a borrow from the subtraction XER$_{CA}$==1, means no borrow. (XER$_{CA}$==0 means borrow.) The result is placed into register RT. This instruction sets the XERCA bit.

If the subfeo[.] form of the instruction is used, then the overflow and summary overflow bits of the XER are set if overflow occurs.

If the subfe[o]. form of the instruction is used, then CR0 is updated.

subfic
integer subtract from (immediate addressing, carrying)

0	8	5	6	RT	10	11	RA	15	16	si	31

subfic[.] RT, RA, si

$$RT \leftarrow \left({}^{16}si_{16} \parallel si_{16, 31} \right) - (RA)$$

The subfic instruction subtracts the contents of RA from the sign extended 16-bit immediate field, placing the result into RT. The XERCA bit is updated with the carry out of the addition.

subfme[o][.]
subtract from minus one (extended)

0	31	5	6	RT	10	11	RA	15	16	/	20	Oe	21	22	232	30	Rc	31

subfme[o][.] RT, RA

$$RT \leftarrow (\overline{RA}) + XER_{CA} - 1$$

The subfme[o][.] instruction subtracts the contents of RA from -1 and uses the carry bit from the XER (XER$_{CA}$) as a borrow from the subtraction XER$_{CA}$==1, means no borrow. (XER$_{CA}$==0 means borrow.) The result is placed into register RT. This instruction sets the XERCA bit.

If the subfmeo[.] form of the instruction is used, then the overflow and summary overflow bits of the XER are set if overflow occurs.

If the subfme[o]. form of the instruction is used, then CR0 is updated.

subfze[o][.]
subtract from (zero extended)

0	31	5	6	RT	10	11	RA	15	16	/	20	Oe	21	22	200	30	Rc	31

subfze[o][.] RT, RA

$$RT \leftarrow (\overline{RA}) + XER_{CA}$$

The subfze[o][.] instruction subtracts the contents of RA from 0. The XERCA bit is a carry (borrow) into the subtraction. The result is placed into register RT. This instruction sets the XERCA bit.

If the subfzeo[.] form of the instruction is used, then the overflow and summary overflow bits of the XER are set if overflow occurs.

If the subfze[o]. form of the instruction is used, then CR0 is updated.

subi
subtract immediate

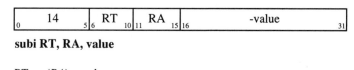

subi RT, RA, value

$RT \leftarrow (RA) - value$

The subi instruction subtracts the sign extended immediate field from the contents of register RA. This is an extended mnemonic for the add immediate (addi) instruction:

addi RT, RA, -value

subis
subtract immediate shifted

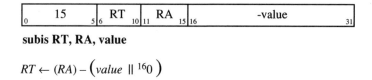

subis RT, RA, value

$RT \leftarrow (RA) - \left(value \parallel {}^{16}0 \right)$

The subis instruction subtracts the immediate field shifted left by 16 bits from the contents of register RA. This is an extended mnemonic for the add immediate (addis) instruction:

addis RT, RA, -value

subic[.]
subtract immediate carrying

6	Rc	RT	RA	-value
0 5	5 6	10 11	15 16	31

subic RT, RA, value

$RT \leftarrow (RA) - value$

The subic[.] instruction subtracts the sign extended immediate field from the contents of register RA. The carry (borrow) out of the subtraction updates the XERCA bit. This is an extended mnemonic for the add immediate (addic) instruction:

addic RT, RA, -value

If the Rc bit is set (subic.), then CR0 is updated.

sync
synchronize

31	///	///	///	598	/
0 5	6 10	11 15	16 20	21 30	31

sync

The sync instruction forms a fence between operations. Operations that occur before the sync instruction are completed with respect to all other operations before operations following the sync are initiated and storage accesses are performed with respect to all other processors and mechanisms.

For weaker ordering, see the eieio instruction.

td
trap doubleword

31	TO	RA	RB	68	/
0 5	6 10	11 15	11 15	16 30	31

td TO, RA, RB

The td instruction compares the contents of register RA to the contents of RB. Five conditions are checked:

- ■ signed less than
- ■ signed greater than
- ■ equal to
- ■ unsigned less than
- ■ unsigned greater than

These conditions are masked by the TO field in the instruction (see Table B.7), and if any true condition corresponds to a one bit in the TO field, then the system trap handler is invoked.

This instruction is defined only for 64-bit implementations.

There are a set of extended mnemonics associated with the trap instructions (see Tables B.7 and B.8).

tdi
trap doubleword immediate

2	TO	RA	si
0 5	6 10	11 15	16 31

tdi TO, RA, si

The tdi instruction compares the contents of register RA to the sign extended immediate field. Five conditions are checked:

- signed less than
- signed greater than
- equal to
- unsigned less than
- unsigned greater than

These conditions are masked by the TO field in the instruction (see Table B.7), and if any true condition corresponds to a one bit in the TO field, then the system trap handler is invoked.

This instruction is defined only for 64-bit implementations.

There are a set of extended mnemonics associated with the trap instructions (see Tables B.7 and B.8).

Table B.7. TO field encoding for extended mnemonics.

Code	Definition	Decimal TO	<	>	=	<u	>u
lt	less than	16	1	0	0	0	0
le	less than or equal to	20	1	0	1	0	0
eq	equal to	4	0	0	1	0	0
ge	greater than or equal to	12	0	1	1	0	0
gt	greater than	8	0	1	0	0	0
nl	not less than	12	0	1	1	0	0
ne	not equal to	24	1	1	0	0	0
ng	not greater than	20	1	0	1	0	0
llt	logically less than	2	0	0	0	1	0
lle	logically less than or equal to	6	0	0	1	1	0
lge	logically greater than or equal to	5	0	0	1	0	1
lgt	logically greater than	1	0	0	0	0	1
lnl	logically not less than	5	0	0	1	0	1
lng	logically not greater than	6	0	0	1	1	0
<none>	unconditional	31	1	1	1	1	1

Table B.8. Extended mnemonics for trap instructions.

Instruction Semantics	32-Bit Trap Instructions		64-Bit Trap Instructions	
	tw	twi	td	tdi
trap unconditionally	trap	—	—	—
trap if less than	twlt	twlti	tdlt	tdlti
trap if less than or equal to	twle	twlei	tdle	tdlei
trap if equal	tweq	tweqi	tdeq	tdeqi
trap if greater than or equal to	twge	twgei	tdge	tdgei
trap if greater than	twgt	twgti	tdgt	tdgti
trap if not less than	twnl	twnli	tdnl	tdnli
trap if not equal to	twne	twnei	tdne	tdnei
trap if not greater than	twng	twngi	tdng	tdngi
trap if logically less than	twllt	twllti	tdllt	tdllti
trap if logically less than or equal to	twlle	twllei	tdlle	tdllei
trap if logically greater than or equal to	twlge	twlgei	tdlge	tdlgei
trap if logically greater than	twlgt	twlgti	tdlgt	tdlgti
trap if logically not less than	twlnl	twlnli	tdlnl	tdlnli
trap if logically not greater than	twlng	twlngi	tdlng	tdlngi

tlbia
TLB invalidate all

31	///	///	///	370	/
0 5	6 10	11 15	16 21	20 30	31

tlbia

The tlbia instruction invalidates all TLB entries in all processors (see Appendix C).

This instruction is privileged and is optional.

tlbie
TLB invalidate entry

tlbie RA

The tlbie instruction invalidates a TLB entry in all processors (see Appendix C). The effective address of the instruction is the contents of RA, and if there is a TLB entry associated with that address in the processor (or any other processor), then that entry is invalidated. The invalidation is done without reference to the segment registers or SLB. All matching entries are invalidated.

This instruction is optional and is privileged.

tlbsync
TLB synchronize

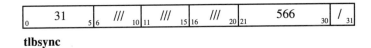

tlbsync

The tlbsync instruction forces all previous tlbie and tlbia instructions to complete on all processors before instructions following the tlbsync instruction can initiate (see Appendix C).

This instruction is optional and is privileged.

tw
trap word

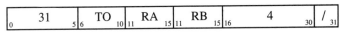

tw TO, RA, RB

The tw instruction compares the contents of register RA to the contents of RB. Five conditions are checked:

■ signed less than
■ signed greater than
■ equal to
■ unsigned less than
■ unsigned greater than

These conditions are masked by the TO field in the instruction (see Table B.7), and if any true condition corresponds to a one bit in the TO field, then the system trap handler is invoked.

There are a set of extended mnemonics associated with the trap instructions (see Tables B.7 and B.8).

twi
trap word immediate

0 3 5	6 TO 10	11 RA 15	16 si 31

twi TO, RA, si

The twi instruction compares the contents of register RA to the sign extended immediate field. Five conditions are checked:

■ signed less than
■ signed greater than
■ equal to
■ unsigned less than
■ unsigned greater than

These conditions are masked by the TO field in the instruction (see Table B.7), and if any true condition corresponds to a one bit in the TO field, then the system trap handler is invoked.

There are a set of extended mnemonics associated with the trap instructions (see Tables B.7 and B.8).

xor[.]
logical XOR

0 31 5	6 RA 10	11 RT 15	16 R_z 20	21 316 30	Rc 31

xor[.] RT, RA, RB

$RT \leftarrow (RA) \oplus (RB)$

The xor[.] instruction performs a logical XOR of the contents of register RA with the contents of register RB. The result is then stored into register RT.

If the Rc bit is set (xor.), then CR0 is updated.

xori
logical XOR immediate

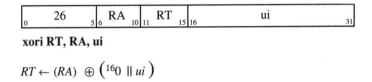

xori RT, RA, ui

$$RT \leftarrow (RA) \oplus \left({}^{16}0 \parallel ui \right)$$

The xori instruction performs a logical XOR of the low-order 16 bits of the contents of register RA with the immediate field ui; the high-order 16 bits of RA are unchanged. The result is then stored into register RT.

xoris
logical XOR shifted immediate

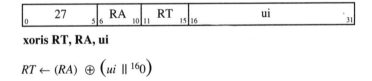

xoris RT, RA, ui

$$RT \leftarrow (RA) \oplus \left(ui \parallel {}^{16}0 \right)$$

The xoris instruction performs a logical XOR of the high-order 16 bits of the contents of register RA with the immediate field ui; the low-order 16 bits of RA are unchanged. The result is then stored into register RT.

C

Operating System Design for PowerPC Processors

This appendix covers parts of the PowerPC processor and system-management architecture that will be most interesting to OS and systems programmers, such as the instructions and architectural features designed for implementing security, virtual memory and protection, interrupts, and interprocess communication and synchronization.

Machine State Register

The machine state register (MSR) is the main processor mode register; bits in this register select supervisor mode, enable and disable some interrupts, and determine how the processor reacts to some system events. The MSR defines the state of the processor. The MSR is 32-bits wide in 32-bit PowerPC implementations (like the 601, 603, and 604 processors), and 64 bits in 64-bit implementations (like the PowerPC 620 processor). At this time, the only difference between the 32-bit and 64-bit MSR is a bit in the upper-order 32 bits that selects 64-bit mode. Therefore, a discussion of the 32-bit MSR, which is identical to the low-order 32 bits of the 64-bit MSR, is sufficient. Figure C.1 shows the format of the MSR. The following list describes the bits in the MSR:

■ Power Management Enable (POW)

If this bit is set to 1 and the processor has hardware to perform dynamic power management, then the dynamic power management is enabled. The actual power-management hardware is implementation dependent (see the User's Manual for the particular implementation you are using).

■ Interrupt Little Endian (ILE)

When an interrupt occurs, this bit is copied into the LE bit (this is described later in this section) to select the endian mode of the interrupt handler.

■ External Interrupt Enable (EE)

If this bit is set to 1, then external and decrementer interrupts are allowed to occur (see "PowerPC Interrupt Architecture," later in this appendix).

■ Problem State (PR)

This bit determines whether the processor is allowed to execute privileged instructions.

■ Floating-Point Available (FP)

If this bit is set to 1, the processor is allowed to execute floating-point instructions. Otherwise, a program interrupt occurs if the processor attempts to execute a floating-point instruction. The operating system may use this bit to determine whether floating-point registers need to be saved during a state save operation.

■ Machine Check Enable (ME)

If this bit is set to 1, machine check interrupts are allowed to occur.

■ Floating-Point Exception Modes 0 and 1 (FE0, FE1)

These bits determine how floating-point interrupts occur. They are described in more detail later in this appendix, with interrupts and with the floating-point execution model.

■ Single-Step Trace Enable (SE)

This bit enables the single step trace mode (which is implementation dependent). For details about this function, see the User's Manual for the particular processor you are using.

■ Branch Trace Enable (BE)

This bit enables the branch trace mode (which is implementation dependent). For details about this function, see the User's Manual for a specific PowerPC processor.

■ Interrupt Prefix (IP)

This bit determines the high-order bits of the interrupt address that are generated when an interrupt occurs (see "PowerPC Interrupt Architecture," later in this appendix).

■ Instruction Relocate (IR)

If this bit is set, the processor performs address translation on all instruction fetch accesses (see "Virtual Memory," later in this appendix). If the bit is 0, then the untranslated effective address is used as the physical address.

■ Data Relocate (DR)

If this bit is set to 1, then the processor performs address translation on all data accesses (see "Virtual Memory," later in this appendix). If the bit is 0, then the effective address is used as the physical address.

■ Recoverable Interrupt (RI)

This bit determines whether certain interrupts are recoverable.

■ Little endian mode (LE)

This bit determines which endian mode is used in the processor for all memory accesses (see Appendix D, "A Detailed Floating-Point Model").

FIGURE C.1.
The machine state register (32-bit MSR shown).

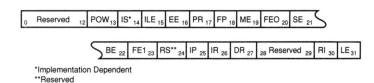

*Implementation Dependent
**Reserved

Problem State

Two problem states are defined in the PowerPC architecture. When the MSR_{PR} bit is one, certain instructions cannot be executed—these are called *privileged instructions,* and the mode is called *non-privileged* mode. When the MSR_{PR} bit is 1, all instructions can be executed. This mode is called privileged or kernal mode . Generally, an operating system sets this bit to one before returning control to a user program. This setting enables the operating system to protect critical resources (such as the MSR, or the virtual memory resources). When an interrupt occurs, control is passed back to the operating system, and this bit is set to zero in order to enable the interrupt handler to run in privileged mode. Another important feature of these problem states is that memory protection can be assigned differently for each of the states (see "Virtual Memory," later in this appendix).

Special-Purpose Registers

In Chapters 3 and 4, you learned about the *move to special-purpose register* (mtspr) and the *move from special-purpose register* (mfspr) instructions, and how you can used them to move data between the general integer registers and the link register (LR), the count register (CTR), and the integer exception register (XER). These instructions can be used to manipulate other special-purpose registers—there are 34 that may be written and 33 that can be read. The general form of these instructions follows:

```
mtspr SPR, RS
mfspr RT, SPR
```

The SPR field is a 10-bit field that identifies the special-purpose register. The RS and RT fields identify the general integer register from which data is read or into which data is stored, respectively. Table C.1 shows a complete list of the special-purpose registers.

Table C.1. Special-purpose registers.

Special-Purpose Register	Encoding Decimal	Hexadecimal	Privileged	Read/ Write
Integer Exception Register (XER)	1	0×001	no	R/W
Link Register (LR)	8	0×008	no	R/W
Count Register (CTR)	9	0×009	no	R/W
Data Storage Interrupt Status Register (DSISR)	18	0×012	yes	R/W
Data Address Register (DAR)	19	0×013	yes	R/W
Decrementor (DEC)	22	0×016	yes	R/W
Storage Descriptor Register 1 (SDR1)	25	0×019	yes	R/W
Machine Status Save/Restore Register 0 (SRR0)	26	0×01A	yes	R/W

Special-Purpose Register	Encoding Decimal	Hexadecimal	Privileged	Read/ Write
Machine Status Save/Restore Register 1 (SRR1)	27	0×01B	yes	R/W
Software Use SPR 0 (SPRG0)	272	0×110	yes	R/W
Software Use SPR 1 (SPRG1)	273	0×111	yes	R/W
Software Use SPR 2 (SPRG2)	274	0×112	yes	R/W
Software Use SPR 3 (SPRG3)	275	0×113	yes	R/W
External Access Register (EAR)	282	0×11A	yes	R/W
Time Base Lower (TBL)	284	0×11C	yes	W
Time Base Upper (TBU)	285	0×11D	yes	W
Processor Version Register (PVR)	287	0×11F	yes	R
Instruction Block Address Translation Upper Register 0 (IBAT0U)	528	0×210	yes	R/W
Instruction Block Address Translation Lower Register 0 (IBAT0L)	529	0×211	yes	R/W
Instruction Block Address Translation Upper Register 1 (IBAT1U)	530	0×212	yes	R/W
Instruction Block Address Translation Lower Register 1 (IBAT1L)	531	0×213	yes	R/W

continues

Table C.1. continued

Special-Purpose Register	Encoding Decimal	Hexadecimal	Privileged	Read/ Write
Instruction Block Address Translation Upper Register 2 (IBAT2U)	532	0×214	yes	R/W
Instruction Block Address Translation Lower Register 2 (IBAT2L)	533	0×215	yes	R/W
Instruction Block Address Translation Upper Register 3 (IBAT3U)	534	0×216	yes	R/W
Instruction Block Address Translation Lower Register 3 (IBAT3L)	535	0×217	yes	R/W
Data Block Address Translation Upper Register 0 (DBAT0U)	536	0×218	yes	R/W
Data Block Address Translation Lower Register 0 (DBAT0L)	537	0×219	yes	R/W
Data Block Address Translation Upper Register 1 (DBAT1U)	538	0×21A	yes	R/W
Data Block Address Translation Lower Register 1 (DBAT1L)	539	0×21B	yes	R/W
Data Block Address Translation Upper Register 2 (DBAT2U)	540	0×21C	yes	R/W
Data Block Address Translation Lower Register 2 (DBAT2L)	541	0×21D	yes	R/W
Data Block Address Translation Upper Register 3 (DBAT3U)	542	0×21E	yes	R/W

Special-Purpose Register	Encoding Decimal	Hexadecimal	Privileged	Read/ Write
Data Block Address Translation Lower Register 3 (DBAT3L)	543	0×21F	yes	R/W
Data Address Breakpoint Register (DABR)	1013	0×3F5	yes	R/W

The XER, LR, and CTR registers were described earlier with the integer and branch instructions. The DSISR, DAR, SRR0, SRR1, TBL, TBU, and DABR registers are described with the interrupt architecture (see below). The SDR1, EAR, 8 DBAT, and 8 IBAT registers are described in the "Virtual Memory" section. This section covers the remaining four SPRG registers and the PVR register.

The *Software-use SPRs* (SPRG0-4) are registers with no specific architectural meaning. These registers are provided as privileged registers reserved for operating system use—such as scratch space for an interrupt handler, or to hold information unique to each processor in a multiprocessor system.

The Processor Version register (PVR) is a read-only register that returns a 32-bit value identifying the processor implementation. This 32-bit value is split into two 16-bit pieces. The upper-order 16-bits are a version number identifying a particular processor number (601, 603, and so on). The lower-order 16 bits identifies a revision number for the particular processor (engineering change level).

Virtual Memory

As described in Chapter 2, "Introduction to the PowerPC Architecture," *virtual memory* is a method of increasing the apparent size of memory by using main memory (typically DRAM memory) as a cache for a larger storage space (such as disk storage). (See the cache descriptions in Chapter 7, "Performance Tuning and Optimization.") You might create a virtual 1GB memory space on a machine with only 4MB of DRAM memory, for example, by using a 1GB hard drive. Whenever a piece of data is requested by a program, the DRAM memory is checked first, and if the data is there, it is accessed. If the data is not there, however, the data is read from the hard drive and placed into the DRAM memory for future use (some other piece of data is displaced from the DRAM memory and put back into the hard drive). The hard drive space is referred to as *paging space*. Why do all this work instead of simply using the hard drive as the only memory device? In a word, *speed.* Access time to DRAM memory is measured in nanoseconds (ns); access time to a hard drive is many orders of magnitude slower, and is measured in milliseconds (ms). The DRAM memory is used as a cache for the much larger, slower paging space device (usually a hard drive). Caches are described in Chapter 7. This particular cache is controlled by software through a number of mechanisms contained in hardware. In this section, the interface to those mechanisms is described.

Virtual memory management generally is in the realm of the operating system, and in the PowerPC architecture, most of the instructions used to manage the virtual memory space are *privileged*, meaning that user programs cannot directly execute the instructions. The PowerPC architecture supports two memory-management schemes: a paging system and a block address translation system. The paging system is discussed first, followed by the block address translation (BAT) mechanism. (The BAT mechanism enables the programmer to map larger pieces of memory with a single translation resource.) There are differences between the 32-bit and the 64-bit virtual memory mechanisms, so these are covered separately in the following sections.

32-Bit Page Translation Mechanism

This section discusses virtual memory management on 32-bit implementations of the PowerPC architecture. The 64-bit virtual memory architecture is discussed in "64-Bit Virtual Memory Architecture," later in this appendix. Recall from Chapter 2 that the PowerPC architecture has a 52-bit virtual address space, which is split into 2^{24} 256MB pieces called *segments*. Each of these segments is broken down further into 2^{16} 4KB chunks called *pages*. Pages are the granule of memory that be moved from the virtual storage device (a hard drive, for example) to the physical storage device (DRAM, for example).

The process uses a 32-bit address that maps to a portion of the virtual address space, which is accessible only by that process (ignoring shared memory spaces for the moment). This address is called an *effective address*, and it is all a programmer normally needs to see. Figure C.2 shows a simplified view of address translation.

The first structure associated with the translation mechanism is the *segment register*. The PowerPC architecture defines 16 segment registers; each contains information about a memory segment and forms the set of active segments in the processor. The most significant 4 bits of the effective address are used to select one of the 16 active segments. The segment register contains several pieces of information, including a virtual segment ID that is a 24-bit value used to uniquely identify the segment being accessed in virtual memory. The 24-bit segment ID with the remainder of the effective address (the low-order 28 bits) concatenated to it forms the 52-bit virtual address. Next, the virtual address must be translated into a physical address. This process involves determining where in physical memory the virtual page for this address currently resides If we assign 16 VSIDs to each process, this results in 1 million processes each with a 32-bit effective address space.

The next structure associated with address translation is the *page table*. The page table contains the mapping of virtual pages to physical pages. When a page is read from the virtual memory storage device and placed into the physical memory storage device, the page table is updated to reflect the new mapping (it lists the virtual page currently contained in each physical page). The page table is searched using a hash function (described in "Page Table Construction," later in this appendix). The virtual segment ID is used with the page index (bits 4 through 19 of the effective address) to access the page table, resulting in a 20-bit real page number. The real page number has the page offset (bits 20 through 31 of the effective address) concatenated to it to form the physical address. The physical address then is used to access system memory.

FIGURE C.2.

A simplified view of address translation.

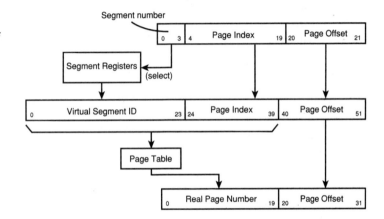

Page Properties

Different pages in memory can have different properties. The properties of a page are specified in the segment register or the page table, and generally are set by the operating system when the page is set up (initialized or brought in from paging space).

Page Protection

The first property that pages have is their page protection settings. Page protection settings can be different, depending on whether the processor is in privileged (operating system) mode or nonprivileged (user) mode. Three types of access permissions are defined by the PowerPC architecture:

- ■ *No access.* Neither loads nor stores are allowed to occur.
- ■ *Read-only access.* Loads are allowed, but stores are not allowed.
- ■ *Read/write access.* Both loads and stores are allowed to occur.

An operating system therefore may choose to control access to some critical system resource by setting the user code permission to No Access, while retaining access rights for itself of Read/Write Access. The user code might have to perform a system call to ask the operating system to read or write that system resource. Another possibility is that the operating system may give one process read/write access, while denying access to all other processes. This could be done by setting the page protection properties one way while that process is running, but changing them when a different process gains control of the CPU.

Cache Policy

Another property that can be defined on a per page basis is how a cache will behave for accesses to that page. Some programs (especially in a multiprogramming environment) rely on certain specific cache behavior. Instructions can be used to force some of this behavior, but this process can be cumbersome or impossible in some cases. The PowerPC architecture therefore defines a set of properties on a page granularity to force certain cache behavior.

A page can be set to *write-through* mode so that accesses to that page always behave as if all levels of cache in the system are write-through caches. This mode means that read accesses to that page behave normally, but stores always propagate out to main memory at the time they occur. If a program requires data in main memory to match data in any caches in the system, the pages containing that data should be set to write-through mode.

A page can be set to *cache-inhibited* mode. In this mode, data accesses to that page behave as if there were no caches in the system at all. In this case, when data is read or written, the access is performed only in main memory, and no data is placed in any cache. An example where cache-inhibited mode would be used is in memory-mapped I/O. For memory-mapped I/O, reading the same location in main memory may result in different data (because the memory location is mapped to some device rather than to a standard memory area). In this case, it would be bad to cache the data from a read, because a second read to the same address should return new data from the device rather than the old data (cached from the previous read). Thus, it is important to disable all caches for these accesses.

A problem can arise when multiple processing devices try to access the same data in main memory. Some devices that may cause this problem to arise are two microprocessors in a multiprocessing system, or a microprocessor and a direct memory access (DMA) controller in a uniprocessor system. The problem is that one device may have data cached locally (in a cache that is not shared by the other device), in which case the other device will get old (stale) data when it performs a read access to that data. To solve this problem, the PowerPC architecture defines a page property of *memory coherence*, which tells the hardware to make sure that all the different devices in the system see the most recent copy of the data within that page. This is discussed in more detail in "Multiprogramming and Multiprocessor Synchronization," later in this chapter.

The final property that pages can have is related to caches but not unique to cache behavior. Often, in modern processors, data is fetched before it is known to be needed. This generally is done invisibly so that the programmer need not be concerned with it, but there are cases where it may not be invisible to the programmer. If a load is executed speculatively, for example, and the address loaded happens to be a memory-mapped I/O device, the results can be disastrous. The device very well may change its data because of the read, and the processor may discover that the load should not have executed and throw away the data it read. That data now is gone forever. As a solution, the PowerPC architecture defines a property for pages called *guarded storage*. If a page is guarded, data cannot be speculatively read from it. Basically, any load that has store semantics (loads to idempotent storage) should be placed in guarded storage.

Block Translation Mechanism

The block address translation (BAT) mechanism in the PowerPC architecture enables the programmer to map a larger than 4-KB piece of memory using a single translation resource. The BAT mechanism uses special-purpose registers, which are entirely software controlled, in order to perform the translation. Each translation resource consists of two BAT registers: an upper register and a lower register (see "Special-Purpose Registers," earlier in this appendix). The BAT mechanism is a single-level translation. The upper-order effective address bits are compared against some bits in the upper BAT register (the block effective page index), and if there is a match, the upper-order bits of the real address are read from the lower BAT register (the block real page number). The PowerPC architecture includes four sets of instruction BAT registers (each set consists of an upper and a lower register) and four sets of data BAT registers.

Not only does the BAT mechanism enable you to map larger spaces, but it also enables you to map different-size spaces. You therefore could map one area (a video frame buffer, for example) into a 4-MB BAT space, and another area (the operating system kernel, for example) into a 1MB BAT space. Each of these mappings would consume one BAT register (as opposed to 1,024 and 256 page table entries each, respectively). The upper BAT register contains an 11-bit mask that is used to select the page size. Table C.2 shows all the possible sizes of memory blocks which can be mapped to a BAT entry.

Table C.2. Allowable BAT sizes/BAT mask values.

BAT Size	BAT Mask
128 KB	000 0000 0000
256 KB	000 0000 0001
512 KB	000 0000 0011
1 MB	000 0000 0111
2 MB	000 0000 1111
4 MB	000 0001 1111
8 MB	000 0011 1111
16 MB	000 0111 1111
32 MB	000 1111 1111
64 MB	001 1111 1111
128 MB	011 1111 1111
256 MB	111 1111 1111

The BAT mechanism supports the same page protection and cache behavior bits as the page mechanism.

32-Bit Virtual Memory Management

This section covers some of the issues associated with managing virtual memory on a 32-bit implementation of the PowerPC architecture. This memory management generally is handled by the operating system.

Segment Registers

The segment registers are accessed whenever the processor needs to translate an address. The format of the segment register is shown in Figure C.3. The fields of a segment register follow:

T	This field selects between two formats for the remaining bits in the segment register. If T=0, this is a normal segment (this is the format described here). If T=1, this is a direct store segment (see the "Direct Store Segments" section later in this appendix).
K_S	This is the page protection key for operating system code ($MSR_{PR} = 0$).
K_P	This is the page protection key for application code ($MSR_{PR} = 1$).
N	If N=1, this segment is a no-execute segment.
VSID	This is the virtual segment ID.

FIGURE C.3.

The segment register format (normal segments).

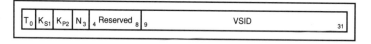

Two instructions can be used to update segment registers. The *move to segment register* instruction (mtsr) copies the contents of a general integer register into a segment register specified in the instruction. The *move to segment register indirect* instruction (mtsrin) copies the contents of a general integer register into a segment register specified in another general integer register.

Similarly, two instructions can be used to read the segment registers. The *move from segment register* instruction (mfsr) copies the contents of a segment register specified in the instruction into a general integer register. The *move from segment register indirect* instruction (mfsrin) copies the contents of a segment register (specified in a general integer register) into a general integer register.

Synchronization requirements are associated with these instructions; these are specified in the section "Synchronization Requirements for Segment Registers, Page Table Entries, and Segment Table Entries," later in this appendix.

Page Table Construction

The page table is a software-controlled table used by the processor during address translation. The table is organized into groups of eight entries, each of which is 64-bits long (see figure C.4). The page table is searched by hardware each time it needs to translate an address. As mentioned previously, the processor uses a hash function to look up page table entries.

FIGURE C.4.

64-bit page table entry: 32-bit architecture.

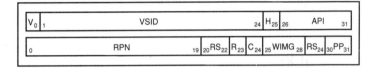

The result of the hash function is the real (physical) address of the page table entry group that should be searched for the translation. The most significant bits of this address come from a special-purpose register: storage description register 1 (SDR1). The high-order 16 bits of this register are called the *hash table origin* (HTABORG), and the least significant 9 bits of SDR1 are called the *hash table mask* (HTABMASK). Between 7 and 16 of the high-order bits of the HTABORG field are used to identify the base address of the page table (see figure C.5). The minimum supported page table size is 64KB, and the maximum supported page table size is 32MB.

FIGURE C.5.

The organization of storage description register 1 (SDR1) and formation of the page table entry group address.

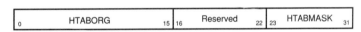

- HTABORG - Real address of the page table.
- HTABMASK - Mask for the page table address.

Page table group physical address generation:

$$\text{HTABORG}_{0:6} \;||\; (\text{HTABORG}_{7:15} \;|\; (\text{HTABMASK} \;\&\; \text{HASH}_{0:8})) \;||\; \text{HASH}_{9:18} \;||\; {}^{6}0$$

(where || is concatenate & | is logical OR)

- HASH - The 20 bit hash value.

The index into the page table comes from a hash value generated using the effective address of the access being translated. Two hash values are generated: a primary hash and a secondary hash. These hash values, together with the values in SDR1, give the physical addresses of two page table entry groups, which are searched for the appropriate translation information (see figure C.5). The primary hash is generated by XORing the low-order 19 bits of the VSID (from the segment register) with three 0s concatenated with the page index (from the effective address). The secondary hash is the 1's complement (logical inversion) of the primary hash.

The page table entry group (PTEG) accessed from the primary hash is called the *primary PTEG*, and the PTEG accessed from the secondary hash is called the *secondary PTEG*. After the addresses of the two page table entry groups have been calculated, these two groups are searched for translation information. Each of these groups consists of eight page table entries (see figure C.5).

A page table entry (PTE) for the current translation is found if the following conditions are met:

■ PTE_H = 0 for the primary PTEG, and 1 for the secondary PTEG.
■ PTE_V = 1.
■ PTE_{VSID} = VSID (from the segment register).
■ PTE_{API} = page index bits 4 through 9.

After a valid PTE is found, the RPN from that PTE is concatenated with the page offset from the effective address to form the 32-bit physical address.

If the page table lookup fails, then a page fault occurs and an instruction storage interrupt (for instruction fetch accesses) or a data store interrupt (for data accesses) is taken (see "PowerPC Interrupt Architecture," later in this appendix).

Example C.1 shows how a page table can be created. A page table entry contains the following fields:

Valid (V)	This bit specifies that the page table entry is valid (this field is set to 1 if this entry is valid).
Virtual Segment ID (VSID)	This field specifies the virtual segment for which this entry is used.
Hash Function Identifier (H)	This bit specifies whether the primary or secondary hash function is used to access this entry.
Abbreviated Page Index (API)	This field is matched with bits 4 through 9 of the effective address (the first 6 bits of the page index).
Real Page Number (RPN)	This field gives the real page number where the access will go in physical memory.
Reference Bit (R)	This bit is set by hardware when a page is accessed using this PTE.
Change Bit (C)	This bit is set by hardware if any data in this page has been changed by an access using this entry during translation.
Write Through, Cache. Inhibited, Coherent, Guarded (WIMG)	These bits specify the cache behavior for this page, and whether the page is guarded.
Page Protection (PP)	These bits specify the page protection for this page.
Reserved (RS)	These bits are reserved and should be set to 0.

EXAMPLE C.1.

Setting up a page table.

In this example, you will set up a page table entry and then see how it is used by hardware. The order in which you perform the various steps is basically a logical order for clarity; it is not necessarily the order in which you actually would perform these steps in a real system (see the section "Synchronization Requirements for Segment Registers, Page Table Entries, and Segment Table Entries," later in this appendix).

The first step in setting up a page table is deciding where it will be in physical memory and how big it will be. The page table is constrained to start on a 64-KB boundary. You will place a 128-KB page table at the start of physical memory (0×00000000). You therefore load the value 0×00000001 into SDR1. The HTABORG field is 0×0000, which corresponds to real address 0×00000000; the HTABMASK field is 0×001, which corresponds to a page table size of 128 KB. The HTABMASK field would be set to 0×000 for a 64-KB table and to 0×003 for a 256-KB table. Note that 0×002, or any setting with any zeros to the right of the first 1 bit is invalid. You also initialize the page table to zeros (so that all entries are initialized to invalid).

Next, assume that an application wants to have a page allocated for its use. Assume that the application tries to access effective address 0×50003000. Because none of the PTEs are valid, the translation of that address fails, and a page fault occurs. The page fault handler is called in the operating system, and now the operating system must decide whether to assign a virtual page to the application so that it can continue to run. For this example, assume that the operating system does assign a page. You will assign virtual segment 0×000001 to this application, and you will map page 0×0003 of this segment into physical memory for this access (this is from the effective address earlier). You will make this page cacheable and coherent, and you will not force caches to write-through stores. It also will not be guarded and will be read/write for both the application and the operating system.

This effective address accesses segment register 5 (from the effective address earlier), so you load segment register 5 with the following values:

T = 0	This is not a direct store segment.
K_s = 1	This is the page protection key for the operating system code (MSR_{PR} = 0).
K_p = 0	This is the page protection key for the application code (MSR_{PR} = 1).
N = 0	This segment can be executed.
VSID = 0×000001	This is the virtual segment number.

Now, you will set up the PTE. You first generate the primary hash value by XORing the low-order 19 bits of the VSID (0×00001) with three binary 0s concatenated with the page index (0×00003). This gives you a primary hash value of 0×00002. Thus, the primary PTEG for this access is found at address 0×00000080 (HTABORG$_{0:14}$ ∥ HASH$_{8:18}$ ∥ ^{6}0). The secondary hash value is the logical inversion of the primary hash value (0×FFFFD). The secondary PTEG for this access is found at address 0×0003FF40. If there were no PTEs available in the primary PTEG, then a PTE in the secondary PTEG could be used (if there were none here, then a page would have to be put back on disk to make room for the new page). In this example, however, none of the PTEs are valid, so the PTE at address 0×00000080 is used for this access, and is set up as the following:

V = 1	This entry now is valid.
VSID = 0×000001	This is the VSID for this access.
H = 0	This is in the primary PTEG for this access.
API = 0×00	The high-order 6 bits of the page index of this access are 0.
RPN = 0×00020	This is the real page number to which you are mapping this virtual page.
R = 0	Hardware will set this bit when it first accesses this page using this PTE.
C = 0	Hardware will set this bit if it changes any data in this page using this PTE.
WIMG = 0b0010	Write-through is not set, Cache inhibited is not set, memory coherent is set, guarded is not set.
PP = 0b10	This sets read/write permission for a page protection key of 0 or 1.

You have mapped physical page 0×00020 in this example, so you must be sure that that page is not already in use (pages 0x00000-0x0001F are used by the page table itself, and no other pages are in use). Control now is passed back to the application, which will try its access over again.

This time, when the application tries to access effective address 0×50003000, it reads segment register 5 and gets a VSID of 0×000001. This result, together with the values you placed into SDR1 and the page index of 0×0003, generates a primary PTEG address of 0×00000080 (HTABORG$_{0:14}$ ∥ HASH$_{8:18}$ ∥ ^{6}0). This PTEG is accessed, and a match is found in the first PTE. This PTE gives an RPN of 0×00020 with read/write permission for the application. The physical address the application accesses is 0×00020000. You therefore translate the effective address 0×50003000 into the physical address 0×00020000.

Translation Lookaside Buffers

In the preceding section, you learned how the processor accesses the page table when it wants to translate an address. If the processor had to access the page table in memory every time it wanted to perform an instruction fetch or data access, it would spend most of its time doing translation and very little of its time actually running your program. In order to solve this problem, all current implementations of the PowerPC architecture contain special caches called *translation lookaside buffers* (TLBs). These caches are used to cache PTE entries. When the operating system changes a PTE entry, it must invalidate the TLB entry corresponding to that PTE so that the processor does not use the old translation.

Two instructions are supplied for manipulating TLBs. The *translation lookaside buffer invalidate entry* (tlbie) instruction invalidates a subset of the TLB based only on the page index. Any entry that may correspond to that page index is invalidated (the invalidation is done without accessing the segment registers). The *translation lookahead buffer invalidate all* (tlbia) instruction invalidates the entire TLB. Synchronization requirements are associated with these instructions, which are described in the section "Synchronization Requirements for Segment Registers, Page Table Entries, and Segment Table Entries."

64-Bit Virtual Memory Architecture

The 64-bit PowerPC virtual memory architecture differs primarily in the segment registers. The formats of the PTEs are different, but the fields and their meanings are the same (see Figure C.6). The same is true of the 64-bit version of SDR1, except that instead of having the HTABMASK field, the 64-bit SDR1 contains a field (HTABSIZE) that specifies the number of 1 bits in the mask, which is used in the same way as the HTABMASK field in the 32-bit architecture (see Figure C.7).

FIGURE C.6.

128-bit page table entry: 64-bit architecture.

0	VSID	$_{51}$ $_{52}$	API	$_{56}$ $_{57}$ Reserved$_{61}$	H$_{62}$	V$_{63}$

| 0 | RPN | $_{51}$ $_{52}$ Reserved$_{64}$ | R$_{55}$ | C$_{56}$ | $_{57}$ WIMG$_{60}$ | RS$_{61}$ | $_{62}$ PP$_{63}$ |

FIGURE C.7.

The organization of storage description register 1 (SDR1) and the formation of the page table entry group address (64-bit architecture).

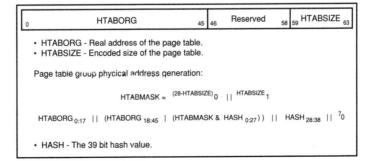

0	HTABORG	$_{45}$ $_{46}$	Reserved	$_{58}$ $_{59}$	HTABSIZE $_{63}$

- HTABORG - Real address of the page table.
- HTABSIZE - Encoded size of the page table.

Page table group physical address generation:

$$HTABMASK = {}^{(28-HTABSIZE)}0 \; || \; {}^{HTABSIZE}1$$

$$HTABORG_{0:17} \; || \; (HTABORG_{18:45} \; | \; (HTABMASK \; \& \; HASH_{0:27})) \; || \; HASH_{28:38} \; || \; {}^{7}0$$

- HASH - The 39 bit hash value.

Instead of the 16 segment registers in the 32-bit architecture, the 64-bit architecture defines a one-page segment table (STAB). The STAB is organized into 32 groups of 8-segment table entries (STEs) (see Figure C.8). Each STE has the following fields:

ESID	Effective segment ID.
V	This is set to 1 for valid STEs.
T	This bit identifies direct store segments. The description given here is for normal segments (T=0).
K_S	This is the page protection key for operating system code ($MSR_{PR} = 0$)
K_P	This is the page protection key for application code ($MSR_{PR} = 1$).
N	If N=1, then this segment is a no-execute segment.
VSID	This is the virtual segment ID.

FIGURE C.8.

The segment table entry format (normal segments).

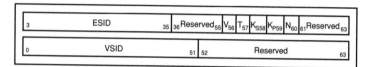

Accessing the STAB is similar to accessing the page table. The address space register (ASR) identifies the real address of the STAB ($ASR_{0:51}$ is the base address of the STAB, and $ASR_{52:63}$ is reserved). Bits 31 through 35 of the effective address identify the index into the STAB of the primary segment table entry group (STEG). The logical inverse of these bits form the offset into the STAB of the secondary STEG. Both the primary and secondary STEGs are searched for an appropriate STE. A match for an effective address is found if $STE_V = 1$, and $STE_{ESID} = EA_{0:35}$. After a matching STE is found, the fields are extracted from the STE and are used in the same way as they were in the 32-bit architecture.

Just like with the page table, hardware typically will have a segment lookaside buffer (SLB) in order to speed up translation. The synchronization requirements for software relative to this structure are described in the section "Synchronization Requirements for Segment Registers, Page Table Entries, and Segment Table Entries," later in this appendix).

Two instructions are provided for managing the SLB. These instructions are available only on 64-bit implementations of the PowerPC architecture. The *SLB invalidate entry* instruction (slbie) invalidates any entries in the SLB that correspond to the effective address of the instruction. The *SLB invalidate all* instruction (slbia) invalidates the entire SLB.

Direct Store Segments

If the T field in a segment register is set to 1, then the segment is a *direct store segment*. These segments are meant for use with I/O devices and are an alternative to using memory-mapped

I/O. The format of the segment register for a direct-store segment is shown in Figure C.9 (32-bit architecture) and Figure C.10 (64-bit architecture).

T	This bit identifies the segment as a direct store segment.
K_S	This is the page protection key for the operating system code ($MSR_{PR} = 0$).
K_P	This is the page protection key for the application code ($MSR_{PR} = 1$).
BUID	Bus unit ID.

The remaining bits have different meanings for different I/O controllers.

FIGURE C.9.

The segment register format (direct store segments).

FIGURE C.10.

The segment table entry format (direct store segments).

When translating a direct store address, translation stops after the segment register lookup. The following information is sent to the controller (identified by the BUID):

■ The page protection key (K_S if $MSR_{PR} = 0$, or K_P if $MSR_{PR} = 1$).

Note that page protection is not implemented in the processor for direct storage segments.

■ Some portion of the segment register (see the User's Manual for the specific implementation you are using).

■ Some portion of the effective address (see the User's Manual for the specific implementation you are using).

The following instructions are not supported for direct store segments (the results of these instructions for T=1 are boundedly undefined):

■ eciwx

■ ecowx

■ ldarx

■ lwarx

■ stdcx.

■ stwcx.

Finally, the following instructions have no effect in direct store segments:

■ dcbf

■ dcbi

■ dcbt

■ dcbst

■ dcbtst

■ dcbz

■ icbi

Synchronization Requirements for Segment Registers, Page Table Entries, and Segment Table Entries

This section describes the synchronization requirements software must follow in order to guarantee correct execution of virtual memory structure manipulation.

Context Synchronizing Instructions

In order to implement the synchronization requirements that follow, context synchronizing instructions typically are used. In order to understand context synchronization, remember that in a typical modern microprocessor, many operations are occurring in parallel; and, unlike in the strict architectural model, operations may occur out of order. Normally, the processor ensures that this out-of-order and concurrent execution of instructions is invisible to the programmer; however, that takes hardware and, in general, slows the execution of instructions. As a compromise, many of the operating-system specific operations (especially ones that are infrequent) are required to have software-synchronization support to ensure correct operation.

An operation is context synchronizing if the following conditions are met:

■ Instructions following this operation are performed in the context set by this operation (context is the machine state, especially MSR, and virtual memory structures).

■ Instructions preceding this operation are performed in the context prior to this operation.

An example of a context-synchronizing instruction is the instruction synchronize instruction (isync). This instruction simply waits for all instructions in front of it to complete and then flushes any following instructions that have begun execution out of the processor (requiring them to be refetched). The isync instruction therefore exactly implements context synchronization.

There are other instructions and events that are context synchronizing (sc, rfi, and most interrupts, for example).

In the following descriptions, lock() and unlock() are subroutines that provide exclusive access to the structure passed. Therefore, if you want to update a shared object, you issue the following code:

```
lock(object)
```

This code gives you exclusive access to that object. When you have finished updating that object, you issue the following code:

```
unlock(object)
```

This code releases the object so that another processor or thread can lock it and update it.

Synchronization for Segment Register Updates

When updating segment registers, the only synchronization required is that a context-synchronizing instruction must be placed on either side of the updating instruction. The following code therefore is a valid way to update segment register 1 (from integer register 0):

```
isync
mtsr sr1, r08
isync
```

Synchronization for Page Table Entry Manipulation

There are three operations on page tables:

- Adding a new PTE
- Modifying an existing PTE
- Deleting a PTE

TLBs are not coherent caches of the page table, so software must ensure coherency between different TLBs.

Adding a Page Table Entry

The following pseudo-code can be used to add a page table entry:

```
lock(PTE)
        PTE_VSID,H,API <- new values
        PTE_RPN,R,C,WIMG,PP <- new values
        sync
        PTE_V <- 0b1
        unlock(PTE)
```

The sync instruction is required to ensure that the PTE is set up before the valid bit is set. Without the sync instruction, an implementation might reorder the storage operations so that the valid bit is set before the rest of the PTE is set up, resulting in a window during which an invalid translation might occur.

Modifying a Page Table Entry

The following pseudo-code can be used to modify a page table entry:

```
lock(PTE)
PTE_v <- 0
sync
tlbie(PTE)
sync
tlbsync
sync
PTE_VSID,H,API <- new values
PTE_RPN,R,C,WIMG,PP <- new values
sync
PTE_v <- 0b1
unlock(PTE)
```

The tlbsync instruction ensures that the preceding tlbie has been seen by all processors in a system.

Deleting a Page Table Entry

The following pseudo-code can be used to delete a page table entry:

```
lock(PTE)
PTE_v <- 0
sync
tlbie(PTE)
sync
tlbsync
sync
unlock(PTE)
```

Synchronization for Segment Table Entry Manipulation

There are three operations on segment tables:

- Adding a new STE
- Modifying an existing STE
- Deleting an STE

Segment LBs are not coherent caches of the segment table, so software must ensure coherency between different SLBs.

Adding a Segment Table Entry

The following pseudo-code can be used to add a segment table entry:

```
lock(STE)
STE_ESID,T,Ks,Kp,N <- new values
if T=0 then
        STE_VSID <- new value
else
```

```
            STE_IO <- new value
sync
STE_V <- 1
unlock(STE)
```

Modifying a Segment Table Entry

The following pseudo-code can be used to modify a segment table entry:

```
lock(STE)
STE_V <- 0
sync
slbie(STE)
sync
STE_ESID,T,Ks,Kp,N <- new values
if T=0 then
            STE_VSID <- new value
else
            STE_IO <- new value
sync
STE_V <- 1
unlock(STE)
```

Deleting a Segment Table Entry

The following pseudo-code can be used to delete a segment table entry:

```
lock(STE)
STE_V <- 0
sync
slbie(STE)
sync
unlock(STE)
```

Multiprogramming and Multiprocessor Synchronization

Some means of avoiding race conditions is necessary to implement preemptive multitasking and cooperating processes in any computer system. Classically, such a mechanism is provided architecturally by an *atomic* read-write memory operation—an instruction that appears to read a value from memory and (perhaps optionally) replace it with a new one. A broad discussion of operating system theory and algorithms is beyond the scope of this book; for a complete discussion of race conditions, mutual exclusion, and an explanation of the reasons for these instructions, see any good operating systems text. This book was written on the assumption that if you're reading this section, you understand the necessity of synchronization primitives for shared memory communications.

The PowerPC instruction set does not provide any atomic read-write memory instructions *per se*. Instead, the architecture provides the capability to implement atomic memory *operations* as sequences of PowerPC instructions. The mechanism that enables this process is called a *reservation*. The architecture defines two instructions based on the reservation principle: *load word and reserve indexed* (lwarx) and *store word conditional indexed with record* (stwcx.). There are corresponding double-word instructions—ldarx and stdcx.—defined for 64-bit implementations. Other than the size of the data reference, they are identical, and are not discussed further.

The reservation concept is fairly simple. When a lwarx instruction is executed, the value held at the memory location is placed in the destination register; additionally, the processor places a reservation on the block of memory containing the loaded word. If the processor still holds the reservation and executes a stwcx. instruction to the same location, the store takes place and the condition code is set (the EQ bit in cr0 is set to 1). Otherwise, the stwcx. instruction has no effect.

The reservation is held by the processor until one of the following occurs:

1. The processor executes another lwarx instruction. The first reservation is lost, and a new one is made. A processor can hold only one reservation at a time.

2. The processor executes a stwcx. instruction, regardless of whether the address matches the current reservation.

3. Another processor executes a store to an address in the same reservation block (see the following sidebar).

4. The processor is interrupted or trapped to supervisor state. Actually, the interrupt itself doesn't release the reservation, but normally, the interrupt handler clears it to avoid problems such as one process improperly inheriting a reservation from another.

The synchronization algorithms used in multiprogramming systems are defined in terms of a particular primitive hardware operation. The reservation concept and the associated PowerPC instructions enable fairly straightforward implementation of popular synchronization primitives and emulation of atomic instructions defined in other machine architectures.

Following are examples of these coded to be called as C functions. An appropriate ANSI C prototype is included in a comment preceding each definition.

Before using any of popular synchronization primitives in your applications, make sure that you understand the concepts of reservation and reservation granularity (see the following sidebar).

RESERVATIONS AND RESERVATION GRANULARITY

The *reservation* mechanism provides a means of implementing an atomic operation with a nonatomic sequence of instructions. Rather than make the sequence of operations atomic, the idea is to assume that the sequence is atomic, and simply detect any event that might cause that assumption to be violated; in that case, the operation is retried.

This is a simple idea, and it's really not new; because few hardware memory devices support an atomic read and conditional write operation, the concept of a reservation or lock on a unit of memory has been used for years to implement the function in hardware.

Understanding the difference between a reservation and a lock can be critical to making sense of the way these functions work. A *lock* on a memory location is like a lock on a door; it prevents any access except by the owner of the lock. A lock is a very powerful mechanism, but it can create problems if a lock is placed but not removed by an errant program.

Unlike a lock, a *reservation* permits access by nonreservation holders, but if such access is given, it causes the original reservation to be canceled. The store conditional instruction provides a mechanism that simultaneously tests to see whether the reservation still is held; it exits harmlessly if it was lost, and notifies the reservation holder that it was lost through a bit in the condition register. Judicious use of reservations by cooperating programs permits the implementation of locks without the undesirable failure modes associated with hardware locks.

Another key concept is *reservation granularity*. It might appear from the definition of the instructions that any word (or doubleword) can have its own reservation. In fact, the reservation actually covers a larger block of memory, and the size of that block varies among the PowerPC processor implementations. If a processor sets a reservation, references to other locations in the same block (a store to an adjacent word, for example) can cause loss of the reservation, so care must be taken in assigning the locations of synchronizing variables. In the PowerPC 601, 603, and 604 processors, the reservation granularity is 32 bytes; the 620 processor granularity is 64 bytes. Also, synchronizing variable addresses must be aligned, on 4-byte boundaries for lwarx and stwcx., and on 8-byte boundaries for ldarx and stdcx..

Fetch and Nop

This function returns the current value of a variable. This primitive allows the fact that the value is being read by one process to be detected by another process that may be in the middle of updating the value (because the store conditional would cause that other process to lose its reservation):

```
# long Fetch_and_Nop (void *Var);
#
.Fetch_and_Nop:
        lwarx   r4,0,r3     # Load and reserve Var
        stwcx.  r4,0,r3     # Store value back
                            # ..if still reserved
        bne-    _fetch_and_nop
                            # Loop if lost reservation
        mr      r3,r4       # Return current value
        bclr
```

Fetch and Store

This operation fetches the current value of a variable, atomically replacing it with a new one. The value of the variable before the replacement is returned:

```
# long Fetch_and_Store (void *Var, long NewVal);
#
.Fetch_and_Store:
            lwarx     r5,0,r3       # Get current value
            stwcx.    r4,0,r3       # Try to replace with NewVal
            bne-      _Fetch_and_Store
                                    # Loop if lost reservation
            mr        r3,r5         # Return previous value
            bclr
```

Fetch and Add

This operation atomically adds to the current value of a variable. The variable's unincremented value is returned:

```
# long Fetch_and_Add (void *Var, long Incr);
#
.Fetch_and_Add:
            lwarx     r5,0,r3       # Get current value
            add       r0,r4,r5      # Add Incr to value
            stwcx.    r0,0,r3       # Try to store it back
            bne-      _Fetch_and_Add
                                    # Retry if reservation lost
            mr        r3,r5         # Return previous value
            bclr
```

Some algorithms use a similar primitive, except performing a Boolean operation such as logical AND or OR on the variable. A Fetch_and_AND or Fetch_and_OR could be implemented by simply replacing the add instruction with the appropriate logical instruction.

Test and Set

Test and Set is a commonly occurring primitive in some algorithms, and even appears as an atomic instruction in some processor architectures. The primitive returns when the value in storage is nonzero. If the current value is nonzero, it is returned. If it is equal to zero, it is set atomically to the provided nonzero value. The caller checks to see whether the returned (previous) value is zero; if so, it is known that Test_and_Set routine replaced it with the caller's value:

```
# long Test_and_Set (void *Var, long NewVal);
  #
  .Test_and_Set:
            lwarx     r5,0,r3       # Get old value and reserve
            cmpi      r5,0          # Old value zero?
            bne-      done          # Branch if no
            stwcx.    r4,0,r3       # Replace zero with NewVal
            bne-      .Test_and_Set
```

```
                              # Retry if reservation lost
done:
        mr      r3,r5         # Return old value
        bclr
```

Compare and Swap

This primitive is based on the definition of the IBM System/370 Compare and Swap instruction. It is similar to Test and Set, except the comparison is with a specified value instead of zero. If the current value of the variable is equal to the specified comparison value, it is replaced with a second value, and the old value is returned. Otherwise, the variable is unchanged, and its current value is returned:

```
# long Compare_and_Swap (void *Var, long CmpVal, long NewVal);
#
.Compare_and_Swap:
        lwarx   r6,0,r3       # Get old value and reserve
        cmp     r4,r6         # old == CmpVal?
        bne-    done          # If not, return current
        stwcx.  r5,0,r3       # If equal, try to replace
        bne-    .Compare_and_Swap
                              # Retry if reservation lost
done:
        mr      r3,r6         # Return previous value
        bclr
```

In all these examples, you code the conditional branch that tests the result of the store-conditional to indicate your expectation that the store will succeed.

Lock and Unlock

The section on virtual memory management ("32-Bit Virtual Memory Management") described earlier used a lock/unlock method of synchronization. Here is an implementation of these primitives using Test and Set:

```
# void lock(void *Var);
#
# Var is unlocked if 0, locked if 1
.lock:
        li      r4,1          #
loop:   bl      .test_and_set
        bne-    loop          # Loop until unlocked
        isync                 # Wait for prior instr
        blr                   # return


# void unlock(void *Var);
#
# Var is unlocked if 0, locked if 1
.unlock:
        sync                  # Wait for any prior stores
        li      r4,0          # Set lock to zero
        stw     r4,0(r3)      #
        blr                   # return
```

PowerPC Interrupt Architecture

The PowerPC exception-handling mechanism enables the processor to change state and react to program requests, signals, errors, or external events. Except for certain catastrophic conditions (like Machine Check or System Reset) PowerPC interrupts are precise, and are handled in program order. If two interrupting instructions are executed out of order, for example, the first interrupt signaled is the one for the instruction that is earlier in program order, regardless of the order in which the instructions actually are executed.

When an interrupt occurs, the following sequence of events is initiated:

1. The current value of the MSR is copied to SRR1. Some additional bits to indicate the type of the interrupt also are placed in SRR1.

2. An instruction address is placed in SRR0. Depending on the type of interrupt, this address may be the effective address of the instruction causing the interrupt; the instruction that would have been executed next had the interrupt not occurred; or, in some cases, an instruction near the point at which the interrupt occurred (in some execution modes, some PowerPC interrupts may be imprecise).

3. The MSR is set to disable instruction and data translation, and to enter supervisor state.

4. Control is transferred to an interrupt vector location corresponding to interrupt type; vector addresses for each interrupt type are shown in Table C.3.

5. Additional information about the interrupt may be present in other PowerPC registers. On a data storage exception, the data address register (DAR) contains the interrupting address (the DAR can be read with the mfspr instruction), for example. Consult the User's Guide for a specific processor for complete details of interrupt signaling.

The interrupt handler invoked to process an exception should examine the machine state and determine what action is required. In some cases, the required action can be performed directly; in other cases, a record of the event is posted to a queue for later processing. Sometimes, execution of the halted program is resumed at the point of interruption. The *return from interrupt* instruction (rfi) provides an operation inverse to an interrupt—it restores the appropriate MSR bits from SRR1, and branches to the location in SRR0.

Care must be taken to ensure that the state of one process is not incorrectly carried across an interrupt-handling boundary. There are two principal concerns: instructions and references executed out of order, and memory reservations. isync may be required in an interrupt handler when it changes the MSR or SRs for turning on DR or IR, for example. Also, a held memory reservation is *not* cleared by an exception; to prevent incorrect inheritance of a reservation across the rfi, the handler may need to execute an stwcx. (or stdcx.) instruction to clear any pending reservations.

Table C.3. PowerPC interrupt vector locations.

Vector Offset (hex)	Interrupt Type
00000	Reserved
00100	System Reset
00200	Machine Check
00300	Data Storage
00400	Instruction Storage
00500	External
00600	Alignment
00700	Program
00800	Floating-Point Unavailable
00900	Decrementer
00A00	Reserved
00B00	Reserved
00C00	System Call
00D00	Trace
00E00	Floating-Point Assist
00E10-00FFF	Reserved
01000-02FFF	Reserved, implementation-specific

D

A Detailed Floating-Point Model

This appendix is supplied primarily for those who want to optimize floating-point code. A basic introduction to floating point is given in Chapter 2, "Introduction to the PowerPC Architecture," and this is probably sufficient for most programmers. If you need to know the exact behavior of floating-point code (to avoid pathological rounding errors, for example) or how to control the exception behavior of floating-point code, however, then this appendix provides those details.

Included in this appendix are the algorithms used for rounding and conversion between integer and floating point values. First we will describe the floating point status and control register in more detail than in previous chapter, including the exception status and control mechanism.

Floating-Point Status and Control Register

The *floating-point status and control register* (FPSCR) is used by software to control certain floating-point operations, and by hardware to report certain conditions that arise during floating-point execution. There are 32 bits in the FPSCR (see Figure D.1). The bits of the FPSCR are described below (see Table D.1). The exception bits are described in the "Floating-Point Exceptions" section.

FIGURE D.1.

The floating point status and control register (FPSCR).

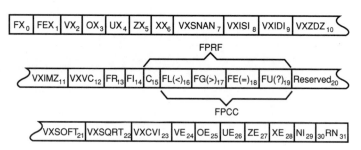

Table D.1. Floating-point status and control registar bit definitions.

bit(s)	Name of field	Meaning of field
0	Floating-Point Exception Summary (**FX**)	The processor sets this bit to one if any of the floating point exception bits in the FPSCR change from zero to one during the execution of an instruction, regardless of the corresponding enable bit for that exception.
1	Floating-Point Enabled Exception Summary (**FEX**)	This bit indicates whether any enabled exceptions have occurred. It is set by ORing all the floating point exception bits in the FPSCR (see below) masked by their enable bits (also in the FPSCR - see below).
2	Floating-Point Invalid Operation Exception Summary (**VX**)	This bit indicates whether any invalid operation exception have occurred. It is set by ORing all the invalid operation exception bits in the FPSCR (see below).
3	Floating-Point Overflow Exception (**OX**)	This indicates whether an overflow exception occurred.
4	Floating-Point Underflow Exception (**UX**)	This indicates whether an underflow exception occurred.
5	Floating-Point Zero Divide Exception (**ZX**)	This indicates whether a divide by zero exception occurred.
6	Floating-Point Inexact Exception (**XX**)	This indicates whether an inexact result exception has occurred. This is a 'sticky' (meaning that instructions set it to one implicitly, but once set, it stays set until explicitly reset) version of the FPSCRFI bit (see below).
7	Floating-Point Invalid Operation Exception (SNaN) (**VXSNAN**)	This bit is set if the floating-point invalid operation exception occurs because an attempt was made to operate on a signaling NaN.
8	Floating-Point Invalid Operation Exception (∞-∞) (**VXISI**)	This bit is set if a floating-point invalid operation exception occurs because an attempt was made to perform a magnitude subtraction of infinities.
9	Floating-Point Invalid Operation Exception (∞/∞) (**VXIDI**)	This bit is set if a floating-point invalid operation exception occurs because an attempt was made to divide infinities
10	Floating-Point Invalid Operation Exception (0/0) (**VXZDZ**)	This bit is set if a floating-point invalid operation exception occurs because an attempt was made to divide zero by zero.
11	Floating-Point Invalid Operation Exception (∞ x 0) (**VXIMZ**)	This bit is set if a floating-point invalid operation exception occurs because an attempt was made to multiply an infinity by zero.
12	Floating-Point Invalid Operation Exception (invalid compare) (**VXVC**)	This bit is set if a floating-point invalid operation exception occurs because an attempt was made to make an ordered comparison involving a NaN.
13	Floating-Point Fraction Rounded (**FR**)	This bit indicates whether the last arithmetic or conversion/rounding instruction to execute that rounded the intermediate result incremented the fraction (rounded away from zero).

continues

Table D.1. continued

bit(s)	Name of field	Meaning of field
14	Floating-Point Fraction Inexact (**FI**)	This bit indicates whether the last arithmetic or conversion/rounding instruction to execute rounded the intermediate result or caused a disabled overflow exception (see FPSCROE below).
15:19	Floating-Point Result Flags (**FPRF**)	This is a 5-bit field consisting of two subfields: the **Floating Point Result Class Descriptor** (**C**), and the **Floating Point Condition Code** (**FPCC**) fields. These bits are set as shown below.

C	**FPCC:** <,>,=,?	Type of value for the result
1	0b0001	Quiet NaN
0	0b1001	Negative Infinity
0	0b1000	Negative Normal Number
1	0b1000	Negative Denormalized Number
1	0b0010	Negative Zero
0	0b0010	Positive Zero
1	0b0100	Positive Denormalized Number
0	0b0100	Positive Normal Number
0	0b0101	Positive Infinity

bit(s)	Name of field	Meaning of field
21	Floating-Point Invalid Operation Exception (Software Request) (**VXSOFT**)	This bit is set explicitly by software in order to request an invalid operation to occur.
22	Floating-Point Invalid Operation Exception (Invalid Square Root) (**VXSQRT**)	This bit is set if a floating-point invalid operation exception occurs because an attempt was made to perform a square root operation on a negative non-zero number.
23	Floating-Point Invalid Operation Exception (Invalid Integer Convert) (**VXCVI**)	This bit is set if a floating-point invalid operation exception occurs because an attempt was made to convert a NaN or a large number to an integer (large meaning outside the representable range for the type of integer requested).
24	Floating-Point Invalid Operation Exception Enable (**VE**)	
25	Floating-Point Overflow Exception Enable (**OE**)	

bit(s)	Name of field	Meaning of field
26	Floating-Point Underflow Exception Enable (**UE**)	
27	Floating-Point Zero Divide Exception Enable (**ZE**)	
28	Floating-Point Inexact Exception Enable (**XE**)	
29	Floating-Point Non-IEEE Mode (NI)	If this bit is set to one, the meanings of all the other FPSCR bits may be different from how they are described here. In addition, the results of floating point operations may differ from the IEEE defined results. If the result of a floating point operation normally would be a denormalized number, then the result is set to zero. In general, if this bit is set to one, the operation of the floating point unit is implementation-specific, and the User's Manual for the particular implementation of interest should be consulted. Note that different implementations may behave differently when this bit is set to one.
30:31	Floating-Point Rounding Control (RN)	This is a 2-bit field that determines the rounding mode used by the processor. The rounding modes are shown below.

$FPSCR_{RN}$	Rounding Mode
0b00	Round to nearest
0b01	Round toward Zero
0b10	Round toward positive infinity
0b11	Round toward negative infinity

Floating-Point Exceptions

Several floating-point exceptions are defined by the PowerPC architecture:

■ Invalid operation exception:

  SNaN

  Infinity minus infinity

  Infinity divided by infinity

  Zero divided by zero

  Invalid compare

  Software request

  Invalid square root

  Invalid integer convert

■ Zero divide exception

■ Overflow exception

■ Underflow exception

■ Inexact exception

These exceptions may occur during computational operations, or if the FPSCR$_{VXSOFT}$ bit is set by software (for the software request invalid operation exception). Each of these exceptions has a bit in the FPSCR that is used to record an occurrence of that exception (including each type of invalid operation exception). In addition, each of these five exception classes has an enable bit in the FPSCR in order to enable or disable that class of exception. Finally, there is a sticky bit for each class of exception that records the occurrence of that class of exceptions (the sticky bits must be reset by software).

When an exception occurs, the result of the operation may be suppressed (the instruction does not update a general floating-point register). The cases when the result is suppressed are enabled invalid operation exceptions, and enabled zero divide exceptions. In all other cases, the result is written to the floating-point register (possibly destroying one of the operands if the target register also is an operand register for that instruction).

In addition to the enable bits in the FPSCR, there are two bits in the machine state register (MSR) that define the action the processor takes when a floating-point exception occurs (see Table D.2 and Appendix C, "Operating System Design for PowerPC Processors").

Table D.2. Definitions of the floating-point exceptions enabled bit in the MSR.

MSRFE0	*MSRFE1*	*Mode*	*Description*
0	0	Ignore exceptions mode	In this mode, the system floating-point exceptions handler is not invoked when a floating-point exception occurs.
0	1	Imprecise nonrecoverable mode	In this mode, the system floating-point exceptions handler is invoked when an enabled floating-point exception occurs. The handler is invoked at some point after the excepting instruction has executed, and the results of that execution may have been used by a subsequent instruction before the handler is invoked.

MSRFE0	MSRFE1	Mode	Description
1	1	Imprecise recoverable mode	In this mode, the system floating-point exceptions handler is invoked when an enabled floating-point exception occurs. The handler is invoked at some point after the excepting instruction has executed, but the results of that execution will not have been used by a subsequent instruction before the handler is invoked.
1	1	Precise mode	In this mode, the system floating-point exceptions handler is invoked when an enabled floating-point exception occurs. The handler is invoked precisely when the excepting instruction executes.

In general, enabling floating-point exceptions is useful for debugging code, but if possible, exceptions should be disabled (in both the FPSCR and MSR) for best performance.

Floating-Point Models

This section contains suggested models for floating-point operation. Some models are presented as algorithms written in pseudo-code.

IEEE Floating-Point Model

This section describes the IEEE double-precision floating-point model. The IEEE single-precision model is analogous to the double-precision model. The magnitude of the fraction portion of an IEEE double-precision floating-point value is 53 bits long. A sign bit is used to specify the sign of the number (this is called *signed-magnitude representation*). The format used for the accumulator that performs the IEEE arithmetic includes several bits in addition to these (see Figure D.2).

FIGURE D.2.

An accumulator used for IEEE floating-point arithmetic.

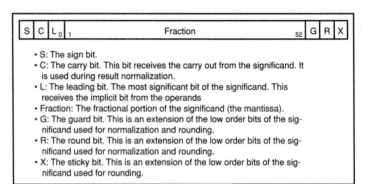

| S | C | L₀ | 1 | Fraction | 52 | G | R | X |

- S: The sign bit.
- C: The carry bit. This bit receives the carry out from the significand. It is used during result normalization.
- L: The leading bit. The most significant bit of the significand. This receives the implicit bit from the operands
- Fraction: The fractional portion of the significand (the mantissa).
- G: The guard bit. This is an extension of the low order bits of the significand used for normalization and rounding.
- R: The round bit. This is an extension of the low order bits of the significand used for normalization and rounding.
- X: The sticky bit. This is an extension of the low order bits of the significand used for rounding.

The guard and round bits are used during normalization of the result. They are shifted left during normalization, with zeros being shifted into the round bit. The carry bit also may be used during normalization. If the carry bit is set, in order to normalize the result, it must be shifted right by 1 bit (so the carry is shifted into the leading bit). The sticky bit is an OR of all bits that are less significant than the round bit. It is not used during normalization. The G, R, and X bits are used during rounding (see Table D.3).

Table D.3. The G, R, and X bits.

G	R	X	*Interpretation*
0	0	0	The intermediate result is exact.
0	0	1	The intermediate result is closer to the next lower
0	1	0	representable number.
0	1	1	
1	0	0	The intermediate result is exactly halfway between the two closest representable numbers.
1	0	1	The intermediate result is closer to the next higher
1	1	0	representable number.
1	1	1	

When the intermediate result is rounded, it is incremented by 1 (rounded up) or not (rounded down). The pseudo-code shown in Model D.1 determines whether the significand is incremented.

MODEL D.1.

```
inc <- 0
lsb <- Fraction₅₂
if FPSCR_RN = 0b00 then
     if S||lsb||G||R||X = 0bx11xx then
     inc <- 1
   if S||lsb||G||R||X = 0bx011x then
     inc <- 1
   if S||lsb||G||R||X = 0bx01x1 then
     inc <- 1
if FPSCR_RN = 0b10 then
   if S||lsb||G||R||X = 0b0x1xx then
     inc <- 1
   if S||lsb||G||R||X = 0b0xx1x then
     inc <- 1
   if S||lsb||G||R||X = 0b0xxx1 then
     inc <- 1
if FPSCR_RN = 0b11 then
   if S||lsb||G||R||X = 0b1x1xx then
     inc <- 1
   if S||lsb||G||R||X = 0b1xx1x then
     inc <- 1
   if S||lsb||G||R||X = 0b1xxx1 then
     inc <- 1
if inc = 1 then
   increment significand
```

Floating-Point Multiply-Add Model

The PowerPC architecture defines an instruction form that performs up to three operations in a single cycle: a multiply, an add, and a negate. The effect of this special form on computational results is a more exact intermediate result for the combined operations than would be obtained by performing separate operations. The intermediate result (the result of the multiply portion of the combined operation) can have as many as 106 significant bits (the product of two 53-bit significands). All 106 bits of this intermediate result are fed into the add portion of the combined operation. The accumulator used for the PowerPC multiply-add model is shown in Figure D.3.

FIGURE D.3.

*Accumulator used for
PowerPC floating-point
multiply-add arithmetic.*

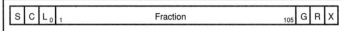

| S | C | L₀ | ₁ | Fraction | ₁₀₅ | G | R | X |

- S: The sign bit.
- C: The carry bit. This bit receives the carry out from the significand. It is used during result normalization.
- L: The leading bit. The most significant bit of the significand. This receives the implicit bit from the operands.
- Fraction: The fractional portion of the significand (the mantissa).
- G: The guard bit. This is an extension of the low order bits of the significand used for normalization and rounding.
- R: The round bit. This is an extension of the low order bits of the significand used for normalization and rounding.
- X: The sticky bit. This is an extension of the low order bits of the significand used for rounding.

Floating-Point Round to Single-Precision Model

The floating point round to single-precision instruction has the following format:

```
frsp[.] FRT, FRB
```

The pseudo-code shown in Model D.2 implements the frsp instruction.

MODEL D.2.

```
if (FRB)₁:₁₁ < 897 and (FRB)₁:₆₃ > 0 then
    if FPSCR_UE = 0 then
        goto DISABLED_UNDERFLOW
    else
        goto ENABLED_UNDERFLOW
if (FRB)₁:₁₁ > 1150 and (FRB)₁:₁₁ < 2047 then
    if FPSCR_OE = 0 then
        goto DISABLED_OVERFLOW
    else
        goto ENABLED_OVERFLOW
if (FRB)₁:₁₁ > 896 and (FRB)₁:₁₁ < 1151 then
    goto NORMAL_OPERAND
if (FRB)₁:₆₃ = 0 then
    goto ZERO_OPERAND
if (FRB)₁:₁₁ = 2047 then
    if (FRB)₁₂:₆₃ = 0 then
        goto INFINITY_OPERAND
    else if (FRB)₁₂ = 1 then
        goto QNAN_OPERAND
    else
        goto SNAN_OPERAND

DISABLED_UNDERFLOW:
    sign <- (FRB)₀
    if (FRB)₁:₁₁ = 0 then
        exp <- -1022
        frac₀:₅₂ <- 0b0 || (FRB)₁₂:₆₃
    if (FRB)₁:₁₁ > 0 then
        exp <- (FRB)₁:₁₁-1023
```

```
      frac₀:₅₂ <- 0b1||(FRB)₁₂:₆₃
DENORMALIZE_OPERAND:
G||R||X <- 0b000
do while exp < -126
    exp <- exp+1
    frac₀:₅₂||G||R||X <- 0b0|| frac₀:₅₂||G||(R|X)
FPSCRᵤₓ <- (frac₂₄:₅₂||G||R||X > 0)
ROUND_SINGLE(sign, exp, frac₀:₅₂,G,R,X)
FPSCRₓₓ <- FPSCRₓₓ | FPSCRꜰᵢ
if frac₀:₅₂ = 0 then
    FRT₀ <- sign
    FRT₁:₆₃ <- 0
    if sign = 0 then
        FPSCRꜰᵖᴿꜰ <- "+zero"
    else
        FPSCRꜰᵖᴿꜰ <- "-zero"
if frac₀:₅₂ > 0 then
    if frac₀ = 1 then
        if sign = 0 then
            FPSCRꜰᵖᴿꜰ <- "+normal number"
        else
            FPSCRꜰᵖᴿꜰ <- "-normal number"
    else
        if sign = 0 then
            FPSCRꜰᵖᴿꜰ <- "+denormalized number"
        else
            FPSCRꜰᵖᴿꜰ <- "-denormalized number"
    NORMALIZE OPERAND:
    do while frac₀ = 0
        exp <- exp-1
        frac₀:₅₂ <- frac₁:₅₂||0b0
    FRT₀ <- sign
    FRT₁:₁₁ <- exp
    FRT₁₂:₆₃ <- frac₁:₅₂
Done.


ENABLED_UNDERFLOW:
 FPSCRUX <- 1
 sign <- (FRB)0
 if (FRB)1:11 = 0 then
    exp <- -1022
    frac₀:₅₂ <- 0b0||(FRB)₁₂:₆₃
 if (FRB)₁:₁₁ > 0 then
    exp <- (FRB)₁:₁₁-1023
    frac₀:₅₂ <- 0b1||(FRB)₁₂:₆₃
 NORMALIZE OPERAND:
 do while frac₀ = 0
    exp <- exp-1
    frac₀:₅₂ <- frac₁:₅₂||0b0
 ROUND_SINGLE(sign, exp, frac0:52, 0, 0, 0)
 FPSCRₓₓ <- FPSCRₓₓ | FPSCRꜰᵢ
 exp <- exp + 192
 FRT0 <- sign
 FRT₁:₁₁ <- exp + 1023
 FRT₁₂:₆₃ <- frac₁:₅₂
 if sign = 0 then
```

```
        FPSCR_FPRF <- "+normal number"
    else
        FPSCR_FPRF <- "-normal number"
    Done.

DISABLED_OVERFLOW:
    FPSCR_OX <- 1
    if FPSCR_RN = 0b00 then /* Round to nearest */
        if (FRB)_0 = 0 then
            FRT <- 0x7FF0 0000 0000 0000
            FPSCR_FPRF <- "+infinity"
        else
            FRT <- 0xFFF0 0000 0000 0000
            FPSCR_FPRF <- "-infinity"
    if FPSCR_RN = 0b01 then /* Round truncate */
        if (FRB)_0 = 0 then
            FRT <- 0x47EF FFFF E000 0000
            FPSCR_FPRF <- "+normal number"
        else
            FRT <- 0xC7EF FFFF E000 0000
            FPSCR_FPRF <- "-normal number"
    if FPSCR_RN = 0b10 then /* Round to + infinity */
        if (FRB)_0 = 0 then
            FRT <- 0x7FF0 0000 0000 0000
            FPSCR_FPRF <- "+infinity"
        else
            FRT <- 0xC7EF FFFF E000 0000
            FPSCR_FPRF <- "-normal number"
    if FPSCR_RN = 0b11 then /* Round to - infinity */
        if (FRB)_0 = 0 then
            FRT <- 0x47EF FFFF E000 0000
            FPSCR_FPRF <- "+normal number"
        else
            FRT <- 0xFFF0 0000 0000 0000
            FPSCR_FPRF <- "-infinity"
    FPSCR_FR <- undefined
    FPSCR_FI <- 1
    FPSCR_XX <- 1
    Done.

ENABLED_OVERFLOW:
    sign <- (FRB)_0
    exp <- (FRB)_1:11 - 1023
    frac_0:52 <- 0b1 || (FRB)_12:63
    ROUND_SINGLE(sign, exp, frac_0:52, 0, 0, 0)
    FPSCR_XX <- FPSCR_XX | FPSCR_FI
    OVERFLOW:
    FPSCR_OX <- 1
    exp <- exp-192
    FRT_0 <- sign
    FRT_1:11 <- exp+1023
    FRT_12:63 <- frac_1:52
    if sign = 0 then
        FPSCR_FPRF <- "+normal number"
    else
        FPSCR_FPRF <- "-normal number"
```

```
Done.
ZERO_OPERAND:
 FRT <- (FRB)
 if (FRB)₀ = 0 then
     FPSCR_FPRF <- "+zero"
 else
     FPSCR_FPRF <- "-zero"
 FPSCR_FR:FI <- 0b00
 Done.
INFINITY_OPERAND:
 FRT <- (FRB)
 if (FRB)₀ = 0 then
     FRT <- 0x7FF0 0000 0000 0000
     FPSCR_FPRF <- "+infinity"
 else
     FRT <- 0xFFF0 0000 0000 0000
     FPSCR_FPRF <- "-infinity"
 FPSCR_FR:FI <- 0b00
 Done.
QNAN_OPERAND:
 FRT <- (FRB)₀:₃₄ ‖ ²⁹0
 FPSCR_FPRF <- "QNaN"
 FPSCR_FR:FI <- 0b00
 Done.


SNAN_OPERAND:
 FPSCR_VXSNAN <- 1
 if FPSCR_VE = 0 then
     FRT₀:₁₁ <- (FRB)₀:₁₁
     FRT₁₂ <- 0b1
     FRT₁₃:₆₃ <- (FRB)₁₃:₃₄ ‖ ²⁹0
     FPSCR_FPRF <- "QNaN"
 FPSCR_FR:FI <- 0b00
 Done.
NORMAL_OPERAND:
 sign <- (FRB)₀
 exp <- (FRB)₁:₁₁ - 1023
 frac₀:₅₂ <- 0b1 ‖ (FRB)₁₂:₆₃
 ROUND_SINGLE(sign, exp, frac₀:₅₂, 0, 0, 0)
 FPSCR_XX <- FPSCR_XX ¦ FPSCR_FI
 if exp > 127 and FPSCR_OE = 0 then
     goto DISABLED_OVERFLOW
 if exp > 127 and FPSCR_OE = 1 then
     goto OVERFLOW
 FRT₀ <- sign
 FRT₁:₁₁ <- exp+1023
 FRT₁₂:₆₃ <- frac₁:₅₂
 if sign = 0 then
     FPSCR_FPRF <- "+normal number"
 else
     FPSCR_FPRF <- "-normal number"
 Done.


ROUND_SINGLE(sign, exp, frac0:52, G, R, X):
 inc <- 0
 lsb <- frac₂₃
```

```
gbit <- frac_24
rbit <- frac_25
xbit <- (frac_26:52||G||R||X = 0
if FPSCR_RN = 0b00 then
    if sign||lsb||gbit||rbit||xbit = 0bx11xx then
        inc <- 1
    if sign||lsb||gbit||rbit||xbit = 0bx011x then
        inc <- 1
    if sign||lsb||gbit||rbit||xbit = 0bx01x1 then
        inc <- 1
if FPSCR_RN = 0b10 then
    if sign||lsb||gbit||rbit||xbit = 0b0x1xx then
        inc <- 1
    if sign||lsb||gbit||rbit||xbit = 0b0xx1x then
        inc <- 1
    if sign||lsb||gbit||rbit||xbit = 0b0xxx1 then
        inc <- 1
if FPSCR_RN = 0b11 then
    if sign||lsb||gbit||rbit||xbit = 0b1x1xx then
        inc <- 1
    if sign||lsb||gbit||rbit||xbit = 0b1xx1x then
        inc <- 1
    if sign||lsb||gbit||rbit||xbit = 0b1xxx1 then
        inc <- 1
frac_0:23 <- frac_0:23 + inc
if carry_out = 1 then
    frac_0:23 <- 0b1||frac_0:22
    exp <- exp + 1
frac_24:52 <- ^29 0
FPSCR_FR <- inc
FPSCR_FI <- gbit | rbit | xbit
Return.
```

Floating-Point Convert-to-Integer Model

The floating-point convert-to-integer instructions have the following form:

```
convert[.] FRT, FRB
```

The operand in floating-point register FRB is converted to an integer and placed into floating register FRT. The pseudo-code shown in Model D.3 implements the PowerPC convert-to-integer model.

MODEL D.3.

```
if instruction = fctiw then
    round_mode <- FPSCR_RN
    precision <- "32-bit integer"
if instruction = fctiwz then
    round_mode <- 0b01
```

```
      precision <- "32-bit integer"
  if instruction = fctid then
     round_mode <- FPSCR_RN
     precision <- "64-bit integer"
  if instruction = fctidz then
     round_mode <- 0b01
     precision <- "64-bit integer"
  sign <- (FRB)_0
  if (FRB)_1:11 = 2047 then
     if (FRB)_12:63 = 0 then
        goto INFINITY_OPERAND
     else if (FRB)12 = 1 then
        goto QNAN_OPERAND
     else
        goto SNAN_OPERAND
  if (FRB)_1:11 > 1086 then
     goto LARGE_OPERAND
  if (FRB)_1:11 > 0 then
     exp <- (FRB)_1:11 - 1023
  if (FRB)_1:11 = 0 then
     exp <- -1022
  if (FRB)_1:11 > 0 then
     frac_0:64 <- 0b01||(FRB)_12:63||^11 0
  if (FRB)_1:11 = 0 then
     frac_0:64 <- 0b00||(FRB)_12:63||^11 0
  gbit||rbit||xbit <- 0b000
  for (i=1; i<=63-exp; i++)
     frac_0:64||gbit||rbit||xbit<-0b0||frac_0:64||gbit||(rbit|xbit)
  ROUND_INTEGER(sign, frac_0:64, gbit, rbit, xbit, round_mode)
  if sign = 1 then
     frac_0:64 <- frac_0:64 + 1
  if precision = "32-bit integer" and frac̄_0:64 > 2^31-1 then
     goto large operand
  if precision = "32-bit integer" and frac̄_0:64 < -2^31 then
     goto large operand
  if precision = "64-bit integer" and frac_0:64 > 2^63-1 then
     goto large operand
  if precision = "64-bit integer" and frac_0:64 > -2^63 then
     goto large operand
  FPSCR_XX <- FPSCR_XX | FPSCR_FI
  if precision = "32-bit integer" then
     FRT <- 0xuuuuuuuu||frac_33:64 /* u is undefined */
  else
     FRT <- frac_1:64
  FPSCR_FPRF <- undefined
  Done.
ROUND_INTEGER(sign,frac0:64,gbit,rbit,xbit,round_mode)
  inc <- 0
  if round_mode = 0b00 then
     if sign||frac_64||gbit||rbit||xbit = 0bx11xx then
        inc <- 1
     if sign||frac_64||gbit||rbit||xbit = 0bx011x then
        inc <- 1
     if sign||frac_64||gbit||rbit||xbit = 0bx01x1 then
        inc <- 1
  if round_mode = 0b10 then
```

```
     if sign||frac₆₄||gbit||rbit||xbit = 0b0x1xx then
         inc <- 1
     if sign||frac₆₄||gbit||rbit||xbit = 0b0xx1x then
         inc <- 1
     if sign||frac₆₄||gbit||rbit||xbit = 0b0xxx1 then
         inc <- 1
 if round_mode = 0b11 then
     if sign||frac₆₄||gbit||rbit||xbit = 0b1x1xx then
         inc <- 1
     if sign||frac₆₄||gbit||rbit||xbit = 0b1xx1x then
         inc <- 1
     if sign||frac₆₄||gbit||rbit||xbit = 0b1xxx1 then
         inc <- 1
 frac₀:₆₄ <- frac₀:₆₄ + inc
 FPSCR_FR <- inc
 FPSCR_FI <- gbit|rbit|xbit
 Return
INFINITY_OPERAND:
 FPSCR_FR,FI,VXCVI <- 0b001
 if FPSCR_VE = 0 then
     if precision = "32-bit integer" then
         if sign = 0 then
             FRT <- 0xuuuu uuuu 7FFF FFFF /* u means undefined */
         else
             FRT <- 0xuuuu uuuu 8000 0000 /* u means undefined */
     else
         if sign = 0 then
             FRT <- 0x7FFF FFFF FFFF FFFF
         else
             FRT <- 0x8000 0000 0000 0000
     FPSCR_FPRF <- undefined
 Done.
SNAN_OPERAND:
 FPSCR_FR,FI,VXSNAN,VXCVI <- 0b0011
 if FPSCR_VE = 0 then
     if precision = "32-bit integer" then
         FRT <- 0xuuuu uuuu 8000 0000 /* u means undefined */
     else
         FRT <- 0x8000 0000 0000 0000
     FPSCR_FPRF <- undefined
 Done.
QNAN_OPERAND:
 FPSCR_FR,FI,VXCVI <- 0b001
 if FPSCR_VE = 0 then
     if precision = "32-bit integer" then
         FRT <- 0xuuuu uuuu 8000 0000 /* u means undefined */
     else
         FRT <- 0x8000 0000 0000 0000
     FPSCR_FPRF <- undefined
 Done.
LARGE_OPERAND: /* same as INFINITY_OPERAND */
 FPSCR_FR,FI,VXCVI <- 0b001
 if FPSCR_VE = 0 then
     if precision = "32-bit integer" then
         if sign = 0 then
             FRT <- 0xuuuu uuuu 7FFF FFFF /* u means undefined */
         else
```

```
            FRT <- 0×uuuu uuuu 8000 0000 /* u means undefined */
    else
        if sign = 0 then
            FRT <- 0×7FFF FFFF FFFF FFFF
        else
            FRT <- 0×8000 0000 0000 0000
    FPSCR_FPRF <- undefined
Done.
```

Floating-Point Convert-from-Integer Model

The floating-point convert-from-integer has the following form:

fcfid[.] FRT, FRB

The contents of FRB are treated as a 64-bit sign integer, which is converted to a floating-point number and stored in FRT. The pseudo-code shown in Model D.4 implements the fcfid instruction.

MODEL D.4.

```
sign <- (FRB)_0
  exp <- 63
  frac_{0:63} <- (FRB)
  if frac_{0:63} = 0 then
      goto ZERO_OPERAND
  if sign = 1 then
      frac_{0:63} <- frac_{0:63} + 1
  while frac_0 = 0 do
      frac_{0:63} <- frac_{1:63}||0b0
      exp <- exp-1
  ROUND_FLOAT(sign, exp, frac_{0:63}, FPSCR_RN)
  if sign = 1 then
      FPSCR_FPRF <- "-normal number"
  else
      FPSCR_FPRF <- "+normal number"
  FRT_0 <- sign
  FRT_{1:11} <- exp + 1023
  FRT_{12:63} <- frac_{1:52}
  Done.
ZERO_OPERAND:
  FPSCR_{FR,FI} <- 0b00
  FPSCR_FPRF <- "+zero"
  FRT <- 0×0000 0000 0000 0000
  Done.
ROUND_FLOAT(sign, exp, frac0:63, round_mode)
  inc <- 0
  lsb <- frac_52
  gbit <- frac_53
  rbit <- frac_54
  xbit <- frac_{55:63} != 0
  if FPSCR_RN = 0b00 then
```

```
        if sign||lsb||gbit||rbit||xbit = 0bx11xx then
            inc <- 1
        if sign||lsb||gbit||rbit||xbit = 0bx011x then
            inc <- 1
        if sign||lsb||gbit||rbit||xbit = 0bx01x1 then
            inc <- 1
if FPSCR_RN = 0b10 then
        if sign||lsb||gbit||rbit||xbit = 0b0x1xx then
            inc <- 1
        if sign||lsb||gbit||rbit||xbit = 0b0xx1x then
            inc <- 1
        if sign||lsb||gbit||rbit||xbit = 0b0xxx1 then
            inc <- 1
if FPSCR_RN = 0b11 then
        if sign||lsb||gbit||rbit||xbit = 0b1x1xx then
            inc <- 1
        if sign||lsb||gbit||rbit||xbit = 0b1xx1x then
            inc <- 1
        if sign||lsb||gbit||rbit||xbit = 0b1xxx1 then
            inc <- 1
frac_0:52 <- frac_0:52 + inc
if carry_out = 1 then
    exp <- exp + 1
FPSCR_FR <- inc
FPSCR_FI <- gbit | rbit | xbit
FPSCR_XX <- FPSCR_XX | FPSCR_FI
Return.
```

E

Portability Notes

Obviously, portions of code developed in assembly language won't run directly on another platform except in emulation, and emulation is not usually a good way to achieve high performance. However, in some cases, the hardware underpinnings can have implications even for high-level language code. Since most software developers strive for platform independence, it's important to understand key differences between processor, system, and software architectures to avoid unnecessary stumbling blocks to portability. To this end, we'll try to outline some of the key computability concerns among PowerPC machines and systems based on other architectures.

Motorola 680x0 and Intel 80x86 Processors

Many of the potential problems in developing code for Apple Macintosh machines based on the Motorola 680x0 processors and PowerPC processors have been solved very neatly by Apple and ISVs developing for the Macintosh platform. Apple provides complete emulation for the 680x0 processor on Power Macs, and virtually all applications written for 680x0 Macs run with good performance without modification on PowerPC Macs. The Mac OS provides ways of packaging applications with native code for both platforms (fat binaries), making it easy to maintain one set of application binaries, even on a network server used by Macs of both types.

From a coding standpoint, there are a few compatibility issues that bear mention. First is the stricter alignment rules for best performance on PowerPC processors; second is the choice of floating-point representation. Better floating-point performance can be achieved with native PowerPC floating point than with Apple's SANE library, which is supported only in emulation on PowerPC Macintoshes.

The Intel 80x86 architecture is used in the IBM PC and compatibles. Aside from the instruction set, a significant difference between PC-compatibles and Macintoshes is the byte ordering in memory (see "Big Endian Versus Little Endian Byte Ordering" later in this chapter). The PowerPC processors support little endian memory access mode, so it would be possible to build an emulation environment like the Power Macintosh for the IBM PC, but there is not currently such a system available. The Microsoft Windows NT operating system depends on little-endian operation, and this OS has been ported to the PowerPC platform.

Like the Apple machines, some IBM PC applications use non-IEEE floating-point arithmetic, and converting applications to run with native PowerPC floating point may require code changes.

IBM POWER and POWER2

The easiest migration path to PowerPC processors is from the IBM RS/6000 workstations. These machines are based on the POWER or POWER2 architecture that served as the basis for the PowerPC architecture. There are some instruction set differences; the MQ register and associated instructions were eliminated from PowerPC in favor of more general multiply and divide instructions, and the lscbx string instruction was dropped in PowerPC. The POWER instructions are all supported in the PowerPC 601 for compatibility but don't appear in the other implementations. The POWER2 architecture has some instructions like the quadword floating-point instructions that allow loading and storing of two floating point registers at a time (which takes advantage of POWER2's 128-bit cache interface).

All of the POWER and POWER2 instructions will be supported through software emulation under IBM's AIX operating system, but best performance can be obtained by avoiding these instructions in code for PowerPC systems. Compilers can be conditioned to generate "intersection" code that only uses instructions that work on all RS/6000 platforms.

PowerPC 601, 603, 604, and 620 Processors

All PowerPC processor implementations run the same applications programs, and from a strictly functional point of view, it's not really necessary to worry about compatibility. However, there are some differences in these implementations that may require changes to system management code in the operating system. Also, the approach taken to implement the PowerPC architecture for each may result in differences in the ways to achieve best performance. Sometimes this is by design, and sometimes due to constraints of the implementation, such as the amount of silicon available for processing resources. For example, the 601 has a unified cache and the 604 has split instruction and data caches. Depending on the resource demands of a particular program, one design approach might yield better performance than another.

It would be impossible to cover in detail all of the ways in which the PowerPC processor implementations differ, let alone explore all of the subtle ways in which performance could be affected, and Table E.1 summarizes some of the important ones.

Table E.1. PowerPC implementation differences.

	601	*603*	*604*	*620*
Architecture	32-bit	32-bit	32-bit	64-bit
Instructions Issued/Cycle	3	3	4	4
Instructions Fetched/Cycle	8	2	4	4
Branch Prediction	Static	Static	Dynamic BHT 512-entry	Dynamic BHT 512-entry
On-chip cache Instruction/Data	32K Unified	8K/8K	16K/16K	32K/32K
Cache Associativity	8-way	2-way/ 2-way	4-way/ 4-way	8-way 8-way
Data bus width	64-bit	32/64-bit	64-bit	128-bit

Big Endian Versus Little Endian Byte Ordering

The obstacle to compatibility among different system architectures is the order in which the bytes of a register are stored in memory when more than one byte is stored at a time. There are two conventions for byte ordering used in computer systems today, and these are commonly known as *big endian* and *little endian*. If a 4-byte word is stored at a memory location, loading the individual bytes of that word, one at a time, yields different results depending on the memory ordering convention used by that system.

To illustrate, suppose a general register contains a hexadecimal register 12345678. The processor issues a store instruction that writes the contents of the register to a word of storage beginning at memory address 100. Then a load instruction to read the *byte* (rather than the word) at location 100 is issued. What value is returned? In a system using big endian byte order, the value is hexadecimal 12. If the ordering is little endian, the hex value is 78. Figure E.1 shows why.

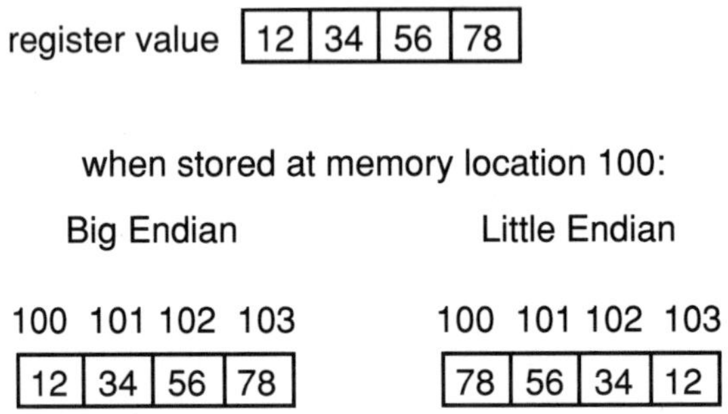

FIGURE E.1.

Big endian versus little endian byte ordering.

register value | 12 | 34 | 56 | 78 |

when stored at memory location 100:

Big Endian   Little Endian

100 101 102 103   100 101 102 103
| 12 | 34 | 56 | 78 | | 78 | 56 | 34 | 12 |

Most of the time, the byte ordering convention is transparent. The order used by a particular machine can only be determined if memory words can be accessed as both words and bytes, or when trying to share data between machines using opposite orderings. Historically, IBM (except for the PC) and Motorola processors have been big endian, while DEC and Intel processors (used in the IBM PC) have been little endian. This creates a dilemma, since the two most popular personal computer architectures, the IBM PC and the Apple Macintosh, use different byte ordering. This makes it difficult to share data between the two machines, and challenging to build one machine that can run code for both with ease.

Several features of PowerPC processors permit them to use either mode of memory access. A bit in a special register (in HID0 for the 601, in the MSR for the others) selects the processor's memory access mode. It is possible to address memory opposite the current mode by using the byte-reversed load and store instructions (lhbrx, lwbrx, sthbrx, and stwbrx). These instructions allow, for example, little endian storage access while running in big endian mode with no performance penalty.

This is important because the current family of PowerPC processors can yield better performance running in big endian mode. There is better hardware handling of misaligned big endian accesses—misaligned references and the multiple-register and string load and store instructions are trapped to software emulation in little endian mode.

Many artifacts of endianness can be handled transparently by a compiler. When coding in assembler, it can be more difficult, but it is still possible in many cases to keep code insensitive to endianness by always manipulating memory in the natural mode width of the scalar data items. Endian-neutral development is discussed in some detail in a two-part article by James Gillig in *Dr. Dobb's Journal.* It is highly recommended for developers concerned with compatibility (see Appendix G).

F

Quick References

Instruction Set

Table F.1. The PowerPC instruction set.

Mnemonic	Arguments	Description	Side Effects
add[o][.]	RT,RA,RB	add	$[XER_{SO},XER_{OV}]$ $[CR_0]$
addc[o][.]	RT,RA,RB	add carrying	XER_{CA} $[XER_{SO},$ $XER_{OV}]$ $[CR_0]$
adde[o][.]	RT,RA,RB	add extended	$[XER_{SO},XER_{OV}]$ $[CR_0]$
addi	RT,Ra^0,SI	add immediate	
addic[.]	RT,RA,SI	add immediate carrying	XER_{CA} $[CR_0]$
addis	RT,Ra^0,SI^s	add immediate shifted	
addme[o][.]	RT,RA	add to minus one extended	$[XER_{SO},XER_{OV}]$ $[CR_0]$
addze[o][.]	RT,RA	add to zero extended	$[XER_{SO},XER_{OV}]$ $[CR_0]$
and[.]	RT,RA,RB	and	$[CR_0]$
andc[.]	RT,RA,RB	and with compliment ($RA \wedge \overline{RB}$)	$[CR_0]$
andi.	RT,RA,UI	and immediate	$[CR_0]$
andis.	RT,RA,UI^s	and immediate shifted	$[CR_0]$
b[l][a]	SI^w	branch	[LR]
bc[l][a]	BO,BI,SI^w	branch conditional	[LR]
bcctr[l]	BO,BI	branch conditional to count register	[LR]
bclr[l]	BO,BI	branch conditional to link register	[LR]
clrldi[.]^x	RT,RA,N	clear left doubleword immediate	$[CR_0]$
clrlsldi[.]^x	RT,RA,MB,N	clear left and shift left doubleword immediate	$[CR_0]$
clrlslwi[.]^x	RT,RA,MB,N	clear left and shift left word immediate	$[CR_0]$
clrlwi[.]^x	RT,RA,MB	clear left word immediate	$[CR_0]$

Mnemonic	Arguments	Description	Side Effects
clrrdi[.]^X	RT,RA,ME	clear right doubleword immediate	[CR$_0$]
clrrwi[.]^X	RT,RA,ME	clear right word immediate	[CR$_0$]
cmp	CRF,L,RA,RB	compare	
cmpd^X	Crf,RA,RB	compare doubleword	
cmpdi^X	CRF,RA,SI	compare doubleword immediate	
cmpld^X	CRF,RA,RB	compare logical doubleword	
cmpldi^X	CRF,RA,UI	compare logical doubleword immediate	
cmpi	CRF,L,RA,SI	compare immediate	
cmpl	CRF,L,RA,RB	compare logical	
cmpli	CRF,L,RA,UI	compare logical immediate	
cmpw^X	CRF,RA,RB	compare word	
cmpwi^X	CRF,RA,SI	compare word immediate	
cmplw^X	CRF,RA,RB	compare logical word	
cmplwi^X	CRF,RA,UI	compare logical word immediate	
cntlzd[.]	RT,RA	count leading zeros doubleword	[CR$_0$]
cntlzw[.]	RT,RA	count leading zeros word	[CR$_0$]
crand	CRBt,CRBa,CRBb	condition register and	
crandc	CRBt,CRBa,CRBb	condition register and with compliment ($CRBa \wedge \overline{CRBb}$)	
crclr^X	CRBt	condition register clear	
creqv	CRBt,CRBa,CRBb	condition register equivalent (xnor)	
crmove^X	CRBt,CRBa	condition register move	
crnand	CRBt,CRBa,CRBb	condition register nand	
crnor	CRBt,CRBa,CRBb	condition register nor	
crnot^X	CRBt,CRBa	condition register not	
cror	CRBt,CRBa,CRBb	condition register or	
crorc	CRBt,CRBa,CRBb	condition register or with compliment ($CRBa\overline{CRBb}$)	
crset^X	CRBt	condition register set	

continues

Table F.1. continued

Mnemonic	Arguments	Description	Side Effects
crxor	CRBt,CRBa,CRBb	condition register xor	
dcbf	Ra^0,RB	data cache block flush	
dcbi^P	Ra^0,RB	data cache block invalidate	
dcbst	Ra^0,RB	data cache block store	
dcbt	Ra^0,RB	data cache block touch	
dcbtst	Ra^0,RB	data cache block touch for store	
dcbz	Ra^0,RB	data cache block set to zero	
divd[o][.]	RT,RA,RB	divide doubleword (RA÷RB)	[XER$_{SO}$,XER$_{OV}$] [CR$_0$]
divdu[o][.]	RT,RA,RB	divide doubleword unsigned (RA÷RB)	[XER$_{SO}$,XER$_{OV}$] [CR$_0$]
divw[o][.]	RT,RA,RB	divide word (RA÷RB)	[XER$_{SO}$,XER$_{OV}$] [CR$_0$]
divwu[o][.]	RT,RA,RB	divide word unsigned (RA÷RB)	[XER$_{SO}$,XER$_{OV}$] [CR$_0$]
eciwx	RT,Ra^0,RB	external control word in	
ecowx	RT,Ra^0,RB	external control word out	
eieio		enforce in-order execution of I/O	
eqv[.]	RT,RA,RB	equivalent (xnor)	[CR$_0$]
extldi^X[.]	RT,RA,N,MB	extract and left justify doubleword immediate	[CR$_0$]
extlwi^X[.]	RT,RA,N,MB	extract and left justify word immediate	[CR$_0$]
extrdi^X[.]	RT,RA,N,MB	extract and right justify doubleword immediate	[CR$_0$]
extrwi^X[.]	RT,RA,N,MB	extract and right justify word immediate	[CR$_0$]
extsh[.]	RT,RA	extend sign byte	[CR$_0$]
extsw[.]	RT,RA	extend sign half	[CR$_0$]
extsb[.]	RT,RA	extend sign word	

Mnemonic	Arguments	Description	Side Effects
fabs[.]	FRT,FRA	floating absolute value	[CR$_1$]
fadd[.]	FRT,FRA,FRB	floating add double precision	FPSCR [CR$_1$]
fadds[.]	FRT,FRA,FRB	floating add single precision	FPSCR [CR$_1$]
fcfid[.]	FRT,FRA	floating convert from integer doubleword	FPSCR [CR$_1$]
fcmpo	CRF,FRA,FRB	floating compare ordered	FPSCR
fcmpu	CRF,FRA,FRB	floating compare unordered	FPSCR
fctid[.]	FRT,FRA	floating convert to integer doubleword	FPSCR [CR$_1$]
fctidz[.]	FRT,FRA	floating convert to integer doubleword with round toward zero	FPSCR [CR$_1$]
fctiw[.]	FRT,FRA	floating convert to integer word	FPSCR [CR$_1$]
fctiwz[.]	FRT,FRA	floating convert to integer word with round toward zero	FPSCR [CR$_1$]
fdiv[.]	FRT,FRA,FRB	floating divide double precision (*FRA÷FRB*)	FPSCR [CR$_1$]
fdivs[.]	FRT,FRA,FRB	floating divide single precision (*FRA÷FRB*)	FPSCR [CR$_1$]
fmadd[.]	FRT,FRA,FRB,FRC	floating multiply add double precision (*FRA×FRB×FRC*)	FPSCR [CR$_1$]
fmadds[.]	FRT,FRA,FRB,FRC	floating multiply add single precision (*FRA×FRB+FRC*)	FPSCR [CR$_1$]
fmr[.]	FRT,FRA	floating move register	[CR$_1$]
fmsub[.]	FRT,FRA,FRB,FRC	floating multiply subtract double precision (*FRA×FRB-FRC*)	FPSCR [CR$_1$]

continues

Table F.1. continued

Mnemonic	Arguments	Description	Side Effects
fmsubs[.]	FRT,FRA,FRB,FRC	floating multiply subtract single precision ($FRA \times FRB\text{-}FRC$)	FPSCR [CR$_1$]
fmul[.]	FRT,FRA,FRB	floating multiply double precision	FPSCR [CR$_1$]
fmuls[.]	FRT,FRA,FRB	floating multiply single precision	FPSCR [CR$_1$]
fnabs[.]	FRT,FRA	floating negative absolute value	[CR$_1$]
fneg[.]	FRT,FRA	floating negate	[CR$_1$]
fnmadd[.]	FRT,FRA,FRB,FRC	floating negative multiply add double precision ($\text{-}[FRA \times FRB\text{+}FRC]$)	FPSCR [CR$_1$]
fnmadds[.]	FRT,FRA,FRB,FRC	floating negative multiply add single precision ($\text{-}[FRA \times FRB\text{+}FRC]$)	FPSCR [CR$_1$]
fnmsub[.]	FRT,FRA,FRB,FRC	floating negative multiply subtract double precision ($\text{-}[FRA \times FRB\text{-}FRC]$)	FPSCR [CR$_1$]
fnmsubs[.]	FRT,FRA,FRB,FRC	floating negative multiply subtract single precision ($\text{-}[FRA \times FRB\text{-}FRC]$)	FPSCR [CR$_1$]
fres[.]	FRT,FRA	floating reciprocal estimate single precision	FPSCR [CR$_1$]
frsp[.]	FRT,FRA	floating round to single precision	FPSCR [CR$_1$]
frsqrte[.]	FRT,FRA	floating estimate reciprocal square root double precision	FPSCR [CR$_1$]
fsel[.]	FRT,FRA,FRB,FRC	floating select	

Mnemonic	Arguments	Description	Side Effects
fsqrt[.]	FRT,FRA	floating square root double precision	FPSCR [CR$_1$]
fsqrts[.]	FRT,FRA	floating square root single precision	FPSCR [CR$_1$]
fsub[.]	FRT,FRA,FRB	floating subtract double precision	FPSCR [CR$_1$]
fsubs[.]	FRT,FRA,FRB	floating subtract single precision	FPSCR [CR$_1$]
icbi	Ra^0,RB	instruction cache block invalidate	
inslwi[.]^X	RT,RA,N,MB	insert from left word immediate	[CR$_0$]
insrdi[.]^X	RT,RA,N,MB	insert from right doubleword immediate	[CR$_0$]
insrwi[.]^X	RT,RA,N,MB	insert from right word immediate	[CR$_0$]
isync		instruction synchronize	
la^X	RT,SI(Ra^0)	load address	
lbz	RT,SI(Ra^0)	load byte and zero	
lbzu	RT,SI(RA)	load byte and zero with update	RA
lbzux	RT,RA,RB	load byte and zero with update indexed	RA
lbzx	RT,Ra^0,RB	load byte and zero indexed	
ld	RT,SI^W(Ra^0)	load doubleword	
ldarx	RT,RA,RB	load doubleword and reserve	RSRV
ldu	RT,SI^W(RA)	load doubleword with update	RA
ldux	RT,RA,RB	load doubleword with update indexed	RA
ldx	RT,Ra^0,RB	load doubleword indexed	
lfd	FRT,SI(Ra^0)	load floating double precision	

continues

Table F.1. continued

Mnemonic	Arguments	Description	Side Effects
lfdu	FRT,SI(RA)	load floating double precision with update	RA
lfdux	FRT,RA,RB	load floating double precision with update indexed	RA
lfdx	FRT,Ra^0,RB	load floating double precision indexed	
lfs	FRT,SI(Ra^0)	load floating single precision	
lfsu	FRT,SI(RA)	load floating single precision with update	RA
lfsux	FRT,RA,RB	load floating single precision with update indexed	RA
lfsx	FRT,Ra^0,RB	load floating single precision indexed	
lha	FRT,SI(Ra^0)	load halfword algebraic	
lhau	RT,SI(RA)	load halfword algebraic with update	RA
lhaux	RT,RA,RB	load halfword algebraic with update indexed	RA
lhax	RT,Ra^0,RB	load halfword algebraic indexed	
lhbrx	RT,Ra^0,RB	load halfword byte-reversed indexed	
lhz	RT,SI(Ra^0)	load halfword and zero	
lhzu	RT,SI(RA)	load halfword and zero with update	RA
lhzux	RT,RA,RB	load halfword and zero with update indexed	RA
lhzx	RT,Ra^0,RB	load halfword and zero indexed	
li^X	RT,SI	load immediate	
lis^X	RT,SI^S	load immediate shifted	

Mnemonic	Arguments	Description	Side Effects
lmw	RT,SI(Ra⁰)	load multiple word	
lswi	RT,RA,N	load string word immediate	
lswx	RT,Ra⁰,RB	load string word indexed	
lwa	RT,SI(Ra⁰)	load word algebraic	
lwarx	RT,Ra⁰,RB	load word and reserve	RSRV
lwau	RT,SI(RA)	load word algebraic with update	RA
lwaux	RT,RA,RB	load word algebraic with update indexed	RA
lwax	RT,Ra⁰,RB	load word algebraic indexed	
lwbrx	RT,Ra⁰,RB	load word byte reversed indexed	
lwz	RT,SI(Ra⁰)	load word and zero	
lwzu	RT,SI(RA)	load word and zero with update	RA
lwzux	RT,RA,RB	load word and zero with update indexed	RA
lwzx	RT,Ra⁰,RB	load word and zero indexed	
mcrf	CRFt,CRFa	move condition register field	
mcrfs	CRFt,FBFa	move to condition register field from FPSCR	FPSCR
mcrxr	CRF	move XER to condition register field	
mfcr	RT	move from condition register (CR)	
mfctr^X	RT	move from count register (CTR)	
mffs[.]	FRT	move from FPSCR	[CR$_1$]
mflr^X	RT	move from link register (LR)	
mfmsr^P	RT	move from machine state register (MSR)	

continues

Table F.1. continued

Mnemonic	*Arguments*	*Description*	*Side Effects*
mfspr[PA]	RT,SPR	move from special purpose register	
mfsr[P]	RT,Sa	move from segment register	
mfsrin[P]	RT,RA	move from segment register indirect	
mftb	RT,TBR	move from time base register (TBR)	
mftb[X]	RT	move from time base	
mftbu[X]	RT	move from time base upper	
mfxer[X]	RT	move from fixed point exception register (XER)	
mr[.][X]	RT,RA	move register	$[CR_0]$
mtcr[X]	RS	move to condition register (CR)	
mtcrf	FXM,RS	move to condition register fields	
mfctr[X]	RS	move to count register (CTR)	
mtfsb0[.]	Fbt	move to FPSCR bit 0 (clear FPSCR bit)	$[CR_1]$
mtfsb1[.]	Fbt	move to FPSCR bit 1 (set FPSCR bit)	$[CR_1]$
mtfsf[.]	FXM,FRS	move to FPSCR fields	$[CR_1]$
mtfsfi[.]	FBFt,UI	move to FPSCR field immediate	$[CR_1]$
mtlr[X]	RS	move to link register (LR)	
mtmsr[P]	RS	move to machine state register (MSR)	
mtspr[PA]	RS,SPR	move to special purpose register	
mtsr[P]	St,RS	move to segment register	
mtsrin[P]	RS,RA	move to segment register indirect	

Mnemonic	Arguments	Description	Side Effects
mtxer[X]	RS	move from fixed point exception register (XER)	
mulhd[.]	RT,RA,RB	multiply high doubleword	$[CR_0]$
mulhdu[.]	RT,RA,RB	multiply high doubleword unsigned	$[CR_0]$
mulhw[.]	RT,RA,RB	multiply high word	$[CR_0]$
mulhwu[.]	RT,RA,RB	multiply high word unsigned	$[CR_0]$
mulld[o][.]	RT,RA,RB	multiply low doubleword	$[XER_{SO},XER_{OV}]$ $[CR_0]$
mulli	RT,RA,SI	multiply low immediate	
mullw[o][.]	RT,RA,RB	multiply low word $[CR_0]$	$[XER_{SO},XER_{OV}]$
nand[.]	RT,RA,RB	nand	$[CR_0]$
neg[o][.]	RT,RA	negate	$[XER_{SO},XER_{OV}]$ $[CR_0]$
nop[X]		no operation	
nor[.]	RT,RA,RB	nor	$[CR_0]$
not[.][X]	RT,RA	not	$[CR_0]$
or[.]	RT,RA,RB	or	$[CR_0]$
orc[.]	RT,RA,RB	or with compliment (*RA/RB*)	$[CR_0]$
ori	RT,RA,UI	or immediate	
oris	RT,RA,UI[S]	or immediate shifted	
rfi		return from interrupt	MSR
rldcl[.]	RT,RS,Rn,MB	rotate left doubleword then clear left	$[CR_0]$
rldcr[.]	RT,RS,Rn,ME	rotate left doubleword then clear right	$[CR_0]$
rldic[.]	RT,RS,N,MB	rotate left doubleword immediate then clear	$[CR_0]$
rldicl[.]	RT,RS,N,MB	rotate left doubleword immediate then clear left	$[CR_0]$
rldicr[.]	RT,RS,N,ME	rotate left doubleword immediate then clear right	$[CR_0]$

continues

Table F.1. continued

Mnemonic	Arguments	Description	Side Effects
rldimi[.]	RT,RS,N,MB	rotate left doubleword immediate then insert mask	$[CR_0]$
rlwimi[.]	RT,RS,N,ME	rotate left word immediate then insert mask	$[CR_0]$
rlwinm[.]	RT,RS,N,MB,ME	rotate left word immediate then and with mask	$[CR_0]$
rlwnm[.]	RT,RS,Rn,MB,ME	rotate left word then and with mask	$[CR_0]$
rotld[.]^X	RT,RS,Rn	rotate left doubleword	$[CR_0]$
rotldi[.]^X	RT,RS,N	rotate left doubleword immediate	$[CR_0]$
rotlw[.]^X	RT,RS,Rn	rotate left word	$[CR_0]$
rotlwi[.]^X	RT,RS,N	rotate left word immediate	$[CR_0]$
rotrdi[.]^X	RT,RS,N	rotate right doubleword immediate	$[CR_0]$
rotrwi[.]^X	RT,RS,N	rotate right word immediate	$[CR_0]$
sc		system call	*
slbia^P		SLB invalidate all	
slbie^P	RA	SLB invalidate entry	
sld[.]	RT,RS,Rn	shift left doubleword	$[CR_0]$
sldi[.]^X	RT,RS,N	shift left doubleword immediate	$[CR_0]$
slw[.]	RT,RS,Rn	shift left word	$[CR_0]$
slwi[.]^X	RT,RS,N	shift left word immediate	$[CR_0]$
srad[.]	RT,RS,Rn	shift right algebraic doubleword	$[CR_0]$
sradi[.]	RT,RS,N	shift right algebraic doubleword immediate	$[CR_0]$
sraw[.]	RT,RS,Rn	shift right algebraic word	$[CR_0]$
srawi[.]	RT,RS,N	shift right algebraic word immediate	$[CR_0]$
srd[.]	RT,RS,Rn	shift right doubleword	$[CR_0]$
srdi[.]	RT,RS,N	shift right doubleword immediate	$[CR_0]$

Mnemonic	Arguments	Description	Side Effects
srw[.]	RT,RS,Rn	shift right word	[CR_0]
srwi[.]	RT,RS,N	shift right word immediate	[CR_0]
stb	RS,SI(Ra^0)	store byte	
stbu	RS,SI(RA)	store byte with update	RA
stbux	RS,RA,RB	store byte with update indexed	RA
stbx	RS,Ra^0,RB	store byte indexed	
std	RS,SI^W(Ra^0)	store doubleword	
stdcx.	RS,Ra^0,RB	store doubleword conditional	
stdu	RS,SI^W(RA)	store doubleword with update indexed	RA
stdux	RS,RA,RB	store doubleword with update indexed	RA
stdx	RS,Ra^0,RB	store doubleword indexed	
stfd	FRS,SI(Ra^0)	store floating double precision	
stfdu	FRS,SI(RA)	store floating double precision with update	RA
stfdux	FRS,RA,RB	store floating double precision with update indexed	RA
stfdx	FRS,Ra^0,RB	store floating double precision indexed	
stfiwx	FRS,Ra^0,RB	store floating as integer word	
stfs	FRS,SI(Ra^0)	store floating single precision	
stfsu	FRS,SI(RA)	store floating single precision with update	RA
stfsux	FRS,RA,RB	store floating single precision with update indexed	RA
stfsx	FRS,Ra^0,RB	store floating single precision indexed	

continues

Table F.1. continued

Mnemonic	Arguments	Description	Side Effects
sth	RS,SI(Ra^0)	store halfword	
sthbrx	RS,Ra^0,RB	store halfword byte-reversed	
sthu	RS,SI(RA)	store halfword with update	RA
sthux	RS,RA,RB	store halfword with update indexed	RA
sthx	RS,Ra^0,RB	store halfword indexed	
stmw	RS,SI(Ra^0)	store multiple word	
stswi	RS,Ra^0,N	store string word immediate	
stswx	RS,Ra^0,RB	store string word	
stw	RS,SI(Ra^0)	store word	
stwbrx	RS,Ra^0,RB	store word byte-reversed	
stwu	RS,SI(RA)	store word with update	RA
stwux	RS,RA,RB	store word with update indexed	RA
stwx	RS,Ra^0,RB	store word indexed	
stwcx.	RS,Ra^0,RB	store word conditional	[RSRV] [CR_0]
sub[o][.]^X	RT,RA,RB	subtract ($RA+\overline{RB}+1$)	[XER_{SO},XER_{OV}] [CR_0]
subc[o][.]^X	RT,RA,RB	subtract carrying	XER_{CA} [XER_{SO},XER_{OV}] [CR_0]
subf[o][.]	RT,RA,RB	subtract from ($RA+\overline{RB}+1$)	[XER_{SO},XER_{OV}] [CR_0]
subfc[o][.]	RT,RA,RB	subtract from carrying ($\overline{RA}+RB+1$)	XER_{CA} [XER_{SO},XER_{OV}] [CR_0]
subfe[o][.]	RT,RA,RB	subtract from extended ($\overline{RA}+RB+CA$)	[XER_{SO},XER_{OV}] [CR_0]
subfic	RT,RA,SI	subtract from immediate carrying ($\overline{RA}+IMM+1$)	XER_{CA}
subfme[o][.]	RT,RA	subtract from minus one extended ($\overline{RA}+XERCA-1$)	[XER_{SO},XER_{OV}] CA [CR_0]

Mnemonic	Arguments	Description	Side Effects
subfze[o][.]	RT,RA	subtract from zero extended ($\overline{RA}+XERCA$)	[XER_{SO},XER_{OV}] CA [CR_0]
subi[X]	RT,RA,SI	subtract immediate ($RA+\overline{IMM}+1$)	
subis[X]	RT,RA,SIS	subtract immediate shifted ($RA+\overline{IMM}+1$)	
subic[.][X]	RT,RA,SI	subtract immediate carrying ($RA+\overline{IMM}+1$)	XER_{CA} [CR_0]
sync		synchronize	
td	TO,RA,RB	trap doubleword	
tdi	TO,RA,SI	trap doubleword immediate	
tlbia[P]		TLB invalidate all	
tlbie[P]	RA	TLB invalidate entry	
tlbsync[P]		TLB synchronize	
tw	TO,RA,RB	trap word	
twi	TO,RA,SI	trap word immediate	
xor[.]	RT,RA,RB	xor	[CR_0]
xori	RT,RA,UI	xor immediate	
xoris	RT,RA,UI[S]	xor immediate shifted	

Table F.2. Key to instruction argument symbols.

Symbol	Description
BI	Conditional branch BI field—selects condition register bit to test.
BO	Conditional branch BO field—selects options for instruction operation.
CRB	Condition register bit.
CRF	Condition register field.
FRn	FPR n.
FB	FPSCR bit.
FBF	FPSCR field.
FXM	Register field mask—one bit per field.

continues

Table F.2. continued

Symbol	Description
L	Compare length bit (set to zero for 32-bit compares, one for 64-bit compares).
MB	Mask begin position.
ME	Mask end position.
N	Count.
Rn	GPR n.
Sn	Segment Register n.
SI	Immediate field which will be sign extended.
TO	Trap TO field - selects conditions for trap.
UI	Immediate field which will be zero extended.

Table F.3. Key to instruction notes.

Symbol	Description
mnem[P]	Instruction is priviledged.
mnem[PA]	Instruction is priviledged for certain arguments.
mnem[X]	Instruction is an extended mnemonic for another instruction.
Ra[0]	When set to 0, this argument is ignored rather than being the contents of GPR 0.
I[S]	The immediate value is shifted left 16 bits.
I[W]	The immediate value must be word aligned
*	Operating system dependent.

Table F.4. Simplified branch mnemonics.

Branch Semantics (X[a])	Target address type			
	(bc) relative	(bca) absolute	(bclr) to link	(bcctr) to count
branch unconditionally	—	—	blr[l]a	bctr[l]
branch if condition true (t)	bt[l]	bt[l]a	btlr[l]	btctr[l]
branch if condition false (f)	bf[l]	bf[l]a	bflr[l]	bfctr[l]

Branch Semantics (X[a])	Target address type (bc) relative	(bca) absolute	(bclr) to link	(bcctr) to count
decrement count and branch if count non-zero (dnz)	bdnz[l]	bdnz[l]a	bdnzlr[l]	—
decrement count and branch if count zero (dz)	bdz[l]	bdz[l]a	bdzlr[l]	—
decrement count and branch if count non-zero and condition true (dnzt)	bdnzt[l]	bdnzt[l]a	bdnztlr[l]	—
decrement count and branch if count non-zero and condition false (dznf)	bdnzf[l]	bdnzf[l]a	bdnzflr[l]	—
decrement count and branch if count zero and condition true (dzt)	bdzt[l]	bdzt[l]a	bdztlr[l]	—
decrement count and branch if count non-zero and condition false (dzf)	bdzf[l]	bdzf[l]a	bdzflr[l]	—

a. The building block which is used to form the mnemonic is shown in parentheses beside the semantic description. The mnemonic for the branch is built out of three components: b[direction mnemonic][target mnemonic].

Table F.5. Simplified branch mnemonics with comparison conditions.

Branch Semantics (X[a])	Target address type (bc) relative	(bca) absolute	(bclr) to link	(bcctr) to count
branch if less than (lt)	blt[l]	nlt[l]a	bltlr[l]	bltctr[l]
branch if less than or equal to (le)	ble[l]	ble[l]a	blelr[l]	blectr[l]
branch if equal to (eq)	beq[l]	beq[l]a	beqlr[l]	beqbtr[l]

continues

Table F.5. continued

| Branch Semantics (X^a) | Target address type | | | |
	(bc) relative	(bca) absolute	(bclr) to link	(bcctr) to count
branch if greater than or equal to (ge)	bge[l]	bge[l]a	bgelr[l]	bgectr[l]
branch if greater than (gt)	bgt[l]	bgt[l]a	bgtlr[l]	bgctr[l]
branch if not less than (nl)	bnl[l]	bnl[l]a	bnllr[l]	bnlctr[l]
branch if not equal to (ne)	bne[l]	bne[l]a	bnelr[l]	bnectr[l]
branch if not greater than (ng)	bng[l]	bng[l]a	bnglr[l]	bngctr[l]
branch if summary overflow (so)	bso[l]	bso[l]a	bsolr[l]	bsoctr[l]
branch if not summary overflow (ns)	bns[l]	bns[l]a	bnslr[l]	bnsctr[l]
branch if unordered (see floating point compare instructions below) (un)	bun[l]	bun[l]a	bunlr[l]	bunctr[l]
branch if not unordered (see floating point compare instructions below) (nu)	bnu[l]	bnu[l]a	bnulr[l]	bnuctr[l]

a. The building block which is used to form the mnemonic is shown in parentheses beside the semantic description. The mnemonic for the branch is built out of three components: b[CR code][target code][l].

Register Set

Table F.6. PowerPC register set.

Symbol	Width	Access	Description
CR	32	User	Condition Register
LR	32,64	User	Link Register

Symbol	Width	Access	Description
CTR	32,64	User	Count Register
GPR 0 - 31	32,64	User	General Purpose Registers
XER	32	User	Fixed Point Exception Register
FPR 0 - 31	64	User	Floating Point Registers
FPSCR	32	User	Floating Point Status and Control Register
MQ	32	User	MQ Register (601 only)
DEC	32	Privileged	Decrementer
SRR 0 - 1	32,64	Privileged	Machine Status Save/ Restore Registers
MSR	32,64	Privileged	Machine State Register
DAR	32,64	Privileged	Data Address Register
DSISR	32	Privileged	Data Storage Interrupt Status Register
SPRG 0 - 3	32,64	Privileged	Software-use Special Purpose Registers
PVR	32	Privileged	Processor Version Register
IBAT 0 - 3 U/L	32,64	Privileged	Instruction Block Address Translation Upper/Lower Registers (8 total)
DBAT 0-3 U/L	32,64	Privileged	Data Block Address Translation Upper/Lower Registers (8 total)
EAR	32	Privileged	External Access Register (optional)
HID 0 - N	Optional	Optional	Implementation-specific SPRs (optional)
TB	64	User Read	Time Base Register
RTCU	32	User Read	Real Time Clock Upper (601 only)
RTCU	32	User Read	Real Time Clock Lower (601 only)
ASR	64	Priviledged	Address Space Register (64-bit implementations only)

Assembler

Assembler Pseudo-Ops

.align   *n*

Forces the alignment of the next assembly element to occur on the next 2^n byte boundary. If the current csect is of type PR or GL, then any alignment padding will be filled with the **nop** instruction.

.byte   *expression*[,*expression*...]

Allocates a byte or region of bytes, initialized to the value of *expression*.

.comm   *name*,*expression*[,*n*]

Defines an uninitialized common block name, of size expression, aligned on a 2^n byte boundary.

.csect   [*name*][[*storage_class*]][,*n*]

Specifies the csect that the following code or data belong in. The alignment of the csect may be set to a 2^n byte boundary.

.double   *expression*

Allocates eight bytes of memory initialized to the double precision floating point value of *expression*. Alignment padding will be added so that the value is word aligned.

.drop   *n*

Stops using register *n* as a base register.

.dsect   *name*

Specifies the dummy csect that the following code or data belong in.

.extern   *name*

Identifies *name* as a symbol from another module.

.float   *expression*

Allocates 4 bytes of memory initialized to the single precision floating point value of *expression*. Alignment padding will be added so that the value is word aligned.

.globl   *name*

Identifies *name* as a global symbol.

.lcomm   *name,expression[,section]*

Defines a block of uninitialized storage *name* of size *expression* in local common section *section*.

.long   *expression[,expression...]*

Allocates words of memory initialized to *expression*. Alignment padding will be added so that the data is word aligned.

.org   *expression*

Sets the value of the current location counter ($).

.rename   *name,string*

Creates external alias *string* for internal symbol *name*.

.set   *name,expression*

Defines a symbolic constant *name* for *expression*.

.short   *expression[,expression...]*

Allocates halfwords of memory initialized to *expression*. Alignment padding will be added so that the data is halfword aligned.

.space   *n*

Allocates *n* bytes of memory initialized to zero.

.string   **string**

Allocates initialized bytes of memory to hold string and terminating null.

.tc   *name[TC],expression[,expression...]*

Creates a TOC entry.

.toc

Indicates the TOC csect.

.tocof   *symbol,name*

Defines local symbol *name* as a reference to another module's TOC which contains the global symbol *symbol*.

.using   *expression,n*

Tells the assembler to use register *n* as a base register and to assume that it contains the value *expression*.

.vbyte   *n,expression*

Allocates *n* bytes (4 maximum) of memory and initializes them to *expression*.

Table F.7. Assembler storage classes.

Class	Section	Description
PR	.text	Program Code
RO	.text	Read Only Data
GL	.text	Glue Code
TC	.data	TOC Entry
UA	.data	Unknown Type
RW	.data	Read Write Data
DS	.data	Function Descriptor
BS	.bss	Uninitialized Read Write Data
UC	.bss	Unnamed Common

Table F.8. Assembler special symbols.

Symbol	Description
$	Current location counter value.
TOC[TC0]	TOC anchor-address of the current module's TOC.

G

Further Reading

General Reference

Hennessy, John L. and David A. Patterson. *Computer Architecture: A Quantitative Approach.* **Palo Alto: Morgan Kaufmann, 1990.**

This computer architecture textbook is considered by many to be the "bible" of RISC architecture.

Hennessy, John L. and David A. Patterson. *Computer Organization and Design.* **Palo Alto: Morgan Kaufmann 1994.**

This sequel to their first book, *Computer Organization and Design* focuses on system design and performance issues, as well as the interface of the processor to software and other system components.

Johnson, Mike. *Superscalar Microprocessor Design.* **New York: Prentice Hall, 1991.**

This book takes up where Hennessy and Patterson leave off, and covers the design of Superscalar (parallel pipeline) processors.

Tanenbaum, Andrew S. *Operating System Design and Implementation.* **Engelwood Cliffs: Prentice Hall, 1987.**

A very readable text that focuses on the real problems of building operating systems, rather than "pretty" theoretical problems that clutter some books on the subject. Includes source code for Minix, a UNIX-like PC operating system.

PowerPC Architecture and Implementations

Books

Duntemann, Jeff and Ron Pronk. *Inside the PowerPC Revolution.* **Scottsdale: Coriolis Group, 1994.**

Where most of the other material written about PowerPC is strictly technical in focus, this is a book about where the computer marketplace and technology has been, where it's going, and how PowerPC fits in. Full of history, insider information (occasionally, misinformation), and technical details, this is more a book about the PowerPC technoculture phenomenon than architecture or programming.

IBM Corporation. *The PowerPC Architecture.* **Palo Alto: Morgan Kaufmann, 1994.**

Books 1, 2, and 3 of the official PowerPC architecture specification are published in this volume (the partnership developed these specifications at four levels, each described by a separate "book"). Books 1 through 3 describe the instruction set and programming environment.

IBM Microelectronics and Motorola. *PowerPC 601 User's Guide.*

IBM Microelectronics and Motorola. *PowerPC 603 User's Guide.*

IBM Microelectronics and Motorola. *PowerPC 604 User's Guide.*

These books describe the respective chip implementation in extensive (and sometimes stupefying) detail. Essential for system developers, these books can also be useful to programmers needing a reference for a particular chip. All include detailed descriptions of instruction timing, pipeline interactions, and a wealth of other minutiae (the 601 and 603 versions include an instruction set reference). These books, and other detailed specifications are available from the manufacturers. Call IBM at 1-800-POWERPC or Motorola at 1-800-845-MOTO to order.

Weiss, Shlomo and James E. Smith. *POWER and PowerPC.* **Palo Alto: Morgan Kaufmann, 1994.**

This book discusses modern computer architecture, studying how principles are applied in the design and implementation of the POWER and PowerPC machines.

Young, Jerry. *Insider's Guide to PowerPC Computing.* **Indianapolis: Que Publishing, 1994.**

This book is a good introduction to the PowerPC architecture and features of the 601 and 603 processor chips. This book is more readable than the specifications or manufacturers' user's Guides, and is a good introduction to PowerPC chips for system designers and programmers alike.

Articles

***Byte,* 18(8), August 1993.**

This issue has several PowerPC articles including details of the PowerPC 601 processor, operating system support, and an introduction to RISC.

***Communications of the ACM,* 37(6), June 1994.**

This issue of *CACM* has a collection of articles on PowerPC, including the history of the architecture and the partnership, the 603 processor, and the compilers and simulators available from Motorola.

***IEEE Micro,* 14(5), October 1994.**

This issue of *IEEE Micro* features several PowerPC articles, including the PowerPC instruction set, some details of the 601 and 604 implementations, and the PowerPC 60X bus design.

"PowerPC 620 Soars." *Byte,* **19(11) November, 1994: 113-120.**

This article describes the features of the 64-bit PowerPC 620.

Optimization and Performance

Books

Thompson, Tom. *Power Macintosh Programming Starter Kit.* **Indianapolis: Hayden Books, 1994.**

A detailed treatment of high-level language development for the Power Macintosh, including a demonstration version of the Metrowerks CodeWarrior development toolset on CD-ROM.

Articles

Gillig, James R. "Endian-Neutral Software, Part 1." *Dr. Dobbs Journal* **220, October 1994.**

Gillig, James R. "Endian-Neutral Software, Part 2." *Dr. Dobbs Journal* **222, November 1994.**

This two-part series discusses strategies for avoiding program incompatability due to different memory byte ordering (endianness) conventions in different systems, and a discussion of the bi-endian features of the PowerPC architecture.

Heisch, R.R. "Trace-directed program restructuring for AIX executables." *IBM Journal of Research and Development* **38(5) September, 1994: 595-604.**

This article describes the methods used in the FDCR (feedback directed code restructuring) tool for optimizing cache performance mentioned in Chapter 7, "Performance Tuning and Optimization."

Thompson, Tom. "Power Mac Code Optimizations." *Byte* **19(11), November 1994: 291-292.**

A short article about improving performance of high-level language Power Macintosh programs, particularly considerations in the OS and library interfaces.

I

Index

M

Add to Your Sams Library Today with the Best Books for Programming, Operating Systems, and New Technologies

The easiest way to order is to pick up the phone and call

1-800-428-5331

between 9:00 a.m. and 5:00 p.m. EST.
For faster service please have your credit card available.

ISBN	Quantity	Description of Item	Unit Cost	Total Cost
0-672-30548-8		Interfacing to the PowerPC Microprocessor	$35.00	
0-672-48470-6		Assembly Language: For Real Programmer's Only! (Book/Disk)	$44.95	
0-672-30286-1		C Programmer's Guide to Serial Communications, Second Edition	$39.95	
0-672-30291-8		DOS 6 Developer's Guide (Book/Disk)	$39.95	
0-672-30500-3		Lotus Notes Developer's Guide (Book/Disk)	$39.99	
0-672-30160-1		Multimedia Developer's Guide (Book/CD-ROM)	$49.95	
0-672-30496-1		Paradox 5 Developer's Guide (Book/Disk)	$49.99	
0-672-30475-9		PC Programmer's Guide to Low-Level Functions and Interrupts (Book/Disk)	$45.00	
0-672-30594-1		Programming WinSock (Book/Disk)	$35.00	
0-672-30568-2		Teach Yourself OLE Programming in 21 Days	$39.99	
0-672-30402-3		UNIX Unleashed (Book/CD-ROM)	$49.99	
❏ 3 ½" Disk		Shipping and Handling: See information below.		
❏ 5 ¼" Disk		TOTAL		

Shipping and Handling: $4.00 for the first book, and $1.75 for each additional book. Floppy disk: add $1.75 for shipping and handling. If you need to have it NOW, we can ship product to you in 24 hours for an additional charge of approximately $18.00, and you will receive your item overnight or in two days. Overseas shipping and handling adds $2.00 per book and $8.00 for up to three disks. Prices subject to change. Call for availability and pricing information on latest editions.

201 W. 103rd Street, Indianapolis, Indiana 46290

1-800-428-5331 — Orders   1-800-835-3202 — FAX   1-800-858-7674 — Customer Service

Book ISBN 0-672-30543-7

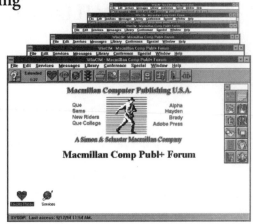

PLUG YOURSELF INTO...

THE MACMILLAN INFORMATION SUPERLIBRARY™

Free information and vast computer resources from the world's leading computer book publisher—online!

FIND THE BOOKS THAT ARE RIGHT FOR YOU!

A complete online catalog, plus sample chapters and tables of contents give you an in-depth look at *all* of our books, including hard-to-find titles. It's the best way to find the books you need!

- STAY INFORMED with the latest computer industry news through our online newsletter, press releases, and customized Information SuperLibrary Reports.

- GET FAST ANSWERS to your questions about MCP books and software.

- VISIT our online bookstore for the latest information and editions!

- COMMUNICATE with our expert authors through e-mail and conferences.

- DOWNLOAD SOFTWARE from the immense MCP library:
    - Source code and files from MCP books
    - The best shareware, freeware, and demos

- DISCOVER HOT SPOTS on other parts of the Internet.

- WIN BOOKS in ongoing contests and giveaways!

TO PLUG INTO MCP: → **WORLD WIDE WEB: http://www.mcp.com**

GOPHER: gopher.mcp.com

FTP: ftp.mcp.com